Passport
to
Life

Autobiographical Reflections on the Holocaust

Emanuel Tanay, M.D.

Forensic press

Printed in the United States of America
10 9 8 7 6 5 4 3 2 1

Library of Congress Control Number: 2004096021
ISBN: 0-9760263-0-9 (PB)
ISBN: 0-9760263-1-7 (CB)

Forensic Press
PO Box 3132
Ann Arbor, MI 48106-3132

"Long ago, *over there,* far from the living, we told ourselves over and over that if we were to come out alive, we would devote every moment of our lives to denouncing by word and deed the cynicism and silence of mankind toward victims past and future. Convinced that the free world knew nothing of the cursed and evil kingdom where death reigned, we encouraged one another. The one among us who would survive would testify for all of us. He would speak and demand justice on our behalf; as our spokesman he would make certain that our memory would penetrate that of humanity. He would do nothing else. His days and nights would be devoted to telling the story. He would turn his entire life into a weapon for our collective memory; thanks to him, it would not be lost."
--And the Sea Is Never Full, Elie Wiesel

Dedicated to the memory of my parents, Betty and Bunim Tenenwurzel, whose love gave me the optimism that made my survival possible; and to their grandchildren Elaine, Anita and David; and their great-grandchildren Aaron, Sara, Jeremy, Rachel and James.

Table of Contents

All humanity is one undivided and indivisible family, and each one of us is responsible for the misdeeds of all the others. I cannot detach myself from the wickedest soul.

-Mohandas Ghandi

Introduction

This book reflects the lessons learned from my fifty years of psychiatric practice with my experiences during the Holocaust. The Holocaust and forensic psychiatry have been the twin poles of my life. My professional life was, for the most part, devoted to the study of people who had killed someone; people who wanted to kill me dominated the early part of my life. The September 11th atrocity has made my story more relevant to all Americans. We know *now* that Nazi Germany was dedicated to the killing of all the European Jews. This historical fact was unimaginable to us in 1939. Before September 11, 2001, it was inconceivable that Islamic holy warriors would wish and be able to kill thousands of Americans. The Holocaust and 9/11 differ in number of victims, but they have in common that they have been inspired by a belief system and were perpetrated in the name of a cause. The 6 million Jews in Europe , and the 3000 Americans in New York were killed for no other reason than national identity. This is the essence of genocide.

This is a book about a teenager's struggle to stay alive in a culture of death. It tells a story of a young adult who, after the ordeal of the Holocaust, lived a good life. It ends with an old man who enjoys family, professional success, health and prosperity. My life was worth living. I became a physician, a professor of psychiatry, and have received many recognitions for my work, but none of it can compare with what I accomplished by the time I was 16 years old.

I made more consequential decisions between the ages of 14 and 17 than in the following 50 years. I helped to save the lives of my mother, my little sister Olenka, my childhood sweetheart Gina, and my own.

The most remarkable thing about me is that I am alive. My greatest triumph is that being a Jew will not be the cause of my death. To die of old age is a rare privilege for a Polish Jew of my generation. My father's heroic death is my greatest sorrow.

What happened to a teenage boy who survived the Holocaust is a fascinating story. What motivated the millions of people who wished to see him dead is both interesting and significant for the future of humanity.

I understand some of the factors that made killing 6 million Jews acceptable to millions of ordinary people. As a forensic psychiatrist, I have evaluated hundreds of homicide perpetrators. Most felt guilty because they caused the death of a human being. Guilt-free mass murder is a subject we must study if we hope to survive as a civilization.

It would take Homer's imagination and Shakespeare's sense of drama to do justice to the lives of Holocaust survivors. It is beyond my ability to describe the unimaginable and to imagine the indescribable. And yet I feel compelled to attempt it.

Religion and ideology are the most common reasons for the ability to kill without guilt. Religion and ideology played a vital, or more accurately, deadly, role in my eventful life. Therefore, reflections about my past include thoughts about belief systems. It is a sad fact that Christianity has had a greater impact upon my existence than Judaism. I am more familiar with Catholicism than Judaism. In order to avoid being killed, I studied to become a Catholic priest.

Judaism, Catholicism, Nazism and Communism shaped the environment in which I lived. None of these belief systems found a follower in me. The spirit of skepticism watched over me until I arrived in New York in January of 1952, ready to take up Americanism as my creed. I treasure this country because it is free of secular and religious ideology as a cultural dogma.

Hate and its psychosocial twin, cruelty, have been part of my personal experience and work as a forensic psychiatrist. The human capacity for love, hate and the ability to cope with the consequences of these emotions are more than theoretical concepts for me. Encounters with self-righteous, ideological and religious fanatics immunized me against the belief in revolutionary solutions to human problems.

Advocating hatred of the Jews was valuable to various movements for practical reasons. Love is cherished but hate is a better recruitment tool than love. It is easier to organize a riot or a pogrom than a love fest. People sacrifice their lives more often out of hate than love. The Islamic holy warriors are a good example of the power of hate.

Hatred, unlike anger, is not a reaction to the behavior of others but a displacement of the repressed rage of those who hate. Scapegoating provides emotional relief, but it is not an effective adaptive mechanism. Before World War II, revenge had been the curse of Germany. The Islamists seek revenge in the 21st century against the "crusaders" (The last crusade took place in 12th century) and pay a great price for this diversion.

I hope that this book will increase the empathy for both victims and perpetrators of the calamity we call the Holocaust and other genocides. A willingness to suspend the perspective of the present is essential for the reconstruction of the Zeitgeist of a bygone period.

Empathy is the ability to put oneself in the shoes of another person. Empathy is the primary tool of a psychiatrist. It is essential to politicians, historians, writers, parents and all others who wish to understand friends and enemies. Without empathy, one could not play a game of chess or cope with a murderous adversary.

The slaughter of innocent human beings is readily declared monstrous. The challenge is to imagine the feelings and thoughts of people who found killing the Jews both a moral necessity and a noble cause.

Had we, the Jews of Europe in the 1930s, empathized with Nazi Germany and grasped that the Germans perceived us as a threat to their survival; we would have realized the danger that lay ahead. The lack of empathy was a significant factor in our belief that Hitler did not mean what he said and that the German people did not support what they so enthusiastically cheered. A belief need not be valid or reasonable to motivate behavior.

Before the September 11th atrocity, wishful thinking and noble sentiments clouded the American image of Radical Islam. We deluded ourselves into thinking that Radical Islam did not mean what it preached and the Islamic masses did not support what they applauded.. Islam is an aggressive culture based upon Arab nationalism and dogmatic religiosity. History does repeat itself; once again Western Civilization is in danger.

I am troubled by distortions of Holocaust history. History is based upon creative remembering of the past, and is constructed of facts, imagination and wishful thinking. History is a work in constant progress. The ability to listen to what one does not want to hear is essential to learning the truth about the past. I recall treating a young woman who survived Auschwitz. She discontinued treatment with me because I was bringing up her Holocaust experiences. A few months later she returned, dissatisfied with her new psychiatrist, "he does not want to hear what I do not want to talk about", she explained.

The prevailing images about the genocide of the Jews during World War II and my memories differ. I was in Warsaw on April 19, 1943, the beginning of the Warsaw Ghetto Uprising; my views about that day are in sharp contrast to the current glorification of this collective suicide. A Jew in German captivity faced the alternative of death and death delayed. Overt resistance made a dangerous situation lethal. Mordechai Anielewicz and his friends decided that the 60,000 still living in the Warsaw Ghetto in April 1943 should die in Warsaw, instead of later in Treblinka. Anielewicz and his few hundred followers had courage and deserve to be admired, but they were not role models for those of us who struggled to survive. Armed resistance makes adaptive sense when there is some likelihood of success. The Jews who resisted wanted to die. When powerless individuals resist a powerful, ruthless enemy, they invariably die. The opposite of Jewish passivity in German captivity was not armed resistance, but the struggle for survival.

Passivity and survival are incompatible. Survival was not a random event, but a contingent process; it nearly always involved active involvement of the survivor. Indomitable courage, resourcefulness and endurance in the face of brutal persecution were essential. There are many studies on the psychopathology of survivors. The virtues that made survival possible have been neglected in the prodigious literature on the Holocaust because little value has been attached to survival. In *Shadows on the Hudson*, Isaac Bashevis Singer has one of his fictional survivor's say: "Before you, you see a dead person. Dead in all respects except that the heart still beats to no end or purpose. They burned me together with the others." This is a popular view of Holocaust survivors, but nothing could be further from truth. Contrary to expectations, most survivors remained alive in body and spirit. I, like most survivors, have had a good and productive life.

It is a common view that the Nazis were assisted in their effort to bring about the final solution by "Jewish police" and the "Judenrats" (Jewish councils). The Judenrats that I remember do not resemble this picture. If any form of cooperation with the enemy was to be avoided, then the Judenrats were illegitimate. If survival was a desirable goal, then the Judenrats were adaptive and useful. I do not recall anyone questioning the legitimacy of the Judenrat in my hometown. The Judenrat, from the German perspective, was an instrument of destruction, but from the Jewish perspective, it was a survival tool.

History rooted in bereavement only has no future because bereavement is, and should be, a time limited process. Holocaust education must shift emphasis from victims to survivors. This means that Raoul Wallenberg will have to share the stage with Rudolph Kasztner, a Hungarian Jew who also saved thousands of Jews but was murdered in Israel as a collaborator. This also means that the head of the Lodz Judenrat, Mordechai Chaim Rumkowski, who saved thousands of Jews but was accused of collaborating with the Germans, must be considered as much a hero as Mordechai Anielewicz, a leader of the Warsaw Ghetto Uprising.

In 1959, I established in Detroit a genocide study group. Professors from Wayne State University, Oakland University and University of Michigan met once a month and presented research on the subject of genocide. We did not call our group a Holocaust Study Group because that word had not as yet been connected to the "Final Solution," as the Germans called the annihilation of Europe Jews.

In 1961, *The Destruction of the European Jews* by Raul Hilberg was published, which to this day is considered the standard on the subject. You will not find the word holocaust or Holocaust in the index. Had the National Holocaust Memorial Museum been established in the 1960s it would have been called the National Genocide Memorial Museum.

We accept uncertainty about the future but our past is equally unpredictable. In 1945, I was a survivor of genocide, some years later I became a Holocaust survivor. My identity has not undergone significant change but the needs of the bystander community imposed upon me a new label. I object to it, but to avoid becoming a linguistic *Don Quixote*, I defer to the common usage.

The word Holocaust has its origin in the religious ritual of burning a sacrifice. It stems from the Greek translation of the Hebrew Bible's oft-repeated word olah, which means "burnt offering." In modern times it has been used to describe a major calamity. The Orthodox Jews embraced this term for religious reasons. The murder of 6 million European Jews is, for the Orthodox Jews, another "Churban," this is the religious Hebrew term for the destruction of the

Second Jerusalem Temple. Churban may be translated as destruction, which is accurate linguistically but misleading nevertheless. Churban, like Holocaust, connotes divine origin; it was imposed upon the Jews by God as punishment. Genocide, unlike Holocaust, is an atrocity perpetrated by people against people. Hilberg's *Destruction of European Jews* makes no mention of God or Holocaust. I would expect a religious person to reject the view that the murder of 6 million Jews was a sacrifice to God. Using the term Holocaust as synonym for the German genocide of the Jews has the virtue of brevity but it also creates conflicts.

Long before Nazi Germany's "Final Solution of the Jewish Question" Arnold Toynbee, in his 1915 book, *The Murder of a Nation*[1], spoke of "Armenian holocaust." (Not capitalized). I am troubled by the fact that we capitalize Holocaust but the term genocide does not receive such special linguistic treatment. All genocides are unique in some respects and all genocides are similar. The genocide of the Jews is unique by the sheer magnitude, the manner of implementation and the fact that it was perpetrated by a nation, which was highly civilized and cultured. The systematic murder of six million Jews confronted the Western world with its age old genocidal mentality. Other genocides are unique in different ways. The genocide of the Jews was neither the first nor the last effort to destroy a group of people because of their identity.

A chapter in this book is called "Home At Last"; it refers to my life in this country. For the first time, I was able to identify with the national ethos of a country. America has become my home because it is free of an ideology that promises to make this planet a paradise. America never offered eternal salvation. America makes promises to make people rich, strong, beautiful and slim. When these schemes fail, no one dies. Americans, in times of peace, are passionate about the good life. To live in such a land is a privilege.

Not the earth, will the good man inherit.
He is a stranger; he goes to roam
And seeks an everlasting home.
-Friedrich Schiller

Chapter 1
Where Am I From?

I was born on the fifth day of March, 1928. The most important day in my life, however, is January 10, 1945. On that day I regained the right to live.

The place of my birth was Wilno, Poland. Today, you will not find Wilno on a map of Poland; it is the capital of Lithuania and its name is Vilnius.

Wilno or Vilnius is not the most important city in my life. That distinction belongs to Miechow. I lived in that sleepy little Polish town between the ages of seven and fourteen, a mere seven years.

I feel that I am from Miechow because seven years of childhood are longer than seven years of young adulthood or forty years of maturity. Miechow is my hometown because there I experienced the fears and joys of childhood. The house I called home was in Miechow. In the house there on Pilsudski Avenue, I had my first sexual experience. In Miechow, I also had my first encounters with anti-Semitism. Sex and anti-Semitism had equal importance when I was growing up.

Poland and Hungary are the countries where my struggle for survival took place. "Zyd", "Jude", and "Zido" are the three words that shaped my life. The first is Jew in Polish, the second is Jew in German, and the last is Jew in Hungarian. In my childhood, the word "Zyd" triggered harassment; in my adolescence "Zyd," "Jude" and "Zido" were death sentences.

In Poland, being a Jewish boy overshadowed all of my other human attributes. When I walk into an American store today, I am just a customer. In Poland, I was a Jewish customer. My parents, even though very much assimilated, were not dentists, but "Jewish dentists." In the Poland of my generation, the collective image of "The Jews" was more important than the individual identity of a Jew.

From time to time, anti-Jewish riots (pogroms) would take place. In 1918, my father, then a fourteen-year-old boy, was severely beaten during a pogrom in Kielce, his hometown. This is the same town where more than forty Holocaust survivors were killed in July 1946 by a murderous Polish mob that believed "The Jews" had abducted a young boy to use his blood to make matzo for Passover.

14

The boy turned up, and it was discovered he had visited his uncle in a nearby village, and simply lied that he was abducted by Jews and then escaped.

When I was growing up, the word "Christian" in Poland and Europe was a synonym for anti-Semitic. It was common to see signs in display windows: "This is a Christian Store." This meant that the owner was not only Christian, but also anti-Semitic, and Jews were not welcome as customers. In 1938, Regent Horthy of Hungary welcomed representatives of the Young Men's Christian Association (YMCA) from America, with an expression of pleasure at meeting "an American anti-Semitic association." He assumed that "Christian" was a synonym for anti-Semitism in America as it was in Europe.

Our apartment building on Pilsudski Avenue was painted a bright white, creating a contrast with the darkness and gloom of the strangely beautiful Catholic cemetery across the street. From the front windows and the balcony, I could see the graveyard, which looked like a park. Jews never ventured onto the holy fields of Catholic burial grounds, full of crosses and figures of saints.

One entered our building through a massive door called "brama", which was a portal locked at certain hours. To enter after hours one had to pay a fee to the concierge. A blue door separated the hallway from the stairway that led up to our apartment. For my 10th birthday, I was given a knife, called a "finka" because it came from Finland. With it, I carved my initials, "E.T." on the blue door. My name then was Emanuel Tenenwurzel. The scolding I received from my father made the day especially memorable.

The rooms of our apartment were large, the ceilings high, and the furniture was modern and of high quality. From the back windows we could see the courtyard; it had a vegetable and flower garden. The kitchen, the dining room, and the dental laboratory were in the rear. My parents' bedroom, the dental office and waiting room occupied the front of the apartment.

The kitchen was a large space, in the center of which was a coal stove. Attached to the kitchen was an alcove with a bed for our maid, Victoria, who we called Vikta. She had been with our family from my early childhood. Vikta was a stocky woman with stern facial features and a morose personality. However, her affection for our family was obvious. The Catholic Church and the Tenenwurzel family were her main interests in life.

The furniture in my parents' bedroom was of light colored wood with elaborate inlays, giving the room a bright and cheerful appearance. Since there were no closets, clothing was kept in massive armoires. Over the bed was a full-bodied portrait of my mother, semi-nude, painted by an artist from Krakow. A French door opened to a balcony that wrapped around the corner of the house. Outside the wrought iron railing on the balcony were flower boxes, and it was my job to water the flowers daily. The dental office could be reached through a separate outside entrance or through the bedroom. We also had a telephone, a rare device in a small town in Poland in those days. Our number was eleven. The Catholic priest naturally had number one.

Our dining room had black mahogany furniture and a large credenza with glass doors held crystal and Rosenthal dishes. On top of the credenza there had been a big crystal fruit bowl imported from Czechoslovakia. When I was about five years old, I was playing ball with a friend in the dining room and knocked the bowl down. Mother, hearing the crash, rushed in from the dental office, and at the sight of the broken bowl, she cried and so did I. After that, the main point of interest in the dining room was a crystal chandelier hanging over an ornate table.

Everyday, precisely at 1 p.m., my parents, myself, and my sister, Olga Ruth, who we called "Olenka," and was five years my junior, would gather around this table to have the main meal of the day, prepared by Mr. Tomasz. Mr. Tomasz had been a restaurant chef in Krakow and after his retirement had moved to a nearby village. Every morning, except on Sunday, he came for a few hours to prepare the food. Vikta resented his presence.

Behind our building was a "podwórko", a fenced in yard that could be entered only from the main hallway or by opening massive gates. In the center of the yard was a small garden, and to the side were sheds for the four apartments and an outhouse, a brick structure with four cubicles. We did not go to the outhouse at night. Under each bed was a chamber pot that would be emptied in the morning into a special bucket and taken to the outhouse. Our family had a cook, live-in maid, and a governess, but we did not have indoor plumbing.

My parents dressed fashionably. Mother usually wore a skirt and suit jacket. It would have been bizarre for women in those days to wear pants unless they were skiing. Mother bought her clothing in Krakow. Occasionally, I heard my parents argue about my mother's clothing expenditures. Father wore tailor made suits and preferred solid blue shirts. The tailor would make two or three visits to the house before a suit was finished. Kids asked me if it was true that my father changed his shirt every day, and not once a week as "normal people" did. The Jews in our town walked on the sidewalk close to the houses so as not to be in "their" way, but my father walked briskly and bareheaded in the roadway, acknowledging the greetings of Poles and Jews who would tip their hats with deference. My parents were not the richest people in our town but they were among the most respected.

Our parents traveled to the resorts of Zakopane and Krynica in the Tatra Mountains. Olenka and I went every year to Rabka, a summer resort popular in Poland. Unlike most Jews in our town, my parents were at home in both the Polish and Jewish cultures.

In the 18th century, Poland had been partitioned and occupied for more than one hundred years by its three mighty neighbors: Russia, Prussia and Austria. Russia and the two Germanic countries, Prussia and Austria, were dramatically different cultures.

The Jews of Poland were either "Litwaks" or "Galizianers" depending in which part of occupied Poland they lived. The term "Litwak" was derived from "Litwa" (Lithuania); it included all the Jews who had lived under Russian occupation before 1918. "Galizianer" described those who had lived under German and Austrian control. Litvaks were practical; their lives were less dominated by religion than the Galitzianers. My maternal grandfather, like most Jews of Wilno, was a *misnaged,* an opponent of mystic religion.

My father had been born and raised in the part of Poland that was occupied by Germany before 1918, so he was a Galizianer and spoke perfect German. Mother, a Litwak, came from the region occupied by Czarist Russia, and spoke fluent Russian. The personality differences of my parents were, in part, the result of the fact that they had grown up in dissimilar environments. Father was orderly, logical, disciplined, and linear in his thinking. Mother spoke and behaved like a Russian. She was emotional, intuitive and expressive. Mother would scream; Father would spank.

Father had blond hair, blue eyes, and light skin; he looked Scandinavian. Mother's pitch-black hair and olive complexion would have made her look Italian in the United States, but she looked Jewish in Poland. I recall Mother singing Russian songs at bedtime and at parties. She was an accomplished singer and dancer. Both of my parents were joyous people. I was often sick, at which time both parents would be even more loving than usual. Father played checkers with me and when I got older, he taught me how to play chess. He was known in town as one of the best chess players, a skill which became quite important during German occupation.

My parents were the only dentists in our town. My mother had a medical degree and was a physician-dentist; father was simply a dentist. Mother was entitled to do more procedures than father. But father was technically more proficient, and this was a cause for some tension between them. She had the title and he had the skill.

The attitudes of the Miechow Jews towards my parents were mixed. As non-observant Jews they were called "apikoros" (heretics). But the Jews of our town were also gratified by the prestige and influence of my parents in the Polish community.

My parents were not religious; however, they observed Passover and Yom Kippur. I enjoyed the Jewish holidays, often celebrated with my grandparents, but I did not understand the songs and prayers. At the high holidays of Rosh Hashanah and Yom Kippur, my father, whom some Jews disparagingly called a "goy," would take me to the synagogue. On those days, Father became a practicing but not a believing Jew. We made these annual visits to assert our Jewish identity.

To the amazement of the town's Jews, my father knew how to "daven." The word means to "pray", but this translation does not fully convey the meaning of the term. "Daven" was a skill gained by lengthy training. The congregation recited the text in a rapid singsong manner, but not in unison. They seemed to be reading it, but most had the prayers memorized. It was a choir of soloists, togetherness without uniformity.

As my father and I would make our way to our seats, the men engaged in animated prayer would greet us warmly and make pleasant comments without stopping their communication with God. The setting was simple: a large, plain space with a high ceiling. The scripture lesson of the day would be read from a raised platform called a "bima". Any Jew could be called to perform this function. The only decoration was on the Ark containing the book of law called the Torah.

There was no visible distinction between the rabbi and other adult males. The room was noisy, and most of the men stood, moving rhythmically in place.

The mass at the Catholic Church in Miechow, where I went with our maid or my friends, was different. There was no animation, no noise, and activity was mostly limited to the priests and acolytes. The church building dominated the town. I was filled with awe and trepidation whenever I entered the Catholic Church. Daylight passed through stained glass windows, creating an eerie atmosphere. The altar was ornate and elevated and the unfamiliar smell of incense was everywhere. Priests performed elaborate religious rituals in Latin, a language understood by only a few of the parishioners. The place commanded reverence, compliance and obedience. Everyone but the priest was either sitting or kneeling. The mass was a ritual in which supplicants symbolically drank the blood of Jesus Christ and ate his body.

In later years I learned that, according to the Church doctrine, Christ is actually present in both the consecrated bread and the consecrated wine in the Eucharist. The mass is a true sacrifice; a priest is necessary for such a complex ritual. The Catholic Holy Mass, unlike the Jewish service, could not be conducted without a priest.

In the synagogue there was no altar, no blood rituals were performed and no sacraments were administered. Yet, Polish folklore abounded in stories about Jewish rituals that required the blood of Christians, especially Christian children. In some churches, paintings depicted Jews with knives performing ritual killing of a Christian child. The Church in the city of Sandomierz to this day displays two paintings of Jews performing ritual murder.[2]

As a child, I believed that Jesus was a Pole. This may seem amusing to an American, but it made perfect sense to children and many adults in Poland. The mother of Jesus was commonly called Queen of Poland; therefore, it seemed logical that her son would be a Pole. German scholars argued otherwise.

Jesus, as depicted in the paintings that were everywhere in Poland, certainly did not look Jewish. He did not have a crooked nose or the shifty eyes attributed to Jews. I remember a joke told in Poland of a woman from a noble family who was entering a convent. Since this was considered a marriage of the woman to Jesus, the family gave a big party. A Jew tried to crash the bash by saying: "I am from the bridegroom's side."

In my childhood I was surrounded by intense piety. Vikta, our maid, was a devout Catholic. She never went to sleep without saying her prayers in a loud whisper. She went to early mass every Sunday, and on a number of occasions I went with her. Our downstairs neighbor was a pious Jew. He placed the phylacteries on his forehead and arms for the morning prayers. Nearly all Jews of Miechow followed the same ritual. Our family was different; we were called non-observant Jews. That was true of the few Jewish families of professionals in our town.

From the balcony of our apartment, one had a view of the main street, named after Marshal Josef Pilsudski. I watched the life of our small Polish town from that platform, though not much happened. Funerals and drunken peasants created occasional excitement. Catholic and Jewish funerals passed in front of our house. A Polish funeral moved slowly. The casket would be ornate, with gold leaf decorations. If the deceased was a young person, the casket was white. Two acolytes, young boys dressed in white garments, preceded the casket, which was carried by pallbearers. A priest walked behind the coffin, wearing crown-like headgear. Mourners, dressed in their best clothes, walked behind the priest with military precision. Pedestrians faced the funeral procession, removed their hats, and made the sign of the cross. Some knelt on the sidewalk. Horse-drawn vehicles pulled to the side of the street, and drivers and passengers got out and stood in respectful silence.

Jewish funerals were different. The casket was a plain black box with handles that rested on the shoulders of pallbearers. Mourners in distinctive Jewish garb surrounded the box. The men wore long, black shiny caftans and black caps, the women black dresses and scarves. Behind the casket walked three or four wailing and screaming women. They were the professional criers. Family and friends followed. The mourners moved as if someone were chasing them. Traffic in the street and on the sidewalk did not stop for Jewish funerals.

Poles called the Jewish cemetery "Kierkow." This was a derogatory term derived from the German language, from Kirchhoff, meaning church yard. The Jewish burial grounds were plain, with small uniform headstones, and there were no trees or flowers along the narrow paths. A wall with a big iron gate surrounded the Catholic cemetery. Inside were impressive monuments with elaborate inscriptions and wide walkways lined with big oak trees. Poles and Jews lived and died differently. In those days, one did not speak of Poles and Jews, but of Catholics and Jews.

Dzidzia Wroblewska, a Catholic girl, was my first childhood sweetheart. She lived downstairs and we amused ourselves by hiding behind the flower boxes on the balcony and squirting people below with water. We used one of my parents' dental instruments. Dzidzia was a beautiful girl, with blue eyes and long blond hair that she wore in two braids. She had the typical non-Jewish look. In Poland, most Jews could be recognized by Jewish facial features. My father, who was blue-eyed and blond, was an exception. I also did not have pronounced Jewish features.

Every day Dzidzia and I walked to school together. Our parents enjoyed and encouraged this childhood romance that bridged the walls of prejudice separating Jews and Christians. My father always let me go outside if I said I was going to play with Dzidzia. I overheard him once say to a family friend "I hope the boy gets interested in girls and starts combing his hair." Little did he know how much I was interested in Dzidzia.

Hide and Seek was the favorite game for the children in our neighborhood. Dzidzia and I liked to hide in the cellar. The cellar had no electricity or daylight; the air was dank and stale, and there were mice and rats. Being frightened was a good excuse to hug and kiss. Dzidzia was not bashful. One time she suggested, "If you show me yours, I'll show you mine." She must have done this with other boys, too, because she told me "Yours looks different." I was very much aware that my penis was unlike that of a Pole. In Poland and the rest of Europe, only Jews were circumcised.

Jewish boys my age wore "yarmulkes" (skullcaps) and had "peyos" (ear locks). After school, they would attend "heder," a religious school, until evening. They had no time to play or do homework. I was the only Jewish boy my age that did not go to the heder. The others began attending heder at the age of three or four. To call heder a school is a charitable description. The heder was owned and operated by a "melamed," an inept scholar of the Torah who made his living teaching little boys the Talmud. If he had been any good, he would have been a rabbi, a man who, unlike a melamed, commanded respect. The melamed taught about fifteen boys in a one room flat. He was typically poor, frustrated, and physically abusive of his pupils. The Jewish boys in my school had to rush to heder as soon as school was out or expect punishment by the melamed for being late. This was a strange world to me. Elie Wiesel, who is my age, recalled in his memoir.[3]

> In my little village, which in winter was blanketed with snow, the Jewish children got up early, very early to go to school - the heder - to say their morning prayers and study the Bible.
> During the winter I lighted my way with an oil lamp. It was dark outside and I was afraid. The early part of my childhood was more or less that: fear of anti-Semitic thugs, fear of demons, fear of God.

Even in a large city like Warsaw, the heder was a pathetic setting for children. Isaac Bashevis Singer writes:

> The heder where I studied was a room in which the teacher ate and slept, and his wife cooked. There I studied not arithmetic, geography, physics, chemistry, or history, but the laws governing an egg laid on a holiday and sacrifices in a temple destroyed two thousand years ago. Although my ancestors had settled in Poland some six or seven hundred years before I was born, I knew only a few words of the Polish language. We lived in Warsaw on Krochmalna Street, which might well have been called a ghetto. [4]

Yiddish was the language of the Jews in Poland. It was a jargon derived from the German language and had no resemblance to Polish. The Yiddish language itself had two major dialects. Litwaks spoke one and the Galizianers used the other. The Polish spoken by most Jews was a distinct Jewish dialect of Polish. Americans assume that the Jews of Poland spoke Polish with a Jewish accent. They know foreigners who speak English with a distinct intonation but that is only part of the story. The Jewish Polish involved more than an accent; the grammar and vocabulary were different. The Polish spoken by most Jews is comparable to the Black English vernacular. Most Polish Jews lived in a linguistic ghetto.

I did not speak Yiddish nor did I speak the Jewish-Polish dialect. Linguistically, I was not a Jew by Polish standards. Many Poles believed that one could always identify a Jew by his or her speech. Jews from unassimilated families spoke Polish poorly; they had Jewish accents and made grammatical errors. The difficulties the Jews had with the intricacies of Polish grammar were the subject of many jokes, such as this one:

A Jew comes to a bakery and wants to buy two loaves of bread. The number two in Polish has a different ending depending on the gender of the noun to which it refers. Bread is masculine, so when you ask for two loaves of bread, you must use the masculine form of number two. Number three has no gender. Since this Jew did not know how to ask for two loaves of bread, he simply said "Please give me three loaves of bread and take one back immediately."

The public elementary school in Miechow was a modern two-story red brick building. It was on the outskirts of town, at least a mile from my home. The hallways were spacious, and the classrooms had big windows. The teachers sat in front of a large crucifix symbolizing that Poland was a Catholic country. A portrait of Marshall Edward Rydz-Smigly, the head of the military, hung on the right side of the crucifix; to the left was a portrait of the President of the Republic, Ignacy Moscicki. The day began and ended with a Catholic prayer. There was only one Jewish teacher in the school and he instructed Jewish children about religion. It was a long Catholic tradition that a Jew could not teach Polish children.

Most of the Jewish boys in my class were poor, and I often gave them food. I sought them out to demonstrate my solidarity with them. The seating in our school reflected the students' academic standing. All Jewish boys, except me, sat in the last row. The first row was for the best students, the last for the worst. I sat in the first row center beside Tadek Dombrowski, the only classmate whose last name I still remember. We were the best students in the class. The other Jewish boys spoke Polish poorly and often had no time to do their homework, as heder was more important to them than the "goyshe" school. This did not apply to Jewish girls, who looked and functioned more like their Polish counterparts. Unlike other Jewish children in our school, I played with Polish boys. I was good at soccer and another ball game called "double fire." I had the biggest collection of lead soldiers and the boys liked to play with them.

One day, a priest came into the classroom to recruit students for the Boy Scouts. He signed up Tadek Dombrowski, and then he asked me to join. I was delighted, as I had read a great deal about scouting. At that point, the teacher walked behind me. The priest looked in her direction, puzzled. I turned around and saw her gesturing intensely. It did not require lip-reading to gather that she was letting him know I was a Jew and therefore could not be a Boy Scout. The priest had mistaken me for a Catholic youngster. Being the best student in the class was not good enough to join the Boy Scouts, if you were a Jew.

School in Miechow was over by noon and I was always at home by 1 p.m., when the family sat down to the main meal of the day. I often related what happened in school or what I saw walking home. That day I did not finish my story because I cried in the middle of telling my parents about my effort to become a scout.

The extent of the hatred that surrounded me in childhood is inconceivable to an American. It was a daily ritual for Polish boys to chase Jewish boys after school and beat them. Because the principal and many teachers were patients of my parents, I was exempt from being chased and beaten and that made me feel guilty. I often intervened. "Why don't you fight with me?" I would ask. I was the biggest boy in my class and because I was not regarded as a typical Jewish kid, a group would not attack me. The "real" Jewish boys were not protected by such a code of honor. I could, and often did, hold my own in a one-on-one fight.

Tormenting Jewish kids after school was at times life threatening. One day, a few Jewish boys were chased onto the thin ice of a pond. They ended up in the water and ran home nearly frozen.

When Czeslaw Milosz, the future Nobel Prize laureate, was twelve years old, he was summoned one day to approach the teacher's desk and empty his bulging pockets. The teacher wanted to know why he had a slingshot in his pocket. "To beat up the Jews", was the answer.[5] Beating up the Jews was a national pastime in Poland, and during my childhood a youngster would proudly tell a teacher about it.

Every Tuesday was market day in our town. After the peasants concluded their transactions, they visited the local taverns. The next activity was for the drunken men to knife each other and beat up the Jews. After school I used to climb a tree and jump on the roof of a marmalade factory adjacent to our house. From this safe location I watched the end of market day activities, which meant violence against Jewish peddlers.

Most Jews in Miechow were shopkeepers, tailors or shoemakers. With rare exceptions, they were very poor and orthodox. The tiny group of assimilated professionals was a minority within a minority. There were two Jewish physicians in Miechow, Dr. Lazer and Dr. Friedman. Dr. Lazer was a short man with a baby-like face. He was friendly but not outgoing, with a serious, confidence-inspiring manner. He was highly respected in our town. Mrs. Lazer was a dainty woman, pleasing in appearance and very proper.

Dr. Friedman was tall, exuberant and very popular among the peasants from surrounding villages who flocked to his practice. Mrs. Friedman was a beautiful and sophisticated woman who was openly contemptuous of her husband's unconventional ways of dealing with his patients. The diet of Polish peasants was protein deficient. They sold chickens and eggs to city folk and ate potatoes and lard. Therefore, Dr. Friedman instructed some of his superstitious peasant patients to kill a black chicken on a Friday at midnight; cook it and eat it before dawn. Many peasants when ill did not turn to physicians; they trusted a "znachor" more than a physician. There is no translation for this term in English, nor is there a similar profession in this country. A znachor practiced folk medicine and magic. Dr. Friedman, in the eyes of the peasants, combined the power of a znachor with the knowledge of a medical doctor. There was widespread belief in the power of the evil eye, and doctors could do nothing about it, but a znachor could. A popular legend told of a father who plucked his eyes out to protect his children from his evil eye. The backwardness of Polish peasants in those years was staggering.

There were also two Jewish attorneys in Miechow; Dr. Menasha and Dr. Wurm. Dr. Menasha was a lean, sour-looking man who had a spinal deformity.

He was single and lived with his parents in a villa, a term used loosely to describe a house occupied by one family. In Poland, the very poor and the very rich lived in single-family dwellings. The middle class lived in apartment buildings.

Dr. Wurm was very short, wiry and funny. Dr. Wurm and Father often played poker and chess. One day, Dr. Wurm lost a lot of money to my father in a poker game. The sum was so large that Father refused to accept it. Dr. Wurm, to ease his conscience, gave me a 12-volume set called "Books of Knowledge" and a large geographic atlas as a gift.

I believe that our home was the only Jewish household in Miechow with a Christmas tree. It was supposed to be for Vikta but we all decorated it and enjoyed it. We spent every Christmas Eve and Christmas Day with our Christian friends, the Kobasa family.

Alexander and Mila Kobasa were my parents' best friends. He was the manager of a large estate called Polanowice, in a village also called Polanowice., about ten kilometers from Miechow. The Kobasa family lived in a mansion-like home at the estate. I called them Uncle Olek and Aunt Mila. He was a Ukrainian and she was a Czech. Aunt Mila was a beautiful woman with a mellow voice; her speech had traces of an accent from her native Czech language. She was loving and lovable. Uncle Olek was a man whose competence and quiet authority were obvious the moment one met him. They had two children, Wlodek and Olenka; both were close to my age. I loved to go there to ride horses and roam around the estate. We spent every Christmas with the Kobasa family, and I went there for a long stay in the summers.

"When I grow up, I will become an agronomist like Uncle Olek," I answered when asked about my vocational plans. The Kobasa family stayed with us often. Such a close friendship between a Christian and a Jewish family was rare in Poland, particularly in a small town.

We had fed the heart on fantasies,
The heart's grown brutal from the fare.
-William Butler Yeats

Chapter 2
National Identity

The brunette teacher who looked like a younger version of my mother asked the class if anyone knew a poem. With the eagerness of a seven-year old boy trying to please the teacher, I recited a popular verse that began with "I am a little Pole and the white Eagle is my sign." My Polish classmates reacted with hilarity; the Jewish children were self-consciously silent. The teacher was puzzled and I was devastated. Everyone but me knew that it was ludicrous for a "Zyd" (a Jew) to say, "Ja jestem Polak maly (I am a little Pole)."

To be Polish, you had to be a Catholic; to be a good Catholic; you had to be an anti-Semite. I was neither, therefore to claim to be a Pole seemed outrageous to some and comical to others. Until that memorable day, I believed myself to be a Jew and a Pole.

When I got older, I understood that Polish identity was a blend of nationalism and Catholicism. During the 100-year-long occupation of Poland by Germany, Russia, and the Austro-Hungarian Empire, a fusion between nationalism and Catholicism took place. Poles acquired most of their views about the Jews from the Church propaganda, which nurtured anti-Semitism. Czeslaw Milosz speaks of:

> ...the peculiar features of Polish Catholicism, which had been shaped by Poland's historical situation as a country of the peripheries of Roman Catholic Europe. This meant, especially in the 19th century, the resistance to Protestant Prussia and Orthodox Russia. Polish culture developed entirely within the orbit of the Vatican. After Poland had disintegrated as a country, and wounded nationalism had made its appearance, the notions of "Pole" and "Catholic" came to be equated. Thus, religion was turned into an institution for preserving national identity; in this respect, the Poles were like the Jews in the Roman Empire.[6]

Milosz also writes that in his childhood:

> The Catholic Church was awesome in her immensity, and she was addressing herself to me with no more than a plea to submit to her discipline while suspending my judgment.[7]

To understand the behavior of the Jews during World War II, one has to have an image of the environment in which Jews lived in Poland before 1939. In my childhood, it was prudent to assume that every Pole was an anti-Semite unless there was evidence to the contrary. During my adolescence, I had to assume that every Pole hated Jews enough to denounce me to the Germans. I had to have valid reasons to believe otherwise. In my old age, I have the luxury to assume that most Poles are friendly towards Jews, unless they demonstrate hostility.

Originally, most Jews in Poland lived on the estates of wealthy landowners. They bought and sold goods, an activity that was below the dignity of the nobility, and above the ability of the peasants. Each nobleman had his own Jew, whose shrewdness and devotion he valued. In the feudal past, the Jews were useful to the gentry. This was an affront to the clergy and it meant that Jews became scapegoats for the peasants.

In 1918, the 100 year-long occupation of Poland by its neighbors ended, and the people of Poland celebrated independence with a wave of pogroms.[8]

Jerzy Tomaszewski, a Polish historian, documented a series of pogroms carried out in the first months of the Polish Republic by the Polish Army.[9]

> A pogrom took place in Lvov, on Nov. 22, 1918. Violence against the Jews was carried out throughout the winter of 1919 by the troops in the Rzeszow Region. The Army organized a pogrom in Warsaw on April 22, 1919; on April 5, 1919 in Pinsk; and on May 27, 1919 in Czestochowa.

General Heller declared that the 10,000 Jews who were in the fledgling Polish Army in 1919 were not loyal, and all Jewish soldiers were placed in Camp Jablono. The remaining troops under his command committed atrocities against the Jewish population. Polish atrocities against the Jews attracted international attention. The Versailles Treaty contained a special provision designed to protect the Jewish minority in Poland.

In January 1934, Poland and Nazi Germany signed a bilateral non-aggression declaration. In September of 1934, Colonel Josef Beck, as Poland's Foreign Minister, announced in Geneva Poland's unilateral cancellation of the Minorities Treaty that had been in force since 1919. The abrogation of the Minorities Protection Treaty resulted in a deterioration of conditions for Polish Jews.[10]

Before the French Revolution, Jews were non-citizens in all European States. But while Jews later became full citizens elsewhere, the emancipation of the Jews was never complete in Poland. They were second-class citizens because they were Jews. "Polak to Catholic," a Pole is a Catholic, was national canon. Religion and national identity were inextricably intertwined and created insurmountable obstacles to amicable coexistence between Poles and Jews.

In inter-war Poland (1918-1939), "Kwestja Zydowska" (The Jewish Question) dominated political life. The national identity card gave the religion of the cardholder and a Jew was identified as a citizen of the Mosaic. "Religia" is the Polish word for religion, but Judaism was designated as "wyznanie," which the dictionary defines as persuasion. Judaism, unlike Catholicism, did not rate the status of a religion in Poland's official terminology.

Poland was not alone. Anti-Semitism in Europe was a respected social movement and a powerful political force; it was part of the mainstream. A self-respecting citizen was proud to be an anti-Semite. In America, anti-Semitism did not have legitimacy and therefore it was masked.

President Eisenhower warned that there was danger that a military-industrial complex might rule the United States. A religious-military complex governed inter-war Poland; The Army and the Church were the two dominant institutions. The dream of every mother was to have her son be either an officer or a priest. There was a popular adage "Humanity begins at the level of the first lieutenant." The famed French author Stendhal, in his novel *The Red and the Black*, made clear that the only chance for social mobility for a lower middle class male in France was to become a priest or an officer. That was certainly true in inter-war Poland.

Poland was a Republic in name only. It was not a theocracy but, from the standpoint of the Church, the next best thing to it. The universities maintained a strict quota system and Jews were forced to sit on separate benches during lectures once they got in. The parliament enacted special laws dealing with Jews. The population viewed the Jews as parasites who harmed the body politic and undermined the religious devotion of the nation. When I say that Poles of my generation were anti-Semitic, I do not mean that all Poles hated Jews but I do believe that most did. There was a social consensus that Jews were evil and undesirable.

Cardinal Hlond, the Primate of Poland, and Marshall Pilsudski, called "WODZ" (The Leader), and his successor Marshall Rydz-Smigly, dominated the country. The President was merely a ceremonial figure. The Prime Minister was a top administrator, not a policy maker.

In our town, the mayor and chief of police were important officials, but like everyone else they deferred to the "Ksiadz Proboszcz" (the head of the parish). This was an awe-inspiring title. I have searched in vain for a title in English which would convey the same intimidating influence. Pastor or parson does not do it.

"Ksiadz Proboszcz" had political and spiritual power. Miechow's Ksiadz Proboszcz was my father's patient, as were the mayor and the chief of police. Unlike everybody else, the Ksiadz Proboszcz did not come to the office, the office went to him. His carriage would take the dental equipment to the palatial residence and Father would follow. It would not be proper for the Ksiadz Proboszcz to come to a Jew, and there was no Polish dentist in Miechow. There was a prohibition in the Catholic doctrine about visiting a Jewish home. Father was reluctant to make this concession to Ksiadz Proboszcz. However, they got along well and I recall that father came back with a bottle of sacramental wine after every visit.

Historically, Poland considered itself the outpost of Catholicism. *Antemurale Christanitatis* was the Latin term for Poland's special status within Christendom. Catholicism was the official state religion of Poland. The Ukrainians and the Byelorussians were Greek-Orthodox and hated the Catholic Church, and the Germans were Protestant. They all-or nearly all- hated the Jews.

The cohesiveness of Americans is based upon a blend of diversity and identity. The divisions, based upon ethnic background, religion and race, are superseded by being American. That was not the case in Poland, or for that matter, in any European country.

The Poland created by the Versailles treaty in 1919 was a land of minorities; 30 percent of citizenry were members of a minority. The Jews were a majority in most small towns and represented 30 percent of the inhabitants of Warsaw, the capital city. The Ukrainians were a majority in southeastern Poland; the Byelorussians were the dominant group in the center of eastern Poland. In Wilno, the town of my birth, there were many Lithuanians. Katowice and western Poland had a sizeable German population.

Cultural pluralism was not celebrated, it was suppressed. Nation and state are synonyms in the United States. The American melting pot was fueled by tolerance. Poland was a boiling pot of nationalism.

Poles were split into the often illiterate peasantry, the sophisticated intelligentsia, the struggling middle class, and the underpaid and often unemployed proletariat. The provincialism of the little towns resulted in distrust of the urban centers. The holders of large estates and subsistence farmers lived side by side.

Geographically, Europe extends to the Ural Mountains, but culturally the continent was divided into two parts. The Western part was a culturally advanced trend setter. The Eastern region was poor and backward. France and Germany had in common contempt for Eastern Europe. The French divided the continent into high Europe and low Europe.

The diverse segments of Polish society had in common a devotion to Catholicism and anti-Semitism.

Fortunately for the Jews, the father of the Second Republic (1918-1939), Marshal Josef Pilsudski, was not anti-Semitic, and he kept the anti-Semitism of the population under control. Marshal Pilsudski had enough stature to be able to politically survive the label "friend of the Jews."

Czeslaw Milosz wrote:

Pilsudski's biggest enemies were Polish nationalists – and because
of his opposition to the right, he was viewed by liberal and leftist
opinion as an ally. [11]

The collective fate of the Jews depended upon the good will of an individual leader. Throughout the history of the Diaspora, the Jews had to seek protection from a powerful and benevolent figure. The death of Marshal Pilsudski in May of 1935 caused national mourning. A portrait of Pilsudski framed in black crepe hung in the window of our home. The Jewish community experienced a profound state of anxiety. With the death of Pilsudski, the hope of Poland being a state tolerant of minorities vanished, and nationalist ideology became dominant. Making life difficult for the Jews became national policy.

The leading political party formed after the death of Pilsudski, OZN, did not accept Jews as members. Endecja, a party dedicated solely to anti-Semitism, was the next most popular movement. The expulsion of the Jews from Poland was seriously debated in leading political circles of the country. In December of 1937, the Polish government negotiated with the French government about settling Polish Jews in Madagascar, the island in the Indian Ocean, then a colony of France. In 1939, before the outbreak of World War II, the Polish legislature debated a law that would prohibit Jewish people from changing their names, even if one converted to Catholicism. There was even legislation proposed to require everyone who on November 11, 1918, was of the "Mosaic religion" to carry the name Israel or Sarah.[12] This was an unabashed imitation of the Nazi policy.

Nazi Germany was poised to conquer Europe, but Polish political parties and the government were preoccupied with "solving" the Jewish question. I have a clear recollection of the nearly daily accounts in the newspapers dealing with the "anti-Semitic excesses." Milosz writes:

That was an ominous period (1937-1939) as the signs of the approaching war went together with the self-imposed blindness of many people. The political climate was ugly. Since the turn of the century, a division into two camps characterized the political life in Poland: liberals and socialists on one side and the Nationalists on the other; but in the late 30s, the second camp seemed to encounter no open resistance. Its chauvinism, its anti-Semitism, its fanning of hatred for other nationalities led to acts of violence, particularly at the universities, where gangs of students would attack their Jewish colleagues. The press was full of inflammatory articles directed against presumed conspiracies of Jews and Free Masons. The paradox was that Poland was threatened by Nazi Germany and determined to defend itself, yet the majority of Poles seemed not to realize they were undermining in their own way the principles of democracy.[13]

Poles and Jews had lived for centuries on the same soil, but now grew apart with every passing decade. A wall of hostility separated them. The Orthodox Jews welcomed the failure of Polish-Jewish encounters as protection against the disappearance of Judaism. The cultural gulf between Poles and Jews did not deprive Poles of the benefits of full citizenship, but it reduced the Jews to second-class citizens. I doubt that there was a day in my childhood when I did not witness anti-Semitic behavior.

Polish Jews were set apart from Poles by language, behavior, and physiognomy and the Jewish men were set apart by their circumcised penises.

28

The Jewish population in inter-war Poland was divided into two major segments. The Orthodox Jews, who formed a separate cultural group with a different language and a distinct manner of clothing and customs, were the majority. The assimilated Jews were a minority within a minority. They adapted to the Polish culture and maintained a secular Jewish identity.

The Zionists advocated the transformation of the Jews into a secular people, and the creation of a Jewish state. Zionism was an outgrowth of the Haskala movement (from Hebrew "shekel," reason), also called the Jewish Enlightenment. Haskala had begun in Germany in the late 18th century in the wake of the emancipation of the Jews by some Christian rulers. It spread to Eastern Europe, where the goal was to introduce the Jews to European secular education.

Some assimilated Jews in Poland belonged to the Bund, a leftist group that advocated secular Jewish culture but did not espouse Zionism. They had in common with the Zionists the vision of a Jew as a full-fledged member of a secular society. The Jewish leftists, communists and socialists wanted to reach this goal by a transformation of the society.

My parents were ardent Zionists and proud of their Jewish heritage. As a child, I collected money for buying land in Eretz Israel, the land of Israel, as the Zionists called Palestine. The Orthodox Jews rejected Zionism as blasphemy. Return to Israel would come with arrival of the Messiah, they believed. To the Orthodox Jews, assimilation was a rejection of Jewish identity, a betrayal. They believed that anti-Semitism was divine punishment for assimilation. This is still their belief. The assimilated Jews were hated by the anti-Semites as interlopers and despised by the Orthodox Jews as renegades.

A rich Jewish culture developed in Poland in spite of the discrimination. Family life was a source of satisfaction. Religious Jews derived support and joy from the observances of rituals and the "learning" (the study) of religious literature. Secular Jews were involved with Polish culture and Zionism.

The prevailing wisdom among the Jews of Poland was that as long as a Jew was humble and poor "they" – the Poles – would leave him alone. Jews were not supposed to be rich, strong or even healthy.

Most Poles believed that Jews were not entitled to the good life because they were involved in "Handel" (commerce) instead of work. "Handel" was disdained by the Polish upper classes and resented by the peasants. My parents were considered rich because we lived like upper class Poles. For a Jew to show wealth was considered poor form and dangerous. Homes of rich Jews were looted during pogroms. Polish officials extracted bribes from wealthy Jews as a condition of doing business. Taxes were based on assessment, and those who displayed wealth paid more than those who appeared to be poor. The affluence of Jews was believed to be one of the causes of Polish anti-Semitism. Poland had many poor Jews, and a few wealthy Jews who pretended to be poor.

At Christmas and Easter, hostility toward the Jews was magnified. The joy that the "Lord and Savior Jesus Christ" was resurrected was combined with hatred of the Jews, who had rejected and crucified him. The Jews kept an especially low profile during Easter. Good Friday was a bad day for the Jews in Poland.

A Jew of my generation cannot be a dispassionate observer because every Jew who lived in Poland between 1918 and 1968 was subjected to systematic persecution. Individual Poles heroically helped some of the Jews to survive the Holocaust, but the majority behaved in a shameful manner. Many actively helped the Germans in the genocidal process and most welcomed it.

Whenever Poland gained freedom, it engaged in violence against the Jews. After the First World War there was an increase of anti-Semitism among the liberated ethnic groups of the fallen empires of Europe. The emergence of nation states relegated the Jews to the status of outsiders. In 1918, Poland celebrated its freedom with pogroms against the Jews.[14] The newly gained political power of the impoverished masses was manipulated by politicians and clergy. The Christian clergy's view that the Jews could not be assimilated – read converted – was exploited by ethnic nationalist leaders. Democracy was a mixed blessing for the Jews in Europe in the post war years, since the majority of Europeans hated the Jews.

The Jedwabne atrocity and similar violence occurred after Eastern Poland was freed from Soviet occupation in 1941. Even after Poland regained freedom from Nazi occupation in 1945, pogroms took place in a number of places. The persecution of Holocaust survivors continued for a number of years. In 1968, Poland declared all Jews as citizens disloyal to Poland and beholden to Israel. Most Jews felt compelled to leave Poland 23 years after liberation. This time, the communists persecuted the Jews.

The civic integration of Jews in the United States was an evolutionary development that grew with the evolving democracy in this multiethnic country. Americans have the tendency to assume that democracy is a cure-all for social ills everywhere but this was not the case for Jews in Poland after World War I.

Poland has been a much abused country; it has suffered oppressive occupation and poverty. As I have said, before 1918, Russia, Prussia and Austria occupied Poland for a hundred years. Czarist Russia exploited and persecuted the Poles. The more the Russians oppressed the Poles, the more the Poles hated the Jews. The Czarist police encouraged violence against the Jews as an outlet for Polish hostility. The Russian military reacted brutally to protests against the occupation but rarely interfered with violence against the Jews.[15]

Call it a clan, call it a network, call it a tribe, call it a family. Whatever you call it, whoever you are, you need one.
-Jane Howard, *Families*

Chapter 3
My Family

On New Year's Eve in 1937, my parents were walking home from a party. A well-known anti-Semitic hooligan accosted my mother, a beautiful woman, and Father beat him up. The next day the man barged into our residence, knife in hand. Father grabbed a chair and held him at bay. At this point, they exchanged angry words but neither one attacked the other. The "hooligan" did not expect resistance and father had no intention of attacking him. The hostile confrontation evolved into a meeting of the minds, and the two men parted on friendly terms. An early morning toast with vodka celebrated the new relationship. The "hooligan" became our handy man. The Jewish community of Miechow talked about this episode for a long time. Polish Jews did not behave this way. The expected Jewish response was flight or submission. My Father did not fit this image.

Across the street from our house was a small grocery owned by a Jew named Aaron Horowicz.(anglicized version is Horowitz as in Vladimir Horowitz) Mr. Horowicz had served in the Polish Army during the 1919 war with the Soviet Union. He suffered injuries to his spine, which gave him a hunched back. As a veteran, he was entitled to a license by the state monopoly to sell alcohol and cigarettes. Even though Jews owned most grocery stores, they were rarely licensed to sell these products.

One day, the members of the anti-Semitic party called "Endeks," staged a boycott of Jewish stores. The usual graffiti "Zydy do Palestyny" (Jews to Palestine) was scrawled on Mr. Horowicz's front door. The head of the Endek Party, a heavy-set man whose menacing face I clearly remember, and a few other party members blocked the entrance to the store. They carried anti-Semitic placards. The Endeks prevented the peasants, who regularly bought vodka, cigarettes, salt, matches and other necessities, from entering the store. We kids watched the scene with horrified fascination.

Suddenly my father appeared, still wearing his white coat. He exchanged angry words and a few shoves with the Endek leader. Father argued that the

Endeks could encourage boycotting but had no right to block the entrance to the store. He prevailed, and the Endeks backed off, making it possible for some of the peasants to enter the store. Shortly thereafter, the Endeks dispersed. Father was the only Jew in town who could get away with such behavior. Any other Jew would have been attacked by the group and severely beaten. Disputes in our town usually were more physical than verbal.

After this mission, father was a hero to Mr. Horowicz. Whenever I went to fetch cigarettes for my father, he would give me candy. Even our governess had kind words to say to my father about this episode. Miss Luba, who was Jewish, and my father frequently argued about politics. She was a leftist, maybe even a communist. My father fired her when she called him a fascist. Miss Luba had flaming red hair. In Poland red hair was considered typically Jewish and ugly. "Ryza Zydowa" children yelled after the elegant Miss Luba, as passing adults smiled in agreement. In English this phrase simply means red headed Jewess, but in Polish it was an ugly slur.

My sister Olenka was my father's favorite. She was cute and self-assured. Our maid Vikta treated Olenka as if she were a princess. I was jealous of all the attention heaped upon Olenka, but I took comfort in knowing that I was the favorite of my grandparents, aunts and uncles.

Although my parents worked all day, they were always close by when needed. Once, when I was about ten years old, I was chopping wood in the courtyard and hit my foot with an ax. Father heard my screams and was there within seconds. A scar on my right foot and the memory of seeing the stark whiteness of bone are still with me.

Politics, for me, was what baseball is for an American boy; a way of relating to my father. My father always followed the political news with great interest. He was an avid newspaper reader and taught me to read by identifying letters on newspaper headlines. Father subscribed to three newspapers: *Kurier Codzienny*, the leading Polish language daily paper; *Przeglad*, a Jewish newspaper printed in Polish; and *Praegaer Zeitung*, a German paper published in Czechoslovakia.

Unlike my father, I was an early riser and read the papers before he got up. While he shaved and was getting ready to see his first patient, I followed him and reported to him the highlights of the news. He read the papers later in the day.

Listening to the news on the radio was a family ritual. I was very well informed about political developments since this was a major topic of conversation at the dinner table. I read books before I was enrolled in school. I was afraid of my father but also proud of him. He was strong and brave; qualities impressive to a young boy.

My parents cultivated confidence in their children by treating us with respect. Every day at lunch, the main meal of the day, I expressed my opinions on a variety of issues.

My parents met with friends every day to drink tea, play cards and, above all, to discuss political developments. I listened eagerly and occasionally provided some information that one of the adults might not have had. Father had contempt for Mussolini, Europe's first dictator. We followed closely Mussolini's war against Ethiopia, and Haile Selassie of Ethiopia had our wholehearted support. We admired his resistance to the attack by the Italian army. Mussolini had to use aerial bombardment and poison gas to achieve victory.

I remember Hitler's occupation of the Rhineland, on March 7, 1936, two days after I turned eight years old. My father listened to Hitler's speeches on the radio and I came to know that voice very well, even though I did not understand German. The tone was harsh and later I realized that the content was brutal. Hitler's verbal violence was soon followed by violent actions. I vividly recall his annexation of Austria in March 1938, which coincided almost to the day with my tenth birthday.

Next to my parents, my grandparents played an important role in my childhood. My paternal grandfather, Hershel Tenenwurzel, was a kind, gray-haired, soft-spoken man. He had been a well-to-do merchant who lost all of his money during the Great Depression. He spent his years of maturity dependent on his sons. His father, Yakov Shraga Tenenwurzel, was the owner of a large estate known as "Piaski Lubelskie." He was as rich as he was pious.

In the 1800's, Yakov Shraga established Batei Warsaw, part of Mea Shearim, in Jerusalem, a housing development for the Orthodox Jews. My most vivid memory of Grandfather Hershel is his visit to a vacation home my parents had rented in the countryside near Slomniki in Poland. Grandfather looked pale; every word required great effort. He was dying of cancer, yet he never complained, and he smiled gently. After his death, we visited Grandmother quite often in Kielce, the capital of our province, only 80 kilometers from Miechow. It was a short ride by horse-driven carriage from the train station to Grandmother's home. When we arrived at Rynek (Town Square) 11, I would run upstairs and ring the doorbell continuously; this was a ritual announcing the arrival of her grandson. Some 50 years later, when I visited the building, I had the strong urge to ring the doorbell in the same manner; instead I stood silently in front of the door and then walked away tearful.

I remember my paternal grandmother as if I saw her yesterday, although she has been dead for over sixty years. Grandmother's hair was milky white, and she was tall and slender. Her face radiated benevolence and strength, and she inspired deference in most people who dealt with her. She was kind and generous and I loved her dearly. Her maiden name was Finkler; her grandfather had been known as "The Radoszycer Cadyk", the Jewish equivalent of a Church Father in Catholicism. Radoszycer means "from Radoszyce," the little town where he held his rabbinical court. Radoszyce was known for a castle built by King Wladyslaw Jagiello in the 14th century.

I recall a portrait of my famous great-great grandfather hanging in the dining room of our home. He was an awesome looking man with a large white beard. Legend had it that Napoleon came to seek his advice before invading Russia in 1812. The town of Radoszyce is located about 25 miles northwest of Kielce. Jews have lived there since 1615 by permission of King Zygmund. (It took a royal decree to permit Jews to live in a given town).

The front of the apartment building in Kielce where my grandparents had lived since the turn of the century was covered with yellow plaster and a few balconies. I remember the dining room where we had festive Passover dinners, and the kitchen where Grandmother baked "makownik," poppy seed cake – my favorite.

Whenever I visited Grandmother, I kissed her and then ran to the armoire in her bedroom. This massive, cherry-colored piece of furniture had a lower drawer where Grandmother always left a present for me.

At the Passover holidays, the whole family gathered in Kielce. The holiday began with the Passover Feast (Seder). Father taught me the four questions in Hebrew, traditionally asked by the youngest child during the ceremony. When Grandfather was alive, he conducted the Seder service. After his death, my father did it. (My father was the eldest of my grandparents' five children). The whole family and a few guests were crowded around the table. The service began with a reading of the Haggada (the narrative of Exodus). Everyone tried to help me understand the Hebrew text of the Passover story. Occasionally there would be controversy as to the translation and interpretation of a passage. I drank the prescribed four cups (small ones) of wine like the adults. After the meal, the proceedings went on late into the night and I was permitted to stay up.

"You shall eat nothing leavened; in all your settlements shall you eat matzoth (unleavened bread)." (Exodus 12:20) was a command strictly followed by my grandparents during the eight day long Passover Holidays. All food and drink made from wheat, barley, rye and oats was removed from the house because it was leavened. There were even special utensils for Passover. In our home in Miechow, however, matzoth and bread lived peacefully side by side.

My mother's parents, Kalman and Hawa Kowarski, lived in Wilno, Poland. After World War I, the Treaty of Versailles established Poland and Lithuania, and each country claimed Wilno. Poland then annexed Wilno by military conquest, depriving Lithuania of its capital. My mother had gone to a Russian elementary school, attended a Lithuanian secondary school and graduated from a Polish university – without ever moving out of town.

Wilno was home to many cultures – Polish, Lithuanian, Byelorussian and Yiddish. With its large Jewish population, Wilno was known as the Northern Jerusalem. Jewish culture flourished there in isolation from the Polish community. Czeslaw Milosz, a native of Wilno, lists many famous Jewish writers from his hometown who gained fame in America or other Western countries. He wrote:

> But we, in the very city where those books were printed, knew literally nothing about them. Several fell into my hands many years later when I bought them in New York – I had to learn English in order to make contact with something that had been only an arm's reach away.[16]

Every summer, my parents, my sister and I traveled across Poland to Wilno to visit my maternal grandparents. I looked forward to these trips. The distance between Miechow and Wilno seemed enormous. The trains in Poland were modern; they ran on time and were impeccably clean. The railroad cars had compartments that were spacious and accommodated six people, but generally a family or a group of friends would have one to themselves. Long corridors ran along each car. This was the place where people would stand and visit with strangers. The locomotives were large, powered by steam engines and fueled by coal; they seemed to us to be technological marvels. The railroad personnel wore crisply pressed dark blue uniforms. These men were proud to be employed by Polish State Railways. There was an air of adventure associated with railroad travel, like airplane travel in the 1950's. On a train, I felt like an explorer observing the changing landscape, the people in villages and small towns. The steady beat of the wheels against the railroad tracks was like music, and as the train sped through the countryside, people lined up, looked at us wistfully and waved. Railroad stations and churches were the most impressive buildings in Polish towns. The stations were located in the center of the city and were a hub of commercial and social activity. But my joyous memories of trains were later replaced by dread. Trains became connected with terror and death camps.[17]

The trip to Wilno took many hours. I wandered among the compartments and made friends with other children on the train. Sometimes we would stop for a day or two in Warsaw to visit my mother's sister, Aunt Clara, a nurse employed by the Warsaw school system. She was Mother's younger sister, similar to her in appearance. She had pitch-black hair, an olive complexion, and large dark eyes. Aunt Clara, unlike Mother, was not excitable; she was able to handle any situation. She lived on Zelazna Street in a typical Warsaw multistory apartment building that had a large entrance hall dominated by a statue of the Virgin Mary. Aunt Clara was sophisticated, active in politics, and usually surrounded by young men.

Warsaw was the seat of government, but also Poland's largest and most modern city, its ancient history notwithstanding. A little boy from a small town required help in such a metropolis. To this day, when I cross a busy street, I hear Aunt Clara's voice, "First look to the left, then to the right." No such precautions were necessary in Miechow.

My grandparents and other relatives would be waiting for us at the Wilno railroad station. A porter with a red cap and black uniform would take the luggage from the compartment as the family exchanged hugs and kisses on the platform. A "doroshka" (horse-driven carriage) took us to my grandparents' apartment.

I remember hearing the phrase that Wilno was "the wonder of art and nature." The river Wilenka joined the larger Wilia River in the center of town. At the mouth of the Wilenka was Castle Mountain with an ancient fort. The contrast of river, valley, and a mountain made the landscape distinctive. Magnificent buildings – churches, synagogues and mansions – testified to the history of the city. Poles and Jews, equally divided, comprised a majority of the population; Lithuanians, Byelorussians and Russians were in evidence in significant numbers. To me, Wilno was a Polish city, yet I kept hearing that it was to be part of Lithuania. I knew a poem by Adam Mickiewicz, Poland's greatest poet, which began "Lithuania, my fatherland." How could Lithuania be the fatherland of a Pole? I wondered. Hearing Wilno called the "Jerusalem of the North" added to my confusion. My mother's parents spoke to each other in Yiddish or Russian.

My parents and aunts conversed in Polish. When I went with Grandfather to the market, I heard him speak Lithuanian to the peasants from whom he was buying eggs and chickens.

The Kowarski family was large – my mother had two younger brothers and four younger sisters. The Kowarski sisters were all beautiful and gregarious. One of my mother's brothers, Uncle Yehoshua, traveled all over the world. He was an artist and lived most of the time in Paris.

My maternal grandmother bordered on being obese. I remember her as kind hearted and always overjoyed to see me. Grandfather was accepting of everyone – the peasants from whom he bought chickens, as well as religious Jews whom he considered superstitious. He treated poor and rich relations in the same manner. But Grandmother was disdainful towards those whom she considered beneath her. She lacked Grandfather's ever-present serenity. Grandfather's face always looked fresh and friendly, but Grandmother often seemed tired. She took naps in the afternoon and this puzzled me. During that time, Grandfather would collect pine cones that were used as fuel for the samovar to prepare the afternoon tea, a daily ritual.

Each summer, my grandparents rented a "dacha" (a summer home) in the dense pine forest surrounding the city. The dacha would be within walking distance of the Wilia River. In the mornings, we would swim and meet other people spending the summer there. The river was busy with slow-moving rafts made from whole trunks of trees being transported to the mills in the city. Everyone – aunts, uncles, cousins, and friends – would swim out to these rafts, ride them downstream for a good distance, and then walk back.

The eastern part of Poland was like a foreign country to me. The hundred years under Russian occupation made Poles of this region different from those who had lived in the west under German and Austrian control. They spoke with a different accent and had different eating habits. Soup was served as the second course during the main meal and every home had a samovar for making tea. I was used to starting a meal with soup, and no one had a samovar in our part of the country. Poland was politically one country, but cultural integration was not accomplished in the short existence of the Second Republic, as the resurrected Poland was called.

....No man is an island, entire of itself...any man's death diminishes me, because I am involved in mankind; and therefore never send to know for whom the bell tolls; it tolls for thee.
-John Donne

Chapter 4
War is in the Air

In September of 1938, one year before Germany's invasion of Poland, I came home from school shouting enthusiastic slogans about the return of "our Cieszyn". This was a border town divided by a river; half of the town was in Czechoslovakia. My father was scornful and called Poland's leader, Marshal Edward Rydz-Smigly, a fool for making bellicose pronouncements against Czechoslovakia and demanding the return of Cieszyn. Father said that Cieszyn was as much "ours" as "theirs." I was confused. My teacher, an attractive brunette whom I liked, had given us a pep talk in favor of the return of the disputed piece of land to Poland. My father, whom I admired, argued that these territorial demands were self-defeating and played into Hitler's efforts to dominate Europe. In March 1938 Germany had annexed Austria now he was trying to subdue a major state.

Czechoslovakia may seem like an insignificant power today, but in 1938, it was almost a military equal of Germany. It took the cooperation of Britain, France, Hungary and Poland to enable Hitler to dismember Czechoslovakia. On September 29, Adolf Hitler, Neville Chamberlain, Edouard Daladier and Benito Mussolini signed the Munich Agreement. Germany was given the Sudetenland starting on October 10, and de facto control over the rest of Czechoslovakia as long as Hitler promised to go no further.

In joining with Nazi Germany in the destruction of Czechoslovakia, the Polish government relied on Hitler's assurance given in his Reichstag Speech, May 21, 1935, when he declared:

> We recognize, with the understanding and the heartfelt friendship of true Nationalists, the Polish State as the home of a great, nationally-conscious people. The German Reich and, in particular, the present German Government, have no other wish than to live on friendly and peaceable terms with all neighboring States."[18]

It is incredible that Poland would cooperate in 1938 with Hitler's efforts to subjugate Czechoslovakia. Of the population of Czechoslovakia, 0.5 percent consisted of Poles who lived in a region adjacent to Poland.

Sir Martin Gilbert writes in *History of the 20th Century*, "the land transferred to Poland contained 132 thousand Czechs, 77 thousand Poles and 20 thousand Germans." It was a strategic blunder to "liberate" such a small group, which in turn, enhanced the power of Nazi Germany.

Czechoslovakia was the most democratic state in Europe and that was its undoing. Minorities formed independent parties and were represented in the legislature and the government. Among the Germans, Hungarians and Slovaks in Czechoslovakia, there was a strong separatist movement seeking the downfall of the republic.

When Austria became a German province in March of 1938, Czechoslovakia was encircled and militarily indefensible. England and France abandoned Czechoslovakia by pursuing the policy of appeasement. Winston Churchill was the lonely voice advocating resistance to the expansionism of Nazi Germany but at that point he was just a backbencher with little influence.

In 1936, while Winston Churchill was regularly warning a complacent British Parliament about the imminent threat of German rearmament, the prime minister, Stanley Baldwin, told a colleague that when Winston was born, "lots of fairies swooped down on his cradle bearing great gifts: imagination, eloquence, industry, ability. But then came a dissenting fairy who said, 'No one person has a right to so many gifts,' and gave Churchill a shake and twist." As a result, Baldwin concluded, "he was denied judgment and wisdom. And that is why, while we delight to listen to him in this House, we do not take his advice."[19]

In March of 1939, just as I turned 11 years old, Czechoslovakia was overrun by Nazi Germany. This naked aggression was the foreseeable result of the 1938 Munich Conference, which rendered the country indefensible. One look at the map after the German occupation of Austria and the Sudetenland shows that Hitler's greatest military victory took place at the Munich conference table.

William Shirer, the American correspondent, historian and novelist, was in Paris on the day when Nazi Germany violated the Munich agreement. He writes in his diary:

> Complete apathy in Paris tonight after Hitler's latest coup. France will not move a finger. Indeed, Bonnet told the Chamber's Foreign Affairs Committee today that Munich guarantees had: "not yet become effective" and therefore France had no obligation to do anything.[20]

The British government held the same view. France and England shamelessly failed to honor their obligations, but soon would discover the meaning of the truism do not ask "for whom the bell tolls; it tolls for thee."

Apathy is about the only thing that Miechow had in common with Paris and London. I am amazed at how normal our life was in spite of the signs of impending disaster. In the summer of 1939, my parents left my little sister Olenka and me with our grandparents in a dacha in Podbrodzie, outside Wilno. This was far away from home, at the other end of Poland. They returned to Miechow to work as in the years past.

My friends and I played war in the deep trenches that were surrounded by barbed wire. These remnants of the First World War crisscrossed the forest around the village of Podbrodzie. Little did we know that World War II was about to erupt.

In August 1939, our stay at the dacha was cut short when our parents arrived to take us home to Miechow. "Suddenly" the threat of war was in the air. The pleasant and leisurely atmosphere of earlier trips was gone. The train was crowded with tense, anxious people. Poland's joy at gaining part of the Czechoslovak territory and declining to deal with the Russians was short-lived. The appeasement did not work, as it never does with an absolutist regime.

After the takeover of Czechoslovakia, Hitler decided to conquer Poland. Once again, a series of demands was made. The British and the French made their usual protests, which we anxiously followed in the press and on the radio.

The defeat of the Polish Army by the German military machine appears at the present to have been inevitable. But in 1939, there was widespread belief that the brave Polish Army, with the help of France, would be victorious in a confrontation with Germany. The belief that within weeks Polish soldiers would be marching into the German capital was widespread. Milosz writes:

> The political fantasy of pre-war Warsaw – with its slogan: 'We Will Not Yield An Inch', with its conviction that if the Germans struck, the Polish Army would occupy Berlin in a matter of days – was only amplified by the defeat, and the whole conspiratorial apparatus fed an illusion, putting into itself, a gloomy national ecstasy.[21]

We found the Jewish community of Miechow changed when we returned from summer vacation. Rumors of war brought newcomers from the Western part of Poland to our town. One night I was awakened by unusual sounds in the courtyard. I heard the gate opening and a horse-drawn wagon being backed up to the rear entrance of the house. I could also hear the voices of young girls. I fantasized that one of the girls would be my age and as beautiful as Dzidzia Wroblewska, who had moved away a few months before.

In the morning, I thought it had all been a dream. However, I found in the courtyard the tracks of horses. I hung around, curious to see whether a girl would materialize. Before long, a beautiful girl with long blond braids and blue eyes appeared. She pretended not to notice me. I took to the "trapeze," a structure for shaking out rugs. I performed a variety of tricks on this contraption, and my efforts paid off. The girl was impressed and started talking to me. So began one of the most important and enduring relationships of our lives. Her name was Gina Olmer and she was the granddaughter of Mrs. Friedenberg, a widow living downstairs.

The peasants called Gina's deceased grandfather "Prawda" (The Truth), as he had been a wheat merchant known for his honesty. I remember his long white beard that extended to his belt. My cap-less, clean shaven, blond father in his fashionable suit, and Mr. Friedenberg in his traditional black shiny caftan and ever present skull cap, were the symbols of the split in the Jewish community.

Gina's mother, who died before the family came to Miechow, was the stepdaughter of Mrs. Friedenberg. Gina and her sister, Lusia, had lived in Huta Krolewska, an industrial town on the German border. Gina's grandmother was religious, unlike her son and grandchildren who were assimilated.

One day I asked Gina which boy she liked best. There was one, she admitted with a giggle, but she would not name him. Finally she gave me his initials, "I. T." I was crushed.; my initials were E.T.. I wondered who the lucky boy was. At last, Gina told me that Emanuel should be spelled "Immanuel," which means, "God is with us" in Hebrew.

Gina and I spent most of our waking hours together. I introduced her to the fields and hills near our house. My father took Gina and I to the nearby Chodow forest for the traditional mushroom gathering excursions. For years, we remembered these trips with great fondness. Little did we know then that the Chodow forest would gain tragic significance for the Jewish community of Miechow. The Germans, assisted by Polish units called Junaki, would soon massacre hundreds of Miechow's Jews in this forest.

In preparation for the war, Gina and I glued strips of paper on the windows to prevent breakage from sound waves from artillery or aerial bombs. We helped to dig ditches next to our house as air-raid shelters. I was overjoyed that the start of school had been postponed indefinitely.

What disturbs people's minds is not events,
but their judgments on events.
-Epictetus, 100 A.D

Chapter 5
The Great Escape

In the early hours of September 1, 1939, the German Army invaded Poland. We were glued to the radio. Father listened to Radio Berlin. The German propaganda claimed that they were responding to a Polish "provocation." The Germans engaged in a deception. German prison inmates were put in Polish Army uniforms and staged an attack on a radio station in the border town of Gleiwitz. Incredible as it may seem, after the German attack on Poland, Chamberlain, once again, made an offer to Germany to mediate the conflict between Poland and Germany, provided that German troops withdrew from Poland. Chamberlain expressed the view that every territorial dispute could be resolved peacefully. Hitler did not even bother to respond. Fortunately, we did not know that the spirit of appeasement continued.

On the 2nd of September, my parents gave a party for high-ranking officers of the Polish Army who were spending the night in our town. They told us that the Polish army was retreating, but the evening was a gala affair. My father dug up some rare cognac from the cellar. The officers, dressed in their beautiful uniforms, were in good spirits and reassured my parents that the retreat was a tactical maneuver; the army would fall back to the Vistula River and then a counter-offensive would begin. The Polish Army, they told us, would soon end up in Berlin. In retrospect, this sounds like a fantasy, but at the time it was reasonable to people consumed by nationalistic pride. We believed that the superiority of German weapons was counterbalanced by the bravery of the Polish soldiers. Shortly before the German attack on Poland, posters had appeared everywhere proclaiming "We Are Strong – We Are United – We Are Ready."

After the self-assured Polish officers left the party, my parents decided that we should take part in "ucieczka" (the flight), so we joined the mass movement of people fleeing eastward to escape the advancing German Army. The belief that German troops would be thrown back by the glorious Polish Army was widespread and motivated the effort to run east for temporary shelter.

We left our home before dawn, each carrying a piece of luggage and a gas mask. As the lucky owners of gas masks, we were the envy of friends and neighbors. Almost everyone thought that the Germans would use poison gas, so it was a matter of life or death to acquire gas masks. My father had gotten these masks a few days before in Krakow; he had used his influence with military authorities to buy them. The masks were British made and came in green canvas pouches. I became proficient at putting on the mask, having demonstrated its use to my friends many times. I wore the pouch with this life protecting device whenever I left the house.

We began our journey on foot. Our first stop was the railroad station. Trains for the evacuation were supposed to be there, but the trains were not running. We went ahead on foot, hoping to get a horse in a nearby village, but the roads were clogged with panic-stricken people. With horse-driven wagons, pushcarts and people on foot, the road resembled a slow-moving river. Everyone wanted to go east, away from the Germans. People were irritable, angry and ready for hostile confrontation.

Our attempts to buy a horse and buggy were unsuccessful and my parents decided that we had to get rid of our belongings. Mother carried a fancy suitcase made of leather and lined with silk, a birthday gift from Father. She did not want to part with it. My parents argued about it briefly, and she was persuaded to leave it by the roadside. Most of our luggage was designed for travel by train and to be carried by porters. We tenaciously hung on to our gas masks. We were prepared for the military use of the poison gas of World War I. This lesson of history was not much help, as gas was not used in military operations during the Second World War.

At the end of the first day, we reached a small town and visited the principal of the local school. He and his wife were patients of my parents. His title in Polish was Pan Kierownik. "Sir Director" in translation, this title carried a great deal of weight in Poland. Pan Kierownik and his wife gave us a cordial reception and promised to get a horse for us.

Pan Kierownik and his wife decided to join us in the effort to escape the German army. We bought a horse and wagon and the two families hit the road together. But before we departed the Polish radio brought wonderful news that France and England had declared war on Hitler. We cheered and hugged each other joyously when we heard this news. We were convinced that it was only a matter of days until the war would be over. The defeat of Poland by Germany was unimaginable. With the help of these two powers there was no doubt about the outcome. The radio played the national anthems of Great Britain and France repeatedly.

We did not know that these Allies had no intention of coming to Poland's aid; or that they used Poland to divert Hitler in the easterly direction. The declaration of war was an empty gesture. Hitler dreaded a second front, which he considered the reason for Germany's defeat in the First World War. In *Mein Kampf*, he writes that England was essential as an ally in Germany's effort "to march along the road of the Teutonic Knights of old," meaning Poland and Russia.[22]

England and France, contrary to the terms of the Mutual Defense Treaty with Poland, took no action when Poland was attacked. They hoped that Hitler's next victim would be the Soviet Union. Western capitalism felt more threatened by Communism than it did by Nazism. Even after the attack on Poland by Nazi Germany, Chamberlain was willing to negotiate about the "Polish Corridor," if Hitler withdrew from Poland.

We had no doubt that America, under President Roosevelt, would quickly come to the aid of Great Britain. We did not know that the United States was in no position to come to anyone's help. American historian Doris Kearns Goodwin noted:

> In the spring of 1940, the United States possessed almost no munitions industry at all. So strong had been the recoil from the war after 1918 that both the government and the private sector had backed away from making weapons. The result was that, while the United States led the world in the mass production of automobiles, washing machines, and other household appliances, their techniques of producing weapons of war had badly atrophied.[23]

We assumed that Allied forces would soon prevail. Inspired by this false hope, the adults decided to cross the Vistula River, which they believed would become the front separating the Polish and German armies. Neither us nor the Polish army knew about the concept of "Blitzkrieg."

The horse-driven wagon carried our friends' belongings and some items we had brought along. My sister and the two women rode in the wagon while the men and I walked alongside. My Father and Pan Kierownik took turns leading the horse. The roads were crowded with terrified people, and we moved slowly.

Suddenly, we heard the sounds of a low-flying plane in the distance. Convinced it was a Polish plane, we waved to it as it began to descend toward the human river. The tiny plane dove and opened machine gun fire on the crowd. Horses bolted and people screamed. The airplane continued down the road, causing mayhem, returning within minutes to repeat the gruesome performance. We ran to the side of the road and hit the ground, burying our faces in the dirt. When we looked up, bloodied people, dead bodies and chaos surrounded us.

Over the next few days, these small planes, usually alone but sometimes in pairs, would perform their deadly mission. People and horses were injured and killed. I could see the faces of some of the young German pilots as they dove toward us. In one such attack, Mother covered Olenka and me with her body as bullets hit the ground and the people around us. I thought that Mother was dead because for a few seconds after the plane had departed, she remained motionless. Another time, instead of hitting the ground, I stood glued to a tree, using it as a shield, which may have saved my life. A few people next to me were injured and some were killed. These barbaric attacks upon helpless civilians should have served as a warning of future German atrocities. There was no military value to these sadistic attacks.

When we reached the Vistula River, we were told that civilians were not allowed to cross to the other shore. Father and Pan Kierownik explored various possibilities of getting to the eastern side of the river, without success. At one point, the adults broke down crying and hugged each other. This was the first time I saw my father weep. We followed a country road and found a village with a school. Pan Kierownik could always gain access to a school building.

The next morning we traveled along a dirt road in the hope of finding a way to safety on the other side of the river. We were looking for someone with a boat. At a distance, we saw a detachment of Polish cavalry approaching at a fast clip. Father ran toward them and I followed. To our amazement, the officer brought the entire unit to a halt. Father told him of our predicament and asked how to get to the other side of the river. I can still hear the officer's calm but firm response:

"All is lost. Poland is defeated. The German tanks are on the other side of the Vistula. We are soldiers and must fight. You are civilians; get into some small village. Let the Germans advance ahead of you and return to your home." Father thanked him, the officer saluted and they dashed away. There was no time to reflect on this terrible news. We located a village with a schoolhouse and stayed there until the Germans tanks were ahead of us. The image of German tanks and Polish cavalry symbolized the futility of Poland's struggle.

This was around September 10th, days before the invasion of Poland by the Red Army in the east on September 17th. In the first week of the war, we found out later, German panzers were on the outskirts of Warsaw. The Polish Air force was destroyed 48 hours after the outbreak of hostilities.

There is a myth that Poland was the victim of a conspiracy between Hitler and Stalin, known as the German-Soviet Non-Aggression Pact. But Germany had defeated Poland before a single Soviet Unit crossed the border.

The origins of the Soviet-Nazi agreement are the policies of Britain, France and Poland, in relation to Germany and the Soviet Union. Stalin's offer to come to the aid of Czechoslovakia before the Munich sellout was rejected by Great Britain and France. The Soviet Union was not even invited to the Munich conference. Stalin's paranoia was reinforced by the reality of being betrayed by England and France. Poland refused to consider allowing the Red Army to come to the defense of Czechoslovakia and joined Germany in its dismemberment.

The Soviets had been repeatedly rebuffed in the effort to form an alliance with Britain and France against Nazi Germany. The last such attempt had taken place at the time of the Munich Conference (September 1938). By early 1939, Stalin faced the prospect of resisting German military expansion in Eastern Europe alone. This was the expectation of the English and French diplomats. Stalin changed his policy, fired his foreign Minister, Maxim Litvinow, a Jew, and replaced him with V. M. Molotov who soon began negotiations with the Nazi foreign minister, Joachim von Ribbentrop, and concluded the agreement. Ancient animosity prevented Poland from forming an alliance with the Soviet Union against Nazi Germany. Stalin's tyranny was in its early stages, and the old aversion to "Moskale" (Moskowites) was the dominant emotion in Poland.

In my elementary school, I was indoctrinated with the images of relentless assaults on Poland by Czarist Russia, and impressed with the threat facing us from the Soviet Union. The history of Polish-Russian relations looks a bit different, if one relies on more unbiased sources.

Poland and Russia had been trying to dominate each other for ages. Military aggression and religious animosity had existed for centuries between these two countries. Stephen Batory, King of Poland (1575-86), defeated Ivan the Terrible in the 16th century; in 1582, a Polish garrison occupied Moscow's Kremlin, and the Polish prince, Wladyslaw, assumed the role of the Tsar. Not only was he a foreigner, but a member of the hated Catholic religion. In the 18th and 19th centuries, Russia subjugated and occupied Poland.

After World War I, when communism became the Russian "religion," a new dimension of hostility was introduced. The Soviet Union and the newly created Poland went to war. In 1919, the fledgling Polish Army under Jozef Pilsudski occupied Kiev, the capitol of Ukraine. In a counter offensive, the Red Army came to the outskirts of Warsaw. Polish forces prevailed in a battle that is known as "The Miracle on the Vistula."

Nationalism, religion, ideology, territorial disputes and military encounters fueled the fratricidal animosity between Poles and Russians, two members of the Slavic family. The efforts to create a Pan-Slavic movement could not overcome the nationalistic and religious rivalries among the various Slav nations. The Germans conquered the Slavic states one by one. Slavs were to Western Europe what the Jews were to the Slavs, an "inferior" people. At the turn of the twentieth century, the only free Slav states in Europe were Bulgaria, Serbia and Russia. German politicians spoke of the contest between Germandom and Slavdom. Eastern Europe was to the Germans what Africa was to Great Britain, a territory to be colonized and Germanized. What was Eastern Germany in the 19th century used to be part of Poland.

The First World War was inspired by the Germans to teach the Slavs a lesson. World War II was another attempt of the "superior" Germanic people to subjugate the "inferior" Slavs and exterminate the Jews and Gypsies. In both wars, the Russians played the decisive role in frustrating the German "Drang Nach Osten" (Thrust into the East). Conquest of the East has been the ancient German motivation for the periodic invasions of Slavic lands. After the First World War, England, contrary to the provisions of the Versailles Treaty, permitted Germany to become a military power. The English politicians assumed that German aggression would be directed east.

Adapt or perish, now as ever, is Nature's inexorable imperative.
-H. G. Wells, *Mind at the End of Its Tether*

Chapter 6
German Captivity

The day after the Germans overran the village that became our temporary refuge; we ventured onto the main road leading and started our return home. Roads were virtually free of civilians, who were still too intimidated to face the Germans. Father, with his usual bravado, approached a German patrol and asked if it was permissible for us to move in the direction of our home. The Germans were delighted that he spoke fluent German and told him that we could go home. They even gave him some cigarettes. The only Germans that could be seen at this stage were members of the *Wehrmacht*, the regular Army.

They were smartly dressed and traveling in imposing military vehicles. They often sang in a high-spirited manner. The motorcycles with sidecars fascinated me. The Germans bothered no one and even seemed friendly. Along the road we saw a few burned-out German tanks, a tribute to Polish bravery in this unequal struggle. Poland had been an easy victim of Hitler's Blitzkrieg. Cavalry against armored vehicles was no match.

We returned to the community where Pan Kierownik lived. The horse and wagon were left with them and we walked on to Miechow. We passed my school, which had become the Wehrmacht Headquarters. As we entered our building, Gina's family, the Olmers, told us that a group of Poles were upstairs with German soldiers looting our home. They warned us not to go upstairs because we might be beaten or killed. My father ignored the warnings and ran upstairs; I followed, against my mother's objections. Vikta was in the apartment; she had tried in vain to protect our property from the intruders.

Father began to shout, demanding that the mob leave our home. They responded with physical threats and anti-Semitic insults. My father turned to the German corporal who, with a few soldiers, was supervising the looting. Speaking in faultless German, he persuaded the noncommissioned officer to order the horde out of the building. Some objected, pointing at my father and repeating the only German word they knew "Jude!" (Jew). The Feldwebel (Corporal) pointed his submachine gun at one of the men who would not part with a stuffed chair he already considered his own. Our home was reclaimed from the Polish mob with the help of a German soldier. In Miechow, the German military kept control over the Polish population eager to assault the Jews. In some smaller communities the Jews were not so fortunate.

The Feldwebel left after a long talk with father. A little later he returned with German canned foods. Vikta prepared "Knoedel" (dumplings), the corporal's favorite.

Father was concerned about the well-being of Grandmother in Kielce. There was no way to communicate with her as neither telephone nor mail service had been re-established. Neither was there any public transportation. The war was not officially over. Poland had collapsed within a week but the brave defenders of Warsaw were still holding the Germans at bay for many days.

A day or two later, the Feldwebel, our newly found German friend, agreed to drive Father to Kielce, 80 kilometers away. My sister and I went along; we were picked up in a German staff car. It was exciting to be in an Opel Kapitäin. I was familiar with the Opel Kadet, a much smaller vehicle.

Since the military operations were not yet completed, there were a number of checkpoints between Miechow and Kielce. The Feldwebel and my father exchanged pleasantries with the German soldiers, who saluted my father with particular deference. They assumed that my father was a high-ranking German official. He was blond, blue eyed, and impeccably dressed, and he had a uniformed Feldwebel as the driver. My sister and I were in the backseat.

Grandmother was overjoyed to see us and surprised that we had come accompanied by a friendly German soldier. The helpfulness of this man made an impact on me; not all Germans were dedicated haters of the Jews. His generous behavior to our family may have contributed to my ability to trust some Germans, which saved my life a few years later.

Grandmother was alone in her big apartment; Uncle Moniek had not returned from the "great escape" eastward and nothing was known about him. Being in Grandmother's home created the illusion of peace and gave us hope, but that soon would be only a memory. A few days after our return to Miechow, I saw German soldiers shearing off an elderly Jew's long white beard. A group of Poles stood by laughing and cheering. The cutting off of the beards of the religious Jews was a harbinger of the atrocities that followed.

Civilian administration, German Police and auxiliary units of Ukrainians, Lithuanians and Latvians, soon replaced the front line soldiers. Polish Police were resurrected under German direction. Persecution of the Jews became the order of the day. Every few days, new directives were issued that made the life of the Jews more grueling. In the beginning of the occupation, Vikta had continued to live with us, but soon there was an order issued that under penalty of death (everything was punishable by death) Jews were prohibited from employing Aryans.

Parting with Vikta was painful; she was like a member of the family. Even though it was against regulations dedicated to racial purity for Vikta to work for us, it was permissible for father to become the dentist of the German soldiers. This was formally agreed upon at the Wehrmacht Headquarters. The soldiers were coming with written referrals. "They pretend they do not know that I am a Jew," father told mother one day.

Since Mother did not speak German, she stayed mostly out of such situations. The Germans who were located in the county building, the civilian administration, controlled our lives and we called them collectively Gestapo or SS. Paramilitary units wearing black uniforms assisted them; they were Ukrainians. Only later did we learn who was who in the German bureaucracy.

One day we could see a Polish mob under the leadership of the Ukrainians, whom we called Schwarze (Blacks) because of their black uniforms, systematically going from home to home, beating Jews and looting their homes. They were approaching our house. From our balcony, we saw this violence working its way towards us. Father was able to contact the German military headquarters by the newly restored phone. The looting of Jewish homes and savage beatings of the Jews stopped merely a few houses from ours. Lying flat on our balcony, I watched through the cracks between flower boxes. This was not morbid curiosity. My father had assigned me this observation post while he was on the phone.

The arrival of German soldiers was greeted with a sigh of relief. This was the second time that the Germans had protected us from our Polish neighbors. The message was clear – we were facing two enemies, the Germans and the Poles. The increase in the intensity of Polish anti-Semitism under the German occupation was puzzling to us. The adage that the enemies of our enemies are our friends did not hold.

We expected any moment that the mighty British Empire and the brave French Army would launch an offensive against Germany. Defeat would follow swiftly in spite of Hitler's pronouncements that the Third German Empire would last a millennium. But there was no news of any military action by the British or the French. The Allies were conducting what Churchill called a "Phony War." He explained in his memoirs:

> The French government requested us to abstain from air attack on
> Germany stating that it would provoke retaliation upon their war
> factories which were unprotected. We contented ourselves with
> dropping pamphlets to rouse the Germans to a higher morality. [24]

Western statesmen did not know their adversaries. After Germany invaded Poland, the Netherlands proclaimed once again its nonaligned status. They relied on Hitler's assurance that Germany would honor Holland's neutrality. The "Phony War" ended in April 1940, as Denmark and Norway were overrun by the Germans soon after they invaded Holland.

On May 10, 1940, Chamberlain was replaced by Winston Churchill as prime minister of Great Britain. We believed that Hitler's assault on France, Belgium and Holland, which took place in the same month, would bring in a massive response from Great Britain and America. We did not know that America was completely unprepared for war. The United States could muster at this point only five fully-equipped divisions. We were convinced that, unlike in World War I, America would intervene at once. It came as shock years later to discover that the conservatives in Great Britain and the Republicans in the United States opposed the involvement of the United States in the European War.

As late as 1940, when Churchill gave his famous "blood and toil" speech, only labor benches cheered, the conservatives were silent until Chamberlain came in."[25]

In mid-June, Father heard on clandestine radio that Winston Churchill had announced that the "battle of France" was over. The French Army collapsed quickly and, unlike Poland, France made peace with Germany.

There was no political will in the United States to go to war. In 1940, America was still suffering from the Great Depression. In the words of the historian Doris Kearns Goodwin:

> [But] by 1940, the New Deal revolution had sputtered to an end. The country was weary of reform, and Congress was in full rebellion against the administration's domestic agenda. A bipartisan coalition of conservative Southern Democrats and Republicans had seized the initiative, crushing the president's housing program, slashing appropriations for relief, killing the federal theater project, and eliminating the administration's undistributed-profits tax.[26]

After the fall of France, England was within Hitler's reach. In July of 1940, Hitler issued Fuehrer Directive #16 entitled: "Preparations for the Landing Operation against England"; however, to the great relief of Britain, Hitler changed his mind.

Our image of the military might of Great Britain was exaggerated. The British Army had merely five divisions of regular Army facing sixty superior German divisions ready for assault. France and Great Britain were politically inept in dealing with Nazi Germany, militarily unprepared and ineffective. The military leaders were veterans of World War I.

The invasion of Britain would have had dreadful consequences for the future of Western Civilization. The "Battle of Britain" was limited to the confrontation between the Royal Air Force and the Luftwaffe. Hitler did not want to destroy England but merely to force it to deal with Germany. He considered the British to be the other Germanic nation. His military plans were dominated by ideology. Jews and Bolsheviks were on his mind.

Sometimes even to live is an act of courage.
-Seneca, Letters to Lucilius

Chapter 7
Courage to Endure

At first, German behavior looked like a more intense version of the harassment to which Jews were accustomed. In the first few months, the German persecution had a relatively moderate impact upon our lives. My parents considered it a hardship when they were notified that a German civilian would occupy one of our rooms. When the prospective lodger appeared, Father welcomed him and expressed pleasure that a German would live in a Jewish home and assured him that the sleeping sofa was clean. "We have recently fumigated this couch to get rid of the bedbugs," Father told him. The bedbug story was invented and it worked. The man left, disgusted. My father used the German propaganda about the "unclean Jews" to our advantage. A few months later it was unthinkable for a German to be assigned to live with Jews.

At the end of 1939, we were ordered to wear an armband with a Star of David. Posters explained to the Polish population that these measures were necessary to protect the public from associating with the "dirty disease-carrying Jews."

In February 1941, the Germans decreed that all Jews living in Miechow were to move into a two-block area, which they called the Jewish Quarter; we called it a ghetto. The ghetto was the first step in the process we now call the Holocaust, which the Germans called "The Final Solution." What seems inevitable in hindsight was unimaginable to us then. We did not imagine that Nazi Germany, unlike past persecutors, did not want to exploit us as slaves, destroy our temples, forcibly convert us or stage a pogrom. Nazi Germany was dedicated to the idea that we were vermin unworthy of living. We assumed that vermin was a metaphor in the minds of the Germans. We viewed the future from the perspective of the past. What is unimaginable is not anticipated. The Jews of Europe did not dream that this mass killing could be planned by a civilized nation. We went about the business of living and celebrating important family events.

The move to the ghetto was scheduled shortly after March 5, my 13th birthday. On that day I would celebrate my Bar Mitzvah.

Bar Mitzvah marks the entry of a Jewish boy into adulthood. Under Jewish Law, children are not obligated to observe the commandments; although they are encouraged to do so. The Bar Mitzvah ceremony formally marks the assumption of that obligation. A boy gains the right to take part in religious services, to enter binding contracts and to testify before religious courts.

The Bar Mitzvah boy delivers a speech (Drosheh), an interpretation of some Talmudic passage, and the congregation listens with benevolent approval.

I had been preparing for this day since I had turned 12 years old. A young rabbi had tutored me secretly, as instruction of Jewish children was forbidden by the Germans. He came to the house three times a week; he taught me Hebrew and we studied the Torah. He considered the Hebrew Bible divinely inspired. But my father, who was knowledgeable about the Talmud, saw it as the Jewish counter-part to Greek mythology.

A few months before my Bar Mitzvah, Father ordered new suits for him and for me. I was proud to get my first pair of long trousers. Boys my age wore short pants in summer and knickers in the winter.

My Bar Mitzvah ceremony took place in the synagogue mere days before the move to the ghetto. The rabbi called upon me to read a passage from the Torah, and later I was told that I did a grand job. My father pulled off the feat of getting wine and a traditional flat cake for everyone who attended the services. There was also a party at our house on Pilsudski Street.

However, gloom hung over the gathering. A foreboding of impending disaster was on the minds of both the children and the adults. We would be losing our home and our neighborhood. The future was uncertain and the present awful. The ghetto was tiny; therefore, most apartments would have to be occupied by a few families. It fell upon the Judenrat (Jewish Council) to make these assignments.

"We will live with the Apfelbaums," Father announced one day as he returned from the offices of the Judenrat. The house assigned to the Apfelbaums was outside the ghetto proper. A fenced alley connected the Apfelbaum house to the ghetto. It was a red brick building, the most modern one in town. It had bathrooms like no other house in Miechow, with a flushing toilet, an electric hot water heater and showers.

The Apfelbaums were to take the upstairs apartment; the Tenenwurzels would live downstairs. Only these two families would live in such comfort in the ghetto. We were included because of the respect and influence my parents had in the community. The fact that father was treating a number of powerful Germans played an important role in our community standing.

Mr. Apfelbaum was the "Commissar der Juden" (Commissar of the Jews). This title was emblazoned on his armband, which he rarely wore. He was the only Jew who had been granted the privilege of not wearing the armband with the Star of David identifying him as a Jew. The Germans made him the highest authority among the Jews of the county of Miechow.

The Apfelbaums had moved to our town shortly after the defeat of Poland in the fall of 1939. They had come from the Western part of the country, which had been annexed by Germany. They spoke German fluently. Jews who spoke

German were given special privileges. Mr. Apfelbaum was a stocky man who was a bundle of energy. He talked and moved rapidly, and he had an air of authority about him. He was viewed as a benevolent intermediary between the Jews and the Germans.

The Apfelbaums had two sons. The older son, named Moniek, was in his late 20s. He had the looks of a movie star – tall, broad shouldered and dark haired. Unlike his father, he moved and talked with deliberation. I remember him as a man who always had a smile and a friendly word. He was his father's deputy. The youngest son, Bronek, was in his early 20's. He was blond and baby-faced. He was the head of the Order Service (Ordnungsdienst), which is nowadays erroneously referred to as the Jewish Police. Mrs. Apfelbaum was a heavy-set, soft-spoken woman.

Father, with his usual resourcefulness and connections, organized the move to the ghetto. Jews were forbidden to hire non-Jews and did not own any horses. Most Jews in Miechow moved their belongings in handcarts and wheelbarrows. Father gained special permission from the Gestapo to hire a Pole with a horse-drawn wagon to transport the office equipment and our furniture. I remember walking behind the wagon, feeling mournful. I was sad to leave our house on Pilsudski Street.

The Germans ordered the Judenrat to erect walls separating the ghetto streets from the Polish side. Fences surrounded the rest of the ghetto. Large brick walls with gates closed off the three points of entry. The Germans ordered that the walls be constructed from bricks coated with white stucco and decorated with a large Star of David painted blue. The neat, meticulously crafted decoration was in stark contrast to the turmoil and misery behind it. Going outside of the ghetto was forbidden under penalty of death.

Life in the ghetto was dominated by the concerns of daily living, and individual inventiveness provided the necessities of existence. Smugglers brought food from the Polish side. This was dangerous but essential for survival. The food, which could be purchased legally through ration cards, was not sufficient to sustain life. Smuggling also stood for resistance to oppression. In the ghetto, as in colonial America, smuggling was considered a heroic activity. Children and adolescents made the best smugglers. They were agile, adventuresome and courageous.

Life for the Jews under German occupation was like living on a different planet, and the difference from normal life increased with every passing week. I became aware of the strangeness of that existence when I tell a story to friends or family about those days. They do not have the concepts that are necessary to fully understand what I am trying to describe. The term "ghetto" is misleading; it makes us think of the Middle Ages. The Germans called it an even more benign name, "Jewish Quarter." In reality it was an urban top-security prison camp.

There was no work in the usual sense. A few craftsmen like tailors, shoemakers, and others, performed services for the Germans and sold some goods on the black market. The Bakalarz brothers made fancy boots for the Germans and my parents fixed their teeth. In return they would get food, cigarettes and other goods. Jewish women cleaned German houses. Jewish tradesmen and day laborers provided services for the Germans. This was not passive compliance but an active effort to endure. Vital resources and information flowed from such contacts and contributed to survival.

In occupied Poland, the economic system regressed to primitive levels. Money had little meaning and a bartering system developed. This was particularly true in the ghetto. Supply and demand reigned supreme. Aside from shelter, food, fuel and clothing were the commodities essential to survival. The Jews used jewelry, furs, artwork, tools, excess clothing and similar luxuries as payment.

The Germans made daily requests for work parties, which would be put together by the Judenrat. Groups of men and women would leave the ghetto to do cleaning jobs, road repair, unloading or loading of railroad cars. This was forced labor, which included physical abuse by the Germans. For the Jews it was an opportunity to occasionally bring some food from the outside. People adapted to these conditions and hoped for the end of war. The lack of reliable information about the war tormented us. The one-page Polish newspaper published by the Germans was pure propaganda. Having a radio, even for Poles, was an act punishable by death. We believed the war would end any day. We thought the Germans had no gasoline or other resources to pursue the war. A typical joke:

"Did you hear the Germans have enough gasoline for two more years?"

"That is awful; are you sure?"

"Oh yes! For their cigarette lighters."

In Miechow, as in other ghettos, the Judenrat made the ordeal endurable. The Judenrats were social institutions that enhanced the collective adaptability of the ghetto population. A semblance of community organization was present in the ghetto. The thousands of people crammed together in two blocks were organized into a viable community. Food distribution, health care, and law and order were maintained. The Judenrat performed life-sustaining functions. There was an improvised hospital, a synagogue and even a ritual bath. Community spirit was preserved. The time spent in the ghetto is part of my childhood memories. The boys played in streets and chased girls. I continued to be in love with Gina Olmer, who had lived downstairs from us on Pilsudski Street, and now lived across the street.

When people speak about the Judenrat, they rarely mention the positive contributions made by this institution. For example, providing heating materials for the Ghetto was an enormous task, which the Germans did not consider. That involved getting coal, since this was the only method of heating. Negotiations and bribery were used to accomplish this purpose.

If any form of cooperation with the enemy was to be avoided, then the Judenrats were illegitimate. But if survival was a desirable goal, then the Judenrats were adaptive and useful. I do not recall anyone questioning the legitimacy of the Judenrat in Miechow.

The Judenrats are accused by purists to have been tools of German oppression or, at best, pawns in the hands of the Germans. They are viewed as symbols of Jewish passivity, submissiveness and collaboration. Compliance of the Jews in German captivity is labeled collaboration.

Compliance with the enemy in the service of survival is not collaboration. Slaves, prisoners, hostages and victims of rape comply or die. In some hostage situations the victim and the captor develop a positive relationship. This phenomenon has become known as the Stockholm syndrome.[27]

There was no evidence of such a development between the Jews and the Germans during the Second World War. A Jew selected to be in the Judenrat could refuse the "honor." But nearly all took on the challenge of plotting means of reducing suffering and death. Adam Czerniakov, the head of the Warsaw Judenrat, kept a diary. The entry in his diary on May 15, 1942 shows how little he knew what was going to happen:

> In town the rumors about deportations continue. People speak of tens of thousands. To work according to plan under such conditions is remarkable. Nevertheless we do the job day by day. I always go back to what Dickens wrote: "A watch is not wound with tears.[28]

In addition to the Judenrat, there were individual Jews who had contact with specific Germans and could influence them. They were called "Macher," which in Yiddish means literally doer or fixer. The Macher was the ghetto counterpart to the lobbyist in America, but with much higher stakes. During the war the Macher was a savior. His ability to sway a powerful German and extract some concession was vital in times of peril. After the war, the Macher was considered a villain, his former virtue, a relationship with the enemy, became a vice. Yet Jews in German captivity who established contact with the Germans had a better chance of survival. That is true in all situations where people are at the utter mercy of an enemy.

The Judenrat had a dual function. From the German perspective it was an instrument of destruction; from the Jewish perspective it was a survival tool. The concentration camp was a quantum leap of destructiveness when compared to the ghetto, because there was no community structure in the camps.

In the ghetto, the collective survivor know-how of a community offered some protection. In the concentration camps, only an individual's will to live opposed the genocidal program. Survivor skills were not acquired suddenly but were developed over time.

The impact of living in the ghetto was, at first, psychosocial, but with the passage of time it became biological. Malnutrition and living under life threatening oppression brought about profound physical changes, but the struggle for existence under conditions of extreme deprivation did not destroy the spirit of cooperation among Jews.

The eminent Holocaust historian Raul Hilberg has shown great mastery of the historical facts, but he lacks empathy with the existential reality of the Jews in the ghetto. He criticized the Judenrat cooperation with the Germans in carrying out the orders to collect taxes and furs. In his classic *Destruction of European Jews*, he writes:

Efficiency in the collection of taxes or furs could bring about more suffering. Thus many of the virtues of Jewish ghetto government became vices. Responsibility was turned into unresponsiveness and salvage into loss. [29]

The term "ghetto government" is misleading. The Judenrats had no control over the German policy or its enforcement. Here is how the collection of fur was accomplished in Miechow. One day Ukrainian and German units surrounded the ghetto. It was announced that all fur was to be delivered to the offices of the Judenrat by nightfall. Whoever had even a tiny piece of fur in his or her possession thereafter would be shot on the spot. I nearly got killed in the effort to smuggle my mother's expensive fur out of the ghetto. I was chased by one of the Ukrainians but managed to get away and delivered the fur to the house of some Polish friends for safekeeping. Had Apfelbaum and the rest of the Jewish Council refused to obey the German order they would have been shot on the spot.

Hilberg deplores the role of the Judenrat in the collection of furs, but he is silent about the soup kitchens, the care of the sick, and the day care for children that was organized by Judenrats in most ghettos. The Judenrats reduced some of the hardships of ghetto living. Communication with the enemy was maintained. Solving problems created by the Germans was the Judenrat's primary activity. The Judenrat could not help the Jews without being useful to the Germans. That was true for the women who cleaned German houses, for the men who did heavy labor and for my parents who fixed the teeth of the Germans.

In the long run, it was counterproductive for the Germans to establish and preserve a Jewish institution in the ghetto. It had the advantage of reducing the number of Germans necessary to operate the system, but it had the disadvantage of providing individual Jews with life sustaining community, which enabled some to survive.

One definition of intelligence is the ability to adjust to a changing environment. The only available means of adapting for the Jews was to make a change in themselves. The Jews of Europe had the courage to endure; they were surviving under conditions incompatible with life. From the perspective of the Germans, the ghetto was a phase in the annihilation process. Everyone knows it now. To us, it was a place where living was made possible for a longer time than the Germans had planned.

Criticism of the role of Jewish councils during the German occupation of Poland neglects the historical roots of this institution. In ancient Babylon, an Exilarch, a Jew, governed the exiled Jews. In the Babylonian exile, the Jews adapted to the demands of the Persian King. Ultimately, King Darius had a vision that God instructed him to rebuild the temple and some Jews regarded him as the Messiah. So in the Babylonian exile there was also cooperation with the enemy instead of confrontation. In Spain and in Poland, Jewish communities created their own governing bodies, which were useful to the oppressors but also vital to the oppressed.

In the ghetto, I became a born-again Jew in a cultural sense. I learned Jewish folklore, particularly Jewish humor. I admired Jewish resourcefulness and adaptability, and the Jewish community spirit. I became a member of a group of five boys. We called ourselves "Ju-H-E-Wo-Abra"; an acronym of our first names; Julek, Heniek, Emek, Wowek and Abramek. A sixth boy was always with us but was not officially part of our pack. We called him "Piesek" (Doggie); he was Julek's cousin.

Piesek was two years younger and therefore did not deserve the honor of being a full member, but he was permitted to follow us in our escapades at a respectful distance. Julek was my best friend. He and his family came from the Western part of Poland that became part of Germany after the defeat of Poland. He was a brilliant boy who was writing a fictional account of the war. He read us excerpts from it. I recall a chapter describing the victory over Germany by the Red Army. He wrote this before Hitler invaded Russia. Julek spoke German and therefore could communicate better with the Germans than the average Jew. I spoke neither Yiddish nor German. Julek's fluency in German would soon save my life.

One day, I climbed an old tree in the garden behind our house. I don't recall what game Julek and I were playing, but it was probably Cowboys and Indians. I was armed with my Finnish knife, which was hanging from my belt. A vicious German named Foehn suddenly appeared below and yelled angrily. I did not understand a word. He pulled out his revolver and pointed it at me; he appeared ready to shoot. Julek began speaking rapidly to him in German. The only words I understood were "Dr. Tenenwurzel." Foehn put his gun back in the holster and motioned for me to come down. He slapped me once on the face and asked for my knife, which he threw on the ground. "There are partisans in this area. Whoever is armed will be shot," he yelled and Julek translated. Then he marched off. Julek said that telling Foehn that I was the son of Dr. Tenenwurzel stopped him from pulling the trigger. Father was the most influential person, next to Apfelbaum, in the ghetto. This was based upon his skill as a dentist, his knowledge of German and his personality.

Foehn was the second in command at the post office. The headman was an older, pleasant German we called "Herr Postmeister," which was his official title. Herr Postmeister was Father's patient and father was on very friendly terms with him, a fact well known to Foehn, an ardent Nazi. Foehn often wore his yellowish-brown SA uniform instead of the postal outfit. He made periodic forays into the ghetto to harass Jews. Occasionally he would shoot Jews for some infraction.

Why would a postal official want to kill a boy who was obviously engaged in a game? He claimed that he was doing his duty to help stamp out partisans. But it takes a certain personality to intend to kill a young boy in a garden on a pleasant summer afternoon. He was not being impulsive; he did not lose his self-control. Had he killed me, it would have been an egosyntonic homicide, a killing acceptable to the ego (personality) of the killer.[30]

Wowek, another member of our bunch, was also a big-city boy, from Bendzin, a city annexed by Germany. He was an inexhaustible source of Jewish

56

jokes, delivered with a deadpan face. He was the first to teach me Jewish expressions. Wowek was smaller than the rest of us but very determined. No one in our group except me could beat him in a fight, and I could do it only when I became very angry.

Heniek was the only other boy from Miechow who was part of our group. He was an excellent soccer player. His father was a barber who had a shop on the corner of Pilsudski Street and the Town Square before the ghetto was established. In the ghetto, he cut hair in his apartment. There was another barber in the ghetto and one day both of them were summoned to the German headquarters in what used to be the county offices. A few hours later, the Judenrat was called to pick up their bodies. No one ever knew why they had been killed. A rumor had it that the Germans had been drinking and decided the Jews did not need barbers.

My friend Abramek was handsome with blond hair and blue-eyes – the typical Aryan looks. His appearance made him very suitable for assuming a Christian identity. He and I were the only two boys of our age group from Miechow to survive the war. A group of five girls who called themselves "Jednosc" (Unity) were our girlfriends. None of them survived.

Existence in the ghetto, particularly for adults, was bleak. We, as children, adapted more easily. Unbeknownst to our parents, we often would leave the ghetto. We scaled fences and climbed roofs to escape. We often gathered in a hilly area outside town known as "Kocie Gorki" (Cat's Hills), ate white bread with sausage (bought on the black market), and kept score of the death penalties we were facing. Leaving the ghetto, being outside city limits, having white bread and meat, and not wearing armbands were offenses for which Jews were killed.

The bravado of leaving the ghetto just for fun had adaptive value. This adolescent rebellion provided a skill that saved my life. The ghetto was a school for survival. We did not know that the ghetto was also the prelude to nearby Auschwitz.

One day, the 19-year-old Chaim Tenenwurzel, leader of the young Zionists, joined us on our escapade to the hills outside of the ghetto. I was proud of my cousin from Kielce, who was hiding in the Miechow ghetto. The Germans in Kielce were eager to kill him as a leftist organizer. Chaim wanted to talk to us as a group. He gave us an inspirational speech about the future that would bring a Jewish state in Palestine.

The education of Jews was forbidden, but it continued in the early stages of the ghetto. I took private lessons outside the ghetto, studying in the home of the Polish school principal, a former patient of my parents. She lived close to the pharmacy in the Town Square. I had to sneak out with my book hidden under my shirt. My parents considered my education important enough to expose me to the risk of leaving the ghetto. I also worked a few hours every day in the dental laboratory, which was part of the apartment. Leon Storch, a young man trained by my father to be a dental technician, was my instructor and like an older brother to me.

The atrocities perpetrated by the Germans inside the ghetto multiplied every week. The German we called "Der Schwarze" was known for his cruelty.

The two streets of the ghetto were usually jammed with people. When word got out that Der Schwarze was coming, the streets would empty. One day, as he marched through the empty ghetto streets, he smelled food being cooked and entered an apartment. A housewife stood by a stove. He found a piece of meat in the pot and shot the woman. This apartment building had a large entryway (brama), which was a favorite hangout for us boys. That afternoon, we were hiding in the staircase when Der Schwarze entered. We heard the shots he fired. Der Schwarze inflicted a penalty prescribed by an official announcement (Bekantmachung) for possession of meat. This was a killing acceptable to him as a person and approved by his society. We never returned as a group to that house, but I did go there often because Gina lived in the building.

The death penalty was a common punishment for various transgressions. The following proclamation was issued by Dr. Ludwig Fischer, the German district governor of Warsaw, on November 10, 1941:

> Concerning the Death Penalty for Illegally Leaving Jewish Residential Districts...Any Jew who illegally leaves the designated residential district will be punished by death. Anyone who deliberately offers refuge to such Jews or who aids them in any other manner (i.e., offering a night's lodging, food, or by taking them into vehicles of any kind, etc.) will be subject to the same punishment. Judgment will be rendered by a Special Court in Warsaw. I forcefully draw the attention of the entire population of the Warsaw District to this new decree, as henceforth it will be applied with the utmost severity.[31]

All Germans were dangerous; they had the power and the right to kill a Jew on a whim. We quickly learned that some of them were more eager than others to exercise this "right." Any German could torment and kill a Jew, but there was a pecking order of dread associated with the various men in uniform. The gray uniforms of the Wehrmacht (German army) were the least menacing. The blue uniforms of the Polish Police, called Polnishe Polizei by the Germans, represented manageable danger. One could talk to them and bribe them. The greenish uniforms of the "Gendarmerie" (German police) carried the danger of arrest, but only rarely beating or execution. The black uniforms of the Ukrainians were viewed with alarm; they portended brutality. The men of the Jewish Ordnungsdienst (order service) did not wear uniforms; they had distinctive hats and the inscription "Ordnungsdienst" on the required armband with the Star of David; they were called Odeman. We were not afraid of them.

Occasionally, we would see the yellowish-brown uniforms of the SA. These were rare but were as frightening as the SS uniforms, which were fear inspiring. The SS were identifiable as an elite organization by their uniforms and vicious behavior. The double lightening flash was the symbol of the SS. Worship of the God-like Führer and hatred of the Jews were the spiritual backbone of the SS. The SS had within itself super elite known as "Sicherheits Dienst" (Security Service) that watched over the behavior of everyone, including the SS. Whenever we spotted the inconspicuous two letters "S.D." on the lower sleeve of an SS officer, we were terrified. There were individual differences of behavior even among the Gestapo. Any German could kill a Jew without feelings of guilt or fear of reprimand. Killing vermin had no ethical or legal consequences. The indiscriminate acts of cruelty and random killings created a state of terror among the Jews. Helplessness was not a state of mind but a stark reality.

One day, a breathless Odeman came running into our ghetto apartment. "Herr Bayerlein (the chief of the Gestapo) wants to see you at once in the Starostwo (county building)," he told Father. Mother and I were frightened. Would we see Father again? Would he be shot or sent to a concentration camp? We imagined the worst.

It was a great relief a few hours later to see him return unharmed. "I beat him at chess," Father announced. Bayerlein had found out that Father was the town's chess champion and wanted to play a game. After that, Bayerlein and Father played chess often, usually at our apartment in the ghetto. The ancient and international game of chess created a bridge between a Gestapoman and a Jew. "Do you let him win?" I asked Father one day. "Oh no, he is too smart for that" was the answer. Bayerlein also became Father's patient.

He was a rotund man who was always polite and soft-spoken and he wore gold-rimmed glasses. He never came to us empty handed. He often asked me some well-mannered question that my father translated. Father was treating at least a dozen other Germans. The chief of the local Gestapo was naturally the most important. This fact gave our family a certain safeguard from random acts of violence by the Germans that made forays into the ghetto.

It was well known that the Germans who came into the ghetto to be treated by Father did not engage in any of the usual cruelties. Medical treatment of a German by a Jew contradicted the notion that the Jews were "vermin"; it also violated the Nazi laws against so-called "Rassenschande" (racial disgrace). However, Germans who were not stationed in Miechow were not aware of the deference given to father by the local Germans.

One day, a truck and a car pulled up in front of our house and four or five SS men entered our apartment. We knew all the Germans stationed in our town, but we did not know these men. They had a few Jews with them whom they had grabbed in the street. The Jews were ordered to carry elegant pieces of our furniture from the living room to the truck. Father, in his white coat, emerged from the office, protesting. One of the SS men gave him a powerful blow to the face; another pointed a submachine gun at him and came very close to killing him. I watched in horror, crouching in the doorway. They paid no attention to me. The SS men exchanged some comments with each other and began to laugh. One of them handed Father a knife with a metal handle and ordered him to cut down the lighted crystal chandelier hanging low over the table. I ran to the entrance hall, removed the main fuse, and hid it. As I peeked into the dining room, I saw with pleasure the disappointed looks on the German faces. They had expected to witness an electrocution. When dealing with the Jews, out-of-town SS men felt free to ignore local arrangements.

Das war ein Vorspiel nur, dort, wo man Bücher verbrennt, verbrennt man auch am Ende Menschen.
- Heinrich Heine (1797-1856)[32]

Chapter 8
The Final Solution

The words "extermination," "death camp," "gas chamber" and "genocide" were as remote to us in Poland as computers and space travel. Language helps people to anticipate experience. It is hard to recognize what you cannot name. In the ghetto, I never heard even a rumor about the existence of death camps or a plan to annihilate all Jews.

Nazi Germany's policy of solving social problems – real or imagined – by state-sponsored killings is now a well-known fact. Actual or potential disagreement within the Nazi party and many other problems were dealt with regularly by murder.

The technology of killing the Jews evolved from that of killing disabled Germans. The Nazis' first victims were handicapped German children. They were designated as "unworthy of life" and physicians administered lethal doses of sedatives to kill them. Disabled German adults were next. They were killed in carbon monoxide gas chambers. And yet the international community did not declare Hitler an outlaw; instead they chose not to believe his behavior.

The lethal malevolence of Nazi Germany was not believable to statesmen in London, Paris and Washington; it should come as no surprise that the leaders of the Jewish community in Poland did not believe it either. The Polish Jews relied upon past familiarity with the Germans who, before 1933, practiced a more civilized form of anti-Semitism than the Russians, Ukrainians and Poles.

In 1914, the Germans replaced the Russians as occupiers of Poland. Eastern European Jews welcomed the Germans as kinder and gentler oppressors. Polish Jews immigrated to Germany before 1933 to seek a better life in Germany than they had in resurrected Poland. Nazi Germany was a new barbaric chapter in the long history of German anti-Semitism.

We did not take Hitler's pronouncements seriously because they were unbelievable. Hitler's writings and speeches advocated the destruction of the Jews. He urged mass killings of the Jews in *Mein Kampf* and in speeches throughout the 1920s. Germany got the message, but the rest of the world dismissed his words as irrational and implausible.

My parents differed in their reactions to the German atrocities. Father viewed them as an aberration. Mother saw the future in catastrophic terms. Father reasoned that even though some Germans were brutal, Germany was a cultured country and would not tolerate a mass slaughter of the Jews. The controversy going on in our household was not unique. Two schools of thought became dominant in the ghetto: one refused to believe what seemed unreasonable, while the other relied upon the intuition that survival was at stake. Mother was guided by her feelings. It took me many years to recognize that intuition is a form of knowledge. Most things we do well, we do intuitively.

Life in the ghetto was hell on earth, and yet, children played, adults made love, friends and strangers helped each other, doctors treated the sick – in short, life went on. Calling a facility committed to oppression and torture a ghetto was wishful thinking; an expression of hope that we faced nothing worse than what our ancestors had endured in the Middle Ages. But the future was more dreadful than the past. Both the victims and the perpetrators used misleading language. The Germans did it out of malice, the Jews out of ignorance and denial.

In 1942, we still had trust in civilized institutions. German behavior was viewed as a higher level of violence called "anti-Semitic excesses" in Poland. Superficially, there were similarities. Human beings interpret observations in terms of past experiences. Something that has never happened before is likely to be interpreted in light of what is known. The Jews of Poland were used to abuse.

The state-sponsored atrocities carried out by the Germans were mistaken for the depravity of a few "bad Germans." In Miechow, the Gestapoman Kossack was viewed as a "bad German." The "Landrat," the head of civilian administration, was a "good German." With the absence of press and radio and with minimal communication between Jewish communities, it was difficult to recognize a pattern.

The most dreaded word in the ghetto was "Aussiedlung," which literally means "out location". The Holocaust literature calls it deportation. The term does not convey the horror of the barbaric shipping of "human cargo" to destinations unknown to the victims. The transportation itself was designed to kill a significant number of people and debilitate all of them.

Father was a so-called "essential Jew," exempt from "Aussiedlung." He was the head of the Hygiene Commission in the ghetto and, above all, he had vitamin P. "P" stood for the Polish word "protekcja" and the German word "Protection." This term loses something in translation; it was more than connections. It meant that he was in the good graces of powerful figures.

The dread of "Aussiedlung" hung over the ghetto like the Sword of Damocles. But the concept of death camps was as remote to us as the Manhattan Project was to the Japanese in Hiroshima before August 6, 1945. It would be ludicrous to find fault with the residents and city fathers of Hiroshima because they did not anticipate nuclear fission and its military application.

The readers of the *Times* in London on the 16th of December in 1939 could read an article entitled "A Stony Way to Extermination." It described the plans for annihilation of the Jews of Europe. There was even a map provided where the camps were located in the area of Lublin, Poland. *The London Times* was as inaccessible to us as if we were on a different planet.

The much-rumored Aussiedlung came to Miechow in the spring of 1942. One day, an Odeman came at dawn to inform Mr. Apfelbaum that Polish police and Ukrainian units we called "Czarni" ("the black ones" because they wore black uniforms) surrounded the ghetto. Local and out-of-town Germans were among them. Father went with Mr. Apfelbaum to the Judenrat and returned later telling us that all inhabitants of the ghetto were to be taken to the railroad station. It seemed that the first Aussiedlung in Miechow would also be the last. Everyone panicked. Mean-looking Ukrainians eager to use their guns guarded the narrow walkway connecting our house to the ghetto. To the north of our house was the German post office, which was outside the ghetto. The backyard of the post office was separated from our yard by a fence with a gate. No one guarded that fence because, after all, a Jew would have to go through the German post office to get outside the ghetto. Father told Mother, Olenka and me to follow him to the post office. The back door was open. We sneaked quietly up to the second floor of the post office, where the German "Postmeister" lived. Father led us into a room and locked the door. A window overlooked the ghetto, which my parents watched from behind a curtain. I can still see their horrified faces as they looked out that window. Olenka and I were forbidden to come close enough to see anything, but we could hear the gunfire and the screams. At the end of the day, there was complete silence; the operation was completed. But my parents noticed that some essential Jews were in the streets. Evidently this was not the final liquidation of the ghetto after all.

In the evening, we slipped out of the post office and returned to our apartment. During our time hiding in the post office, I never saw Herr Postmeister, but I knew it was he who had arranged this hiding place for us. He took a tremendous risk, and I don't even know his real name. I have only a vague notion that it was Meier. I see him clearly before my eyes. He was a heavy-set man who walked slowly, and spoke with a strong voice that was free of the strident sounds I associated with the Germans. When he played chess with Father, he spoke very little. He was one of the few Germans who did not scare me.

After the first Aussiedlung, those of us still in the ghetto were compressed into a single block. Our modern redbrick house behind the post office was no longer part of the ghetto. Our new apartment was relatively spacious. We had two rooms and a kitchen, plus the dental office. We did not have to share our home with another family. There was a long, narrow courtyard with a wooden outhouse, which meant no more indoor plumbing. We lived on the second floor.

The office window faced the ghetto wall and the forbidden "Aryjska strona" (Aryan side). I looked at the normal life on Pilsudski Street with longing and envy. People walked on the sidewalks; horse-drawn wagons and Polish and German cars were in the roadway. Polish vehicles were easily recognized from a distance. They had a contraption attached to them that resembled a modern water heater. It burned wood, creating gases that served as a substitute for gasoline. They moved slowly.

German gendarmes were at the ghetto gates, and Polish policemen patrolled the ghetto's perimeter. An escape from this genocidal environment was virtually impossible. In addition to the physical barrier erected by the Germans, a wall of implacable hostility of our Polish neighbors surrounded the Jews in the ghetto. It was easier to elude the Germans but the Poles were omnipresent and nearly always eager to betray or apprehend a Jewish fugitive. To denounce a neighbor or a member of the underground was worse than treason, but to denounce a Jew was neither sinful nor shameful. Whoever protected a Jew made one friend and many enemies.

We did not know the fate of the Jews who had been placed in the cattle cars and sent away. The Germans claimed they were being resettled in the eastern territories. Why did they take old people, children and women first? Why all the secrecy?

The Miechow Judenrat hired a young Pole to follow the deportation trains and report their destination. All that he could tell us was that the train went east. The isolation of each ghetto was extreme. No telephones, no newspapers and no freedom of movement. There was a sense of peril but no awareness of impending collective annihilation.

My parents constantly discussed ways to circumvent deportation. Surviving in the ghetto seemed the best option. Living outside the ghetto as Christians was possible for assimilated Jews who had false identity papers. However, a male Jew trying to pass for a Catholic had three Achilles' heels; his facial features, a Jewish accent and a circumcised penis. The foremost vulnerability was the penis.

The hostility of the Polish population was uppermost in the mind of a Jew who considered living on false papers. Anyone who was suspected to be a Jew was likely to be denounced to the Germans by the Poles. Unmasked Jews were often executed on the spot.

From time to time the Germans conducted an "Akcja," a Polish equivalent of the German word "Aktion," roughly translated as "roundup." Usually the purpose was to get workers for forced labor for a day. At other times, they searched for those who were in the ghetto illegally. Whatever the objective, every intrusion into the ghetto by the Germans and the Ukrainian paramilitary units resulted in atrocities.

One day, a group of Gestapo men came looking for an old Jew who had killed a Pole many years ago. He had acted in self-defense, and a Polish court had acquitted him. There was uproar in the Polish community about the verdict, leading to a pogrom. The acquitted man escaped and lived in hiding in Krakow. Some Poles found out that he had returned to Miechow and reported this to the Gestapo. He was killed along with the members of his family.

My parents felt relatively secure as "essential Jews." But I, a 14-year-old unemployed boy, was vulnerable. Father worked out a plan to protect me. Mr. Popielski, the owner of a large estate known as Czaple Wielkie, had been a patient of my parents from before the war. At Father's suggestion, Mr. Popielski made a request for farm labor to the German Arbeitsamt (labor office). The

German head of that office was Father's patient; he approved the request, and I became part of that work party.

The work detail consisted of four girls and me. The girls lived with other female farmhands at the working end of the estate. I lived with the Popielski family in the manor house, which was surrounded by a park. I was treated as a guest of the family and ate with them. The girls worked in the gardens and fields. I wanted to join them but Mr. Popielski would not hear of it; he considered it inappropriate for the son of Dr. Tenenwurzel to work in the fields.

He was a tall man whose appearance and bearing left no doubt that he was a nobleman. He was an outstanding horseman. Mrs. Popielski was a pretty woman, in her late 40s; she was kind and even-tempered. They had two teenage daughters.

The manor house was located a good distance from the road, on a gently rising hill. The road to the manor was clearly visible, which gave a sense of security. The one-story structure overlooked a private park with a small stream running through it. A stonewall surrounded it. The front of the house looked over a sloping meadow at the bottom of which were the farm buildings and the living quarters of the farmhands. I spent most of my time in the park, reading and walking. The setting was in such contrast to the ghetto – peaceful and secure. But I was lonely and anxious, worried about my parents, sister and friends. When would the next Aussiedlung come? Would my family be spared? Would I ever see them again? Sitting or walking in the park, I listened to the cuckoo birds and I made them my oracles. I would repeat, "We will survive. We will not survive." If the birdcalls stopped at "We will not survive," this was a bad omen, but it so happened that most of the time it stopped at "We will survive." We had used this method in better times to determine if a girl "loves me or loves me not."

At the end of the day, I would walk over to the farming area and visit with the four girls. I felt guilty that I was being treated in a preferential way. The youngest one of them was barely a year or two older than I. Her first name was Sala. I was attracted to her and enjoyed her company. She was pretty; her blond hair and blue eyes reminded me of Gina.

One day, while sitting in the park, I saw Mrs. Popielski walking in my direction. She was in a hurry. "Quickly, come with me," Mrs. Popielski instructed in an anxious voice. As we walked towards the mansion, she said, "Two Polish policemen came to pick up the Jewish workers and took them directly to the Miechow railroad station for deportation. We told them you escaped. We will hide you."

She took me to the dining room where I was told to stand behind the thick drapes. Mrs. Popielski went into the kitchen. I could hear her order the cook and his helpers to go on some errand. Mr. Popielski came and motioned me to follow him into the kitchen. A large credenza was positioned in the kitchen across a corner, leaving an empty space behind it. Mr. Popielski moved it and told me to get behind, and then he shoved it back. The kitchen was a large room where food was prepared and where some of the farm workers ate.

I sat quietly in the corner when the kitchen help returned. Not long after, the workers came in for lunch, the main meal of the day in Poland. Mrs. Popielski engaged them in conversation. Two young men serving in a Polish labor troop called "Junaki" joined the lunch group. These units were organized by the Germans to perform manual labor. They marched in military fashion, carrying shovels on their shoulders, as if they were guns. The Germans used Junaki like a paramilitary force. Germans did not entrust Poles, unlike Ukrainians and Lithuanians, with guns unless they were policemen.

The two young visitors on the other side of the credenza had assisted in the liquidation of the ghetto. They described how the Germans took hundreds of Miechow Jews into the Chodow forest and systematically shot them. This was the same forest to which father had taken Gina and I for early morning excursions. One Jew pulled a knife and stabbed a German[33] in his neck. He was not shot, instead he was torn to pieces by dogs.

"Some of the Jews were just injured. We finished them off with the shovels before we buried them," one of the young men said. "The rest of the Jews from the ghetto were deported," the other explained. These atrocities were described without the slightest sense of feeling. There were comments of approval. Behind the credenza I could not utter a sound, even though I wanted to scream. Survival required silence.

Mrs. Popielski no doubt empathized with me but was unable to do anything. She did not dare to interfere with the lightheartedness of the conversation and the anti-Semitic comments of her help. After the lunch, the help was dismissed and Mr. Popielski retrieved me from my hiding place. Mrs. Popielski and her daughter hugged me. I began to cry uncontrollably. The two women put me to bed and gave me "tincture Valerian." These were drops used to calm exited people. To this day, whenever I try to tell this story, I break down crying. The horror of what I had heard, the belief that my parents and sister were most likely murdered, the unfeeling account, and the kindness of the Popielski family were emotionally overwhelming. This is the first of a number of moments in life that feel as if they took place yesterday.

After I calmed down, Mr. Popielski told me that he would ride his horse to Miechow to find out what had happened. I stood at the window and watched him mount his horse and gallop away. Two hours later, he was back with terrible news. There was no sign of life in the ghetto. Suddenly I was alone in the world. Would I ever see my parents and my little sister? Where would I go now? I could not stay on the estate. I was in despair and Mr. and Mrs. Popielski were in an awkward situation, stuck with a Jewish boy. What would they do? I had no papers and was homeless.

I cried myself to sleep. In the middle of the night, the barking of dogs and a loud banging on the front door awakened me. I assumed the Germans had come to get me. I was ready to escape through the back door. Mr. Popielski was also up.

"This is Max Kubinski. Please open up," a voice announced. "I know him," I told Mr. Popielski. Max Kubinski was also a patient of my parents. He was a well-to-do peasant who kept us supplied with farm products. Mr. Kubinski, upon entering, quickly removed his hat and made a deferential bow to Mr. Popielski but he spoke to me first. "Your parents and sister are safe in my barn. I have come to get you." Within minutes I was ready. I said goodbye to Mr. and Mrs. Popielski, and followed Mr. Kubinski into the darkness of the night.

All of a sudden, I was no longer an orphan. I remember walking with Mr. Kubinski, but have no recollection of my feelings, yet the reunion with my parents in Mr. Kubinski's barn is vivid in my mind.

It was completely dark and there was a strong smell of hay. It reminded me of happy visits to farms. We climbed two ladders and removed a large bale of hay behind which was a nest-like space. My parents hugged me, Mother cried quietly; Olenka did not even wake up. We stayed in the barn for a few days. One part of the enclosure was a blank wall of the barn with cracks in it; through those we could see the farmyard and the road. Mr. Kubinski was a wealthy farmer. His hired hands did not know that he harbored Jews, an offense punishable by death.

In the evening, Mr. Kubinski came to bring us food and take away the bucket we used as a toilet. At night we climbed down the ladders and walked around in the barn.

"The Germans have made a new one-block ghetto. Mr. Apfelbaum says it is safe for Dr. Tenenwurzel to return," I overheard Mr. Kubinski whisper to my parents when he returned from Miechow one day. My parents agonized about our options. Mr. Kubinski was prepared to keep us in our hiding place "till the end of war." That was Mother's choice; Father argued against it. So they agreed to return to the ghetto. Our parting with Mr. Kubinski was emotional; he had saved our lives out of friendship. This was the last time we saw him. Some months later he provided shelter for another Jewish family. His neighbors denounced him to the Germans. The Germans killed him and the Jews he was hiding and set his farm afire.

Back in the ghetto, we moved again, this time to Dr. Lazer's apartment. Dr. Lazer and his wife had committed suicide during the last Aussiedlung. He injected Mrs. Lazer and himself with a large dose of morphine, and they lived for days in a coma. Father enlisted the help of the Gestapoman Kossack to have them admitted to the Polish hospital, where they died. Father saw to it that they were buried in the Jewish cemetery. The Lazers died convinced that their two children would live because they had placed the children with some trusted Polish friends, whom they paid a large sum of money. Unknown to them, the Poles took the children to the Gestapo, where they were put on a freight train headed for the death camps. The story of the Lazer children was known to every Jew and every Pole in Miechow.

Dr. Lazer's apartment was a small structure with two rooms; one was used as a residence, the other was an office. Now the office contained my parents' dental equipment. German patients still used their professional services, performed almost entirely by my father.

We were told that the Gestapoman Kossack had stopped the deportation train from leaving Miechow, looking for my father among the human cargo. This surprised my father because the two of them had had a confrontation a few weeks before the Aussiedlung, which I had witnessed. Kossack was complaining to Father that some Jews had caused trouble by living on false papers. It was his "unpleasant duty" to shoot a beautiful blonde woman who had a false Kennkarte (German ID card). Suddenly, Father moved away from his patient, slumped into a nearby chair and said, "Das war meine Cusine" ("That was my cousin"). He asked Kossack to leave. Visibly angry, Kossack got up from the chair, walked away and slammed the door. After this episode, Kossack stopped being a patient and Father expected to be arrested since he had revealed to Kossack that he knew that his cousin, Miriam Cukier, had been living on false papers. Nevertheless, Kossack tried to save father from being placed on the train.

The little ghetto was like a large vault loaded with corpses-to-be. Death could come at any moment by execution or the final liquidation of the ghetto. We behaved as if we knew that the Germans intended to kill all of us, but we did not openly acknowledge it. Unexpressed grief for the loss of loved ones hung in the air.

The population of the ghetto consisted of about 200 legal inhabitants who were essential to the cleanup operation, and other "illegals" who had escaped the Aussiedlung and returned to the ghetto or had come out of hiding in the ghetto itself. When discovered by the Germans, these illegal people were shot. There were only four children in the ghetto now; Gina, Rutka, Olenka and I. We were illegal but protected by the influence of our parents.

A few teenagers pretended to be young adults to get job assignments. Sala, age 16, one of the girls who had worked with me at Stare Czaple, was among the illegal residents of the ghetto. She told me that one of the Polish policemen who had picked up the girls from Stare Czaple had helped her to escape into the forest. The other three girls were delivered to the deportation train. I asked Father to help her become legal and he made her an assistant to Leon, the dental technician.

Sala slept in the crawl space below the roof of our little house, which was reached by a ladder. One day I went up there with her. We talked about Stare Czaple, her escape, my being hidden behind the credenza and hearing the terrible report of the young peasants who finished off with shovels the nearly dead Jews.

This was the first time I had told anyone that story and I burst out crying. She hugged me, and then we kissed. I tried to sexually approach her and she cried out: "Don't! Don't! That's what the Polish policeman did to me before he let me escape. He raped me." For years the memory of Sala crying came to mind whenever I began sexual advances.

Nothing can save us that is
Possible:
We who must die demand a
Miracle.
– W. H. Auden

Chapter 9
Monastery

One day I overheard Father telling Mother, "You cannot believe every rumor you hear." He sounded irritated.

"I want him out of the ghetto tonight. Mrs. Terlecka said she will keep him." Mother sounded desperate.

My parents spoke in hushed tones in the dental office that was part of the small house in the new ghetto. I heard them clearly in the bedroom, which was separated from the office by a thin partition. I did not want to be caught eavesdropping, so I left the bedroom. A few minutes later, Father called me in from the kitchen.

"Your name will be Jan Wojcik," Father told me in a low voice as he pulled a Roman Catholic baptismal certificate from under the mattress.

Mother, trying to control her tears, put her arms around me, and Father patted me on the back. For a long time no one said a word. I understood that I was being sent away to live on Aryan papers as a Christian. Where? With whom would I live? What would happen to my parents? I had these and many other questions but said nothing.

Father was the first to break the silence; Mother continued to hug me. He said that I was to find a way to escape from the ghetto and get myself to the apartment of Mrs. Terlecka in the Rynek (Central Square). "You know how to do that," he said with a faint smile. This was half reproach and half praise. I had slipped out of the ghetto many times just for fun and had been punished by my parents for taking the risk of being killed.

"Mrs. Terlecka has a friend who we hope will take you to a monastery near Krakow. We are not certain he will do it; he is coming this evening from Czestochowa. He used to be a monk at the Mogila Monastery," Mother told me, trying to hold back tears.

The piece of paper I held in my hand with handwritten entries attested to the birth and baptism of a boy named Jan Wojcik. It was my passport to life. It was hard to believe that this flimsy piece of paper could protect me from being killed.

I noticed that under my new identity, I was 3 months younger. My birthday was no longer in March, but in June.

The year was the same (1928), which made me 14, and in need of a "Kennkarte," an identity card issued by the Germans to all Poles of that age. A baptismal certificate was only sufficient for a child. Thus, I would not be legal even if I were a Pole and not a Jew.

Most important was my "dobry wyglod," or "good appearance" in literal translation, meaning no Jewish features. I was a tall, skinny boy. Unlike most Jews, I had no Jewish accent. But I was circumcised and understood that my penis would reveal my identity.

There was little choice at this point, since it was clear that I would be put into the cattle cars at the next selection of the ghetto. My little sister was also at risk but too young to be sent into the dangerous Christian world on her own. Nearly all my friends were already deported to the unknown.

Mother had been obsessed for weeks with getting Olenka and me out of the ghetto. She chased all over town and pleaded with friends for help. None of our Polish friends were willing to give us assistance with living on the Aryan side. Mother, in desperation, talked to acquaintances, even to strangers. As a doctor she had a permit to leave the ghetto at certain hours. Father was focused on making our position more secure in the ghetto by cultivating his connections with German patients. He was aware of the dangers of living on false papers and agonized about it. Father relied upon reason; he believed that we were less at risk in the ghetto than in the hostile Polish world. Yet he was the most suitable for living on the "Aryan side" because of his blond hair and blue eyes.

Mrs. Terlecka was not a family friend; she was a former patient of mother's. She owned a sweet shop in the rynek (town square); we used to buy pastries from her. Mother explained that when she told Mrs. Terlecka that I and my sister would be taken away at the next deportation, Mrs. Terlecka offered to help. She said that her friend, who had been a monk, could arrange for me to be accepted into the Mogila Monastery.

"There is a rumor that the final liquidation of the ghetto will be tomorrow, therefore you must leave today," my father said. Mother and Father hugged me, which was my signal to leave. I don't remember the details because I repressed this traumatic event; it was the end of my childhood.

Mrs. Terlecka lived above the store in the rynek. I knew that security had been increased, giving rise to the talk that the ghetto would suffer final liquidation soon. Ukrainian units and Polish police, supervised by Germans, guarded the gates. At first I tried the usual way of leaving the ghetto by climbing a fence and jumping on the Aryan side, but two Ukrainian paramilitaries ran toward me. They fired their guns at me but missed. I climbed the fence back into the ghetto. Jewish Odemans pretended they were chasing me. I realized that all of the tiny ghetto was under tight scrutiny.

I ran to the house of Rutka Friedrich, one of the four remaining children in the ghetto. Next to Gina, she was my favored girlfriend. The building in which she lived was next to a house which was outside the ghetto. I climbed from the balcony of their apartment to the roof. I then jumped onto the roof of a building outside the ghetto and slid down the gutter into the courtyard on the Christian side.

I pretended to be a shopper as I entered the store of Mrs. Terlecka. She ordered me in a stern voice to get out because she would not sell anything to a Jew. She winked at me as she said it. A customer and a salesgirl were in the shop. It was dangerous to sell something to a Jewish boy who was not wearing an armband. I guessed that she wanted me to get into her apartment. I went outside, got through the gate of her building and walked up the staircase. Soon she was there.

Mrs. Terlecka was a serene, good-looking woman. She greeted me warmly, and her calmness was reassuring. "You can walk around the bedroom without shoes. Make no noise. I must return to the store," she said and disappeared. I was alone with my fears and doubts. What would happen if her friend would not take me to the monastery when he came in the morning?

Soon I became absorbed in looking out of the bedroom window and observing the normal life in the city square. Well-dressed men and women were strolling along the sidewalks. The shops were open. The familiar gold letters on a black background, APTEKA (pharmacy), appeared as dignified as ever. I had gone there often in the past to pick up medication for my parents and had been treated every time with candy by the gray-haired pharmacist.

The German occupation of Poland was brutal, but by comparison to the ghetto, this was paradise. People walked leisurely, they talked and moved like they had before the war. There was something fundamentally different about how people staggered in the ghetto compared to the steady walk of people on the Aryan side. I could see people coming out of the nearby restaurant. This was an establishment unknown in the ghetto.

Mrs. Terlecka returned a few hours later. She prepared a meal for us and answered many questions I was too timid to ask. Her friend, Mr. Gadomski was coming by train; he would take me to the Mogila Monastery near Krakow. After supper, Mrs. Terlecka put me to bed on her couch. She covered me with a blanket and lovingly stroked me, aware of my fears. I fell asleep before Stanislaw Gadomski arrived.

I was awakened in early morning by Mrs. Terlecka and was introduced to Mr. Gadomski. He was a short man with a pronounced hunchback. He wore a black suit and had a pinched, haggard face. He was unattractive and had an unpleasant sugary sweet manner. He called me "Jasiu," a diminutive form of "Janek," which was a diminutive of Jan. He was the first person to use my new name. His voice was high pitched and intense.

Mrs. Terlecka told me that the final liquidation of the ghetto had begun. Were my parents and Olenka being herded into the cattle cars? Would I ever see them again? I knew that my parents had Aryan papers but they had no place to go. They could not climb a roof and scale down a gutter. My little sister would have no chance to avoid being shoved into the cattle car. We could hear occasional gunshots from the nearby ghetto. Mr. Gadomski said he would take me to the monastery but he made no promises that the prior would accept me.

70

"You walk to the railroad station and Mr. Gadomski will walk behind you. If anything happens on the way or at the railroad station, pretend you don't know him," Mrs. Terlecka instructed me. I understood that it was dangerous for him to walk down the street with me. People might recognize and denounce me.

For the first time in my life, I was entirely on my own. On the day of deportation, getting to the station was risky but there was no other way. As we walked from the Rynek we could see Jews in long columns being herded in the middle of the road in the direction of the railroad station. I looked to see whether my parents and Olenka were among them.

A new chapter in my life had begun. The transition between childhood and adulthood was compressed to a few hours. Emanuel Tenenwurzel ceased to exist and Jan Wojcik took his place. The former was a young boy looked after by his parents, the latter was an orphan on his own. I had to quickly invent the Catholic me; the real me had to be hidden from the world.

I left behind the hazard of being shipped into the unknown in a freight car. I was now at risk of being unmasked as a Jew pretending to be a Pole. It was not clear which was the greater danger. Being caught as a fugitive Jew would result in death by execution. Would I be killed like my cousin Miriam Cukier? I was aware that if I made one false move I would die.

As we walked, I gave Mr. Gadomski my coat. I wanted to be less conspicuous and ready to run should the need arise. Mother had insisted that I wear a coat, even though it was warm weather. I pretended to be a carefree youngster. No one gave me a script of how to act, but I knew that this was the role I had to play. No one told me that poor performance was punishable by death, but I had no doubt about it. I dreaded the unknown. I had never visited a monastery.

I was without the protective presence of my parents. All parents are powerful in the eyes of a youngster. However, being the son of Dr. Tenenwurzel, even in the ghetto, gave me a special status. Suddenly I was without that protection and in a world that wanted me dead.

I had never lived alone. Would I be separated from mother, father and sister forever? Would I ever see my friends again? The people around me had the right to live but I did not. The only friend I had was this strange little man walking at a safe distance behind me.

I made it safely to the station. The ticket agent may have recognized me but said nothing, for which I was grateful. Would he change his mind and denounce me as I stood on the platform waiting for the train to arrive? How many other people could identify me? Every one of them had my life in their hands. Being recognized as the son of doctors Tenenwurzel no longer was an honor.

Being "free" outside the ghetto was scarier than living in the ghetto. Getting into the overcrowded train was a struggle, which involved shoving and many angry glances. Any moment I feared someone would say "Get away you dirty Jew" (Parszywy Zydzie) a common phrase in those days. Once the train was outside Miechow, Gadomski joined me. He was a stranger but all-important to me. His language was overblown and unnatural, unlike my father's straightforward, blunt speech. With father you always knew where you stood. Mr. Gadomski's unsettling demeanor made me distrustful of him.

From the Krakow railroad station, we took a streetcar to the city limits and walked to the village of Mogila. In Polish, "mogila" means "grave" or "tomb" – an odd name for a place where I was seeking lifesaving help.

Mr. Gadomski told me his plan. "I will tell the prior that your family converted to Catholicism when you were a baby. This makes you a Christian in the eyes of the Church, but a Jew for the Germans."

This was an important lesson; half-truths are more believable than total lies. My survival depended on being believable. As we approached Mogila, we could see the huge monastery complex dominating the landscape. The church and the monastery faced Monastery Street. The church entrance was grand; the monastery gate was a small and unobtrusive door. The exterior of the church was plastered over brick, giving it a pinkish, friendly look.

Once we entered the church, I was startled by its size and frightened by what I saw. A gigantic wooden cross held a lifelike figure of Christ. The long flowing human hair made him look real. Above was the inscription "Rex Judeorum Est." I knew enough Latin to understand that it meant, "He is the King of the Jews." Prayer at this cross, I was later told, resulted in many miracles. Inside the church, Gadomski made the sign of the cross and genuflected in front of the altar. I watched closely and did the same. Did I do it right? I had never crossed myself before.

"Kneel down and pray. I will talk to Father Kuchar. I hope he will take you in," Gadomski said before leaving me. He entered the monastery from the church through an inside passageway. I kneeled and pretended to pray, my eyes fixed on the carved figure of Christ. A crucifix was a familiar sight; I had seen it in classrooms, in homes and in government offices, but I had never studied one so intensely.

"The prior wants to talk to you before he makes his decision," Mr. Gadomski whispered when he returned. He told me to follow him. I walked behind him in silence, stunned by the unfamiliar surroundings.

Father Robert Kuchar was a huge man; friendliness and kindness flowed from his pudgy face and twinkling eyes. He had a pleasant, loud laugh. His booming voice was not intimidating, it was reassuring. Father Kuchar greeted me as if he had known me for a long time. He asked about the trip from Miechow and expressed encouragement and sympathy for my having to leave home. He assured me that I would like it in Mogila. There were no questions asked about my past, no need to tell any lies to this kind old man.

Father Kuchar had a foreign accent; I found out later that he was a Serb from Yugoslavia. He called one of the brothers and asked that I be given a cell across from his quarters. This turned out to be a lovely room with a bed, a small table and a nightstand that held a basin and a pitcher. The ceiling had a colorful painting of a scene from the New Testament. "One of the brothers was an accomplished artist," Mr. Gadomski explained. He then announced that he would remain in the monastery for a few days to assist me. I needed a lot of help in order to pass as a Catholic boy eager to become a priest.

72

Mr. Gadomski offered more than instruction for passing as a Catholic boy; he tried to persuade me to become one. He glorified the "true faith" and made demeaning remarks about the Jews.

"You are such a nice boy, no one would think you came from a Jewish family," he told me. He had a lot of misinformation about Judaism. He believed that Jews tortured animals and used Christian blood to make Passover matzo. He was convinced that Jews were responsible for the spread of typhus because they were so dirty. He asked such questions as: "Why do Jews do everything backward like write from right to left, and rest on Saturday instead of Sunday?"

I had to share a bed with him in my cell. His hunchback took up more space than his body and I was afraid to bump into it. He smelled bad. But Mr. Gadomski was my benefactor and I needed him desperately, though he was difficult to like.

I was more secure with Gadomski around, but he frequently hugged me, which I found repulsive. I wanted his tutelage, but I hoped that he would leave soon. A few days after we arrived in the monastery, as we lay in the narrow bed in my cell, he touched my penis and masturbated me. He then placed his penis between my legs and ejaculated. I was horrified, but could not resist. My life depended on him as he was the only person who could help me to adjust to the strange environment of a monastery.

I had to present a new identity based on falsehoods – not an easy task on a day's notice for a 14-year-old boy. I had no preparation for my new role. My knowledge of Catholic prayers and customs was superficial. Jan Wojcik was a Catholic boy born and raised in a village. Emanuel Tenenwurzel was a city boy, from a family of professionals, and a Jew. A peasant background was implicit in the name "Wojcik" and my birthplace, a village not far from Miechow. In those days in Poland, speech and appearance were usually consistent with social class. I did not know the peasant dialect. I did not have the looks or manners of a villager. Upward social mobility in inter-war Poland was rare.

The story I told was that my father was a dental technician who became a POW in September 1939. He was a lieutenant in the Polish Army and was somewhere in a German camp for prisoners of war. My mother was a nurse from Wilno. She had met my father in eastern Poland when he had served in the KOP (an elite Polish border defense corps), which would account for my genteel manner and speech. Telling these stories was easier than performing the functions expected of a Catholic boy living in a monastery.

Only days before, I was in the ghetto with my parents and friends. In the ghetto we fought for survival collectively; now I was on my own. Gone were the days when my parents and my environment ensured my safety. I had to replace the external protection with my own ingenuity. Gut feeling or intuition became a critical survival tool.

I was thrown into the ocean of Catholicism without a single swimming lesson. A boy who wanted to be a priest had to have more than a casual knowledge of catechism and religious practices. I had to acquire these skills as I went along, without revealing my ignorance. I observed and imitated what I saw.

My entire daily life was centered upon an unfamiliar religion. Catholicism is full of rituals that do not allow for variation. There was no room for trial and error. My performance had to be consistent and precise.

The first night, I memorized the daily prayers to be recited at breakfast. In the following days I studied the catechism intensely and memorized the Latin liturgy of the Holy Mass. I read the life stories of the saints. I was assigned to a choir a few days after arrival and had to sing songs I didn't know. I listened attentively and relied on split-second delay. Sometimes I gave words the wrong endings.

I was called on to serve at mass and required to take advanced religious instruction. I knew that I had to act and think like a Catholic, though I did not feel like one.

Unlike some of the other Jewish youngsters hidden in monasteries and convents, I did not undergo a change in my identity. The exposure to the Catholic teachings increased my knowledge of Catholicism but it did not affect my beliefs. My spiritual roots were firmly planted in the secularism of my parents. Had I been a religious Jew it would have been more difficult to assume this part.

I had always been an avid reader, but in the monastery I read about Catholicism with the determination of a boy fighting for his life. I was fascinated by the life of Jesus who, unlike his followers, accepted everything and everyone. It was a supreme irony under my circumstances to read that according to Jesus, the first commandment is to love God; the second commandment is to "love your neighbor as yourself." I was a neighbor and yet the followers of Jesus had a "duty" to hate me. I learned that in the eyes of the Roman Catholic Church, I was a member of an evil category of people called the Jews. I was instructed that there were two subcategories of infidels: the pagans who have no religion at all and the Jews, who are guilty of rejection of the true Messiah.

The Jews committed the sin of perfidy because they chose to remain outside of the Church. The pagan infidels were not culpable; they were ignorant and unable to recognize the truth. The other "bad people" were the heretics, the Christians who chose to believe false teachings and refused to recognize the authority of the Roman Pontiff.

I memorized the catechism and prayers well, but never wore a religious medallion around my neck. Externally I was a Pole and Catholic; internally I remained a Jew. To me, being a Jew was not a religion, but a nationality. The heavy exposure to Catholicism in the monastery and the efforts of Mr. Gadomski to convert me failed to change my beliefs. The religious people around me were not my friends. I was certain that if they found out that I was a Jew they would have denounced me to the Germans. My intuitive judgment proved correct.

In the ghetto, the enemy was clearly defined. In the monastery, everyone, with the exception of Father Kuchar and Gadomski, was my enemy. Frequent anti-Semitic comments made me aware that I was in constant danger. I had no real papers showing that I was not a Jew and, even if I were a Pole, I was in violation of the law for not having a valid identity card. All I had was a handwritten baptismal certificate. Thus, it was vital for me to have the identity card. The Germans issued this document, which was very difficult to counterfeit because it

74

was printed on special cloth. Each Kennkarte contained a photograph, fingerprints, and an intricate German seal.

A forged Kennkarte was expensive. The Germans, if suspicious that a Kennkarte was a fake, called the issuing office; through a coding system they could determine that the document was not genuine. To get a Kennkarte, one had to go to the local German police office. The administrative work was done by Poles and "Volksdeutsch" (ethnic Germans), born and raised in Poland. They had the power of a German and the ability of a Pole to identify Jews.

It was a gamble for me to apply for a Kennkarte. I would arouse suspicion because I had not gotten this document in a timely manner. Waiting made the situation worse every day. One was asked for documents frequently in occupied Poland. Yet, going to the German police office could end up badly for me. I had to make a fateful decision and after much contemplation, I chose to apply and subject myself to the scrutiny of the officials.

Mogila did not have a German police office, so I traveled to Krakow with passport size photos and my baptismal certificate. The official, a Pole or a Volksdeutsch, interrogated me in flawless Polish. I gave living in a monastery as an excuse for not having applied for the Kennkarte in a timely manner.

He asked: "Since you are in a monastery, let me see how well you can recite the prayers." This was a sure sign he suspected that I was a Jew. He asked other similar questions, which I answered correctly, I thought. When he disappeared behind a door, I was afraid he was calling a "gendarme," as the German policemen were called. I was tempted to run before the police arrived.

I positioned myself near the exit door, pretending to be looking for someone. The official returned alone, the cherished Kennkarte in his hand. I walked out of that office holding a real passport to life. It was valid until 1947. "I hope I will not need it that long," I thought quietly.

In 1942, while in the monastery, I paid close attention to the military successes of the German war machine. I was aware that the duration of war would determine whether I lived or died.

My only source of information about the war was the German-published Polish newspaper. In November of 1942, the situation of the Soviet Union seemed hopeless. The Germans pushed the front in a line from Leningrad in the north to Stalingrad, and beyond to the Black Sea. They were not far from Moscow. The Western allies were as inactive as ever. Since May of 1941, all of Europe had been under the control of the Third Reich. Nazi Germany was on the verge of winning the War.

My position in the monastery was that of a novice who would take his vows in the future. The education took place in secrecy as the Germans forbade instruction of Polish children beyond the first few elementary grades. The only other boy my age was also named Janek. He and I had in common the curse of adolescence – pimples. Janek was a serious fellow of peasant background; becoming a priest was his dream.

The priests were called "Fathers," and the monks who were not ordained were called "Brothers." The Fathers dressed in white robes over which they wore a black scapular (a sleeveless garment hanging from the shoulders). The

Brothers wore brown habits. They did manual labor in addition to the prayers and meditation. The Fathers performed priestly duties and did scholarly work. Janek wore the white robe without the black scapular that signified an ordained priest. I was eager to get the same "uniform," it had protective value for me.

Brother Anthony was also close in age to me. A handsome man in his early 20s, he was from Warsaw, and was outgoing, witty and lazy. He was too sophisticated for the brothers, who mostly came from villages, and were not educated enough to be priests. His life's ambition was to become a priest, but he did not have the will power to study. Brother Anthony, Janek and I became friends.

The Mogila monastery had been established in 1202 by the Order called the "White Monks" because of the white habits they wore under the black scapulars. The official name was the Order of Cistercians, established in 1098 in Citeaux France (called Cistercium in Latin). The founder was Saint Robert of Melesme; his group was devoted to strict interpretation of the monastic rules set forth by St. Benedict of Nursia in 540. Being a novice in a monastery that followed the Benedictine rule was an ideal place for a Jewish boy on false papers because I was isolated from the dangerous outside world. The monastery was dedicated to contemplative life, and the daily routine minimized contact with outsiders, which suited my purpose.

The Mogila monastery was not an example of austerity. There was evidence of the power and wealth of the Church everywhere. The Mogila monastery resembled a castle. If architecture is frozen music, as Goethe said, then this structure was Beethoven's Ninth Symphony. The Gothic style church was magnificent; when you entered it, you felt dwarfed. The monastery, attached to the church, was also imposing. There were beautiful gardens and an iron fence that enclosed the church courtyard. Massive walls surrounded the entire complex. The message was that Catholicism is a majestic religion. The monastery was a blend of secular splendor and spiritual humility. The grandiosity of the surroundings and the imposing liturgy were in contrast to the creed that humility was a virtue and pride a deadly sin.

To this day, whenever I hear chanting, I am transported in my mind to the inspiring surroundings of Mogila Monastery. Powerful music emanated from an enormous organ. The organist was an important figure in every church, and in the Mogila monastery, the priest who played the organ was a virtuoso. It was as if an entire orchestra played along with him.

Over the years, I have visited many famous churches and cathedrals throughout the world, but none seemed as majestic and intimidating as the Mogila monastery. I was not surprised when it was named a basilica.

The only person I trusted in the monastery was Father Kuchar, and he trusted me. He gave me a variety of special duties. I emptied the church collection boxes at the end of the day. I was responsible for picking up the mail from the village post office; money and food packages were received by mail. I shined his shoes and helped him at bedtime. He giggled like a baby when I covered him with a blanket.

Every day I marched through the village to the post office with a large leather pouch with the inscription "Klasztor" (monastery) hanging from my shoulder. I was known in the village as "Janek from the monastery." One day, a column of Jews from the Plaszow concentration camp, under SS guard, approached me from the opposite direction. The camp was a few kilometers from Mogila. As I passed the group, I realized that a few were from Miechow. Being nearsighted, I recognized familiar faces only when they were next to me. It was wonderful to see Jews alive, even under SS guard. But this turned out to be a dangerous encounter. Szymek Sosnowski, a boy from Miechow, who was not especially bright, began to yell, "Emek! Emek!" He was waving at me. I was terrified but kept on walking as if this had nothing to do with me.

Another Miechow boy whose name I don't remember, hit Szymek on the back of his head and yelled, "Keep on moving, you idiot." I hoped that none of the Poles in the street had become aware of what was happening.

On my return to the monastery, I tried to give up the honor of being the trusted messenger, but Father Kuchar was unwilling to assign someone else to this job. Seeing the Miechow Jews intensified my anguish about the fate of my parents and sister. I had no contact with them and did not know if they were dead or alive.

A few weeks after my arrival in Mogila, I had a visitor. He was a man in his 30s, short and very fidgety. I had never met him before. When we were alone, he told me that my mother had sent him to me. "Come with me," he demanded, without explanation. I did as I was told. He did not have the appearance of an official and was too uncomfortable to be a Szmalcownik (Jew hunter).

Once we were outside, the man whom I will call Mr. Novak (I don't recall his name) told me that Mother and Olenka were hidden in his flat. "Your mother wants to see you," he said gruffly. He made it clear that he considered it a foolish idea and a sign of weakness for him to go along with Mother's wish. "I understand your mother. I have children also," was his comment a bit later when he was less anxious. We had begun walking to his apartment when he told me that my Father was alive and working as a dentist in the labor camp known as "Lotnisko," a Polish word for airport. Mr. Novak worked in maintenance in the same place. I was surprised that Mother's hiding place and Father's camp were only a few kilometers from the monastery. I knew that the Lotnisko labor camp was considered a safe place for the Jews because it was essential to the war effort. The Jews were not under the direct control of the SS; they were in the hands of the Luftwaffe personnel.

"Your father fixes the teeth of the Germans and Polish workers, that is how I met him," Mr. Novak explained. He had been persuaded by Father to hide Mother and Olenka. He did not know how Mother had escaped from Miechow and how Father had gotten to Lotnisko.

The Novak family lived on the third floor of a rundown apartment building near the airport. The three room flats were a shabby, dark place. Mrs. Novak, a pretty brunette in her late 20s, did not acknowledge my polite greeting and berated her husband for getting mixed up with the Jews. I wondered how such a good-looking woman could be so mean. The grim-faced Mr. Novak made no response.

After assuring himself that there was no one on the staircase, Mr. Novak took me to the attic. Mother and Olenka were in a tiny compartment; they were scared and dirty. Olenka complained of being hungry. It was an emotional reunion; Mother wept quietly as she hugged me, Olenka giggled with pleasure. I was near tears but did not cry. I felt happy but not joyful. Mother and Olenka were alive, but in a rotten place and still in danger. Our time together was limited. Through a round, small window of the attic, I could see the airport. I had never seen so many airplanes in one place. I spotted a group of Jews working on runway improvements. My father was somewhere in those buildings.

I found out from Mother that she and Olenka had escaped during the last liquidation of the ghetto. I no longer remember how they pulled this off. They made their way to the house of a Polish family willing to hide them for a few days. The neighbors noticed them coming in and notified the Polish police. Mother and Olenka were apprehended and were being taken to the deportation place. On the way to the railroad station, Mother gave the policeman her diamond ring and he let them escape again. Mother found another Polish family who agreed to hide them. That house was also searched while Mother and Olenka were there. "We hid under a table covered with a large tablecloth and the police did not find us," my little sister informed me.

Father had been taken from the ghetto, with all the dental equipment, by truck to the Lotnisko labor camp. He arranged for Leon, his dental technician, to come along. I do not remember how Mother got in touch with Father at the Lotnisko camp and learned of the arranged hiding place at the Novak home. This was to be temporary, as Mother planned to go to a resort town and rent a small apartment. She had fake papers in the name of Aniela Rojek. The new name given to my sister was Irene or "Irka" for short. Change of name was not enough; to pass for a Christian it was essential to change Mother's hair color. Her black hair would arouse suspicion that she was a Jew. This was before women could color their hair effectively at home and the services of a city professional would be necessary to transform her black hair into an auburn color. Mother's complexion precluded making her a blond. The risk was that a hairdresser would guess why Mother wanted to change her beautiful black hair into nondescript brown, and denounce her. Then there was the problem of transportation. It would be dangerous to go by streetcar. I told Mother I would find a way to solve the problem.

As I walked back to the monastery, I had the wonderful feeling of having a family again. My parents and sister had risen from the dead. Finding a beautician who would color Mother's hair was also on my mind. Would one of the laundry girls know one? One of the brothers who cut our hair used to be a barber. Could he help? On my return to the monastery, I talked to Father Kuchar about the problem. I wanted to get his advice and moral support; he gave a great deal more. He arranged for a trusted beautician in Krakow to do the job.

The monastery had a farm and the prior had the use of a horse-drawn carriage with a liveried driver. Father Kuchar offered to take Mother in his carriage into the city. A few days later, I walked to the Novak building. I waited outside to intercept Mr. Novak as he came from work. I did not dare meet his wife. He was not happy to see me. I told him that the next day, at 9 a.m., the prior's carriage would pick Mother up and bring her back. He insisted Mother be picked up and dropped off on a corner two blocks away.

The next morning, Father Kuchar and I set out to pick up mother and Olenka. Father Kuchar, who wore a big black hat, looked like a cardinal. Mother wore an elegant suit and hat that covered her hair. The grubby look of the attic hideout was gone. Father Kuchar and Mother sat next to each other, Olenka and I sat facing them. We drove into Krakow in grand style. I listened with satisfaction as the horse-drawn landau clip-clopped on the cobblestones of the ancient city. Mother and Olenka were dropped off at the hairdresser's, and I went to run a few errands. A few hours later, Father Kuchar picked us up. Mother looked odd to me with her brown hair.

In Krakow, I went to see an eye doctor, which turned out to be a dangerous move. I knew that I was nearsighted. The doctor confirmed it and gave me a pair of eyeglasses. Being able to see well seemed important, particularly in my situation. "With those glasses, you look like a Jew," my friend Janek said jokingly when he saw me. In Poland, glasses were a trademark of a Jew. Fortunately, he was the first person I came upon when I returned to the monastery. That was the last time I wore glasses while living in Poland. There were countless ways that aroused suspicion that a person was a Jew: eating onions, mispronouncing a word, being a bookworm, being good with numbers, using one's hands while talking, and, above all, having certain facial features.

In those days, Poles had an uncanny ability to identify Jews. Many anti-Semitic Poles took pride in informing against Jews trying to pass as Christians. Many bragged, "One look and I can spot a Jew." Fortunately, this was not always true. Assimilated Jews who did not have Semitic features and spoke Polish without Jewish traits could escape from a ghetto, just as light-skinned slaves before America's Civil War could run away from a plantation. But most Polish Jews could be easily recognized as fugitives by appearance and speech. The linguistic pitfalls were particularly treacherous. Grammatical and phonological characteristics of speech identified most Jews in Poland. A Jew on false papers was often recognized through body language, such as "talking with hands," and also such subtle gestures as a manner of shrugging shoulders and facial expressions.

Unlike a Pole, a German could not recognize an assimilated Jew with good papers. It is a sad fact that the Nazi axiom "The only good Jew is a dead Jew" was accepted by many Poles. I often heard in the monastery the quotation "For the wages of sin is death" (Romans VI. 23). My offense was that I was born a Jew.

I told a Polish friend many years after the War about living in constant fear that I would be denounced by Poles as a Jew. He pointed out that Poles denounced other Poles also. The reality is that the denunciation of Poles was not a badge of honor; it often occurred through anonymous letters. If a Pole were to publicly identify a member of the underground in a streetcar or on the train, he would be beaten to death. But it was not uncommon to hear someone scream "Catch the Jew," and for other Poles to follow, as happened to me on two occasions. The motive for denouncing a Pole was invariably a personal hatred of the given individual. Jews were denounced for ideological reasons shared by large segments of the population.

In addition to Poles who denounced Jews for "idealistic" reasons, there were also professional Jew hunters called "Szmalcownik" (blackmailers). The term was derived from the word "szmalec," meaning lard, used colloquially for money. Poles who seemed to suspect that I was a Jew, frequently stalked me. A blackmailer had the choice to extort money from the Jew or to claim the reward the Germans were giving for denouncing the Jew. They served the same role as the trackers who pursued runaway slaves in the American South before the Civil War. The difference was that slaves who ran away would be punished but not killed, because slaves had economic value to their masters. We had no value to the Germans, as we were "life unworthy of living."

Janek and Anthony were my "friends" and therefore most likely to discover that I was a Jew. I knew that I could not trust them with my secret. The three of us took walks to the village in our free time. We sat together during meals. We also made what we euphemistically called "excursions" to the laundry. The laundry was just outside the walls of the monastery, and it employed young village girls. We took our clothing there to be washed and ironed. Brother Anthony arranged for three pretty girls to meet us there at night. After Vespers, the routine was to walk in silence in the large hall for an hour and retreat to our cells for contemplation. Instead, the three of us sneaked out into the garden, climbed the high wall, and met the girls in the laundry. The doors were locked but a window was left open and we climbed in. Three girls were waiting for us. At first we talked in whispers, excited by the escapade. Brother Anthony, as the oldest, set the tone. He disappeared with one of the girls. Neither Janek nor I had the nerve to follow his example. The next day Brother Anthony ridiculed us for our timidity. He claimed that he had intercourse with his girl. He bragged a lot about his successes with women. Just before the war, he had enlisted in the KOP (Korpus Ochrony Pogranicza), an elite military unit guarding the borders. "Women go for uniforms," he told us. A monk's habit, in his view, was almost as good as a military uniform. He relied on his Cistercian robes for sexual appeal. Brother Anthony did not consider celibacy a key to salvation.

"You guys get one more chance," he announced. A few days later he arranged another laundry visit. This time, Janek and I were less bashful, and each of us paired off with a girl. I did not have intercourse because I was scared the girl would recognize that I was circumcised. I was too anxious to get an erection and would not allow the girl to touch my penis when she tried to. She was dainty in appearance and well spoken for a village girl. I liked her and went back on "official business" often. My laundry was washed more often than necessary. The night laundry excursions posed a dilemma for me because I knew that if I were caught violating monastery rules, I could be expelled. On the other hand, I did not want to appear too concerned to my friends, and I was eager to do something for fun. Although the monastery was located in beautiful surroundings, it was a joyless community. All pleasures that young men might pursue were sinful. Food was sustenance. Sex was taboo. Even reading for pleasure was forbidden. Ora et Labora (pray and work) was the guiding principle. The monastery existed for the glory of God, not for the satisfaction of human needs. Our secret laundry excursions violated everything the monastery stood for. The rule was that all of us had taken a vow of chastity. Any transgression of this vow was a grievous sin.

I was assigned to work in the monastery's library. It was a glorious place with stained-glass windows overlooking a pond. There were long tables and massive bookcases in a large hall with high, ornate ceilings. I worked in the library alone. This arrangement suited me very well. I felt safe in the library and I was free to read whatever I wanted. My job was to stamp the name of the monastery on the leather bound volumes. Father Kuchar assumed that the Germans would loot the valuable collection of books. I was to stamp pages 7, 17, 107 and so on, to make recovery after the war easier. In my parents' office, I used to take the business stamp and put it on anything I could lay my hands on. At times I put the stamp on inappropriate items and was scolded for it. Now it was my official assignment.

I read a lot, particularly the books with the caution "To be read with permission of the prior only." This restriction was put on books that questioned Church doctrine. My primary incentive for studying Christian teachings was apprehension. Ignorance of Christianity could expose me as a Jew. I read when I awakened in the morning and fell asleep with a book in my hand.

It was unexpected that the monastery's book collection reinforced my lack of enthusiasm for all religion. I read Baruch Spinoza, who argued that it was blasphemy for the Jews and the Christians to claim that their stories came from God. Diderot's Encyclopedia described Judaism and Christianity as absurd and intolerant. David Hume wrote that the existence of God could never be proven; therefore it was ridiculous to persecute those who did not believe a particular religion.

The monastery's library had a number of books describing the reigns of the Popes. I was fascinated by these accounts because they presented great stories. These guardians of faith were not immune to the failings of ordinary human beings. Some were saintly, where others were sinful. It was amusing to read that Pope Alexander VI appointed his son Ceasare Borgia to be a cardinal.

I learned that the policies and actions of Christian authorities in the Church were governed by myths about Jewish "devilishness," "money-grabbing," and "ritual murder" of Christian children. The fate of the Jews in Christendom depended on the whims of the reigning pontiff. Gregory the Great (590-604 A.D.) protected the Jews, stopped the practice of forced conversion and ordered the restitution of confiscated property. Alexander VI Borgia (1492-1503) allowed the Jews to live freely in the Papal State; while on July 26, 1556 Paul IV, the former Grand Inquisitor John Peter Cardinal Carafa, issued an order for the segregation of the Jews. The first Jewish quarter was established in Venice. A gated wall surrounded it; the Jews could leave only during the day and had to wear a distinctive marking on their clothes.

Only two sources of livelihood were allowed: selling old clothes and lending money, a business prohibited to the Christians by anti-usury laws. These occupations induced hostility toward the Jews.

I read about the First Crusade that took place in 1099. The victorious Christians slaughtered all the Muslims in Jerusalem and burned the Jews alive in a synagogue. People have killed throughout the ages in the name of a good cause. In Biblical times, they stoned the heretics; during the Holy Inquisition, they burned them at the stake.

In the monastery, "Patristics," the study of the Church Fathers, was a required subject. I still see before my eyes a multi-volume work bound in red leather entitled "Church Fathers." Jews and women were depicted as dangerous to the Christians. Jews, blood, and sex were an obsession of the Catholic Church. The long row of red books soon became frightening to me. I had dreams about them.

Jews were accused of poisoning wells, desecrating the Host, and killing Christian children and drinking their blood. They had to be separated from the Christian community because they were disgusting, and emanated "foetor judaicus," the Jewish stink. I wanted to scream that it was not true. Why did these saints hate the Jews so vehemently?

When I arrived in the monastery, I did not know that my baptismal name was John Chrysostom. I assumed that there was only one John, John the Baptist. This mistake nearly unmasked me as a Jew when Janek and I discussed our respective name days. In Poland, Catholics, unlike Jews, did not celebrate birthdays but name days. The saint whose name is chosen becomes a special patron who protects and guides the one who bears his name. When I discovered that my patron saint was not John the Baptist, but John Chrysostom, I immediately went to the library and read about my namesake. He was the archbishop of Constantinople (died Sept. 14th, 407) known for his preaching, which earned him the Greek surname Chrysostom. (*Chrysostomos*, "golden-mouthed," so called because of his eloquence).

He hated the Jews with a passion. What irony that I, a Jewish boy, carried the name of a ferocious despiser of the Jews. Contrary to the library policy, I took out the volume to my cell and read it at night. His bloodthirsty tirades against the Jews sounded terrifying. John Chrysostom had this to say about the Jews:

The Jews sacrifice their children to Satan . . . They are worse than wild beasts . . . The synagogue is a brothel, a den of scoundrels, the temple of demons devoted to idolatrous cults, a criminal assembly of Jews, a place of meeting for the assassins of Christ, a house of ill fame, a dwelling of inequity, a gulf and abyss of perdition. The synagogue is a curse. Obstinate in her error, she refuses to see or hear; she has deliberately perverted her judgment; she has extinguished within herself the light of the Holy Spirit . . . [the Jews] had fallen into a condition lower than the vilest animals. Debauchery and drunkenness had brought them to the level of the lusty goat and the pig. They know only one thing: to satisfy their stomachs, to get drunk, to kill and beat each other up like stage villains and coachmen . . . I hate the Jews, because they violate the Law. I hate the Synagogue because it has the Law and the Prophets. It is the duty of all Christians to hate the Jews.[34] (Emphasis mine)

The pious men with whom I lived in the monastery *had a religious obligation to hate me as soon as they found out who I was.* The eminent historian Steven T. Katz wrote:

Make no mistake – every major church father is a great hater of Judaism and the Jewish people. Not all the saints rival Chrysostom's passion, and none rivals his coarse prose, but his sentiments are in no sense atypical.[35]

The Christian duty to hate the Jews, advocated by my "heavenly intercessor," played a critical role in my everyday life. Living as a Catholic among Catholics made me aware that most of them hated the Jews intensely. I had not realized before how the Church demonized us.

The American author James Carroll, a former Catholic priest, points out that it is not surprising that shortly after the diatribes of the Archbishop Chrysostom, there was murderous violence against Jews, and the great synagogue of Antioch was demolished. In 414, a large-scale pogrom occurred against the prestigious Jewish community of Alexandria.

Saint Chrysostom wrote:

A place where a whore stands on display is a whorehouse. What is more, the synagogue is not only a whorehouse and a theater; it is also a den of thieves and a haunt of wild animals...No better disposed than pigs or goats, (the Jews) live by the rule of debauchery and inordinate gluttony. Only one thing they understand: to gorge themselves and to get drunk. When animals have been fattened by having all they want to eat, they get stubborn and hard to manage...When animals are unfit for work, they are marked for slaughter, and this is the very thing which the Jews have experienced. By making themselves unfit for work, they have become ready for slaughter. This is why Christ said: "And for my enemies, who did not want me to reign over them, bring them here and slay them before me."[36]

In the monastery, the symbols of the crucifixion surrounded me. The great relic of the monastery was an enormous wooden crucifix. I read the crucifixion story with horrified disbelief. The New English version of the New Testament tells the gruesome story:

Now it was the custom at festival time for the governor to release any prisoner whom the people chose. And it happened that at this time they had a notorious prisoner called Barabas, so when they assembled to make their usual request, Pilate said to them, "Which one do you want me to free, Barabas or Jesus called Christ?" For he knew very well that the latter had been handed over to him through sheer malice.

...but the chief priests and elders persuaded the mob to ask for Barabas and demanded Jesus' execution. Then the governor spoke to them, "Which of these two are you asking me to release?" "Barabas!" they cried. "Then what am I to do with Jesus who is called Christ?" asked Pilate. "Have him crucified," they all cried."

We are told that Pilate found for the Prisoner, saying "I find no guilt in this man," and sent Him off to Herod. (Matthew 22:1-7)

Herod also refused to commit, so the Temple leaders again came before Pilate. Calling upon the Jewish custom of releasing a condemned prisoner on Passover, Pilate spoke to the growing crowd and offered to release Jesus. To no avail. (Luke 23:13-25)

It was then that Pilate sat down on "the judgment seat." Then, he received a communication from his wife, concerning a dream she had had and begging him to have nothing to do "with that righteous man." (Matthew 27:19) The crowd pressed for Jesus' death. At last, Pilate took water and washed his hands in front of the multitude, declaring himself innocent of Christ's blood. The crowd didn't care, for they cried out, "His blood be on us and on our children." (Matthew 27:24,25)

Since hand washing was a Jewish custom, it made no sense to me that Pilate would perform this ritual. The reading of the scriptures in the monastery led me to different views from those held by my teachers. They blamed the Jews and exonerated the Romans for the execution of Jesus. Matthew's Gospel portrayed the Romans as benevolent, subservient to the Jewish elders and compliant with the wishes of a Jewish mob.

To me, Pontius Pilate was like Dr. Hans Frank, the German governor-general of occupied Poland. He was the dreaded Nazi tyrant living in the ancient royal castle of Wavel. I could never imagine Dr. Frank being influenced by Polish clergy or trying to please a Polish mob. But what was apparent to a 14-year-old boy was not obvious to the scholarly men who had access to the same literature as I did. Faith, not reason, determined what they believed.

Who killed Christ was not an abstract philosophical matter; it had vital significance to my generation of Poles and to me. The fate of the Jews was determined by this narrative. Saint Paul wrote that those responsible for the crucifixion were "the rulers of this age" (1 Cor 2:8). This hardly described the Jews under Roman occupation.

In Christian dogma, each human being is born into the condition or state of sin. Adam and Eve disobeyed God in eating the forbidden fruit and their sin was transmitted by heredity to all descendants.

The Christian concept of sin blames a person or a group (collective guilt) for a situation that is not of their making. The hereditary transmission of guilt made little sense to me. Why should the sin and guilt of Adam be transferred to every human being?

84

The Hebrew Bible, which, according to Christian lore, preaches vengeance, takes a different view. The Old Testament makes no mention of the transmission of hereditary guilt. It treats Adam's behavior as a mistake; the notion of sin in the Christian sense does not exist in the Jewish religion. "Fathers shall not be put to death for their children, nor children put to death for their fathers; each is to die for his own sins" (Deuteronomy 24; 16).

We spent a great deal of time in the monastery learning about the varieties of sin. St. Augustine defined mortal sin as something said, done or desired contrary to the eternal law. The seven deadly sins are: (1) vainglory, or pride; (2) covetousness; (3) lust, excessive or illicit sexual desire; (4) envy; (5) gluttony, (6) anger; and (7) sloth. There was the sin of the pleasure of a sinful thought or idea. There was the sin of complacency regarding sins already committed, and the desire for what is sinful.

Saint Paul was the originator of the Christian concept of sin. He believed that Adam brought us sin and death but that Christ gave us the opportunity for eternal life and grace. The Christian teachings on sin, Christ, and the Antichrist justified hatred of the Jews. "Who is a liar, but he who denies that Jesus is the Christ? This is Antichrist, who denies the Father and the Son" (1 John 2:22); was interpreted as referring to the wicked Jews.

Even if one assumes that Jews induced Romans to crucify Jesus, is it reasonable for Christians to persecute the Jews for something that took place 2,000 years ago? I was tempted to ask my teachers this question but wisely refrained from doing so. Finding contradictions, while studying the New Testament, was a tradition from my childhood when we, the secular boys, made fun of the youngsters studying Talmud. I noted in the monastery, that the description by Luke of the Crucifixion, mentions that one of the two criminals executed along side of Jesus, mocked him; whereas, the other scolded his companion and declared his faith in Christ. Christ said to his supporter that he will be with him in heaven. What brought my attention to Luke's description of the thieves was a sermon in which Saint Augustine was cited, "Do not despair, one of the thieves was saved". I soon discovered that of the four evangelists, only Luke conveys this hopeful message. Matthew tells us that both thieves insulted the Savior. The two others do not mention the thieves at all.

Next to the passages dealing with the Jews, sexual references were particularly interesting to me. The Polish word "niepokalana" means, "Unviolated." The English equivalent is "Immaculate Conception." Mary was a virgin when she gave birth to Jesus, and yet I read that Jesus "was born of the seed of David according to the flesh." (Romans I, 3-4). Jesus was the Son of God, but he was also the Son of David. How could he be both at the same time? While Joseph and Mary were betrothed, Joseph is referred to as Mary's "husband" (Matt. 1: 19). However, at first, Joseph believed Mary to have been unfaithful and was minded to "put her away" (Matt. 1: 19).

The Trinitarian doctrine was difficult to comprehend. I had to struggle with it in order to grasp it. The Father is God as is the Son and the Holy Spirit and yet there are not three Gods but one God. They were all made of the same substance. I was not surprised that there were disputes within the Church on this subject.

I derived a secret pleasure from these inconsistencies; they protected me from the efforts of Mr. Gadomski to convert me to Catholicism. He visited the monastery from time to time and stayed in my cell. During his visits, he continued his proselytizing, which was not as distasteful to me as his other activities.

He did not attempt to hide his disdain for Judaism. He wanted to save my soul by making me a Christian believer. He liked me, but had a strong aversion to "the Jews." Mr. Gadomski was unaware that his derogatory references to Judaism were painful to me. He quoted the New Testament often, trying to show me the erroneous ways of the Jews.

One day the monastery's gatekeeper got me out of choir practice and told me, "There is a strange-looking fellow at the gate asking for you." I wondered who it could be. With the exception of my parents, no one knew that I was in the monastery. With concealed apprehension, I rushed to the portal. A man in his 20's was waiting for me. He had what in Poland was called "Zydowski wyglad" (a Jewish look); dark hair and a crooked nose. Now I understood why the gatekeeper spoke of a strange-looking fellow. I hoped that my alarm did not show when I said, "I am Jan Wojcik. You wanted to see me?" He handed me an envelope containing a sheet of paper. "Please help him; he must survive" was the unsigned, one-sentence message. I recognized my father's handwriting. The gatekeeper kept a watchful eye on the two of us.

I pretended to be reading a letter as I was thinking about what to do. "Thank you. Let us go outside," I told my visitor in a loud and harsh voice. As soon as we were in the courtyard I took him into the church, to the same pew where, a few months before, Mr. Gadomski had told me to pray and wait. "Pretend that you are praying; I will come back soon," I told the young man without taking the time to explain. I returned at once to the monastery gate. "If that fellow comes back, please tell him that I am not here," I told the gatekeeper as I re-entered the monastery. I pretended that I was returning to choir practice. I then snuck out to the church through the hidden passage. I guided my visitor through the monastery halls to my cell. As we walked, I addressed him with the honorific "Pan" (Mister). "Call me Szmulek," he said. "I'll call you anything but Szmulek," I said. Both of us laughed. Szmulek was a typical Jewish name.

Fortunately, we encountered no one on the way to my cell. But before we had a chance to talk, there was a knock on the door. I told Szmulek to crawl under my bed, the only hiding place in my cell. Janek was at the door; he had come to pick me up on the way to our lectures. When I returned two hours later, my guest was still under the bed. He had fallen asleep.

Szmulek was a cousin of my friend Ruth Friedrich. He had escaped from the Treblinka Death Camp. I don't remember how he got in touch with my father in the Luftwaffe camp. He had no papers; his Polish was quite good, but not perfect. "I will get Aryan papers in a week. Can you keep me that long?" he asked. I naturally agreed. The information Szmulek had to convey was so important that my father had felt justified in exposing me to the risk of his visit and concealment.

86

I kept Szmulek for a week in my cell without anyone discovering his presence. My room had no toilet and I had no access to food; our meals were served in the communal dining room. I pocketed food in the dining room and brought it to him. I carried a pail to the toilet. My concern was that Mr. Gadomski would come for a visit any day.

Szmulek told me horrifying details about Treblinka. He had been part of a crew of inmates who removed ashes from the crematoria. The mounds of ashes were transported to a location from which it was possible to escape. Szmulek had dug out a pit in the heaps of ashes and hid in it. At night, he dug further and managed to get out of the camp. I do not recall all the particulars of his escape. He wore layers of clothing that he intended to use as payment to peasants. The first Polish peasant that he met took his clothing and chased him away; another peasant had helped him.

His story seemed unreal. It was like a gruesome fairy tale. It was whispered to me during the night, which contributed to my feeling that it was a figment of my imagination. I buried the account in my mind, and it became an abscess in my memory.

Szmulek left the monastery the way he came – secretly. We embraced warmly before we parted. I had little hope he would survive. He looked too Jewish to live on false papers. Years later, Ruth Friedrich told me that Szmulek was apprehended shortly after he left me and was never heard from again. The chances of survival for a Jew trying to pass as a Pole were poor. We know about the few who survived on false identity papers. There is no way to know how many perished in a desperate struggle to survive.

A boy my age could not remain in the monastery for Christmas because it would arouse the suspicion that I did not have a family. The only person I knew was Gadomski, who lived in Czestochowa. I dreaded being with Gadomski but had no other choice than to spend the holidays with him. On December 24, 1942, I traveled from Krakow to Czestochowa to visit Gadomski—my "family". The railroad station was nearly empty. I was accustomed to being swept into the train by a throng of people.

A rumor had it that Hitler said, "If I see a Jew alive on January 1, 1943, I will tip my hat to him." Staying alive, at least to that day, was my goal. Sitting alone in a railroad car, I recall thinking, "Only seven days left to my victory over Hitler."

I arrived safely at Mr. Gadomski's tiny apartment. On Christmas Day we went to the Basilica of Jasna Gora ("Shining Mountain") to attend the Holy Mass in the sanctuary of the Virgin Mary, Poland's most holy shrine. Every year thousands of people went by our house on Pilsudski Street on a pilgrimage to Czestochowa. Young and old walked hundreds of kilometers from all over Poland to worship before this miracle-making icon. In Poland, the cult of the Virgin Mother rivaled that of Christ.

Full of awe, I entered the church. This was the first time I was going to see the painting of the Black Madonna. The crowd had a sense of ecstasy. Suddenly, as everybody was kneeling and praying, two SS men entered the church. They talked loudly to each other in German, never removed their caps, and marched in front of the assembled congregation to the Black Madonna and stood there for a while, talking and laughing. It was a deliberate humiliation. The crowd was aghast. Hatred of the Germans was palpable but no one dared to make a move.

My return trip to Krakow on January 2, 1943 was delayed. The usual multitude of people filled the railroad station but the early evening train did not arrive. I did not want to return to Mr. Gadomski's apartment, or it may have been after the curfew. Like hundreds of others, I slept on the floor of the station. From time to time, the Germans came, asked for documents and searched luggage for contraband. Every so often, they hauled some person away.

The Polish employees of the railroad turned off the lights to reduce the harassment. I was lying next to a young woman. We talked in whispers, and then we hugged and kissed. We ended up having intercourse in the dark. This girl made me feel part of humanity. I was just a boy she liked; we were two strangers affirming life. It was like an island of tenderness in the ocean of hatred and apprehension. "The artist is the creator of beautiful things," said Oscar Wilde. What about people who create beautiful feelings? Beautiful acts?

A life force bridged the abyss of hate that separated "them" from "us." In the monastery, the "laundry excursions" made me part of the normal world. Erotic energy fueled the will to fight for survival. For a short time, when the sexual impulse dominated, apprehension was not my foremost feeling. Otherwise, fear was my constant emotional companion.

Showing apprehension was like blood in the water for sharks. Being anxious was a giveaway; being sad was even worse. People often boasted, "I can tell a Jew by his sad eyes." Every few days, someone told a story about a Jew being unmasked in an unlikely place.

I was relieved to be back in the monastery, where I was less exposed to what was called "polowanie na Zydow"(hunting for Jews). However, even in that sheltered setting I was in danger. "Would you believe the post office clerk turned out to be a Mosiek (a derogatory form of the name Moses used for all Jews)?" Janek asked me one day. He was my best friend in the monastery and knew more about me than anyone else. Did he suspect that I was a Jew, like the post office clerk? Would he betray me?

I had limited contact with most of the monks in the monastery. They were older and aloof and I remember only a few of them. My primary instructor was a priest I will call Father Joseph, as I don't recall his real name. He was a handsome, energetic man, in his late twenties or early thirties. Father Joseph, like so many priests in Poland, came from a peasant family. For Polish peasants to have a son who became a priest was a dream come true.

Father Augustine (his real name) was my favorite teacher. Like the Saint whose name he chose, he was scholarly and a true intellectual. He gave inspiring but moderate sermons. Unlike Father Joseph, he was not preoccupied with the Jews. He walked at a leisurely pace through the halls of the monastery whereas Father Joseph moved rapidly, full of purpose. There was something predatory about Father Joseph. He had a smile I associated with righteous hostility. I classified him as "falszywy," a Polish word that is difficult to translate; it implies insincerity.

Father Joseph was a heavy smoker, and cigarettes were hard to come by. In a subtle but unmistakable way, he let me know that if I could scrounge cigarettes for him, he would appreciate it. I wanted to be on his good side and bought some cigarettes on the black market for him. I did not trust him; I disliked his pretentiousness and his frequent anti-Semitic comments. But he was bright, articulate, and an excellent teacher.

His Sunday sermons were delivered with passion. He never missed an opportunity to include an anti-Semitic comment in his homily. During one of his Sunday exhortations, he was berating the parishioners for trading goods on Sunday. "In the past, the Jews conducted business secretly on the Lord's Day. Thank God, we have gotten rid of them," he shouted as I cringed. "The Jews did it," he explained, "to desecrate Sunday, the day dedicated to the commemoration of Christ's resurrection."

In Poland, it was against the law to keep stores open on Sunday. Some Jewish shopkeepers, who usually lived above their stores, sold goods to peasants on Sunday, through the back door. The peasants walked to towns on Sunday from villages that had neither churches nor stores.

Hearing a priest thanking God for the annihilation of the Jews from an "ambona" (pulpit) was a powerful jolt to my sense of security. The word pulpit does not convey the majesty of the sound of the word "ambona" in Polish. In the Mogila monastery it was a semi-enclosed space surrounded by elaborate carvings high above the congregation and attached to a pillar. People looked up to the priest not only spiritually but literally as well.

Sermons played an important role in forming the attitudes of the population in Poland. The liturgy was symbolic, conducted in Latin; but a sermon was an understandable direct communication. The Polish word "Kazanie" for sermon is derived from the infinitive "kazac" meaning "to order" or "to direct." The combination of hate-promoting preaching and the reenactments of the torture of Jesus did not encourage good will to the Jews.

Every Sunday our Church was packed with ardent believers. I looked at them with apprehension from the choir loft or from the elevation of the altar when I was an acolyte. I had no doubt that most would be eager to denounce me and cause my death.

Even Father Kuchar, a man dear to my heart, felt compelled to baptize me without my consent. One Sunday during the celebration of the mass, Father Kuchar stopped in front of me, sprinkled me generously with holy water and whispered something in Latin. I asked him about it later and he answered with laughter in German, "Sicher is Sicher," the equivalent of the English "better safe than sorry." Father Kuchar said that he was making sure that I was sanctified to everlasting life by the sacrament of baptism. Mr. Gadomski might have told him that the initial story that I had been baptized in my childhood was not true.

Father Kuchar had lived for years in Rome and must have known that Pope Pius IX ordered the "legal" removal of the six-year-old Jewish boy Edgardo Mortara from his parents. A servant had secretly baptized Edgardo. She loved the boy and wanted him to have the eternal life that comes only with baptism.

The Pope and the Italian government considered the parents unfit to raise a baptized child and he was legally taken away from his family.

The Pope and Father Kuchar felt justified in violating the requirement that there must be a profession of faith or, in the case of an infant, vicarious consent by a Godparent, for baptism. Thomas Aquinas did not approve of baptism without consent but he cites the argument of those who do:

> It seems that children of Jews or other unbelievers should be baptized against the will of their parents. For it is a matter of greater urgency to rescue a man from the danger of eternal death than from the danger of temporal death. But one ought to rescue a child that is threatened by the danger of temporal death, even if its parents through malice try to prevent its being rescued. Therefore much more reason is there for rescuing the children of unbelievers from the danger of eternal death, even against their parents' will.[37]

Many years later, I stood in the Sistine Chapel admiring frescoes by Michelangelo. I noticed that the story of the "Old Testament" begins with the depiction of circumcision. The story of Christianity starts with the portrayal of baptism. I have the dubious distinction of having been subjected to both of these rituals without my consent.

My faith in Janek's loyalty increased when one day he came running into the library, pulled me aside and whispered, "Quick, hide. There are two civilian Germans outside the gate asking for you. One of them must be a Volksdeutsch. He speaks perfect Polish." They came with a "doroshka" (horse-driven carriage used as a taxi). I assumed naturally that it was the Gestapo trying to arrest me. I had little doubt that someone had denounced me. I considered running to the garden, jumping the wall and going to Czestochowa to Mr. Gadomski. But at the last minute I changed my mind and decided to look. I left the library and went into the church through the inner passage. This made it possible for me to get outside without using the main entrance to the monastery.

Once in the courtyard, I was able to see the entrance gate without being seen. There were two men standing at the gate. One of them was dark-haired, wearing a black suit; the other was blond, wearing a sports jacket and officer's high boots. I took another look, doubting my eyesight. There could be no mistake. It was my father. I approached the two men with a mixture of joy and alarm. "Janek! We came to visit you. May we come in?" Father said, for the obvious benefit of the gatekeeper who stood outside chatting. It was strange to hear Father call me Janek. This was the first time a member of my family had used my Christian name. Father's companion smiled, but did not say a word. He looked German and had the familiar red swastika on his lapel indicating membership in the Nazi Party.

I wondered what was going on while leading my guests in silence through the corridors of the monastery to my cell. Once we were in the privacy of my room, Father threw his arms around me, and the German smiled with obvious satisfaction. "He is a German working for the Luftwaffe. I trust him completely. He wears the swastika for show; he is a communist," Father explained. "Das ist

Herr Schwarzer," father said to me in German, introducing his companion. We shook hands and then he gave me a few bars of chocolate. "He is truly my friend," father said. He then told me that the commander of the airport, a major in Luftwaffe, knew that Father was outside the camp that afternoon buying dental supplies. "The major is a good German and he is very friendly with me," father told me.

What stands out most in my mind about that visit was Father's reaction to my Kennkarte. I still can see his beaming smile and expressions of approval. "Eine echte Kennkarte" (a genuine identity card), Father said to Herr Schwarzer as he showed him the document with obvious pride. He explained in German how I had gotten this precious item. Father pulled out his own Kennkarte, which he had hidden inside one of his high boots. It was a good fake. Father's Christian name was Stanislaw Niedziela. I do not recall last names of childhood friends but remember distinctly this name, which I saw only once in 1943. I tried to persuade Father to escape from the camp and live on false papers. I told him that Father Kuchar would accept him in the monastery. "Ten Jews will get killed if I escape. I am trying to have myself declared dead, then I will get away and no one will get hurt," he said.

Father and Herr Schwarzer came to visit at least two more times, each time on a Sunday. I no longer remember what explanation I gave for my strange visitors but I was delighted with these visits, even though they were dangerous for Father, Herr Schwarzer, and me. Anything that called attention to me was fraught with danger.

One day, in March 1943, I saw Father Joseph in the Grand Hall of the monastery. He was a good distance away. He motioned me to come to him. I no longer remember our conversation, but I will never forget the encounter. During our chat, Father Joseph casually corrected my verb conjugation, a mistake typically made by Jews. Verb conjugation in Polish is a complex process of changing a verb to reflect its subject and tense. Native speakers intuitively knew it; Jews who learned Polish as a second language had trouble with it.

He scrutinized me with the look of a man who had found what he had been looking for. To me, it was like the sound of an air raid siren. In Poland, many Jews mispronounced ordinary words and made grammatical errors, but I did not have a Jewish accent and made no grammatical errors. I could not help but notice the triumphant smile on his lips. He may as well have cried out "I know you are a Jew." Father Joseph was unwittingly putting me on notice that I was in danger. His many anti-Semitic sermons and his thanking God for the elimination of the Jews made me sensitive to his demeanor. Father Joseph had no intention of letting me know that he suspected that I was a Jew.

I walked away casually towards my cell, full of apprehension. The white habit I wore and the walls of the monastery no longer offered protection. I had the feeling that I had no time to lose and yet I could not be sure that I had been denounced. I did not want burn my bridges by running away, besides, I had no place to go to.

Across from my cell was a door that opened onto a small windowless cubicle, which had a door to the steps leading to the church. Another door from this space gave access to the top of the bellows of the church organ. The bellows were nearly one story high. Because the bellows were constructed like an inverted cone, there was a space at the bottom not visible from the top. I had previously looked for a hideout in case of a raid by the Germans and had decided that this was the best place for my purpose; I called it my bunker. "I am going to sleep inside the organ tonight," I told Mr. Gadomski, who was visiting. I explained that while praying, I had had a strange premonition that the Germans might come to get me. He was more likely to be impressed by my clairvoyance than my interpretation of Father Joseph's behavior.

Mr. Gadomski decided that he would sleep in a different cell also. I did not dare to go to the refectory for the evening meal. I spent the evening inside the organ hungry and frightened. During the night I heard banging that left no doubt that the Germans had come looking for me. For years I told myself that I could not have heard, but merely imagined the Gestapo breaking my door. Years later, when I visited the monastery and told this to the prior he showed me that I had been only a few meters away from the door to my cell and certainly would have heard the Germans bursting though the door.

In the morning, Mr. Gadomski came to my hiding place and told me that the Gestapo had smashed the door to my cell. To everyone's surprise, they had not found me. It was no longer possible for me to remain in the monastery. "There is a suspicious fellow walking around the gates," Mr. Gadomski told me. Evidently, the Gestapo suspected that I was within the monastery walls. "You must get out of here before they start searching the place," he whispered to me. He offered to take me to a friend in the village of Stary-Korczyn, located next to the little town of Nowy-Korczyn, who might take me in. We agreed that he would walk down the road and I would sneak into the garden, climb the wall, and meet him at a designated place. We had to get to the railroad station in Krakow and travel to Nowy-Korczyn, about 100 kilometers away. Mr. Gadomski and I took the same path we had walked only a few months earlier on the way to the monastery. Once again, I was on the run. The weather was strangely out of tune with my mood. Why is the sun always shining, the sky free of clouds and blue when I am frightened and gloomy? I thought. The weather had also been sunny on the day that I believed my parents had been killed in Miechow.

Gratitude is not only the greatest of virtues, but the parent of all others.
— Cicero

Chapter 10
The Forbidden Life

Mr. Gadomski told me during the trip to Nowy-Korczyn that his friend Stefan was a hero of the resistance movement. "He blew up an ammunition factory. He lives in the village called Stary-Korczyn, under the assumed name of Joseph Smalec, and pretends to repair the church organ. If the Germans got hold of him, they would kill him."

It was painful to leave the monastery. Within the walls of this small community I had had a feeling of relative security. I had also made some friends there. I could read and study in the library. There was plenty of food, which was hard to come by in occupied Poland.

I have a clear image of entering the village of Stary-Korczyn full of trepidation about my future. Once again, I was in unfamiliar surroundings. We walked to the church that dominated the village. The building was empty; it was before noon. Gadomski told me, "Jasiu, let us pray to the Good Lord and the Virgin Mary that Stefan takes you in." We then knelt together and prayed in silence. I said the only Hebrew prayer I knew "Shma Israel." This was more affirmation of Jewish identity than a plea for divine intercession. I never had the notion that a supernatural force could help me.

Mr. Gadomski had to return immediately to the monastery to avoid suspicion that he was involved in my disappearance. After he left, I looked around the empty church. The entire population of Stary-Korczyn would not fill it up. Sunlight coming through the large stained-glass windows reflected in the metal organ pipes. My appreciation of this instrument had increased in the last 24 hours. I rose from my kneeling position and walked to the back of the church. The silvery organ pipes seemed cheerful in the otherwise gloomy church. I climbed the stone steps leading to the organ. Stefan Jagodzinski was working on the instrument. If he agreed to accept me, would I be working with him on the organ? I wondered.

What would I do if he was not willing to risk his life to help me? Gadomski was the only person in the world I could turn to, and I had the feeling that he wanted to get rid of me as quickly as possible. My father was in the camp and I did not know the whereabouts of Mother.

Hearing the church portal opening, I quickly returned to the pew. A young man entered the church. He crossed himself as he walked to the altar and then went into the sacristy. He returned and looked at me again as he went by. I wondered who he was and naturally became alarmed. Soon he was back. He walked directly to me, laid his left hand on my shoulder and extended his right hand to me. "I am Stefan. My official name is Josef Szmalec. From today on, you are my nephew. Come along."

Stefan was a vigorous and cordial man, in his early 20s. I liked him instantly. I followed him to his rented room in one of the largest houses in the village. The owner, Felix Dembski, was a rich peasant.

Stefan was friendly but he did not have the unctuous sweetness of Gadomski. I sensed his capacity for compassion and loyalty. He was unfailingly upbeat despite the dreadful situation. We became friends from the moment we met.

Stefan helped me to survive and I helped him after the war to live his life more comfortably, but our friendship came first. I was grateful to Gadomski but we never became friends. My mixed feelings about Gadomski made me feel guilty. He risked his life to help me and had the courage that some of our friends were lacking. Gadomski was helping me in spite of his belief that Jews were despicable; helping me was no doubt a source of some inner conflict for him. I was thankful for his help but troubled by his anti-Semitism. He was a hypocrite who did not eat meat on Friday, but sexually abused young boys. He spoke hateful words about the Jews, but he never harmed one. Gadomski, unlike some anti-Semites, did not carry out acts of hate, and acts, not words, were important to my survival. Stefan and Gadomski were men of uncommon courage; they risked their lives for altruistic reasons. The Germans would kill them or at very least send them to a concentration camp if it became known that they were helping a Jew; and fellow Poles would not approve their actions either.

The Dembski house, where Stefan lived, was unlike most of the other dwellings in Stary-Korczyn. It was constructed of brick and had a tile roof. Most of the homes were built of wood and had thatched roofs. It was painted white and a large, heavy door led to a corridor. Stefan's room was to the left of the entrance and occupied a whole corner of the house. One window faced the main road; another opened into the farmyard. I noted the escape routes. There was a potbellied stove in a corner. A large crucifix hung over the bed, with a picture of Jesus on one side and the Black Madonna of Czestochowa on the other. When we entered the room, Stefan knelt by the bed and prayed for a few minutes. Unlike Gadomski, he did not ask me to join him in prayer. Stefan was not in the conversion business.

My first day in Stary-Korczyn went very well, but I was worried by the proximity of Stary-Korczyn to Miechow and the village where, according to my documents, I was born.

The most pressing problem was that my Kennkarte was still at the monastery. I no longer recall why I did not have it when I escaped from Mogila.

94

Stefan decided that he should go to the Mogila to retrieve it. It was dangerous for me to be without this document. Polish police and the Germans were frequent visitors to the village and could ask for the Kennkarte at any time.

Stefan was supposed to be gone for only two days. On the fourth day, I became alarmed by his long absence and decided to call the monastery. The only telephone in the village was in the house of the Soltys (the village elder). As I approached the Soltys' house I was stopped by two Polish policemen. They pointed their rifles at me and demanded that I raise my hands over my head. There were partisans in the area, they said, and I did not look like a villager nor did I speak like one. They searched me thoroughly and discovered that I had neither guns nor documents. In the process of searching me, one of the policemen said to the other, "The kid looks like a Jew." I immediately replied with laughter, "I don't take that to be a compliment."

Both of the policemen laughed with me. At this point, the one searching me had his hand between my legs looking for a hidden gun. "Next he will unbutton my pants, and that will be the end of me," I thought, trying to act casual. I had heard that in nearby Krakow, it was common for the Germans to round up men in the streets, place them in a large hall, and inspect their genitalia with a flashlight. This was called the "Schwantz Parade" in German (Parade of Tails).

"How come you have no documents?" one of the policemen asked. "I left them at home," I said. At this point, the Soltys emerged from his home and asked, "What is going on?"

"Do you know this boy?" demanded the policeman.

"Oh, yes, I know him very well. He lives a few houses from here." I had never seen the man before but he knew that I lived with Stefan. The senior policeman announced that being without documents was an offense punishable by jail or a fine. The Soltys, Kazimierz Czurlik, paid my fine, which seemed more like a bribe, and I was free to go. I doubt that the Soltys would have been so helpful had he suspected that I was a Jew. I believe that he assumed that I was involved with the underground like Stefan.

When Stefan returned the next day, we repaid the money to the Soltys and gave him a bottle of vodka. Stefan had brought my Kennkarte and wonderful news. He had visited my father at the Luftwaffe camp. That seemed to me like traveling to the moon and back.

Stefan told me that after my narrow escape, Father had showed up once again to visit me at the monastery with Herr Schwarzer and had talked to Gadomski, who was still in the monastery. Father had told Gadomski that he could be visited by going to the gate of the military airport and asking for the Commandant. The password was to announce, "Please tell the Commandant that I am a salesman selling brushes for cleaning airplanes." The Commandant of the airport, a major in the Luftwaffe, was father's patient and was helpful to him.

Stefan had done just that, and the Commandant had received him in his office. A few minutes later, my father showed up. "Your father is so handsome, blond and blue-eyed; he speaks perfect Polish. No one would believe he is a Jew," said Stefan.

Stefan also visited Father's dental office, where he met Leon Storch, the dental technician. Leon had come to the camp with father from Ghetto Miechow. Father asked Stefan to provide help for Mother and Olenka because they could no longer stay where they were. There was no time to waste, so Stefan somehow picked them up and took them by boat to a village not far from Stary-Korczyn. One of Stefan's many girlfriends, a schoolteacher, lived there. Stefan told her that Mother was a cousin and was wanted by the Germans for underground activities. The teacher agreed to have Mother and Olenka live with her. Mother paid her very well.

Once I had my Kennkarte in hand, we could go about the business of making money by smuggling. The Polish word for smuggling, "szmuglowac," had heroic overtones in those days. To be a smuggler was a badge of honor. People in the cities could not survive on the rations allocated by the Germans. Bringing food into the cities was a way to make money and be anti-German. It was a dangerous occupation, punishable by being sent to a concentration camp. The type of goods and the whim of the Germans determined the punishment. Possession of meat and bacon, when found in some quantities, was punishable by death. All the trains leading to big cities were full of people, most of whom smuggled food for themselves or to offer for sale. Meat and bacon, because of their high value and the risk of punishment, were concealed on one's body. Potatoes, beans, beets and other vegetables were carried in bags and abandoned when the Germans conducted a search. The Polish police could be handled with bribes.

Stefan discovered a technique of smuggling by using the ships on the Vistula River. These boats were propelled by steam engines; therefore large amounts of coal had to be kept below the deck. The bribed crew members would hide our contraband in the coal. When the ships arrived in Krakow, the Germans searched the people and their luggage. We carried small amounts of vegetables and got through the searches without difficulty. A few hours later we would return and retrieve the illegal goods from the ship's crew. We smuggled goods every day except on Sunday. Stefan was a devout Catholic. He attended church regularly and I naturally went with him.

On our trips to Krakow, I often saw Jews marched to labor assignments. At times, I walked to the ghetto wall as an expression of my loyalty to Judaism. But I was scrupulously "Polish" in my behavior and habits. So now I disliked onions, and ate bacon and ham eagerly whenever they were available. I listened to anti-Semitic remarks without protest but never made anti-Semitic comments myself. But I could not resist going near the ghetto and seeing what was happening. I had the hope of seeing someone I knew. The Ghetto was the real world. I lived in a world of fantasy that could collapse any day.

The most profitable trips and the most dangerous ones were to Warsaw. To travel on the train from Krakow to Warsaw was a feat by itself. The overcrowding was horrendous. Being an agile boy, I could get into a compartment by climbing though the window. Stefan would hand me the luggage and then fight his way till he reached the compartment where I was. We would take food into the city and bring back "bimber" (homemade vodka).

Warsaw was a world unto itself. The black market seemed the primary occupation of the city. Certain sections were full of black marketers, mostly young people and children. "Black market" was not a derogatory term; it was recognized as essential to staying alive. Partisans fought the Germans with guns. Black marketers fought them by making it possible for the people to stay alive. The underground economy consisted of illegal producers, wholesale smugglers and retailers known as "handlarze" (traders). Vodka was produced and sold in the old part of town, near the ghetto. The Warsaw Ghetto was enclosed with a brick wall 10 feet high and 11 miles long.

Vodka made in the countryside had a foul smell and occasionally caused blindness. The home-brewed vodka from Warsaw was indistinguishable from liquor produced by the government monopoly. The bottles had official labels indicating that the vodka had been produced before the war. The adjective "przedwojenny" (produced before war) meant high quality. All goods, including vodka, were separated into these two categories – made before, or during the war. Being caught with such contraband was likely to result in being sent to a concentration camp. We did this only a few times, the last one being April 19, 1943, the day of the Warsaw Ghetto Uprising.

April 19, 1943 was a sunny spring day in Warsaw. Stefan and I were walking to the railroad station carrying two six-liter packages of bimber. That day the German patrols were unusually active. We were stopped a few times by agitated motorcycle-riding SS men, their submachine guns ready. They even asked in broken Polish, "Have you seen any Jews?" At the railroad station we were told, "The Jews started an uprising in the ghetto." This explained the German hyperactivity in the streets. I was frightened and troubled by this act of desperation of the Jews in Warsaw Ghetto.

When Stefan and I returned from Warsaw, we had to deal with the Easter holiday problem. It would arouse suspicion if we remained in Stary-Korczyn for Easter; it was customary to go home for the holiday. At Easter, Jews were on everyone's mind. Unfortunately, we had no home to go to. Therefore, we decided to visit my mother and little sister in the home of the schoolteacher. We walked to the village, whose name I no longer remember. The schoolteacher was an attractive woman in her 20s, though Stefan was not particularly interested in her because she was too heavy. He called her, with disdain, "gruba" (the fat one). She operated a one-room schoolhouse, with attached living quarters for the teacher, consisting of a bedroom and kitchen. Mother and Olenka slept in the classroom. It was a secret that Mother and I were related. It was wonderful to see mother and Olenka but it was peculiar not to be able to kiss and hug them. My little sister understood that she was to act as if I was a stranger. I do not recall if mother and I had a chance to speak in private. Mother looked good and was able to act casual.

It was strange to address mother by the formal "Pani (Madame) Rojek," indicating that we were not related. Stefan called Mother by her first name "Aniela," and used the familiar "you" limited to Polish to relatives and very close friends.

Easter Sunday included a festive meal to which the local priest was invited. We all sat around the kitchen table. During the meal, the conversation turned a few times to the Jews. It was rare in Poland to have a gathering without some comments about the Jews. The priest wondered how it was possible for Jews to hide or live on false papers.

"I would recognize a Jew in the darkness of the night if he just said good evening," said the priest and everyone laughed. Like most Poles he believed that speech would invariably identify a person as a Jew. Little did he know that the joke was on him. Out of the six people around that table, three were Jews.

After the meal, we all lay down on the classroom floor and sang songs. It soon became completely dark. There was, naturally, no electricity. The priest left and we were all falling asleep. The teacher began to hug me. She pressed her body against me and then took my hands and placed them on her breast. I was embarrassed and frightened but participated with enthusiasm. I assumed that this would be the limit. Not so! She unbuttoned my pants and reached for my penis with her hand; she used her other hand to place my fingers in her vagina. I was in a state of panic. My mother and sister were nearby, which was bad enough. I assumed that the teacher's interest was not sexual; she was reaching for my penis to find out if I was circumcised and therefore a Jew. I considered myself unattractive. A woman of her good looks and age could not be sexually drawn to a pimple-faced, skinny boy like me. This was not a seduction but an inspection, was my first thought. I immediately lost my erection. She did not give up, but no amount of manipulation produced the desired result. I was excited and terrified. Ultimately, she found a solution to the problem. She turned her back lifted her skirt (she wore no underwear), and placed my soft penis against her vagina by holding it with her hand. I had an erection and was able to have intercourse. But I was petrified. It was likely that I had been unmasked as a Jew. However, having had sex with an adult woman who was also a teacher pleased me.

Leaving the schoolteacher's home next day, I carried a terrible secret with me. Should I tell Stefan what had happened? Would he be jealous? Did she realize that I was a Jew and that Mrs. Rojek was my mother? Would she denounce my mother as a Jew? I did not tell Stefan. We walked very slowly towards Stary-Korczyn since we had to be away from the village for a respectable period. In the afternoon we would enter some village, go to the house of the Soltys (village elder). It was an old Polish custom for a Soltys to assign a stranger to the home of a peasant for an overnight stay.

On the last day of our Easter "vacation," we were walking along the Vistula, "the queen of Polish rivers." In those days, the river was clean and blue. To the right was a high embankment that extended over many kilometers along the river for flood control. On top of this earth barrier was a narrow path. The day was sunny and beautiful, and we sat down facing the river. Suddenly we heard horses' hooves. Two Germans, on horseback, were approaching, preceded by a civilian on a bicycle. They spotted us and came to an abrupt halt. The Germans pointed their submachine guns and yelled the familiar "Haende Hoch!" (Hands up). We did as we were told. At this point, one of the Germans yelled in Polish

"Do wody!" This meant "into the water." We were convinced that turning our backs would provide the Germans with an excuse to shoot us in the back for trying to run away.

"Janek! You run to the left and I will run to the right. One of us might get away," Stefan whispered. I was about to take off when the civilian, evidently aware of what we were about to do, shouted in Jewish-accented Polish, "Hey, boys, don't you have any documents?"

These few words probably saved our lives. "Dowody" (one word) is the synonym for the Polish word "documenty" meaning documents "do wody" (2 words) means "into the water." We reached for our documents and climbed up the bank. The civilian on the bicycle was a Jew, who was still kept at the Korczyn Gendarmerie post. He served as a living mine detector. Partisans in the area would lay mines in the path of German patrols. These Jews on bicycles would activate the booby traps first. The Germans inspected our documents carefully. To my horror, they passed my Kennkarte to each other with comments that I did not hear. I was then asked directly "Wie alt bist Du?" (How old are you?). I pretended not to understand. The Jew translated and I gave my age in Polish. One German commented that I looked older than 15. "They don't believe you are only 15," said the Jew helpfully. I was asked to come closer, and after a long look at the Kennkarte and me, Stefan and I were permitted to go. A soon as we were out of range of their guns Stefan invoked a historic phrase by saying this was our "Miracle on the Wistula" (Cud nad Wisla). This was a historical reference to a 1920 battle around Warsaw between Polish and Bolshevik forces.[38]

Upon our return to Stary-Korczyn, we continued our usual activities, pretending to be working on the church organ and smuggling food to Krakow. As days went by, I was feeling less guilty about my involvement with the schoolteacher. No news from Mother meant that maybe the teacher did not recognize me as a Jew by the shape of my penis.

From time to time Stefan went away by himself. I assumed he was involved in some underground missions. I felt lonely and scared without him; I did not trust the villagers. They often talked about Jews, usually with a great deal of hostility. I took long walks by myself along the shores of the river. I had a favorite spot, with weeping willows and wild flowers. I lay in the high grass and watched the water and the clouds. I used to daydream about joining the Yugoslav partisans. I believed that they, unlike the Polish underground, were not anti-Semitic. I called this location my "Jasna Gora" (Bright Mountain), which was the name of the monastery of the Black Madonna, known for her miraculous cures.

One day when Stefan was away, I felt a severe pain in my belly. I was convinced that I had appendicitis. In those days, a ruptured appendix meant certain death. In England, penicillin came into use in 1940. In occupied Europe it was non-existent. Early surgery was lifesaving. Whenever I had a bellyache at home, Father and Mother would check my abdomen for tenderness in the right lower area above the groin. That was exactly where I had my pain. I could not go to a doctor; he would examine me, see my penis and I would be exposed as a Jew. A ruptured appendix was less dangerous than being recognized as a Jew.

It was a sunny day. I lay in the grass, exposing my belly to the warmth of the sun. After a few hours, I pronounced myself miraculously cured. It seemed that whenever Stefan was away, something bad happened.

Another time, in his absence, I woke up with a high fever and chills. I lay in bed shivering, unable even to get to the outhouse. We had a large oleander plant in our room. I urinated into the plant and felt very guilty about it. I did not want the landlords to know that I was sick for they might call a doctor. The fever was very high and I became delirious. Whenever I was sick at home, my parents lovingly cared for me. Now I had to keep my illness a secret. If only mother were here, I thought. Suddenly I heard Mother's voice and dismissed it as a fantasy. The voice persisted. I dragged myself to the window. There were Mother and Olenka, talking to a peasant who was unloading a suitcase from the horse-drawn wagon. The next thing I remember is waking up many hours later, with my mother putting cold towels on my overheated body. The fever subsided and I recovered.

Mother told me that she was found out as a Jew by the teacher, who threatened to call the police. The teacher took Mother's expensive fur coat and chased her out of the house. Mother told our landlady that she was Stefan's cousin and had come to visit him. I was amazed that Mother found where Stefan and I lived. I was happy to see Mother and Olenka but terribly worried. Did our landlady catch on that Pani (Madame) Rojek was related to me? Did she suspect that she might be Jewish? What would happen to mother now?

Fortunately, Stefan arrived the next day. After a long discussion, we decided that Stefan would take Mother and Olenka to Krakow to a friend of his. He was confident that Mrs. Siedlecka, a widow he knew, would be willing to hide them in her apartment for a reasonable fee. Once again, Stefan was gone and I was left feeling more insecure in Stary-Korczyn.

My intuition was sending emergency signals. After Stefan returned, he too became concerned. He heard in the village comments of suspicion about "that nephew of yours." Some people expressed doubts that we were related. It was only a matter of time that I would be denounced as a Jew. We decided that I could not remain much longer in the village. I wanted to leave at once, but Stefan was less apprehensive. "We have time to find you a new place," he told me. He was in an optimistic mood, befitting a man who was in love. He had returned from Krakow with a dark haired beauty in her early twenties. Her name was Rose (Roza in Polish). She had recently left a convent and fallen in love with Stefan. He found a sleeping room for her in a nearby house. He was spending most of his time with her. Stefan told Rose that we were involved with the underground and were in danger of being denounced in Stary-Korczyn. After a few days, Stefan and Rose left to find a place for me somewhere else.

The German police in Nowy-Korczyn were paying a bounty for the delivery or denouncement of a Jew. I heard peasants talk about it on a number of occasions, and I was afraid that a party of bounty hunters would come and get me. I slept in my clothes, ready to leap through the window on a moment's notice. Most raids were conducted at night. I was reminded of this years later when I read Dr. Martin Luther King's words: "Midnight is the hour when men desperately seek to obey the Eleventh Commandment, 'Thou shalt not get caught'."

One late afternoon, two Polish policemen drove by our house in a wagon. They were sitting behind the driver with rifles in their hands. I stepped outside and sat down on the stoop trying to act casual. The horses came to a stop at the house of the Soltys (the village elder). The policemen went inside, the driver stayed with the horses. Suddenly, I saw the policemen furtively approach our house. They must have left the Solyts' house through a back door and were sneaking up to catch me, I thought. I could not run from the front of the house – they were too close and had rifles ready to fire. I leaped into the house, nearly colliding with the landlady who was heading for the entrance door. I bolted into the back yard, jumped the fence to a side road and ran as fast as I could towards the fields. People were looking at me in amazement. I reached the first path separating the wheat fields. In Poland, the small plots of land are separated by narrow walkways that form an elaborate patchwork covering a great deal of the countryside. I ran along these strips; the wheat was chest high. I made frequent turns until I fell exhausted on the ground. No one seemed to pursue me. I was safe for a moment.

What do I do next, I wondered? I decided to return to the house after the policemen left the village, but I had to wait for Stefan. I was certain that the two Polish policemen would not dare to stay overnight in the village. They would be afraid of becoming a target for the underground army. If the landlord wanted to grab me I would escape. I slowly made my way to an area overlooking the road from the village of Stary-Korczyn to the little town of Nowy-Korczyn. The wagon with the policemen would have to take this road on its way back.

It was almost completely dark when I heard the horses' hooves, and soon afterwards, I could hear the men talking and laughing. No doubt some vodka had been consumed during this visit. I sneaked back into the village, greeted by the barking of the dogs. The house was locked up and I had to knock on the window to wake up Mr. Dembski. Before I could say anything, he explained, "The police came to confiscate two of my horses." My vigilance got me in trouble; I had blown my cover for nothing. The whole village knew now that I was scared of the Polish police. Poles in the underground had little to fear in a village from the "granatowa policja" (blue police), as they were called. Their collaboration with the Germans included various activities on behalf of the Germans, but they would never act against members of the underground army. They were used often in rounding up Jews.

Stefan and Rose arrived the next day, and I told Stefan what happened. To my surprise, he did not blame me. "I will go into the village to survey the enemy territory," he said cheerfully. He returned in a somber mood. He took me aside so that Rose could not hear him. "They suspect you are a Jew and a group was formed to catch you. You must leave at once in secret," he said.

The plan was that I would run into the fields and find my way to Krakow alone. Stefan and Rose would meet me the next day at the main railroad station and we would go to the Niepolomice Forest. Rose had an uncle who lived next to the forest. Once again I headed for the wheat fields and walked to Nowy-Korczyn avoiding the road. I took the next ship going to Krakow. After the riverboat pulled into port at Krakow, I had no place to go. I walked to the railroad station and spent the night there sleeping on the floor. The next day I wandered around the city until the first movie house opened. I felt safe in a movie theater, protected by darkness from people who might recognize me as a Jew. My self-assurance had been shaken by the recent developments.

I met Stefan and Rose at the agreed upon time and we traveled by train to Niepolomice. We then walked to the edge of the forest where Rose's uncle lived on a subsistence farm. The family did not have a real home. They had a barn, which housed animals; one corner had a room where the peasant and his family lived. Stefan, Rose, and I slept in the hayloft. One night we were summoned by our host to assist in the delivery of a calf; it was a breech presentation. The peasant tied a rope to the unborn calf's foot. The men pulled on the rope and the women lovingly encouraged the cow. I pulled with all my strength; it was the first time I could do something useful for my host. A healthy calf was delivered to the joyous outcries of the family. A bottle of vodka appeared to celebrate the event. A day or two later Stefan went to Krakow to find a safe place for me there. He was planning to go back to Stary-Korczyn. While Stefan was away, Rose and I were alone in the hayloft, except for the rats. I kept a set of "cepy," a long pole with a short stick attached by two leather straps to the end of it. It was used in Poland for threshing wheat. Every so often, I beat the surrounding area to scare away the rats. Rose and I cuddled together in dread of the rats. We became aroused and ultimately had sexual relations. I felt guilty for having slept with my "uncle's" woman, and I became terrified when she insisted on handling my penis to bring about a repeat performance. She proudly called herself "zachlanna" (insatiable). I was afraid that Rose would recognize that I was circumcised. She did not know that I was a Jew. She believed that I, like Stefan, was a member of the underground. Stefan had told her that I could not stay in Stary-Korczyn because I had blown my cover by running from the police.

Rose left Niepolomice before Stefan returned, to see her mother who lived in Krakow. I was left alone and quite insecure. During the day I wandered in the forest, getting to know the area in case I had to escape. At other times I sat in the tiny room while the family worked in the fields. I kept a careful lookout, apprehensive that someone might show up. Then I was to crawl under the bed. Two days after Rose left, I saw two Polish policemen approaching the house from two different directions. This time there could be no doubt that their purpose was to capture me.

They went to the back of the house, which had the only door. At this point I jumped from the window and ran towards the nearby tree line. They saw me running and fired their guns, but I managed to reach the forest unharmed. They did not dare to go into the forest, fearing to encounter partisans. I knew my way to the nearby railroad tracks. There was a spot where the train had to slow down and I could jump on a railroad car. On one of my walks, I had worked it out as part of my routine to anticipate dangers and ways to escape. I was hoping for a train going west to Krakow. Unfortunately, the first train, which I could hear by putting my ear to the railroad tracks, was going east.

102

Suddenly, I could hear another train, which was going west. It was raining heavily but I managed to get on the train without any problem. I was soaking wet in my short pants and shirt. Fortunately, I never parted with my documents and money. Once I was inside, a few young fellows viewed me with great suspicion. "Did you see the conductor?" I asked, trying to imply that I was evading payment of the fare.

When the train arrived in Krakow, I had to find Stefan, my helper and my link to my father and mother. I knew only two people who would know his whereabouts; his girlfriend Rose and Mrs. Wieczorkowska, an older lady whom he visited when he was in Krakow. I went to Rose's apartment first. She lived in one of the typical Krakow buildings in the center of town. Her apartment was located on the second floor. Rose greeted me warmly and introduced me to her mother, a woman in her forties. Her mother did not appear to be friendly and soon departed on some errand. I told Rose what had happened in the Niepolomice.

She did not know where Stefan was but she added sheepishly, "My mother thinks you are a Jew and she went to get a policeman."

"You, of all people, would know that I am not a Jew," I said.

"How would I know?" she asked.

"You don't remember?" I said, pointing to my genital area.

"Oh yes, but then you can prove that to the police."

"Don't you realize my underground connection? I have false papers." I yelled angrily.

"You are right, I am sorry. I should have stopped my mother," she said, genuinely distressed.

As we looked out from the kitchen window into the courtyard, we saw her mother in the company of two Polish policemen.

"Delay them for a few minutes," I yelled, and ran out the door and went upstairs to the third floor. From there, I could watch the entrance to Rose's apartment. It was all in her hands. If she told them that I had gone upstairs, I was lost. I saw the policemen enter the apartment, and I ran downstairs. The entrance to each apartment was from a circular inner balcony, which meant that I had to run by Rose's kitchen door and kitchen windows. The policemen saw me and ran after me but they were not able to catch up with a boy running for his life. I got lost in the crowd.

Was it coincidence that Rose left Niepolomice before the police came to get me? Had she denounced me? Did her mother instantly recognize that I was a Jew on false papers or was it something she found out from her daughter? I am not certain to this day. The demeanor of a person let me know if he or she suspected that I was Jewish. A facial expression, a tone of voice, or a comment could act as a danger signal. As far as I recall, Rose's mother was the only person whose intention to denounce me I did not recognize.

My next and only hope of finding Stefan after escaping Rose's trap was Mrs. Wieczorkowska, and I knew that Stefan kept in touch with her. I found her apartment and asked for Josef Smalec. The woman responded in an angry voice, "You have the wrong address. I have never heard of such a person.

Please go away." I asked if she knew Stefan Jagodzinski. She became irritated and insisted that I go away. It seemed I was at the end of my resources. Now I was cut off from contact with anyone I could trust and had no way to get in touch with Father in the camp. I also did not know where my mother and Olenka were.

Suddenly I remembered "Schwarzer," the German who used to smuggle my father out of the labor camp at the military airport, bringing him to the monastery to visit me. I knew that he lived in the German Quarter in Krakow; this was a section of newly constructed buildings on one of the main thoroughfares. Herr Schwarzer could get in touch with my father in the camp and might know how I could get in touch with Stefan. I walked from one house to another, asking for Herr Schwarzer. The German households had Polish maids with whom I could talk. After a few tries, I was directed to the residence of the Schwarzer family.

Herr Schwarzer opened the door. He immediately recognized me and invited me inside. In those years I spoke virtually no German. I tried to let him know that I wanted him to take a note to my father and bring back a response. He readily understood and agreed to take a note to father in the morning. He invited me to have supper with him and his wife. I thanked him but made him aware that I had to be off the street before the curfew. I intended to sleep at the railroad station. Herr Schwarzer offered an overnight stay in the apartment, which I accepted. The next morning he went to work. His wife was also working somewhere; they left together. For the first time in many days, I felt secure, since I was in the house of a German. I was amazed by Schwarzer's generosity. He was risking his life by providing a hiding place for me.

About midday, he returned with a note from my father who simply wrote, "Contact Mrs. Wieczorkowska." Once again, I presented myself at her door. She became very irate with me and threatened me with the police if I did not go away. I walked away. Suddenly she yelled to me, "Please come back." The door opened and I saw my mother and little sister. I had not known that this was my mother's hiding place. Mrs. Wieczorkowska suspected that I was a blackmailer, but Olenka recognized my voice and insisted that I be called back.

After the reunion with Mother and Olenka at Mrs. Wieczorkowska's home, I left without telling Mother that I had no place to go. Establishing contact with my mother and sister gave me no practical help but emotionally it gave me a great boost. Mother told me that Stefan would be visiting in a few days. I walked the streets but there was not much time left before curfew. I could not go to a hotel since I looked like a street urchin. I wore short pants, a shabby looking shirt, and had no luggage. I was truly homeless. The railroad station was my traditional hotel of last resort. One could stay there after curfew waiting for a train. I bought a ticket to Miechow for a train departing early the next morning. Naturally, I had no intention of going there. People were lying wall to wall in the waiting rooms, sleeping or waiting for trains departing after curfew. I found a spot on the platform next to a teenage girl. We began to talk. She was traveling alone, returning to Kielce, my father's hometown. We talked for some time, and then fell asleep. I put my head on her traveling bag since I had no luggage. Germans shouting commands awakened us. They ordered us inside the building; there was room now since some people had departed. The document inspection was repeated a few times during the night. The girl and I whispered curses against the Germans and began to hug and kiss each other once the waiting room became dark. We fell asleep in each other's arms. I remember it as a significant intimate relationship that rekindled my will to live.

The next morning I felt invigorated. I felt safer in the anonymity of a metropolitan setting. Here, the Poles were less a threat to my life than in the countryside.

The anonymity of a big city had a big advantage in that suspicions were not communicated to others. In the village of Stary Korczyn, or in the monastery, a Pole who suspected that I was a Jew would tell others, who would watch me more carefully. In Krakow there were a great many Germans but they did not scare me. It was easier for me protect myself against the Germans than the Poles.

I decided to rent a room and find a job. My first task was to make myself look presentable. I still had some money; I found a used clothing store and purchased a pair of pants and a shirt. I then checked into the "Hotel Francuzki' (French Hotel) where my parents used to stay before the war. It was a fancy place. Walking down the street, I saw a sign saying "Dentist and Dental Laboratory." I walked in and asked to speak to the dentist. "My father is a dentist," I told him, "I used to help in his dental lab. He is a prisoner of war in Germany." I recall the doctor vividly. He was a round faced, kind looking man who, after a few questions, hired me as an apprentice in the dental lab. I don't remember his name; I will call him Dr. Zielinski. Getting a job was a condition for living in the city. Now I was legitimate and could register with the "Meldungsamt" (Registration Office). Everyone was required to report to that office upon moving into a locality.

I wanted to rent a room that would be more private and therefore safer but I could not afford such luxury. So I found a sleeping bed in a small apartment with an old lady. She told me I could move in the next day. I returned to the used clothing store, bought a few other items and an old suitcase to create the appearance of a regular boy coming from a small town to work in a big city.

Just before the curfew, I returned to the hotel. I went to the reception desk and asked for the key to my room. I spoke Polish. A few SS-men were standing at the desk chatting with the clerk. That the clerk spoke Polish surprised them; he was evidently an ethnic German.

"Are Poles permitted to stay in this hotel?" one of them asked with amazement.

"We have all kinds of nationalities – Hungarians, Slovaks and others as guests," The clerk replied. Another SS-man remarked that no doubt they had no Jews. Everybody laughed except me; I pretended not to understand a word of German. I was thrilled that the joke was on them.

The next day I moved in with the old lady and began working in the dental lab. The work was not a problem, but my coworkers gave me concern. Three young men worked in the lab in addition to an older technician. It became obvious they suspected that I might be a Jew. They talked about Jews a lot. They kept inviting me to join them in their occasional after work drinking parties. I understood that they wanted to get me drunk and find out if I were a Jew. I had no choice but to go with them at least once. They insisted on picking me up at my place, which was within walking distance from work. I told them that I lived with an aunt. Naturally, I usually addressed my elderly landlady with the honorific "Pani" (Mrs.), which would have made it clear that we were not related. To solve this problem I told my landlady that I was too embarrassed to tell my coworkers that I could afford only a sleeping bed, not a private room; therefore, I had told my buddies that I lived with my Aunt Mary. She smiled and accepted my story. When my coworkers arrived, I repeatedly called her "Aunt Mary." Since she was beyond suspicion of being a Jew, I earned some points towards dispelling doubts about my identity.

We headed for the streetcar to get to the illegal-drinking place. It was little known that one could purchase a monthly, or maybe even yearly, streetcar pass. I got it because it was an additional document with a photo. Each time we got on the streetcar, I went in first, showed my card discreetly to the driver who let me on without taking my fare. I knew that the guys would ask me about it, which they did. I was evasive, trying in a clumsy way to hide why I was able to ride the streetcars without paying. I would tell them the "truth" when I was drunk. I knew that I had to drink a lot but avoid getting drunk. In Poland, competitive drinking was a popular sport. One proved one's manhood by how much vodka one could hold. The shots of vodka were consumed in one big gulp. I made two or three trips to the toilet and made myself throw up. I got tipsy but pretended to be drunk. I confessed to my "friends" that my father was a dentist but it was not true that he was a prisoner of war in Germany. My parents were living on false papers in Krakow. Father was active in the underground army. The Germans tried to arrest him in our hometown of Warsaw but we escaped to Krakow. "The two streetcar drivers are members of the underground. That's why they did not ask me for a fare," I explained.

The conviviality of the occasion and my stories made me part of the group and dispelled the suspicions that I could be a Jew. The party did not last long because of the curfew. After this affair, I felt more secure at work but increasingly less self-confident in the streets. Everywhere people talked about Jews pretending to be Poles. Living on false papers was a never-ending crisis. Hatred of the Jews seemed to be increasing.

I missed living with Stefan. Living on false papers was a lonely existence. Surrounded by hostility and malice, I needed friendship to sustain my will to live. Stefan was such a person for me. I was isolated from family, friends and community and was in peril of death at all times. It was a lonely fight for survival against all odds. The life-threatening encounters were separated by a constant expectation of a disaster.

The contact with Stefan was important to me for emotional reasons. He understood that and came to see me from time to time. One day, I told him that I had read an advertisement that the "Postamt" (German Post Office) was hiring young Poles to deliver telegrams. I had seen these boys in their dark blue uniforms and impressive hats with stiff rims. My dental technician job did not pose an immediate risk of being denounced, but the longer I was in one location the more likely it was that someone would catch on. I showed Stefan the ad. "Who would dare to suspect that I am a Jew if I wore such a uniform?" I told Stefan. He agreed and both of us walked to the main Post Office, an intimidating gray building in the center of town.

The post office was an important governmental agency. The Polish word "urzad" and the German word "Amt" are used only for a place where governmental functions are performed. There is no corresponding term in the English language. The word "office" lacks the intimidating quality of "urzad" or "Amt." A person working in a governmental agency was not called an employee but an "urzendnik" in Polish or "Beamte" in German; these titles inspired respect and fear. During the occupation, the Germans ran the post office, but it employed many Poles who wore the old Polish uniforms without the national emblem. I entered the building with anxious hopefulness. I knew that I would be interrogated and scrutinized, which was risky. On the other hand, I saw myself leaving wearing a protective uniform. The administrative offices were located on the second floor. The place was swarming with Germans in military uniforms. A Polish secretary gave me an application and instructions on how to fill it out. I returned the application to her with my Kennkarte attached to it, as instructed. "It looks good," she said, with a strange smile. "Does she suspect that I am a Jew?" I asked myself.

I waited for a long time, feeling increasingly more anxious. Stefan was waiting for me outside the post office. I did not dare to go outside without a document proving that I was not a Jew. Without my Kennkarte, I felt naked. Why does it take so long? Are they checking the entries on my application? Is there an order for my arrest because of my escape from the monastery? were the thoughts going through my mind.

"Mr. Director will see you now," the secretary told me. I was ushered into a large office. A civilian sat behind the desk, a man in his late 30s, blond, blue eyed; I still remember his sinister smile. The door to the left of his desk was open. I could see an even larger office occupied by a uniformed German who was sitting behind a desk talking on the telephone. The personnel director motioned to me to sit down. Without saying a word, he picked up my Kennkarte and studied it carefully. As soon as the uniformed man next door was off the telephone, the personnel director approached him and they talked in German. "Please follow me," the director instructed me, in perfect Polish. I wondered if he was a Pole or an ethnic German. He opened the door to a room to the right of his desk, a tiny windowless space with a small table and two chairs. After some preliminary interrogation, he asked sharply, "Your father is in a German POW camp?" "Yes," I answered. He wanted to know the name of the camp. I told him that I did not know the name of the camp. A postcard would come every few weeks; it had a response card attached to it with a number of the POW camp. "That's not true," he yelled. I knew that I was right and told him so. His arrogant and contemptuous manner left no doubt that he was convinced that I was a Jew on false papers.

Next, he ordered me to recite prayers. First he asked for Ojcze Nasz (The Lord Our Father). I did that with ease. "How about Aniol Panski?" (Angel of the Lord), a less known prayer – no, that too was no problem. He was getting angry and began to test my familiarity with the catechism and the New Testament. My monastery education was paying off. He was no match for my knowledge of Catholic doctrine and gave up in frustration. His conviction that I was a Jew was not shaken by my faultless performance. Soon, I thought, he would ask me to drop my pants, a test I could not pass. In such situations I always thought of the most informative part of my anatomy.

"I will be back soon," he said, leaving me in the windowless room. He locked the door. I could not see through the keyhole because the key was in it. I put my ear to the door and listened to the conversation between the two men in the next room. The word "Jude" (Jew) was used a few times by the personnel director as he talked in agitated manner to the uniformed German. There seemed no way out. My career as a Catholic had ended. At any moment, the Gestapo would come to claim me. Then my fearful ruminations were interrupted by the turn of the key. "Follow me," my tormentor commanded.

We entered the office of the German who obviously was in charge. "Sitzen Sie, bitte," (sit down please) the elderly man said to me pleasantly. The word "bitte" (please) and his use of "Sie" (third person pronoun) instead of "Du" (you) gave me encouragement. He asked how old I was. I smiled in response but pretended not to understand. "He wants to know how old you are," my persecutor standing in the door translated. I responded by saying "15" in broken German and writing 15 with my finger in the air.

At this point, the telephone rang. The German picked up my Kennkarte and talked to someone on the phone about me. He spelled my name. When he finished, he turned to the personnel director and spoke a German phrase, which I will never forget, "Das ist eine echte Kennkarte" (This is a genuine identity card). "He is a Jew nevertheless," the director said in German. "Wir sind keine Polizisten." (We are not policemen) "Ende, Schluss!" (This is the end. Nothing more), he said with finality.

He then turned to me and said "Sie kennen gehen" (you can leave). He handed me my identity card and motioned to the frustrated Jew-hunter to step aside and let me out. This brave German man granted me the equivalent of a stay of execution.

A few seconds later I was in the street running with a perplexed Stefan following me. Once I was sure that I was not being followed, I explained to Stefan what had happened.

Some weeks later, I encountered the personnel director at the Krakow railroad station. He tried to catch me and yelled, "Catch the Jew," but I ran and disappeared into the crowd. This postal official with aspirations of being a Gestapo man has a prominent place in my gallery of villains. He stands next to Father Joseph, the two even looked similar. Both of them were blond, handsome and in their twenties. Both hated me enough to eagerly seek my death. They hated me, but knew nothing about me, other than that I might be a Jew. Such dedicated hatred is impressive and puzzling.

I was on the brink of a disaster nearly every day. Sometimes in a single day I had to struggle several times to get out of the net of my persecutors. Every narrow escape was a temporary reprieve. Each escape accomplished only that I did not get killed in that particular confrontation. New danger was around the corner. I was living in a minefield and the explosives were hidden everywhere. The constant danger made me preternaturally alert.

A few days after my post office encounter, two Polish policemen in a crowded streetcar were working their way in my direction. I noticed that a man had talked to them with some intensity. One of the policemen glanced in my direction. Wasting no time, I jumped from the moving streetcar and ran. Just before I jumped, one of the policemen yelled to the passengers to grab me. There was no doubt that they were after me. The man talking to them could have been from Miechow and recognized me.

One day, I entered a restaurant on a side street of the main market square in Krakow. As soon as I sat down, a waitress took my order. She looked at me suspiciously. I knew what she was thinking. I was sensitive to these looks. I was coming across them with increasing frequency. I made a few comments in a confident voice to dispel her doubts about my identity. I felt reassured when she brought me food, and not a policeman. I ate quickly and left.

"Can they smell that I am a Jew? Is there some physical trait in me that signals to these Poles that I am on false papers?" I asked myself many times.

My survival depended on recognizing the suspicions and dealing with them before they became actions. The choice was to run or to drive out the suspicion in the person's mind.

The magic of speech worked nearly every time. Absence of a Jewish accent and a voice free of fear did the trick most the time. But it had not worked with Rose's mother. It failed on a few occasions with the professional Jew hunters. The ability to lie persuasively was essential to my survival. I was not used to lying and that was good. Habitual liars are poor liars. Only a truthful person can lie persuasively.

Guilt interferes with effective lying. Lying without guilt or shame is the birthright of psychopaths. Honest people lie at times because of necessity, which absolves them of guilt. I, like all children, had been taught that it is bad to lie, but now my life depended on deception, and I do not recall having any internal conflict about lying in service of survival.

The efforts to unmask me were immoral; therefore I had no guilt about my behavior. Deception performed for just reasons is easier to carry out than similar behavior that is contrary to the conscience of the actor.

I had been very effective in my role as a Catholic boy eager to become a priest. And yet someone recognized that I was a Jewish teenager and denounced me. My high incentive and talent were not enough to deceive everyone.

It is difficult to lie effectively and it is equally difficult to unmask a good liar. This may seem contradictory, but on reflection, it makes perfect sense. Our daily experience proves it. It is easy to recognize a lie told by a little child. An experienced and talented actor makes us believe, as if he or she was not acting.

The pervasiveness of anti-Semitism was a problem for all Jews trying to survive on false papers in Poland. There was a general state of suspiciousness and willingness to denounce a Jew trying to pass for a Christian. My task was to mislead people who suspected that I might be an imposter. Most of the time there were no direct confrontations. I had to recognize that someone suspected that I was a Jew and dispel his or her suspicions without directly saying so.

Intuitively, we grasp a great deal in daily encounters with strangers. The voice, the facial expressions and body movements send a multitude of cues that are processed in our unconscious. Most people make little use of this information.

To survive on Aryan papers, one had to have a mixture of contradictory attributes. The ability to trust was essential, how else could you seek out people who would give lifesaving help? A high index of suspiciousness was even more important; how else would you avoid the vultures trying to destroy you? One had to be both shrewd and trusting. The dialectic of trust and suspicion dominated my thinking. All social interactions were to me like police interrogations of a man suspected of being a fugitive from justice. Every man, woman and child were to me like police investigators. Intrusiveness in wartime Poland was as natural as breathing. "Where are you from? What do you do? Do you know so-and-so?" were routine questions that were rather difficult to answer for a fifteen-year-old boy living alone.

I was constantly both vigilant and casual, as if I did not have a care in the world. Anxiety was a survival tool but overt fearfulness invited suspicion.

To survive on Aryan papers it was not enough to be resourceful, cunning, smart, observant, and courageous, have Aryan looks, speak Polish without a Jewish accent, know the Catholic religion, and be suspicious and trusting. One had to have also what Montaigne has called "contempt of death," which he believed to be the "greatest benefit that virtue confers upon us."

Acceptance of death came to me as a sudden insight. An inner voice reassuringly said, "The worst that can happen to you - - you will die." I would repeat these words in my mind whenever I was at risk of being terrified, and all fear would disappear. These ten words became my survival mantra. They protected me from panic, which would be deadly in my situation. Acceptance of death gave me the courage to see danger and thus enhanced chances of my survival.

Survival in those days meant not being killed as a Jew. Other dangers to life, like sickness, accidents and bombs, were not my concern. I jumped from trains without fear, I smuggled bimber (moonshine) from Warsaw to Krakow, for which I could have been killed or sent to a concentration camp. I did not consider these activities perilous.

Exposure as a Jew was the only danger that mattered. Being a Jew was an evil secret. It had to be evil because it was punishable by death. Being alive was a crime for a Jew. I was a fugitive. My presence in a house or village was dangerous to my hosts. I could be the cause of suffering and death. I was forbidden; contact with me was to be avoided, if not out of hate, then out of self-love. Whoever invited me into his house ran the risk of being killed. Only the deviant, the heroic, or the ignorant would welcome me in their midst. My life depended upon subterfuge. I was an imposter. I could not be "me" and live.

In the lives of ordinary people, there are two cardinal events, birth and death. We, the Holocaust survivors, have three milestones: being born, survival, and death. None of us can exercise power over being born or when we die, except for suicide. Survival was to a significant degree our achievement.

Natural selection, according to Darwin, is "the preservation of favorable variations and the rejection of injurious variations." Some characteristics are adaptive for certain environments. My father's blue eyes, blond hair, and his knowledge of German had no survival value in September of 1939 when German airplanes repeatedly aimed machine gun fire at us. But in the summer of 1942, his "Aryan features" saved his life. During the liquidation of the ghetto, he approached the ghetto gate and engaged the SS-men in conversation in German. He then saluted them with a "Heil Hitler" and walked out. It was his luck that these SS-men were from out of town. They did not know him and assumed he was a German civilian.

Speaking faultless Polish had little survival value in a camp but it was essential to those who lived on false papers pretending to be Christians. Had I spoken Yiddish as a child, I would not be alive today.

Some Jews survived in the camps because they had musical or mechanical talents useful to the Germans. Others were "selected" for more rapid extermination because they were very young or very old.

The term "selection" was used to describe the German process of determining who from the ghetto should be sent to a death camp and who could remain in the ghetto and stay alive a while longer.

Once in a death camp, another selection process took place where it was determined who should go to the gas chamber. The Germans relied upon observable physical characteristics, like age, health and fitness for work. I doubt that the term "selection" was chosen for this process in deference to the theories of Charles Darwin. Nevertheless, Darwinian principals applied. People engaged in what could be called "instant mutation."

Beards were shaved off, rouge was applied to pale checks, people dressed to appear more robust. Similar factors had a survival value before selection. Those who spoke German certainly had a much better chance than those who did not. Certain professions and personality traits played a similar role. My father, who spoke perfect German, became a dentist for the Germans. My mother, who did not speak German, was limited to providing dental care for the Jews. My father's blond hair and blue eyes was a great asset for living on false papers. My mother's black hair and complexion raised suspicion that she might be a Jew. Personality differences between my parents determined that mother survived on false papers and father, who was ideally suited for living on false papers, delayed making his move until it was too late. He was less anxiety prone than mother.

The genocidal environment created by Nazi Germany ensured the total extinction of the Jewish population of Europe if given sufficient time. It was possible for some Jews to survive for a limited period. Sooner or later, every Jew would have been denounced and killed.

German occupation limited the Polish population's freedom of action. "To do nothing is in every man's power," said Dr. Samuel Johnson. The Poles retained the freedom of inaction. My survival was dependent upon the absence of hostile behavior of Poles who hated Jews.

Many years after the end of the war, I was telling a Polish friend in Detroit about the dangers of living on false papers and that any moment my penis could be my undoing. Suddenly, I remembered Gadomski and his sexual exploitation of my helpless state. I could not finish my story because I began to cry. It seemed unbelievable that I, a seasoned forensic psychiatrist, who had heard many gruesome stories, would be so bothered by the memory of being sexually abused by this man.

"Did you tell your psychoanalyst about this sexual abuse during your ten years of psychoanalysis?" she wondered. I decided to find out. "You have never told me about it. I am certain that I would have remembered this particular part of your history," my psychoanalyst, Dr. August, insisted when I asked him. He only remembered that we had talked about Gadomski a great deal as my "rescuer."

Why was this memory such a secret? Why was so much painful emotion connected with it? I do not think the sexual abuse alone accounts for it. I believe that Gadomski is a metaphor for my relationship to Poland. I have mixed feelings about him and my native land. I remember Gadomski as a person who saved my life. I remember him also as a dedicated anti-Semite and a man whose sexual needs were gratified by abusing a young man placed in his care. He was my savior and my abuser.

Poland is my motherland; Polish is my native language. Poles helped me to survive the Holocaust. I remember gratefully the few who were my protectors. I resent the many that harmed countless Jews, and the millions who were eager to do so.

The few friendly people willing to help me were all I needed to survive on false papers. The trouble was not lack of friends, but the multitude of enemies. The denunciations of the Jews who were hiding or were on false papers were not a sporadic activity, but an endemic problem. Virtually all Poles resisted, passively or actively, the German occupation. However, the majority of the Polish population assisted the Germans in their effort to annihilate the Jews.

We should not expect ordinary, decent people to take heroic actions. There is no moral obligation to be a hero, but it is a criminal offense to be an accessory to murder. Whoever denounced a Jew on false papers was a cowardly killer. The death of my cousin Miriam Cukier was a joint project of Poles and Germans. A similar fate no doubt met Szmulek, whom I had sheltered in the monastery.

In the Soviet Union, Pavlik Marazov, a young boy who denounced his parents, was declared an official Soviet hero. In his village he was not considered a hero, but an outcast and was brutally murdered by the local people. In Nazi Germany, children were encouraged to report if their parents were not loyal to the Third Reich. Some of the Poles who denounced Jews used religious excuses; they invoked God's Will or anti-Semitic political principles.

I have heard many times people speak of "Polowanie na Zydow" (Jew Hunting). This was a deliberate roaming of public places to unmask a Jew on false papers. My coworkers in the dental lab invited me to join them in such an expedition. I had to endure the casual talk on trains and other gathering places about the killing of the Jews. The efforts to unmask and denounce Jews who were in hiding were talked about with joyful glee. I do not recall anyone ever objecting or expressing any type of reservation. A fellow survivor wrote to me in January, 2003:

> You know, we live with such dichotomies in our lives. One Polish family saved my life while another Pole (neighbor) turned my mother over to the Gestapo 4 months before liberation. He found her hiding in his barn. He grabbed her and tied her to his manure wagon and drove her into town and turned her over to the German Gestapo. He called his neighbor to help him do this dastardly deed.

Another survivor wrote to me:

> My father's sister went through the same horrific events but with an eight month old baby. Her husband and her little boy were taken away to a concentration camp at the beginning of the war and she never saw them again. However, her baby girl she managed to give to a Polish woman that worked for her family as a housekeeper for 25 years, and this is what kept my aunt alive during her confinement in the Kloga Slave Labour Camp in Estonia, knowing this woman had her baby for safekeeping. It was, however, not to be! After she returned from the camp she went to this horrible woman to claim her baby.
>
> The first words out of the woman's mouth were "I thought that you would be killed along with all the other Jews!!!" She told my aunt that she did not want a "Zydowka" in her home!! She told her that she took the baby to the Gestapo headquarters and did not know what they did with her! But, we all know what they did to her, don't we? That is what some seemingly "nice" Polish Catholics did to us!

I do not know of any consequences suffered by Poles whose denunciations of the Jews resulted in loss of lives. I know that such claims are made now. Virtually all Jews who died trying to pass as Poles or in hiding were killed because a Pole had denounced them to the Germans. The same holds true for Poles who were killed by the Germans for hiding Jews. For years, many Poles who helped Jews to survive kept it a secret to avoid the contempt or persecution by fellow countrymen. When I visited Stefan in 1987, members of his family did not know that he had helped me survive.

Most Jews on false papers concentrated in Krakow and Warsaw because large cities provided anonymity. In the villages, there were no Germans but the risk of being denounced to the Germans by Poles was higher. In a big city like

Krakow, contacts with people were superficial but in a small town or village there was dangerous intimacy.

A Jew living on false papers in occupied Poland was in mortal danger in nearly every encounter with Poles. I looked into every Polish face for an answer to the only question that mattered, "Does he or she suspect that I am a Jew?" There was no time to explore attitudes. I had to instantly categorize every person. Inquiring friendliness was as much a danger signal as silent antagonism. Only indifference was reassuring. Unfortunately, that was rare in relation to the Jews. There is talk about too few Poles being helpful to the Jews during the Holocaust. When I entered a streetcar, a train or a shop, I did not need friends. All I hoped for was the absence of Poles who were eager to ferret out Jews and denounce them.

I developed great sensitivity to the penetrating stare of a Jew hunter. Whenever my emotional radar registered that someone might be thinking, "The boy may be a Jew," I had to act. Like an animal in the jungle, I made intuitive choices to "fight" or take flight. Rarely did I run; that would reveal fear. My usual response was to approach the person with a bold question or aggressive comment. I could tell when the triumphant "The kid is a Jew" gave way to "He may look Jewish but he isn't."

I prayed fervently on my knees to the picture of the Virgin Mary in the privacy of my bedroom when I knew that a suspicious landlady was looking through the keyhole. I left unfinished letters to an imaginary girlfriend containing details confirming my Christian identity. At other times I jumped from trains, climbed rooftops, and ran from pursuing policemen. I bluffed my way out of seemingly hopeless situations. Survival depended upon improvisation and calculating shrewdness. I made decisions based upon my intuition and then stuck to them. Every dangerous episode could end in disaster. Survival was like a large quilt fashioned out of many little squares. Each had to be perfect. Getting killed was easy; one failure was enough.

Why were so many Poles eager to denounce me? In the monastery I learned that there was a special obligation imposed by a decree of the Holy Office of the Catholic Church to denounce heretics, magicians and others guilty of similar crimes to the Inquisition. Did I fall into one of these categories? Why did they want me dead? What made Stefan so different?

Poles that have helped Jews are, as they should be, celebrated by Jews; but those who are responsible for denouncing Jews are forgotten. And yet the respected editor of Poland's leading newspaper, Adam Michnik, writes:

> ...I read so often in Polish and foreign newspapers about the murderers who killed Jews, and note the deep silence about those who rescued Jews. Do the murderers deserve more recognition than the righteous?[39]

In reality, the Jews have gone overboard in celebrating, even exaggerating, help given to them by Christians; the Poles who killed Jews themselves or denounced them to Germans did so with impunity.

In the fight for survival, a tie or split decision simply will not do.
-Merle L. Meacham

Chapter 11
Escaping the Inevitable

One day, in a crowded Krakow streetcar, two young men watched me intently. They had a "we know you are a Jew" look. I got off the tram at the next stop; they followed and quickly caught up with me. I usually had no trouble outrunning adult Jew hunters but these were teenagers and they quickly caught up with me. "You can't get off that easy. Give us a thousand zloty and we won't call the police," one of them announced arrogantly.

"Fuck off," I said defiantly.

"Zydek knows how to use profanity. Did they teach you to talk like that in heder?"

"Oh, you think I'm a Jew?" I asked with feigned astonishment. His next shout clings in my ears in its Polish version. "Wypierasz sie Zydlaku?[40] (You are denying it, you Jew boy?), he asked in a mocking tone, affecting a Jewish accent.

"I'm not a Jew," I said calmly.

"Show us your prick and we'll believe you," said the bigger one who then tried to grab me. In the distance, I saw two Polish policemen walking the beat. "Police! Police!" I screamed and ran toward them. My tormentors looked amazed. "They tried to take my watch," I told the cops when I reached them. The three of us pursued the Szmalcowniki (professional Jew hunters), but fortunately they got away.

My mother and Olenka would not have been able to get out of this type of situation. I constantly worried about them. I met mother daily at prearranged times in various places in the city. I could not visit her, which would arouse suspicions since we were not officially related. I always addressed mother as Madame (Pani) Rojek.

In the fall of 1943, the combination of Jew-killing Germans and Jew-hating Poles made living on false papers nearly impossible. It became apparent that in order to survive, we had to do something different and it had to take place soon. I did not know how to do it, but I knew we had to get away from interacting with

Poles. We could not wait; the next crisis would end in our death. My first idea was to go to Germany to work.

The Germans conducted raids among the Polish population and sent thousands to Germany as forced labor, usually in factories. They also had a voluntary worker program that offered a choice of work place. Some Poles who were in dire economic circumstances chose to work in Germany. The volunteers could choose to work for a German farmer. It meant plenty of food, no exposure to bombing raids and most important for us, being away from Poles who could recognize us as Jews.

I had to persuade mother to go along with this idea. "The Germans are too dumb to recognize a Jew on false papers," I told mother. She agreed and I went about organizing this move. I had to find out if Olenka could accompany mother, I was old enough to be a worker, but was she?

I visited the office that processed the volunteers for labor in Germany. All the preliminary arrangements were made when I discovered that the induction station had communal showers and a delousing procedure. A Polish doctor conducted physical examinations. I would have to expose the forbidden part of my body. One glance at my penis and I would be unmasked as a Jew. I gave up this plan after trying in vain to persuade Mother to go alone with Olenka. It was a good idea but not workable for a circumcised man.

Years later I found out that my friend Sabina Schwartz and her sister Helen took that route and survived. They escaped from the ghetto in Piotrkow and found temporary refuge in the attic of a friendly Polish woman whose anti-Semitic husband was unaware of their presence. The girls had false papers and were told by their father to volunteer for labor in Germany. They walked to nearby Radomsko where they were not known and signed up at the employment office for labor in Germany. They survived in the town of Regensburg, Bavaria working as Polish maids in a hotel.

I gave up the "German plan" after one more visit to the induction station. I saw that the men not only took showers together but were nude when examined by the doctors. Only a Jewish woman could escape detection under these circumstances. Men had better chance to survive in ghettos and concentration camps; women were less at risk on false papers.

One day I read an advertisement that the Germans were looking for Polish dentists willing to work in the Eastern territories, a German euphemism for the occupied Soviet Union. "This is our chance. We must get a false diploma for you," I told Mother as I showed her the newspaper.

"I am out of practice; I have not worked as a dentist for nearly a year," Mother objected. But she reluctantly agreed to go along with this plan. Transforming Aniela Rojek into Pani Doktor Rojek was my next challenge. Doktor Zielinski, in whose dental lab I was working, was the first person I approached.

"Pani Aniela Rojek is a dentist who is living on false papers because of her work for the Underground. The Germans are searching for her; she needs help. Would you be willing to talk to her?" I asked him. He agreed without hesitation.

The next day, I introduced Mother as Pani Rojek to him. Good manners dictated that a young person not be present when adults talked about serious matters. Besides, they were doctors, and I was only a laboratory boy. I was terrified that Mother would somehow reveal that we were related or that she was a Jew. I had little trust in Mother's ability to perform covert activities. She was to tell him that she wanted to work as a dentist but did not have her diploma since she had to assume a false identity after her husband was arrested because of underground activities.

Mother later told me that Dr. Zielinski had been very pleasant, but was unable to help her with getting a false diploma. Instead, Mother thought it was a good idea to see Professor Golab, who she trusted even though he was merely an acquaintance. Professor Golab had been the head of the Medical Board (Izba Lekarska) before the war and was a professor at The Jagelonian University of Krakow (Universitas Jagellonica Cracoviensis). He was not a family friend, but a person my parents praised as fair to the Jews. The University was a hot bed of anti-Semitism, but he was one of the few professors who had objected to the rule that Jewish students must sit on separate benches during lectures.

I found his address in an old Krakow telephone book. I made sure he still lived there by ringing the doorbell and asking if a young boy named Zbigniew Golab lived there. I avoided exposing Mother to the risk of being in the street. The next day I took Mother to Professor Golab's building. I waited outside.

Mother introduced herself as Pani Doktor Rojek to the housekeeper who answered the door. Professor Golab would recognize her as Dr. Kowarski-Tenenwurzel. What would he do? We were convinced that he would not denounce mother, but vigilance was by now a habit. I walked to the corner of the building. If the police came from either direction, I would have time to run in and warn Mother.

"He was wonderful," Mother told me when she finally was back on the street. Professor Golab did not know how to get a counterfeit diploma, but he was willing to make inquiries. As an afterthought, Mother mentioned that Professor Golab had told her about a Jew on false papers who was smuggling other Jews to Hungary. He suggested that mother contact him. Professor Golab could not give us what we wanted, but he identified with our plight and came up with a dangerous but promising idea.

"But that's ridiculous. What would we do in a foreign country?" Mother told me. Hungary was to Mother a faraway, unfriendly land. I knew that Hungary was an ally of Nazi Germany and was not under German occupation. "We don't know anybody there; we know nothing about conditions there", she argued.

"The war will last at least one more year, but we will not manage to survive the next few weeks," I told mother. She considered going to Hungary to be a wild notion. But the idea of going to Hungary appealed to me; we had little to lose. I understood that one had to take risks to avoid being killed.

When my reasons failed to persuade her, I yelled. I had never talked to my mother like that before. Mother went along with the idea more under the impact of my emotions than my reasoning. This was a turning point in our relationship. From that day on I was in charge. Mother returned to Professor Golab and got the name of the smuggler. He told mother how to get in touch with Mr. Wiater, the organizer of the smuggling operation. This was his assumed name.

We met Mr. Wiater the next day. He was a short, heavy-set man in his 50s, with distinct Jewish features. We sat in a small restaurant near Planty Park. He was relaxed and friendly, but I was anxious in his presence because he looked so Jewish. "How do you manage to live on false papers with your looks?" I finally asked. He laughed as if my question was a joke and not a matter of life and death.

"I don't look like a Jew; I look like a Czech." This was a play on words. "Czech" and "three" sound the same in Polish. He meant he looked like three Jews. "I look so Jewish that no one would think that I would have the chutzpah to be on false papers," he added with confidence. Mr. Wiater was a generous man; he agreed to have us smuggled to Hungary for all the money we had, which was a third of his normal fee. He described Hungary as the Promised Land. Jews were free there. There was also plenty of food. We decided we would leave within the week. I was to deliver the money to him the next day. We were instructed to go on Sunday at 2 p.m. to the train station and find the train going to Nowy Sacz. A man with a white handkerchief wrapped around his left hand would wait for us on the platform and he would take us by train to Makowice. We would be smuggled to Slovakia, across the Beskid Mountain range by mountain people, called "gorale." From Slovakia, other guides would take us to Hungary. "Why don't you take people to Hungary directly?" I asked. Poland and Hungary had a common border. "The Ukrainians in that region catch and murder Jews," Wiater explained.

After meeting with Mr. Wiater, I immediately found Stefan and asked him to take a letter to father at the Luftwaffe (Lotnisko) labor camp. In the letter I pleaded with Father to go with us to Hungary. Stefan brought back a response the same day. Father wrote that he could not go with us at this time. "Stefan will explain why not. I will follow you soon," he promised. He wanted to know how to get in touch with the smuggler. Stefan told me what father had said at the monastery—that ten Jews would be executed as punishment if he escaped. "He is working on having himself declared dead, then he can escape," Stefan reminded me.

Father had bad news about Gina's father. "Mr. Olmer has been killed. Stefan will tell you the details. Gina is in a village called Czerna near Krzeszowice. The name of the man in whose home she is living is Joseph Kaczmarczyk. Take the girl with you, if you can, since the Poles will turn her over to the Germans when they get no money from her father." To this day I marvel at how my father could know in the Lotnisko Camp what had happened at the notorious Plaszow Camp, which was run by the sadistic Commandant, Amon Goeth. Once again, father was looking after another person in distress just as he had with Szmulek.

Mother accepted the idea that Gina should go with us if I could find her. I went to see Mr. Wiater and persuaded him to include Gina in our group. To get in touch with her was my next problem. It would be too dangerous to travel to her village and we were leaving in two days. Therefore, I sent her a telegram asking her to arrive at the railroad station in Krakow on a specific train from a community close to the village where she was living. I agonized over the wording of the telegram. I had to let her know who I was without revealing life-endangering information. Yet if I made it too obscure, she would not come.

The message had to say that she would meet Emek, a Jewish-sounding name, but it had to be signed by Jan Wojcik. I do not recall how I solved this predicament. I obviously could not give a return address. It was uncertain if she would come or even if the message would be delivered to her.

I waited for the train with apprehension. If she came would the police or a Szmalcownik (Jew hunter) follow her? I found a spot from which I could watch the platform without being seen. When the train arrived, Gina was one of the first to get off. It would be hard to miss her. Her blonde hair, in a single long braid reaching to her waist, made her noticeable. She was as beautiful as ever, slim, wearing a colorful dress. She looked around, expecting someone to meet her. I wanted to run to her and greet her, but that would have been foolish. I had to make sure that no one had followed her. I knew that my telegram could have been her undoing. I found out later that Mrs. Kaczmarczyk was understandably furious, as the telegram placed them at risk of being suspect of hiding a Jewish child.

Gina went into the waiting room, looked around, and then went out into the street and walked as if she had a destination. I trailed behind, my heart pounding with excitement. When I was convinced she was not being followed, I caught up with her. "Gina! Nice to see you," I said, trying to act casual.

"You have so many pimples on your face," was one of her first comments. I blushed intensely. We walked the streets for a few hours. I told her we were going to Hungary and wanted her to go with us. She said she could not go because her father was getting South American papers and she would be going with him overseas. I had to tell her that her father had been killed. Gina doubted my information. "How can your father be sure in Lotnisko that my father was killed in Plaszow?" she asked. "Your father was shot in the presence of the entire camp," I said. This was not quite true. I knew from Stefan that vicious dogs belonging to Goeth had killed Mr. Olmer.

I told her that her father would no longer be able to pay and Mr. Kaczmarczyk would no longer keep her. She had great faith in Mr. Kaczmarczyk, whom she believed would take care of her without being paid, but she had no hesitation in going with us to Hungary. Neither one of us had the luxury of showing much emotion while walking in the street in Krakow. Attracting attention by any display of feelings was dangerous.

Gina returned to the village to pick up some of her belongings. She had some money, which we needed to give to Mr. Wiater. A new chapter in our struggle for survival was about to begin.

The miserable have no other medicine
But only hope:
I've hope to live, but am prepared to die.
- Claudio in *Measure for Measure* by Shakespeare

Chapter 12
Adventures of Survival

Our escape from Poland to Hungary took place on a sunny October day in 1943. We were instructed by the smugglers to buy tickets to the border town of Nowy Sacz. In a specific area of the railroad station we would find a man with a handkerchief tied around his left hand. He would be our smuggler across the border to Slovakia; from there we would be guided to Hungary.

My mother, Olenka and Gina went to the Krakow central railroad station separately. Whenever possible I stayed away from mother and the girls because to identify a boy as a Jew by circumcision was easy. My presence endangered them.

I was walking at a leisurely pace to the railroad station, carrying a backpack with all of my worldly possessions. Suddenly, I heard the familiar cry "Lapanka! Lapanka!" This meant that the Germans were conducting a human roundup. The most common reason for this exercise was snatching Poles for forced labor in Germany; at times, the Germans would grab Poles for execution in retaliation for some act of sabotage.

I ran into an old building, climbed into the attic and up unto the roof. From there I could see the Germans seizing people and loading them onto a truck. I returned to the street as soon as it seemed safe. The train was leaving in 15 minutes, and I was at least 30 minutes away from the station on foot. Fortunately, I saw a "doroshka" (a carriage for hire). I told the driver I would give him three times his usual fare if he really hurried. When I ran onto the platform, my train was moving; I ran as fast as I could and got on one of the last wagons. I could see a man with a white handkerchief on his hand leaning out a window. I made my way through the crowded train to where mother and the girls were. My progress was slow. People were crowded together like sardines in a can. I wanted to reach Mother; I knew she would be despondent. "Oh, my God!" Mother exclaimed when I finally reached them. I pretended not to know them.

At Nowy Sawcz, we were taken from the station by a horse-drawn wagon to a village at the foothills of the Carpathian Mountains. I had doubts that Mother,

Olenka, and Gina would be able to cross the mountain range that loomed on the horizon. We drove through the village and ended up near an isolated farmhouse. The smugglers told us to hide in a cluster of trees, and that they would come to get us when it got dark. Later, one of them showed up and led us to a barn full of fresh-smelling hay. Through a crack in the barn door, we could see the farmhouse. It felt good to settle snugly away from the overcrowded train and the danger of hiding in the woods.

A few hours later I saw two men approach the barn. They wore the garb of Polish mountain people: tight pants, moccasin-like shoes, capes draped over their shoulders, and round black hats. The taller of the two had a moustache; he also seemed older. Inside the barn, they introduced themselves to us as Jozek, the older one, and Stasiek, who had two gold crowns on his front teeth. Father always refused to put gold crowns on the good teeth of the peasants who requested it. A gold crown was a status symbol. Jozek told us that we would get going soon. One of them would walk ahead and the other would follow with us. "It is a good night to cross the border; there are clouds. It will be pitch-black in the mountains. If you get separated, don't talk; just give a sound like a cricket and the other person will respond in the same way," Jozek told us. He was obviously in charge. He and his companion spoke Polish with a dialect typical of Polish mountain people.

When we got on our way, Stasiek was the point man. Mother and Olenka walked behind him, Gina was next and I was the last. At first we followed a path through fields that led us into a forest. The Beskid Mountain range, unlike the adjoining Tartra Mountains, was covered by a thick growth of trees. The area was familiar to us; my parents had visited the fashionable spa in Beskid known as Krynica regularly. We had often spent our vacation in Zakopane at the foot of the Tartra Mountains.

We climbed in complete darkness through the forest. It was mystifying how our guides knew where to go. At one point, Olenka refused to take one more step. She did not cry; she simply announced, "I will not walk anymore. You can leave me here."

Jozek put her on his back. After a short time, she was ready to walk on her own. Whenever we had to cross a road, our guides became apprehensive. Before going to the other side, we stood for a short time in silence. We welcomed these brief rests. Jozek explained that the roads were dangerous because the Germans patrolled them on foot. They would hide in the roadside ditches, but they rarely ventured into the forest.

"What would happen if the Germans came upon us?" Gina asked me during one of these stops.

"The gorale (mountain people) are like mountain goats; they would run away." I said.

"What would happen to us?" she asked.

"They would catch us and kill us," I said with uncharacteristic pessimism. The probability of walking into a German ambush was on my mind. A few hours later, Gina's question and my familiarity with the lore of American Indians saved our lives.

Like all boys in Poland, I was an avid reader of Karl May, who wrote juvenile adventure stories about American Indians in the Wild West. May was a German writer whose books were best sellers throughout Europe. Karl May told the exploits of the Indian chief Winnetou, in three volumes that I had read more than once.

The adventures described by Karl May became the instructional texts of my survival. The basic message was to never give up and always look for a way out. Thanks to him I was steeped in the methods of outwitting the enemy.

"Halt! Halt!" we suddenly heard Germans shout as we were making one of our road crossings. We saw flashlights. Rapid gunfire followed. The guides ran like mountain goats. In the excitement I kept up with them. Seconds later I stopped as if I had hit a brick wall and turned around. I could see Gina, followed by Mother and Olenka, running in my direction. To my left was a narrow ravine with a mountain stream. At once I knew what to do. As Gina approached, I grabbed her and shoved her down the deep ravine. She fell and rolled down the steep bank into the stream. I did the same with Mother and Olenka, and then I leaped into the creek myself. Shortly after I landed in the water, I heard the stomping of German boots above us as they tried in vain to catch up with the mountain people. I heard barking dogs in the distance. "Quick, get up. We must walk upstream," I whispered. I made them walk in the water until I was satisfied it was safe to climb up on the bank of the stream, hoping that the dogs would have lost our scent. Afraid and cold, we huddled together. It was a chilly night, and we were wet. Mother was weeping, Olenka was sobbing. Gina and I, in whispers, tried to figure out what to do. Neither Gina nor I panicked; we were calm and deliberate, as if oblivious to the danger. We agreed that at dawn I would go looking for the guides. "I can find the village where they live," I claimed, with the bravado of a 15 year-old with his girlfriend by his side.

Daybreak was approaching. All at once we spotted, on the opposite side of the valley, two figures moving slowly as if searching for something. "They are Germans," Gina said, "I can see their helmets." "No, they are not helmets and they have no guns, they could be our guides," I said. We argued briefly about it but there was no time to lose. Soon they would be out of sight. I gave the cricket signal.

There is no sweeter musical tone on Earth than the response we heard; it was also the sound of a cricket. We were suddenly energized and ran over to the guides. They told us to follow them straight up the mountain; we were led to a small clearing where we remained for two days. We were told that it was dangerous to move because the Germans would be searching the area. The guides brought us food and blankets. The weather was beautiful and we were able to dry our clothes and gather berries. I enjoyed the praise I received from Jozek and Stasiek for my actions; Mother was very proud also and I cherished Gina's unspoken admiration. "If only Father were here," I thought. I told our guides, "My father will be coming through here soon, if you see him tell him we made it safely to Slovakia." I was convinced that we would succeed in reaching the "promised land."

On the second night after the encounter with the German patrol, we resumed the effort to get to Slovakia. After a few hours of trekking through the mountains, we slipped into the barn of a Slovakian peasant. These were our Slovakian smugglers.

They greeted us cordially. The similarity between Polish and Slovakian languages made communication possible. We ate our first hot meal in days; it was a variety of grits. They fed us in a large kitchen and we sat at a table as if we were visiting guests. Unlike the Poles, the Slovaks were not fearful of their neighbors' suspicions. When the time came to say goodbye to Stasiek and Jozek, we hugged them gratefully. Money alone was not the only motive for the courage these simple strangers had shown. To us they were heroes.

The bad news was that the Slovakian smugglers expected money from us. They were not paid. We had none. Mr. Wiater had told us that escapees from occupied Poland apprehended within 30 kilometers of the border were handed over by the Slovakian police to the Germans. If they were Jews, they were shot on the spot. Slovakia was a German puppet state; we feared the Slovakian police slightly less than we feared the Germans. I knew that in 1938, when Czechoslovakia was dismembered, a Slovak state had been created with Jozef Tiso, a Catholic priest, as President. The "independent" Slovakia was collaborating with its German benefactors to solve the Jewish problem.

Our host told us that the town of Mikulas was our destination. From there we would be smuggled to Kosice, which, at that point, belonged to Hungary and was called Kassa. From Kosice we would travel by train to Budapest. He claimed that Slovakian border police, contrary to regulations, did not turn escapees over to the Germans but took them to headquarters in Presov and released them to a Jewish community in Mikulas. This sounded incredible to us. We suspected that the smugglers, who did not get their money, were trying to get rid of us. "You go to the border police station and surrender to them and everything will turn out all right," we were told repeatedly. "Tell them you just came across but don't tell them you were in my house. Now get some sleep. We will take care of it in the morning," the man of the house told us.

In the privacy of the barn, we talked over the situation. Could it be true that the police were helpful to Jews who had escaped the Germans? Should we slip out of the barn and keep going south until we were beyond the 30-kilometer zone and less likely to be handed over to the Germans? Our host anticipated this move; he told us that he knew what the border police would do. If regular police apprehended us, then the outcome was unclear. As usual, I relied upon my intuition and decided to trust the advice of the smugglers. By now, Mother was leaving such decisions up to me.

At daybreak, our host woke us up, "Walk down the road, the police station is easy to find. It's the only building with the Slovak flag." A few minutes later we stood in front of a brick building. It seemed strange to surrender to police and tell them we were Jews. What would they do to us?

Gina and I entered; Mother and Olenka stayed outside. Once inside, the sight of one lonely policeman sleeping in a chair, his rifle propped against the wall, startled us. It took some effort to wake him up. The policeman was a handsome blond fellow in his early 20s. We explained our situation. He was pleasant and friendly. I went outside and got Mother and Olenka to join us. "I have to take you to the headquarters," he explained. We started at once on foot along a path. The young policeman encouraged us to take rest stops. At one point he gave me his rifle and he carried our meager belongings. I could hardly believe my eyes, a prisoner holding the rifle, the policeman carrying the luggage. Would anyone believe that in Krakow?

We were brought to what seemed like the regional headquarters of the border police. The man in charge was friendly and told us that we would be taken to Mikulas soon. A few hours later we were placed on a regular bus accompanied by an older policeman. The bus was crowded with people going into the city. We looked more like tourists than prisoners.

Once we arrived at our destination, our escort took us to the police station. To our surprise, we were placed in a dingy cell in the local jail. It was not a pleasant setting. We became alarmed about our future. The cell had two jail bunks, Olenka insisted on being next to Mother. I would not admit my eagerness to share the bed with Gina and slept on the floor.

The next day I was taken from the cell to an office and interrogated by two detectives. I told them that we were Jews who had escaped from occupied Poland. "Did you say your father was born in Hungary?" one of the men asked casually. I took the hint. "Yes," was my response. The rest was easy, it developed through a question and answer exchange that my father had been born in Budapest and was living there now. My mother, my two sisters (they assumed Gina was my sister) and I were visiting relatives in Poland when we were trapped by the outbreak of the war. There was no doubt that the police were trying to help. They were writing a fictitious report that we were not Polish but Hungarian Jews. Later I found out that they were bribed by the Slovak Jews to protect the Jews who were apprehended at the border.

When I returned to the cell, Mother and Gina were eager to know what had happened. "We have nothing to worry about. The Slovak police are on our side. Just remember we are Hungarian Jews returning home," I told them.

The next day we were transferred to a "detention facility" which turned out to be a small schoolhouse with a classroom filled with bunk beds. It was nominally under police supervision, but was operated by the Jewish Community Council of Mikulas. There must have been at least 20 to 30 Polish Jews there, mostly women. The "inmates" surrounded us, eager to hear news from Poland. We were told that no one supervised the place. The residents did their own cooking and cleaning. The head of the Jewish Council or another member of the group came once a day for a visit. From time to time, a group of four or five people would be taken to the Hungarian border and smuggled across.

A few days after our arrival, the head of the Jewish Council picked me to be in charge; I looked older than my 15 years. My responsibility was to assign cleaning and cooking duties. The sleeping-living area had no electrical lights. The kitchen was upstairs and had one electric bulb and a table.

Gina and I became friends with Heniek Westereich, who was the only other teenager in the place. Olenka and Heniek's little brother were the only children. Heniek and his brother were alone. I chose three older women to do the cooking, but Gina, Heniek and I washed the dishes after supper. This gave us a chance to be in a room with a light.

"Isn't technology wonderful? If I survive, I will become an engineer," Heniek exclaimed when we turned on the light.

"Look at our condition. If I survive, I will study people," was my response. He became a professor of physics at MIT and Boston University. His name now is Bar-Yam. I am a professor of psychiatry at Wayne State University in Detroit.

One of the residents of the Mikulas "camp" recognized my mother. He was from Slomniki, a little town half way between Krakow and Miechow. My parents had practiced dentistry there before moving to Miechow. Slomniki had a large Jewish population. This man, named Blat, was related to Bialybroda, whom the Germans had named the "Kommissar der Juden" for Slomniki. Blat was very deferential to my mother, constantly calling her "Pani Doktor." His obsequiousness was a combination of respect and fear. He was concerned that we would denounce him as a collaborator. He was the head of the OD (Order Service) of the Judenrat in Slomniki. He had abused his power and was hated by the Jews of Slomniki. I don't remember his first name. To undermine our credibility, he later spread the rumor that we were Jews who converted to Catholicism before the war. We found that out after he was sent ahead of us to Hungary. He was killed by a member of the Jewish Zionist group a few months later.

I remember Mikulas also as the place where I earned money by my own physical labor. For two days, I moved furniture and was paid an hourly wage.

It seems incredible that in the fall of 1943, Jews in Slovakia were able to assist Polish Jews in an organized manner. It is even hard to believe that a Jewish community existed so late into the Final Solution and was able to organize and support a whole network dedicated to the protection of Polish Jews. The danger and expense must have been enormous. I have been unable to find any mention of these altruistic efforts in any book dealing with the Holocaust.

"Tonight is your family's turn. Be ready at 10 o'clock in the evening. Good luck!" the head of the Jewish Council told me one day. At the appointed hour, a car drove up to the schoolhouse. We were at long last on our way to safety. Mother, Gina and Olenka were told by the driver to take the back seat; I sat next to the driver. It was the first time I had been in a car since the trip to Grandmother's in September of 1939. We were driven to a village near the Slovak-Hungarian border and once again, we ended up in a barn. Our driver handed us to a Slovak farmer and his son.

"They will take you on foot in the early hours of the morning to Kosice, which is now a Hungarian town. They will put you on a train to Budapest. When you get off the train, wrap a handkerchief around your left hand; someone will meet you," the driver told us. Our host gave us some blankets and encouraged us to get some sleep.

It was still dark when our guides awakened us. There was a full moon. Our guides were relaxed and casual. Illegal crossing of the border from Slovakia to Hungary was less dangerous than leaving German-occupied Poland. There were also no mountains. We walked along a road until we got to a forest. "On the other side of these trees is Hungary," the guide told us. Less than an hour later, we were on the outskirts of a sizable town. We were spread out, the guides were ahead, I was next, and then mother and the girls followed. Suddenly, armed men in uniforms were all around us, shouting in a language we did not understand. It looked like an ambush. I stood motionless as they moved around me. Mother and the girls were a little distance behind me. The armed men, who I believed were border policemen, paid no attention to me. They pointed guns at each other and walked away laughing. I realized that these were Hungarian soldiers on maneuvers.

But our guides had gotten frightened and disappeared. I kept on walking, expecting the guides to reappear just like their Polish counterparts did before. Mother and the girls followed me, unaware that I had no one to follow. What to do? I had been told in Mikulas that Hungarians, unlike the Slovaks, turned escapees from Poland over to the Germans. I did not know a single word in Hungarian. Should I look for the railroad station? If I walked slowly, maybe the guides would turn up? After at least half an hour of looking around, I gave up hope that the guides would return. We were on our own in a strange city, which by now was coming alive. People were going to work and shopping. The store windows were loaded with goods. I looked in the window of a food store with a large sign; part of the inscription contained a Jewish name that I believe was "Steinberg" or something like it. "That's it!" was my next thought. This was our chance to get help. I entered the store; a few customers were inside. Behind the counter were an older man with a beard, a woman, and a boy about my age. They looked Jewish.

Mother and the girls followed me and stood by the door. I approached the man and tried to tell him our predicament in Yiddish. The trouble was that my Yiddish was virtually non-existent. The man told me in Slovak to wait and be quiet; he seemed scared. He said something to the boy in Hungarian who came from behind the counter and motioned us to follow him. He took us to a storage room; after a few minutes, Mr. Steinberg appeared. He paid little attention to me and began to talk in Yiddish with Mother, who was fluent in Yiddish. I had already explained to Mother that our guides were gone and that we had to get away from the border town and get to Budapest. Mr. Steinberg left our strange room looking worried, but he promised to help.

It took a long time before he returned with his son and told us to follow the boy. We were taken to a synagogue and placed in a small room. Some people appeared with food and blankets, and assured us that they would find a way to get us out of Kassa, as the town was called in Hungarian. The Jews in this town, unlike those of Mikulas, seemed scared and less organized. Evidently this was a new challenge that I had created for them by walking into the store. They were improvising. Our survival was in their hands. We had no doubt that these Jewish strangers would find a way to help us. We did not sleep most of the night, but our expectations were not disappointed. The Jewish Community of Kassa took care of us.

The next morning, the young Steinberg showed up. He took us to the railroad station, bought tickets, and waited with us on the platform. In spite of the fear, being in a foreign country fascinated me. The language was incomprehensible. The clothing was different. People were relaxed and well fed. As usual, I kept separate from Mother and the girls while waiting for the train. This was our standard operating procedure that I followed at all times.

I walked up and down the platform trying to look casual. Then to my shock, a rifle-carrying, uniformed man with black feathers in his hat approached me and asked something in Hungarian. I looked at him bewildered. Then, in a moment of sudden inspiration, I stuck out my tongue, gave a shriek and walked away. He looked puzzled and put his finger to the side of his head in a gesture pronouncing me crazy. I assumed he was a policeman asking for documents. I had it half right. "He was a state policeman; he asked what time it was," the young Steinberg explained later when he had seated us in a train compartment.

"Er is a kluger jing" (He is a smart boy), our guide said to my mother in Yiddish, shaking his head with admiration for my getting out of a confrontation with one of the feared "Csenders" gendarmes.

Shortly afterwards, we were on our way to Budapest. Looking out the windows of the train, we saw tidy villages, cars and trucks. People and even the horses looked prosperous. There were no bombed out houses, and no German military vehicles. The train was clean and not overcrowded. Everyone seemed comfortable. The contrast with occupied Poland was striking. We smiled at the conductor but could not say one word in Hungarian. We pretended to be asleep when another traveler entered our compartment.

In Budapest, we got off the train like everyone else but we had no place to go and no one to turn to. The chain of contacts had been broken in Kosice when our guides disappeared and we did not take the designated train. We were on our own in a strange city; without papers or familiarity with the language, and we had no money.

I found a comfortable waiting room in the station for Mother and Olenka. "We will find some Polish Jews – they will help us," I told Mother. This turned out to be simpler than I expected. Gina and I had barely walked a block when we heard a man and a woman who looked Jewish speaking in Polish. We told them our plight and they were eager to help.

They went with us to the railroad station to pick up Mother and Olenka and took us to a café on Király Utca (King St.), a gathering place for Polish Jews. It had been a long time since I had seen so many free Jews. They gathered around us, asking questions about Poland. We were fed, given money and plenty of advice. A man knew of a nearby room for rent; he took us there and paid for our overnight stay. We marveled at his ability to speak Hungarian. We could not go to a hotel because we had no papers as legal Polish refugees. The room was a shabby space behind the workshop of a luggage repairman. They used the place to dry their laundry. Water dripped on our beds from the wet wash. The family lived next to the workroom. "Get some rest and come back to the Király Utca coffee house in the morning. Everything will be fine," were the parting words of our unknown Good Samaritan.

The finest praise any man can receive is to be satisfied himself, with what he has accomplished...
– George McGovern

Chapter 13
War and Peace

The next day we found our way to the Király Utca café. Walking the streets of Budapest seemed like a dream. There was no evidence of war, starvation, or oppression. The wonder of a city and a country at peace was startling to us.

Mr. Abramczyk, a Jew from Miechow who knew my parents and was a close friend of Gina's father, was one of the first people we saw in the coffee house. He told us that the three Bakalarz brothers from Miechow were also in Budapest.

Mr. Abramczyk took us to the "Pension" Krakowitz, a European equivalent of a bed and breakfast. It was located in the heart of town on Koszut Lajos Street, number 13. Polish Jews who belonged to a Zionist organization named Hanoar Hazioni were the only residents. Many of the members of the group were from Gina's hometown and knew her father. They were very solicitous of her. We were given a room in the pension. The group was under the leadership of Leon Blatt, a charismatic man in his 20s, who was a legend in the Zionist underground.

"Tomorrow at 9 a.m. Kasia (everyone used Polish names) will take you to the Polish agency, you will use your Christian papers and you'll become legal Polish refugees. Make sure you don't tell them you are Jews," Leon Blatt said, in the manner of a man used to giving orders.

The Polish Agency represented the Polish government in exile located in London. Hungary was an ally of Germany but maintained a friendly liaison with the enemies of Germany. Regent Horthy and Miklós Kállay, the Premier, conducted a balancing act – protecting Hungary's Jews and cooperating with Nazi Germany. They hoped for the victory of the Western Allies but they hated the Soviet Union. They promised to surrender unconditionally when the Allied troops reached Hungary's frontiers. This was called the Kallay Dance, that like Hungary's national dance, the Czardas, required one step to the left and one to the right.

In September of 1939, units of the defeated Polish Army had crossed into Hungary. The soldiers were disarmed and placed in designated villages with peasants. This arrangement was called a "camp" to satisfy the Germans. To be officially recognized as a Polish refugee and be assigned to a refugee camp, one had to show up at the office of the Polish Agency and claim that one escaped occupied Poland for political reasons. Mother, Gina, Olenka and I went to the offices of the Agency and were interrogated by a Polish official who believed or pretended to believe that we were Polish Christians.

Shortly after we accomplished our purpose, we ran into Mr. Wiater. "I have bad news. Your husband was transferred from Lotnisko to Plaszow," he told us. Mother began to cry uncontrollably. We knew that Plaszow was a terrible place where Jews were killed like flies. Mother's crying concerned me. It was dangerous to attract attention; we did not yet have our papers and were illegal. Naturally, I too was worried about Father, but I tried to console mother. I opened a door to a small broom closet where Mother, Olenka and I huddled. I hugged mother and kept repeating, "Mr. Wiater said that there were people trying to have him transferred to Emalia," a work camp operated by Oscar Schindler. The broom closet episode is vivid in my memory, kept alive by recurrent nightmares. I can see clearly the tiny space under the steps leading to the second floor; it smelled of soap. The mops and rags must have been used that morning because they were still wet. From that day on, we had doubts that we would ever see Father again. He was in the dreadful Plaszow camp at the same time we were in the safety and luxury of a civilized peacetime city.

We were amazed by the wonders of Budapest. Wide streets were full of handsome, relaxed and cheerful people. No Germans patrolled the streets. The river Danube, Europe's largest river after the Volga, divided the city. On the left bank of the Danube was the more modern "Pest," on the right bank, the ancient city of Buda. Gina and I stood on the corner of Rakoczy Street and marveled at the never-ending stream of clean streetcars that were not crowded. In Krakow or Warsaw, the streetcars looked like human beehives. It was a struggle to get on and a struggle to get off. The weak and the timid were left behind. In Budapest, men let women and the elderly go first.

The political situation in Hungary was hard for us to understand. The country was a kingdom without a king, governed by an admiral without a fleet. We learned that Admiral Miklós Horthy was a hero in the Austro-Hungarian Empire for his exploits as a Naval Commander. After the First World War, Hungary became a landlocked nation without a navy and a king. In March 1919, the Communist Bela Kun seized power and established the Hungarian Soviet Republic. The regime collapsed on Aug. 1, 1919, and Kun fled to Vienna. In March, 1920, the National Assembly of Hungary proclaimed the country a monarchy and Horthy was named Regent for an indefinite period of time. He was the de facto king referred to as Regent. The country was officially anti-Semitic but Jews lived normal lives and were assimilated. Anti-Jewish legislation had existed since 1938.[41]

In Budapest, I was no longer the mastermind of an undercover operation, making life and death decisions. It was nice to just be a fifteen-year-old boy, in love with Gina. Overnight, Mother once again became "Pani Doktor." We were still on false papers but no one was worried about being unmasked. Gina and I wandered the streets, bought candy in the sweet shops that seemed to be everywhere, and went to the movies. We saw "Baron Munchausen" two or three times. This lighthearted farce was the first color movie we had ever seen. It was in German with Hungarian sub-titles. In the movie, I held Gina's hand; I was too embarrassed to do so in the street. We no longer hugged and kissed on the cheeks like we did when we were younger. I dreamt of making love to Gina but did not dare to kiss her.

My sexual fantasies were curbed by an embarrassing secret. I had pubic lice, a souvenir of having had sex with Rose. In Krakow, I had begun to itch terribly in the pubic area. At first, I thought I had a venereal disease. Then I discovered the tiny creatures firmly attached to my skin. I tried to get rid of them by pulling them off one by one. It was a losing battle. I could not tell my mother about it. I did not have enough money to go to a doctor and I had no male friends to ask for advice. So one day, I found a pharmacy operated by an elderly man and waited until there were no customers in the store. Since I did not speak Hungarian, I had to rely on sign language. His sympathetic smile told me that he recognized my predicament. I was given a safety razor and instructed by pantomime to shave my pubic hair, and then to apply an ointment to the area. I was self-conscious but the pharmacist was amused. He refused payment for one of the most effective treatments I have experienced to this day.

Hungarians were very friendly to Poles. Hungary and Poland shared a narrow strip of border. When Germany attacked Poland on September 1, 1939, Hungary refused to allow German troops to cross into Hungarian territory to pursue them. "Hungarians and Poles are brothers" was a popular Hungarian saying. That did not hold true for Czechs and Slovaks, who were abhorred, as were the Romanians and the Serbs – all neighboring nations. The French philosopher and historian Ernst Renan once wrote that a nation "is a group of people united by a mistaken view about the past and a hatred of its neighbors." That certainly applied to Hungary.

The similarity of the Polish language to Czech and Slovak occasionally led to miss-identification. We quickly learned the word "Lengel," meaning Pole. It worked like magic.

Our dealings with Hungarian Jews were more complicated. When you wanted to find Jews, it was natural to go to a house of worship. There was a splendid synagogue not far from our pension on Dohany Utca. It looked more like a church than a Jewish temple. Gina and I walked in one Saturday morning and were taken by surprise; organ music was being played as part of the service. This would be preposterous in Poland, where organ music was found only in a Christian church. This synagogue symbolized the degree of assimilation of Hungarian Jews. We realized that it was not accurate to speak of Hungarian Jews; they were Jewish Hungarians who saw themselves as different from the Eastern European Jews. Many of them believed that the uncultured and backward Polish and Russian Jews caused anti-Semitism. When the "foreign Jews," most of them Polish, were deported over the border from Hungary to German-occupied Poland, there was neither alarm nor protest among the

Hungarian Jews. The majority of the Hungarian Jewish community, particularly in Budapest, was intensely patriotic.

In Hungary, the code name for Eastern Jews was "foreign Jews." Hungarian Jews talked, looked, and lived like their Christian compatriots. Most had Hungarian first and last names. I remember that one of the leaders of the Hungarian leftist Zionist group called Hashomer Hazair was named Ernoe Szilagyi, hardly a Jewish name. Nearly ten percent of Hungarian Jews had converted to Christianity.

In 1943, the Hungarian Jews in Budapest lived a charmed life in spite of anti-Semitism. It was hard to believe that only a few hundred kilometers away, Jews were killed like vermin. Our friends in Pension Krakowitz told us "The Hungarian Jews did not believe our horror stories; if you tell them anything, they will accuse you of spreading rumors or threaten you with the police." We were too naïve to realize that the messenger who brings bad tidings is more likely to be despised than welcomed. "I am a Hungarian citizen," was a common response of Hungarian Jews to our warnings. At this point, the Hungarian Jews still had various options that could save them.

The tiny group of Polish Jews who escaped German captivity received virtually no help from the Hungarian Jewish community. Yehuda Bauer, an authority on Holocaust history, estimates that 2,000 to 2,500 Polish Jews escaped to Hungary between 1942 and 1944. I accept that number, even though my impression was that the number was lower. Assisting such a small number of people would not have been an undue burden on the Hungarian-Jewish community. But I do not recall a single case of assistance by a Hungarian Jewish organization or a Hungarian Jew to a Polish Jew. They avoided us. This is in marked contrast to Slovak Jews who, as a community and as individuals, were instrumental in my survival. Even in Budapest, the Jews who were helping me were Polish, Slovak or Czech. I am fully aware of the role Dr. Rudolph Kasztner and his committee played in an effort to save lives of Hungarian Jews. Their work in no way contradicts my observations that Hungarian Jews as a community were not helpful to us.

The significance of the phrase, "I am a Hungarian citizen" was not clear to me in 1943. Now I know that the Hungarian government pleaded with the Germans to deport (euphemism for murder) its foreign Jews as early as July 1941, and assured Hungarian Jews that they would be protected. The foreign Jews were rounded up in 1941 and the SS and Ukrainian units killed fourteen or fifteen thousand of them in Kamenets Podolsk.

The Hungarian-born Menahem Schmelzer, Professor of Medieval Hebrew Literature at the Jewish Theological Seminary of America, writes:

> In the newspaper that appeared around the date of the Nazi invasion of Hungary, March 19, 1944, an uncle of mine placed an advertisement, looking for a nanny for his daughter. The same issue carried advertisements for Passover products. Clearly, this was an expression of a certain measure of normalcy.[42]

Professor Schmelzer writes, "When, in May and June of 1944, the large transports of Hungarian Jews were arriving in Auschwitz, well-dressed and well-fed, with neat bundles and suitcases, the Polish Jews were totally emaciated."

After a few weeks of living in Budapest, we received our assignment to an "internment camp" for Polish refuges in the village of Uszod. We were given tickets to the town of Kalocsa, which was the closest railway station to our new location. I was disappointed that Gina would not be coming along. Gina's friends wanted to keep her in the glamorous city of Budapest. My feelings were hurt that Gina made the choice to stay with them. Kalocsa was less than a hundred kilometers away from Budapest but it seemed like the middle of nowhere.

We traveled by train south of Budapest to the Hungarian plains. The area is known as Alfold, the Hungarian breadbasket. The village of Uszod was on the shores of the Danube. We were assigned to the home of Sandor Baci, a jovial rotund farmer in his fifties. His wife, whose name I don't remember, was an equally pleasant, obese woman. Sandor was selected as our host because he had served in the Austro-Hungarian cavalry in the First World War and was supposed to speak German. Whenever I asked him for a Hungarian translation of a German word, he looked thoughtfully to the sky, pulled on his moustache, and said, "I forgot." It turned out that his comprehension of German never extended beyond military drill commands.

The farm was a large compound. Next to the owner's home was a separate structure, which was essentially a bread baking oven behind which was a tiny space with a dirt floor. It had one bed, one chair, and a basin. These were our quarters. Mother and Olenka slept in the bed; I slept next to them on the floor on a sheepskin that served as the bed covering during the daytime. Uszod was a large village; it had a few churches and a number of taverns. The Polish refugee "camp" consisted of half a dozen Jewish families pretending to be Christian Poles and about ten former Polish soldiers. The Poles kept themselves separate from the Jews, whom they easily recognized as such. Naturally, no one admitted being a Jew. Neither the Jews nor the Poles were certain about our identity. I socialized with the young ex-soldiers of the Polish Army. I particularly admired one of them whose first name, I believe, was Edek.

As a prisoner of war, he was taken to Germany in 1939. He escaped to Hungary, managed to get to France, joined a Polish military unit, was captured again by the Germans in 1940, and escaped for the second time from German captivity. Edek was the leader of the group and most eager to find out if we were Jews. One day he invited me to join the guys in a tavern. It was obvious that they intended to get me drunk and find out the truth. I had been through this exercise before in Poland. This time it was prudent not to admit that we were Jews but our lives did not depend upon keeping it a secret. I "confessed" that Pani Rojek was my mother, that my father was arrested by the Germans for underground activities. The Germans were eager to arrest my mother, and that's why we had escaped from Poland.

They must have gotten me very drunk, because I awoke the next morning in bed. My mother and sister were sleeping on the floor. I had no memory of how I got home. I was told later that a woman approached me in the tavern with a glass of wine, put her arm around me, and proposed a toast in honor of Poland. I splashed a glass of wine in her face. I was also told that some Hungarian men attacked me; the Poles rose to my defense but were defeated. I was then bodily thrown out of the tavern. From that day on, the Poles believed that I was not a Jew and treated me as part of the group.

But I considered myself very much a Jew and decided to enhance my Jewish identity and Zionism. The village had a Jewish shoemaker. His young son was a Talmudic scholar fluent in Hebrew. I wanted to improve my Hebrew. I visited the shoemaker's shop, told him that I was a Jew and that I wanted his son to teach me Hebrew. He agreed to do so, but only through study of the Torah, because Hebrew was a sacred language and could not be used for secular purposes. The young man and his father were opposed to Zionism. I was amazed to hear that the rabbi of Satmar declared that the persecution of the Jews in Europe was divine punishment for the sins of Zionism. I accepted their condition and came once a week for an hour to be taught. Obviously, I was taking a great risk of being unmasked as a Jew.

Olenka and I were making rapid progress in learning Hungarian. We did not have a Polish-Hungarian dictionary. We learned the language the way a child learns its native tongue, by interacting with people. "What do you call this?" I asked Sandor Baci the first day we arrived in Uszod. I was pointing to a dove sitting on the roof. His answer did not seem right. I pointed again and he gave me the word for the sky. At this point, I flapped my arms and he said "Golab." The same word means "pigeon" in Polish.

We continued to pretend that we were Christian, and went on Sunday to the only church in the village of Uszod. This was quite a surprise. The church looked more like a synagogue than a Church in Poland. Everything was simple; it was a plain room, without icons or decorations of any kind. We were not aware that the village of Uszod was Protestant. This was my first encounter with non-Catholic Christians. If we wanted to go to a Catholic church, we had to travel to the nearby Kalocsa, which had an impressive Catholic church.

Our Hungarian landlords invited us to supper a number of times. Hungarian villagers were gourmet cooks. We made potato pancakes, which was a novelty to them. I volunteered to help with the farm work. Paprika and wine grapes were the farm's major crops. They also raised hogs that were slaughtered on the farm. For breakfast, they ate smoked solid fat (fatback) dipped in paprika. I soon discovered that one had to be a Hungarian to eat what they called "King's Paprika." This variety was too sharp for me.

It would be an overstatement to call our living space a room. And yet, it became a dental office of sorts. We bought a used foot-operated dental drill and some dental instruments. Mother became the camp dentist. Occasionally, a Hungarian came in as a patient. We even made a few bridges and crowns. I say "we" because I provided the foot power for the drill and at times helped Mother to yank out the gypsum molds that became too hard. I took the molds to the town of Kalocsa, which had a dental laboratory.

Gina and I wrote to each other every few days. A few weeks later she was coming to visit us. In anticipation of her visit, I constructed her and my initials out of stones on the shores of the Danube. This was an indirect declaration of love that I was too bashful to make directly. She arrived on a beautiful sunny fall day. I still see before my eyes the small ship pulling alongside the wharf with Gina sitting on a deck chair. Her beauty turned heads as she walked on shore. The first chance I had, I took Gina to the shores of the Danube for a walk. I could not find the spot with the stones arranged to form G and E. I climbed a tree for a better view of the area. In the process, I split my pants in the crotch and was terribly embarrassed. To my great disappointment, we never found my "artwork." I could not verbally express my love for Gina and did not make any sexual advances. A few days later Gina returned to Budapest and we resumed our correspondence. Little did I know that I would see her soon, again due to unanticipated political developments.

Communication with the outside world was limited. We had no radio. The Hungarian newspaper could be bought in nearby Kalocsa, and I bought one whenever I went to town. By this time I could make out many simple words. I was eager to read about the progress the Soviets were making against the Germans. I was hoping for another Stalingrad. The Hungarians were oblivious of the impending invasion of the Soviets, whom they hated and whom we considered our liberators.

There was regular daily service between Uszod and Kalocsa by a horse-driven wagon with benches. The passengers were mostly women going to shop. The Hungarian peasant women wore colorful hoop skirts that reminded me of the Meissen porcelain figurines that we had had at home. On my first trip to town, the farm cart stopped in the middle of nowhere; a woman got off and stood next to the cart, continuing to chat with the rest of the passengers. I was puzzled. The purpose of her mission became obvious when she got back on the wagon and left a patch of yellow snow. Nothing like this would have happened in Poland.

These things aren't like gravity or the second law of thermo-dynamics;
they don't have to happen. They happen only if people are stupid enough to let
them happen...

Chapter 14
The Germans Again

Our tranquil life in the village of Uszod came to an abrupt end on March 19th, 1944. The rumor was that the Germans had occupied Hungary. This turned out later to be not quite the case. On March 15th, 1944, Regent Horthy was given the choice to have German occupation of Hungary or a German-approved government. Horthy chose the latter. On March 22nd, the collaborationist government of Döme Sztójay was instituted.[43]

We heard that members of the Nyilas Party, also known as the Arrow Cross Party, were attacking Hungarian Jews in nearby Kalocsa. The Nyilas were the Hungarian Nazis. They wore black uniforms with armbands; instead of a swastika, they used the arrow cross. From a distance they looked like their German role models. Ferenc Szálasi was the founder and leader of the Party. He was intensely anti-Semitic, advocating a German-type solution of the Jewish Question in Hungary.

In 1939, the Hungarian Prime Minister Pál Teleki (February 1939–April 1941) had suppressed the Arrow Cross Party, and imprisoned many of its adherents. The Government enacted anti-Jewish laws that did not satisfy the virulent anti-Semitism of Hungarian fascists. In March of 1944, when the Germans set up the collaborationist government of Döme Sztójay, the Arrow Cross Party received official approval from the new government, and popular support.

Admiral Horthy was forced to accept a German plenipotentiary, Emund Veesenmayer, who was an expert on the subject of the elimination of the Jews in the Balkan countries. Veesenmayer provided the diplomatic cover for Adolf Eichmann and his Einsatzgruppe. It was established at the Nuremberg trial that the Einsatzgruppe trained for the mission of rounding up the Hungarian Jews in the camp of Mauthausen weeks before the March 19th invasion of Hungary.

The day after the frightening news that the Germans had occupied Hungary reached Uszod, two men came to see me. One of them we called "Prezes," meaning chairman in Polish. He and two other men were jokingly called

"Our Judenrat." They were the informal leaders of our tiny community. They told me that there was a rumor that in the nearby village located on the main highway, all Jews pretending to be Poles had been arrested. They told me that, being the youngest and speaking Hungarian better than anyone else, I was best suited to go on a reconnaissance mission. I agreed to do it on the condition that my mother would not know about it. "You will take care of my mother and sister if I don't come back?" I asked our informal leader. He promised, but I made him raise his right arm and say the magic word "Przysiegam" (I swear). They got a bicycle for me, which was the quickest mode of getting around. It was too dangerous to use the roads.

I rode the bike on a path along the embankment of the Danube. I did not dare show myself on the road. When I got close to the neighboring village, I hid my bike in the bushes and walked the rest of the way. I knew where a family of Polish Jews lived and strolled casually in that direction. A group of youngsters were gathered outside the house – a sure sign that something happened.

I recognized some of the refugee women walking in and out. After some hesitation, I entered the house. The place had been ransacked. The women told me that a Nyilas group came in and took some of the men. Others had escaped. Some families took the train to Budapest, but now they were checking for foreigners at the railroad station in Kalocsa.

While peddling furiously back to Uszod, I was deciding what to do. Staying in the village was now out of question. The Kalocsa region was studded with Polish refugee "camps," ideal targets for the Nyilas and the gendarmes searching for foreign Jews.

It was time to run back to Budapest and seek the anonymity of a big city. I knew that after I reported to our group what I had discovered on my mission, everyone else would reach the same conclusion.

"We must go to Budapest at once," I told Mother after my return from the surveillance mission. Trains were the only method of transportation to Budapest, which was north of us. I was not about to take the risk of trying to catch a train in nearby Kalocsa, where the Hungarian Nazis where looking for foreign Jews. I decided that we should go south to Baja, a large town with a major railroad station. There was an express train going from Baja to Budapest, which did not stop in Kalocsa.

My plan was that in the early hours of the morning, mother would develop severe abdominal cramps. We would hire a horse driven wagon in the village to take her to the hospital in Baja. I woke Sandor Baci at dawn telling him about my mother's medical emergency. He helped me to get a driver with a horse-driven wagon to Baja. It was a very cold morning. I remember shivering during the long ride. I sat next to the driver; Mother and Olenka were cuddled in the backseat. When we got to Baja, I told the driver that we had changed our mind. Instead of going to the hospital, we would go to a hospital in Budapest. He took us to the railroad station.

I gave the driver a note to deliver to a member of our group, telling them that taking the express train from Baja to Budapest was a good way to avoid the Kalocsa area. They were not as familiar with the region as I was.

The trip to Budapest was uneventful. We welcomed the anonymity that the city provided. We knew no one and we had very little money. We saw in the streets of Budapest a Hungarian gendarme with an Arrow Cross band on his arm; this was frightening.

For the first time, Olenka and I took up talking to each other in Hungarian. It was no longer safe to be Polish. That meant that Mother, who spoke virtually no Hungarian, could not talk to us openly.

When we arrived in Budapest, it was evening. We could not go to a hotel, it was too expensive and one had to register and give one's papers. We were not certain at this point if our documents identifying us as Polish refugees would not result in an arrest. The luggage maker's place where we had spent our first night in Budapest in 1943 was close to the railroad station. The familiar sign "Luggage Repair" was on the door but the door was locked. We sat on the steps and waited. We spent all night in that location. We were not troubled by the discomfort; our major concern was that someone would call the police. We told the neighbors that we were expected.

True enough, in the early hours of the morning, our prospective hosts arrived. They recognized us instantly and were pleased that this time Olenka and I could converse with them in Hungarian. We told them that Mother had to see a special doctor and that is why we had traveled to Budapest. Once again, we had the same space located behind the workshop. It was filthy and musty, but it was relatively safe.

Olenka and I set out on a reconnaissance mission of the city. Our first stop was the Király Utca Coffee House where Jews used to gather. Having my ten-year-old sister by my side was reassuring; it also made me less suspect. Last, but not least, her Hungarian was impeccable. I was concerned that my Hungarian might reveal that I was a foreigner. The cafe was open but there were no Polish Jews noticeable. We did not dare to go in.

Our next destination was the Pension Krakowitz. I was hoping to find Gina there. We found Leon Blatt and some of the other members of the Zionist group. I was told that Gina was staying with a family and would probably come by in the afternoon. Everyone was anxious. I never liked the idea of living as a group in a pension; it seemed to be too much of a target.

When I got into the street, I ran into Kurt Strahlberg. I had seen him somewhere before, but we had never talked. We got into a conversation and he told me that he belonged to a clandestine Zionist group called "Polay Zion." His father belonged to that organization and members of it in Budapest were helping him and his mother. His father had been killed in Poland. Kurt and I became instant friends. He was a few years older than I. There was an air of calm competence about him, essential in a struggle for survival. Kurt told me that the most effective underground Zionist group was Hashomer Hazair, a leftist group that was run by a group of Slovak Jews. I considered myself leftist and I wanted to join them. Kurt told me that there was no such thing as joining. They looked after their own members only. "If you tell them that your father was a member, they may accept you," he said. Kurt knew of a park where one of the Hashomer leaders met the members of the group. He told me to look for a tall, dark-haired fellow carrying a briefcase.

I found the park that Kurt described and wandered around, hoping to come across the man who was our only hope. There was no one else we could turn to in this large city. After an hour or two of aimless roaming, I spotted a dark-haired fellow with a briefcase. I approached him and told him our predicament. I also told him that my father was a member of Hashomer Hazair in Poland. I believed this to be a lie; years later I found out it was the truth.

He asked a few questions and told me that mother and sister and I had to find an apartment somewhere, preferably away from the center of the city. He cautioned me that the city was full of regular detectives and special police called "alien police" looking for illegal foreigners. Even as Christian Poles, we were illegal away from our detention camp. With this warning he handed me a wad of money.

"That's for the apartment, food, and don't forget to buy some more decent clothing," he said with a smile. His first name was Mimis. Years later I found out that his last name was Herbst. He was just as handsome as he was cordial. Within a few minutes we became friends. Little did know that I had just met a man who would become one of my heroes.

A few hours later, Mother, Olenka and I got on a streetcar and rode to a fancy area of Budapest. On my previous stay in Budapest, I had admired this area but we could not afford living there. I always felt safer in affluent neighborhoods.

We rented a two bedroom, lower level apartment in an elegant villa. It had been the maid's quarters. Our apartment had a separate entrance from the street. The landlady, Mrs. Csorba, took a great liking to my mother, even though she couldn't speak with her. My sister and I functioned as interpreters. Mrs. Csorba was a gracious woman. She must have been in her late fifties. Her daughter, Clara, was a famous Hungarian actress who lived in America and her other daughter, Sari, was married to an important government official. Our living quarters were the best since we had left home.

The garden around the villa was beautiful. Elegant men and women sauntered along the boulevard. Mrs. Csorba had a part-time chauffeur who drove her occasionally to the opera or theater. The imposing German car stood idle in the large garage that was originally a carriage house. We felt relatively safe in this affluent setting.

When I told Mimis where we lived, he was greatly impressed. "You are in the lion's cage," he said with obvious pleasure. He told me that Hungarian aristocracy and government officials lived in that neighborhood.

Mimis was a Slovak Jew who spoke Hungarian fluently; he lived in Budapest on false papers as a Hungarian. Later I was introduced to Pil, the second in command, and Rafi, who was the leader of the organization. They too were Slovak Jews. Rafi was blond and blue-eyed. He had the looks of a movie star and could be a poster child for the Nazi concept of the "Nordic" race. According to rumors, he was a half Jew and had the major asset of not being circumcised. His last name was Friedel. These three men became like my older brothers. Mimis was tall, dark-haired, and looked like a typical Hungarian. Pil was the tallest, and distinguished-looking, like a young banker. These three men were kind, gentle and always ready to help no matter what risk was involved. They inspired confidence and to this day, have my profound respect and gratitude.

Every day brought new developments. The Hungarian authorities were enacting a variety of anti-Jewish measures. In April 1944, the Jews in the provinces of Hungary were driven into ghettos. On May 15, 1944, the systematic mass deportations began. In merely a few weeks, over 434,000 Hungarian Jews from the provinces were deported. Veesenmayer proudly reported this fact to his superiors in Berlin by telegram. By early July, all of Hungary, with the sole exception of Budapest, was virtually *Judenrein* (Jew clean). Between June 17th and June 23rd, 1944 the 164,000 Jews of Budapest were forced to relocate into specially designated Yellow-Star houses. The stage was set for their deportation from Hungary. However, on July 7, 1944, on the eve of the beginning of the mass deportations from Budapest, the Regent of Hungary, Admiral Horthy, decided to suspend the deportation. Five days earlier, Allied aircraft had conducted a devastating attack against Budapest.

Time was running out for the efforts to eliminate the Jews; the Russians were not far away.

The Hungarian Jews no longer called us fear mongers. A few months before, most of them thought that it was peculiar that I continued to pretend to be a Christian after escaping from German captivity to the safety of Hungary. Now Hungarian Jews were trying to live on false papers. One Friday afternoon, I visited one of Budapest's many pissoirs. Two young orthodox Jews were at the urinal next to me. They wore the yellow stars. "If I had a prick like he does, I would get Aryan papers," one said to the other in Yiddish. I could not resist and said to them "A Guten Shabes," the traditional greeting used on the eve of Shabbat.

I remembered this line from a story Father used to tell. In the 1920s, Father worked in Chenciny, a small town about 10 kilometers from his hometown of Kielce. One Friday afternoon, he tried to get home before Shabbat. The last horse-driven coach was full of Jews trying to make it home before sundown. Father, blue-eyed and blond, spoke to them in Polish asking for a ride. Some of the passengers told the Jewish driver to refuse; it would be too crowded. Others insisted in Yiddish that "the Goy" must be accepted to avoid trouble. When father got off the carriage in Kielce he shouted "A Guten Shabes" (Good Sabbath) and in this way identified himself as a Jew. The passengers were not amused and yelled obscenities at him.

The war news was encouraging. The Soviets were making amazing progress against the Germans. A rumor circulated in Budapest that the Germans had occupied Hungary because Regent Horthy had tried to make a separate peace with the Soviets. We hoped that any day the long overdue second front by the American and British Forces would materialize and Nazi Germany would collapse. It was frightening to see in the city SS uniforms and Germans in civilian clothing. German military vehicles were in the streets. Every day someone close to us was arrested and taken to the Foe Street prison. Part of that building became a Gestapo prison.

Overnight, our "promised land" was transformed into the familiar hell of persecution. The Hungarian gendarmes and the Nyilas thugs no longer relied upon inspection of documents. If in doubt about a man's "racial" origin, they inspected his penis.

In one of our park bench meetings, Mimis told me that plans were made to get male members of our group to Romania, which now was safe for Jews. The staunchly anti-Semitic Romanian dictator, General Ion Antonescu, was having second thoughts about his alliance with Hitler. Romania was getting ready to desert the Axis powers. Mimis said that from Romania, ships took Jews to Palestine. This sounded more like fantasy than reality.

A few days later, June 1st or 2nd of 1944, I was walking down Rakoczy Street in Budapest, the city's main boulevard, when a member of our group caught up with me and announced breathlessly, "I have been searching for you. You must be at the railroad station at the train going to Mako, buy a ticket and go into the second car from the locomotive. You have been selected to go with Mimis to Romania and then to Palestine."

I had little more than an hour to get home, get ready and, above all, to say goodbye to my mother and sister. Mother knew that our leaders were planning to send male members of our group to Romania. I did not expect to be in the first group and in the company of one of our leaders.

Mother accepted the news bravely. She was aware of the special hazard facing me as a boy. Once again, we would be separated. Olenka began to cry. She wanted all of us to go. Mother took her gold watch off her wrist, the only valuable item we had at this point. "You may need it more than I do." She insisted that I take it. It was a Tissot Swiss watch, father's birthday present to her. In those days, men's jackets had generous padding in the shoulders. Mother slipped the watch between the layers and sewed it up. Another valuable item was the certificate of entry into Palestine that had been sent to us by Mother's sisters. As soon as we had gotten to Budapest, Mother had written to her sisters Kacia and Rywa in Tel Aviv. Both had left Poland for Palestine as pioneers in the early 30's. They sent us a certificate of entry within a few weeks. Since we did not have passports, there was no way to use it. We kept it, even though it was dangerous. If discovered in our possession, it would identify us as Jews, as it was made out to Betty Kowarska-Tenenwurzel, and her children Emanuel and Ruth. Mother sewed the folded certificate in the belt area of my pants.

I knew that Mako was located in the southeastern part of Hungary on the Romanian border. We had studied the map of the region because of our prior plans or fantasies to go to Yugoslavia and join the partisans. I arrived at the railroad station shortly before 4 p.m. On the platform next to the train going to Mako, I was surprised and pleased to see Gina. I was surprised because she did not belong to our Hashomer Hazair group. When I saw Leon Blatt next to her, I understood that this was a joint project of the Zionist underground. A little distance from them I could see Mimis, his wife Suzie, and Amikam, a boy my age that I had seen previously. He was a Palestinian Jew who had come to visit his grandparents in Budapest and was unable to return to Tel Aviv. There were a few others whose names I don't remember.

Two trains were going to Mako, about a half an hour apart. Mimis knew that I was in love with Gina and had asked Leon Blatt if I could go with their group, and Leon had agreed. I had to make a choice. I would have liked to go with Gina but my sense of loyalty prevailed. I went with our group. I was excited to travel in the company of Mimis, whom I admired greatly. His wife Suzie impressed me with her competence and cheerfulness. They told me that a guide would meet us in Mako and take us across the border to Romania. We would travel by train to Bucharest and from there to Constantia on the Black Sea. There we would board a ship that would take us to Haifa in Palestine. "Don't be worried about your mother and sister, Rafi will take good care of them," Suzie told me, recognizing from my facial expression what was on my mind. Rafi remained in Budapest. His blond hair and blue eyes, in addition to not being circumcised, made him less vulnerable than Mimis.

We got off the train at Mako, a small border town. We had to be careful not to attract attention. The much-feared Hungarian gendarmes seemed to be everywhere. We were met by a guide and followed him into a wooded area. When it got completely dark, we walked single file along a path. After about an hour of walking, the guide told us to stop; he had to go ahead and check if it was safe to proceed. We were in Romania already. As we stood in a huddle, suddenly there were flashlights everywhere, shouts of "Hands up!" and gunfire. We were surrounded by Hungarian gendarmes, handcuffed, and marched to a truck. It was obvious that we had walked into a trap set by the Hungarian border police. We were driven to Szabadka (Subotica to the Serbs), a town located in the Bacska region of Yugoslavia. Hungary had annexed it in April of 1941. In January of 1942, Hungarian forces killed a thousand Serbian Jews in Bacska. Hungarians, like the Germans, behaved particularly viciously in occupied territories.

At the gendarmerie post, we were lined up against a blank wall, noses touching the surface. A policeman's club or butt of a gun hit whoever moved. We stood in that position for hours. A few people fainted.

Every so often, one of us was taken into a nearby room. Screams, alternating with thuds, left little doubt what was happening there. I was particularly distraught when Suzie was interrogated and abused. Finally, my turn came. I was led into a brightly lit room and was greeted by a smiling rotund man in short sleeves. He was the first civilian I had seen since we were captured. He was wearing gold-rimmed glasses. "Are you nearsighted?" was his first question.

"Yes, I am." I said.

"So am I. How many diopters are your glasses?" he asked in a friendly manner. I told him and he asked to see my glasses, which I had begun wearing again in Hungary. He held the lens to the light to count the rings that show the strength of corrective lenses. Suddenly, a powerful blow of his fist landed on my face followed by many more. "You get more if you tell me lies," he yelled. I was ordered to sit down. A younger man took notes of what I said. The interrogator informed me that he was an officer of the Hungarian anti-espionage agency and he knew all about the activities of our group. He believed that I was part of a group that had contact with British espionage and smuggled arms into Hungary.

I told him the truth. I was a Jew from Poland; I gave him my real name. I knew nothing about the smuggling of arms; my only contact was with Mimis, who occasionally provided me with some money as a friend. He kept insisting that we were in contact with the British Armed Forces. Whenever he did not like an answer, he would come from behind the desk, shove me against the wall, and threaten bodily harm. He went into a great many details that I no longer remember. I gave him the luggage maker's home as our address in Budapest.

He asked for my mother's maiden name. "Betty Kowarski" I said, truthfully. To my surprise, that got me another blow on my face; this time he broke my glasses, which were back on my nose. "That's a lie! Are you trying to claim that she's not Jewish?" he shouted. "Tell me her real name," he demanded. I made a false "confession" and admitted that my mother's name was "Shapiro, Betty Shapiro." This lie made him happy.

At this point, he stopped the interrogation and strip-searched me. He missed the gold watch in my shoulder pad but found the certificate of entry to Palestine sewn into my pants. I was anxious and worried that the English document with a British insignia would reinforce his suspicion that I had some connection to England. I decided to take the initiative.

"Let me prove to you that I don't lie," I said quickly and pointed to the name "Betty Kowarski" on the certificate, which he, a few minutes before, would not accept as my mother's maiden name. He was impressed. "I thought you were trying to claim that you are a converted Jew."

It sounded almost like an apology. His attitude to me changed. I did not know then that baptized Jews in Hungary were exempt from some anti-Jewish laws thanks to the intervention of the Vatican. After the interrogation ordeal was completed, those of us in our group were permitted to sit on the floor, and even to talk to each other.

The next morning we were loaded on a truck and taken to the town of Szeged and placed into the notorious Csillag prison, the Hungarian equivalent of Sing Sing. Architecturally, it resembled more of a fortress or a medieval prison. It was a large, maximum-security facility. Every aspect of life was strictly controlled. I shared a tiny cell with a Hungarian criminal. He was a man in his fifties and assumed a paternal attitude towards me.

At an appointed hour, prisoners from my block were ordered into the courtyard where we walked briskly, single file, in circles. One day a prisoner behind me whispered, "The Allies have landed in Normandy. Pass it on." At long last, the much-awaited event had occurred. American and English military had become a presence in continental Europe. It strengthened hope that liberation was not too far in the future. This episode also became a chronological marker for me. I had no awareness of dates; later I could say with confidence that on June 6, 1944, I was in the Csillag prison.

The landing on the beaches of Normandy gave me new hope. We never understood why the Americans and the British forces had not created the second front sooner. Many historians agree that the British, for political reasons, diverted

Americans from Operation Roundup, the code name for the cross-Channel invasion planned for 1943. At that point Germany did not have the defenses that it had by 1944. The delay in the mounting of the second front prolonged World War II by many months. A book entitled *1943: The Victory That Never Was* by John Grigg (Hill and Wang, 1980) makes this argument persuasively.

The Soviet Union surprised the West and Nazi Germany by nearly defeating the Germans before the second front became a reality. Hatred of the oppressive Soviet Union should not obscure its contributions to the defeat of Nazi Germany. More Red Army soldiers were confined to German prisoner of war camps than United States had soldiers oversees. Over 80 percent of Allied casualties were Soviet.

The Second Front was established when Germany was nearly defeated by the Soviet Union. The "D" in D-Day should stand for delay. The beaches of Normandy were stormed just in time to ensure a role for the United States and England in post-war Europe.

The Allies could hardly dictate terms at Yalta to the Soviet Union, whose army fought its way from the outskirts of Moscow to the conquest of Berlin. The most strident critics of Yalta are the people whose political ancestors made it inevitable: The Baltic states that in the '30s supported Nazi Germany; the Vatican, which in 1935 established a Concordat with Hitler; Poland, which joined hands in 1938 with Germany in the dismemberment of Czechoslovakia; American conservatives who wanted to stay out of the European conflict.

The Soviet domination of Eastern Europe at the end of World War II has its roots in the spirit of Munich of the 1930s. The appeasement of Nazi Germany made the Soviet Union the essential partner of Great Britain and the United States. These allies of convenience always maintained a high level of suspicion vis-à-vis each other even before the Cold War.

Hitler and Stalin have many similarities; one of them is their phenomenal, even though relatively short-lived, success. Stalin gained complete control of the USSR in spite of being a much less important figure than Trotsky in the 1917 Revolution. He outmaneuvered England and France in their efforts to isolate the USSR and deliver it to the tender mercy of Nazi Germany. Under the leadership of Stalin, the Soviet Union nearly defeated Nazi Germany before a single allied soldier landed in occupied France. He did this in spite of being a paranoid, cruel tyrant who killed the leadership of the Red Army and caused the death of millions of Soviet citizens.

Hitler transformed a small party of 20-some members into a political force in the Weimar Republic. He became the Chancellor of the Republic that he hated and in 1933, he destroyed it. He became the absolute ruler of the Third Reich and abrogated the despised Versailles Treaty that all Germans loved to hate. He proved all his generals wrong by annexing Austria and acquired Sudetenland and Czechoslovakia without firing a single shot. Hitler defeated Poland in 1939 and, with the conquest of France in 1940, became the most powerful leader in the world and the most popular head of state that Germany ever had. This entire agenda he accomplished in a short seven years. In spite of being a murderous sadist, he was more loved than feared by his grateful nation. Niccolo Machiavelli was a role model to both Hitler and Stalin; Stalin kept a copy of *The Prince* at his bedside.

This too, I know – and wise it were if each could know the same
That every prison that men build is built with bricks of shame,
And bound with bars lest Christ should see how men their brothers maim.
– Oscar Wilde, "The Ballad of Reading Gaol"

Chapter 15
Concentration Camp

One day, I was called out of my cell and marched to a truck, where I joined the rest of our group. In addition to the familiar faces, I noticed two older men. They were twins in their forties or early fifties.

Each of the twins had his wrists wrapped in bandages. They were Polish Jews who had been apprehended with the previous group. They had attempted to kill themselves by cutting their wrists. We were heavily guarded by gendarmes who sat with us; two civilians were sitting in the truck cab next to the driver. After a short ride, we ended up at an elegant villa. An SS sentry stood in front of it. This was the Gestapo headquarters in Szeged.

We were marched through the front entrance into a backyard where two Gestapo officers, accompanied by two SS men with sub-machine guns, waited for us. One of the Hungarian civilians who spoke German made a brief presentation reading from a prepared document.

He described the apprehension, investigation and interrogation of our group. He claimed that we were part of a larger conspiracy of Jews with connections to Great Britain. He enumerated our real and false names. He then handed a box with documents pertaining to us over to the Gestapo chief. One of the SS men took possession of the carton. The Gestapo Chief and the Hungarian official shook hands. The Germans saluted, and the Hungarian gendarmes who guarded us saluted back.

After the Hungarians had completed the ceremony and departed, the Germans broke out in laughter; the Gestapo chief yelled to an underling and said, "Zehn Juden" (Ten Jews). The Hungarians had not caught on yet that a Jew was merely a number to the Germans, devoid of personal identity.

Another SS man rummaged briefly though the box. Attached to my file was the photo of Gina, and this attracted his attention. I was singled out for separate interrogation and was beaten for having an "Aryan" girlfriend. He took Gina's picture and put it in his pocket. The rest of the documents were thrown on to a heap of garbage.

On the left side of the courtyard, if one stood with his back turned to the villa, there was a small one-story house that had been converted into a jail. The windows had bars and the reinforced door had a large outside padlock. We were ordered inside. The house was entirely empty; it consisted of two rooms and a small kitchen with a wooden stove and one pot. Formerly these had been servants' quarters. For the first time since the war began, the Germans held me prisoner. It seemed that years of running from them had accomplished nothing. It was a desperate situation but, strangely enough, I don't recall feeling desperate. My optimism endured.

Being with Mimis and Suzie gave me a sense of confidence. They had treated me like a brother. I had been more dejected in the Csillag prison than in the custody of the Gestapo. I was hopeful because this looked like a place one could escape from. Mimis, Suzie, Hans, Lusia and I talked about a breakout as soon as we were inside. A quick survey revealed that the windows only opened into the courtyard and they had bars. An SS man with a submachine gun was patrolling the small courtyard.

I became one of the organizers, in spite of being the youngest. Amikam was a few years older but he was not part of the inner circle. He lacked street smarts and could not be counted upon. Samek was the next oldest; he may have been nineteen years old. He was reliable but did not have much initiative and seemed depressed. The two older men, the twins, could not be relied upon because of age, dejection and their self-inflicted injuries. Hans and Lusia, who did not belong to Hashomer Hazair, were in their early twenties, and we had a natural affinity with them. I believe there may have been one more person but I'm not certain of it. Mimis was the natural leader of our group. Everyone could sense the strength of his personality, his resourcefulness and kindness. Masterminding an escape was our goal.

Escape was also a concern for the Gestapo. An older SS man whom we nicknamed "Der Alte" (the old man) ordered us to get out into the courtyard. He was in charge of the SS detachment. His relatively mild manner made an impression upon us. He told us to line up and stand at attention. After a few moments, the Gestapo chief, wearing white gloves, appeared. He told us that we would be well treated if we obeyed, worked diligently and did not attempt to escape. If one escaped, five people would be shot. If more than one ran away, the rest would be shot. After the chief departed, der Alte told us that we would cook our own meals. This turned out to be an overstatement. We were given potatoes to cook as our main meal and a small ration of black bread.

Standing in the courtyard, we saw that a massive gate separated the courtyard from the street; a high wall ran opposite our makeshift prison. The end of the courtyard was enclosed by a structure with a low roof, which we later found out was a pigsty.

We were a curiosity to the staff of the Gestapo headquarters. The first few days, they came to the windows to take a look. Some asked questions, others made contemptuous remarks. On the second day of our confinement, I stood by the window, looking out through the bars. A tall broad-shouldered civilian engaged me in a friendly conversation. He soon realized that my familiarity with

146

German was limited. He switched to Hungarian, which he spoke like a native. I told him that I was from Poland and he then began to talk to me in Serbian. His name was Milan; he was an ethnic German from the town that was called Neu Sandez in German; Uj Videk, in Hungarian; and Novi Sad, in Serbian. It was a multi-ethnic town. The term "ethnic German" sounds innocuous. The German word for this, used in Polish also, was "Volksdeutsch," which carried the connotation of lack of allegiance to the native country.

During daylight hours, the door to our quarters was open. We worked in the yard, washing cars, motorcycles and tending the pigs. A pigsty behind a swanky villa seemed out of place. Working in the pigsty was a desirable job; one was out of sight of the SS men in the yard. The pigs were fed stale white bread. We would grab pieces of bread from the trough and eat it surreptitiously. Hunger pains caused me great distress. The Germans, unlike the Hungarians, kept us on a starvation diet.

Some of the Germans delighted in tormenting us. A young Gestapo man told Amikam to wash a car. "Mach schnell" (work quickly) was their favorite phrase. Amikam worked rapidly and finished the assignment. The Gestapo man gave it the finger test and found some dirt. He berated the frightened boy and made him do pushups as punishment. The same man ordered me to clean a motorcycle. I worked fast but never declared my job finished until he said that it was good enough. I escaped being abused by using this tactic.

Next to the stove in the kitchen was a box of wood and we decided to dig a hole in the wall behind it. Items found in the courtyard served as digging tools. We did more scraping than digging since noise had to be avoided, but the job turned out to be much easier than we expected. The back wall was mostly plaster. The work was done primarily at night. The biggest problem was to dispose of the chunks. During the daytime we would walk in, put pieces in our pockets and then get rid of them as we worked in the yard. In a few days, the wall was ready for a break through. The plan was that we would make the opening to freedom sometime after midnight that night when everyone was asleep. Excitement was high. There was a great deal of anxiety that some of us would get captured after the breakout. The challenge was to get away from Szeged as quickly as possible. One advantage we had was our papers. The box which the Hungarian anti-espionage agents had delivered to the Gestapo and which they unceremoniously disposed of had the documents identifying us as Christians. We retrieved them.

Around midnight, Mimis, Hans and I crawled in the direction of the kitchen. Standing up was dangerous because a light from the courtyard was shining into the room, and a sentry looked in from time to time. To our surprise, we found the bodies of the twins obstructed the entrance to the kitchen. "We will not let you do this. You are young, you will escape but we will be caught and shot," they whispered. Neither persuasion nor threats changed their determination to prevent the escape.

Once it became apparent that we could not escape as a group, we decided that each one of us was on his or her own. Our bonds of loyalty to each other were suspended. It was understood that whoever got a chance to escape should do so with the full awareness that others would be punished for it. The two older men not affiliated with our group obviously did not agree with us and watched us carefully as we went about our business during the working day. Our conception of fairness and theirs was different.

One day, der Alte told me to comb my hair, which was an unusual request. Since I did not have a comb, I used my fingers. He then told me to follow him. I noticed that he was carrying a sub-machine gun; usually he only had a side arm. I became alarmed, as did my friends. Why was I being singled out? I was led into the villa itself and was ordered to stand in the hallway and der Alte walked into a room. An SS man was guarding the exit door. After a few minutes, der Alte returned and motioned me to follow him into the street. It was the first time since being captured that I was out in the open. I was still in the dark as to where he was taking me; he said that I was going to work. I had my doubts about this assurance. Execution seemed more likely and I was looking for an opportunity to escape.

We walked in silence through the streets of Szeged until we reached a luxurious villa. A German woman, who turned out to be a governess, and a little girl, probably five years old, greeted us at the entrance. There were two Hungarian servants in the house. Der Alte and the governess were delighted to see each other. I was led into a garden. I quickly noted that a high fence enclosed it. Der Alte showed me a small structure with a few angora rabbits. It was my job to paint the cages, he told me. My fears of execution turned out to be unfounded. Der Alte made himself comfortable at a table and the governess brought him coffee and cookies. He was flirting with her. As I painted, the little girl wandered over to me and called me "uncle," which was cause for laughter for the SS man and the governess. This was the house of the Chief of the Gestapo and the little girl was his child. She did not know yet that I could not be her uncle because her elders had declared me vermin. I was hoping to get an opportunity to escape but der Alte never let go of the submachine gun and the wall was too high to bound over it quickly.

On the way back, der Alte was in good mood and asked me a variety of personal questions. He was relaxed, even friendly. As we walked through the streets of Szeged, I looked for an opportunity to run. I was hoping that we would get into a crowded area, but that never happened. The sub-machine gun hanging over his chest gave me second thoughts about running in an open area. "What would happen if I started running?" I asked, emboldened by his friendliness. "I would shoot you. Don't make me do it," he said. I knew he meant it. He was an ordinary, decent man who had been kind and gentle with the little German girl, but somehow it was acceptable to him to kill a teenage boy because he was a Jew. We walked back the rest of the way in silence. My friends were happy to see me alive; they feared that I had been picked for execution.

It was a beautiful summer day and I was washing a car in the courtyard. The rest of our group was doing other chores. Suddenly, I saw the twin brothers running up to the SS man in charge of guarding us. I can hear the words distinctly, "Ich melde gehorsam . . ." (I report dutifully three have escaped). I had suspected as much when I saw Mimis, Suzie, and Hans enter the pigsty together. It turned out that they broke the wall of the flimsy structure and ran to freedom. The SS man fired a salvo from his sub-machine gun into the air, and pandemonium broke out. The courtyard filled with Germans. The remaining five or six of us were herded into our quarters and lined up against the back wall. An SS man stayed inside this time. We could hear motorcycles and cars leaving the courtyard.

After a short time, the Gestapo chief appeared. We were ordered to turn around and approach the windows. He stood outside the window bars. He yelled at us and concluded his tirade with a demand; "I want three volunteers to step out. They will be shot as an example for the rest of you." It occurred to me immediately that it was unlikely that they would shoot the three who would volunteer, under the assumption that whoever wanted to die was not an escape risk. As I was debating whether to offer myself for execution, Samek, who was desperate, did so. I was the next one to step out. Samek volunteered because he wanted to die; I did the same because I wanted to live.

At the same time as the Gestapo chief was calling for a third volunteer, we could hear excited German voices. "They are captured!" The Gestapo chief and his entourage left, leaving us with our guard. Hans and Suzie were dragged in by a group of SS men. It was obvious that they had been beaten severely. Suzie collapsed on the floor, but being kicked revived her. Once again, we were lined up against the wall. "What happened to Mimis? Was he killed? Did he manage to run away?" was on our minds. An SS-man brought a gramophone into the courtyard and we were taken aback by the loud playing of the popular German song "An der Kaserne" (In Front of the Barracks). Shortly thereafter, the chief and a few SS men returned. They brought bullwhips with them. Now we understood that the purpose of the music was to cover up our screams. The chief told us that we all would be punished. Some of us would be killed. "This is all the fault of these two." He pointed to Hans and Suzie. He then asked volunteers to beat Suzie. An SS man was going to take care of Hans. No one volunteered. Suzie was a woman we all loved and respected. The Germans selected Amikam. He was hitting her gingerly and she was taking it stoically. This infuriated the chief; an SS man took the whip and beat Amikam. "Now you do it to her the right way, or you'll get it again." Amikam resumed the beating in a manner that still did not satisfy our tormentors. He was beaten again and began to cry. Suzie had a full skirt made of heavy material. If she bent over, the skirt would absorb most of the force, was my thinking. I volunteered to beat her. "Bend down and scream loudly," I whispered. I lifted the whip high and was hitting her with great force, parallel to her buttocks. She screamed and the music blared outside the windows. I will never forget the song An der Kaserne, playing over and over on the gramophone.

That night, Milan appeared at the window. He asked for Janos, which was my Christian name in Hungarian. Even though I no longer pretended to be Christian, I was still called by that name. Milan told me that no one would be executed but the original plan was to shoot those who had not volunteered. In a few days we would be sent to a concentration camp named Topolya, in occupied Yugoslavia. He was friendly, and made inquiries about the condition of the two that were apprehended. "Your tall friend got away safely," he told me in a whisper. This was great news. Milan also gave me a few cigarettes that were a much-cherished commodity. I did not smoke and gave them to the smokers in our group, keeping two for some future use. We were no longer required to work in the yard and spent the entire day in confinement.

The next evening, Milan was at the window once more. This time there was an air about him of a man with a mission. He asked for me. He told me that he was a "Volksdeutsch" but considered himself a Serb. His father was a German and had died some years ago. His mother was a Serb who did not even speak German. He claimed to work for the partisans and wanted to help us. I liked him and trusted him. I mentioned my mother and he asked for her address, saying that with her help he could possibly work something out for us. I trusted my intuition and believed the incredible story that he was a double agent. I gave him my mother's real address. The fate of my mother and sister was now in his hands.

There are many episodes that I remember that I have difficulty believing. None of them compare to entrusting the lives of my mother and sister to the veracity of a Gestapo agent. The Hungarian anti-espionage agent could not beat out of me my mother's Budapest address, but I gave it willingly to Milan. As I recall this incredible decision, I am reminded of the words of Isaiah Berlin who said: "We are doomed to choose and every choice may entail irreparable loss."

Milan elicited in me a feeling of trust. In my work as a physician and psychiatrist I have discovered that logical thinking is more useful in organizing past experiences than in determining future conduct. We call it in medicine clinical judgment. I did not follow prudent ways of decision making, not out of recklessness, but necessity. I could not reflect upon the best course of action because there was none. I could not rely upon experience because I had none. I had to follow my feelings.

The amazing human instrument we call the mind is not put to full use when we rely rigidly on logic. More information is stored in the unconscious than is held in conscious awareness. To this day I rely greatly on my first impressions; most people do the same, but are reluctant to admit it. Why did Milan pick me to confide in, to tell me who he was? He trusted me before I trusted him.

He watched me volunteer to beat Suzie and heard me tell her in Hungarian to scream as loud as she could. Unlike the rest of the Gestapo agents, he understood Hungarian. Ralph Waldo Emerson writes: "The primary wisdom is intuition. In that deep force, the last fact behind which analysis cannot go, all things find their origin."

Was it reckless to give Milan my mother's address? Was it suicidal to volunteer to be executed? Was it opportunistic to volunteer to beat Suzie? Had the results been different I could have been blamed. Suzie suffered less when I took over the beating and she was grateful. I was not executed and my dealings with a Gestapo agent had positive consequences for us. An ethical purist would reject this consequentialist approach and maintain that cooperating with the enemy is always wrong. I did not reflect on ethics, but acted spontaneously.

A day or two after my talk with Milan, we were loaded on a truck and driven to the concentration camp Topolya, which was located in old military barracks. We were unloaded just beyond the heavily guarded gate. Watchtowers and barbed wire surrounded the grounds. Lusia and Suzie were separated from the men. Under the guard of two SS men, we were marched to a large two-story building. On the way we encountered groups of bedraggled and starved-looking inmates. The young SS men supervising them shouted orders in a menacing way. Being in a concentration camp was one more confirmation that I had lost my private war with the Germans. I was reduced from a fugitive to an inmate of the dreaded Nazi penal colony, called by its German acronym KZ.

Once in the building, we were handed over to a Capo, a middle-aged Serb who acted sternly as long as the SS men were around. Once they left, he told us in a pleasant way that we would join a group of other foreign Jews on the second floor. During our march to the building, we realized that most of the inmates were Serbs. We encountered only a few men and women wearing yellow stars, which meant they were Hungarian Jews. The Jews from the town of Topolya had been sent to Auschwitz in April of 1944.

To our surprise, Leon Blatt and others whom we assumed had made it safely to Romania greeted us. Leon explained how it came about that we ended up in a trap set up by the Hungarians. The guide was in the pay of the Hungarian anti-espionage agency and betrayed the first group. It was prearranged that the first group, after arriving safely in Romania, would send a note. There was a secret code indicating that the note was written under duress. A man in the first group whose name I don't remember and who I shall call "Fink" was tortured and told that if the note did not produce the arrival of the next group, he would be shot. He wrote the note that told us that the group had passed safely to Romania. "That's him." Blatt pointed to a short, frail man who was in his forties. He was sitting on the floor by himself. "They made him a *'Schreiber'* (the clerk for the building)." This meant he did not have to go to work but stayed inside after the morning line up. He was too scrawny to become a capo.

I asked Leon about Gina, but he did not know what had happened to her. When they were arrested on the border crossing and taken to the border patrol station, Gina was not in the group. The rest of his group did not know what had happened to her. She was not with them when they were apprehended.

Suddenly, Leon called out in a loud voice "Achtung" (attention) and everyone jumped and stood at attention. The camp commandant, an SS-officer, came in to inspect the new arrivals. He delivered a stern lecture about work and punishment for escape. After the commandant departed, Leon resumed introducing us to the rules of life in KZ. He told us that the first person that saw a German walking into an area should yell out "Achtung" and everyone must stand motionless.

Every building had a Capo, as did every hall within the building. Our group, which had just recently been formed, did not yet have a Capo. We wanted Leon to be the Capo since he was our undisputed leader. Whenever a German came in, we let Leon yell out "Achtung" even if someone else noticed the German first. Occasionally, he would push someone who did not react immediately, to show himself to be Capo material. Our wishes were fulfilled; he was named the *Stubenalteste* (The Hall Elder), which was the official title for a Capo. Leon had a very large diamond on his person which he would swallow every day, after he retrieved it from his feces. Every evening when we were alone, he would tell us stories of his exploits, which were legendary. He had escaped from a notorious Gestapo prison in Vienna during an interrogation on the fourth floor, by going out the window and sliding down the downspout.

One morning, an SS-Scharffuehrer (sergeant) came into our hall before we went to work and selected some of us to remain inside until further orders. We immediately noted that he chose all of the young men, including me. Something important was happening; the Scharffuehrer was the second in command of the camp. He asked if anyone was from the Katowitz area. Blatt and a few others were, but they did not admit it. A little later, we were marched to the administrative building next to the gate. One by one, we were told to go to a window, which was covered by a blanket, and stand facing it until ordered to move on. Leon Blatt whispered to me, "They are looking for me. Cover me so I can get rid of my moustache." He had a razor blade in his pocket and he shaved off his moustache in a few seconds. He walked by the window but was permitted to move on with the rest of us.

Behind the window there was someone who did not want to be recognized by us. We suspected that it was Fink. Whoever it was, he chose not to name Blatt and returned with us to our hall.

Life in the camp began at 5 a.m. with "Appell" (roll call). There was at least an hour or more of standing at attention and being abused by the SS men. Minor infractions real or imagined were used as excuse for torture. Breakfast consisted of warm liquid that was a coffee substitute made of roasted wheat. A ration of bread was distributed in the late afternoon, which was to cover the evening meal and breakfast the following day. A small round loaf was given to every four men. One of the four would be selected to divide it into four equal pieces. At 11 a.m. we were dished out a bowl of bean soup.

We worked all day long. We carried buckets of water to barrels, filled them up, and then turned them over, repeating this for hours. The "work" was non-productive torture. Daniel Goldhagen writes:

> The phenomenon of Jewish 'work' was such a triumph of politics and ideology over economic self-interest not only because the Germans killed irreplaceable workers, but also in the more profound sense that even when they were not killing them, Germans, owing to the character of their racial antipathy, had great difficulties employing Jews rationally in the economy.[44]

At other times, some of us were taken out of the camp to perform real work. I was often selected for these off-camp expeditions. Working outside the camp gave us a chance to scrounge for food, but it was also an occasion for the Germans to torment us. They insisted, for example, that we carry heavy sacks of cement off a railroad car on our shoulders. Most of us would collapse under the load and be beaten for doing so. It would have been simple for two men to carry the heavy sack but that was not permitted. Work that was useful was also used as torture.

One of the worst experiences I remember was the unloading of a whole trainload of pigs. Most had been dead for days and were in various stages of disintegration. One would grab a leg and it would separate from the rest of the body. The stench of the decayed flesh was overpowering. To make matters worse, the railroad cars used for the shipping of pigs were divided into upper and lower floors. We had to crawl to get to the dead animals.

On another occasion, we were loading cows on to railroad cars. The cows were emaciated, having been kept in makeshift stockyards without food for a long time. They were unable to move and had to be pulled and dragged into the wagons. I found an empty tin can and went out of sight of the SS man. I milked the cows, only able to extricate a few drops from each starving animal. Shortly after this "feast," I developed a high fever. I immediately thought that I had typhus, which in those days was an incurable illness. I reported to the infirmary that was operated by a few prisoner physicians. From their comments, I understood that if I had typhus, I would be shot.

They recommended that I continue to work, which I did. At the end of the day, I realized that I would collapse if I worked one more day with the fever. In that case, I would be shot for sure. I had to hide myself. We were sleeping on burlap sacks filled with straw. These "mattresses" were stacked up one upon the other against the wall every morning. I hid among them and remained there for a few days.

Fink, whom I treated decently, took care of me. He brought me some food and above all, water. He also listed me as being in the infirmary. Years later, I discovered that I did not have typhus, but recurrent fever, caused by drinking the milk from the dozens of emaciated cows.

One day, about 20 of us were marched outside the camp into the adjacent settlement where the SS guards were living. We were to do some road repair work. It was a pleasant summer afternoon; the young Germans were sitting on the porches of the tidy houses, drinking beer. They were cheerful, well fed members of the master race. We were bedraggled starved subhuman creatures. Suddenly, one of them leaped to his feet and yelled "Halt!" The column of slaves came to a standstill. He motioned to me to step out. "Du hasst uns Du Schweinehund!" (You hate us, you pig dog), he yelled as he shoved me against the wall, ready, in his words, to teach me a lesson. His comrades restrained him and I was permitted to return to the group. He perceived that I was alive, not only in body but also in spirit. It was offensive to this SS man that I was not dehumanized. Even now, the memory of this episode evokes a triumphant feeling. Amidst the destruction of my world, they did not break me. For a Jew to challenge the Germans was suicidal, it was even dangerous to appear human.

My short confinement to a concentration camp made me aware of the range of human behavior among the Germans. Some were sadistic, yet others did not tolerate the abuse of prisoners. A group of us were taken to the railroad station to clean up slag. The steam locomotives used coal as fuel, and the coal did not burn completely, leaving more cinder than ashes. Piles of slag were dumped next to the railroad tracks at the Topolya railroad station.

Six of us were loading slag onto a truck, guarded by a young SS man, who was an ethnic German from Croatia and known for his cruelty. He imposed an exhausting speed of work. The fully loaded truck pulled away, giving us a brief respite. We stood around the heap of slag resting on our shovels. This sight provoked our SS guard, who ordered us to do push ups on top of the cinders. Whoever stopped was hit with the butt of his submachine gun, or kicked. While he was busy tormenting another fellow, I lay motionless; when he was close, I resumed the push-ups. He caught on to my ploy. Screaming, he ran to me, put his boot on my neck and began to hit me with the butt of his gun.

Suddenly a burst of gunfire caught everyone's attention. It came from the freight train loaded with German desert troops (Afrika Korps), wearing the typical beige uniforms. An officer standing in the open door of the freight car yelled to our guard, "Du Schweinehund! (You pig dog), we are fighting a war and you are playing games. Stop or I will shoot you." The SS man ordered us to stand up. The soldiers surrounding the officer cheered and laughed. A few minutes later, the train with my unknown German hero pulled away.

We expected at this point to be punished with vengeance by the humiliated SS man, but the opposite happened. He stood at a distance watching us load the slag onto the trailer without demanding unreasonable speed. At the end of the day, a truck came from the camp to take us back. The push-up ordeal made our muscles sore and exhausted. We had great difficulty climbing onto the truck. We helped each other without any objection from the SS man, which was not his style.

To have shoes in good condition was important in the camp, particularly if an escape opportunity presented itself. There were shoemakers in the camp that did shoe repair for the German guards, but a prisoner could get his shoes repaired if he gave something of value to one of the shoemakers. My shoes were in disrepair and I planned on using the two cigarettes that Milan had given me in Szeged to pay the shoemakers to fix them. I soon learned that a fellow prisoner, a passionate cigarette smoker who slept next to me, stole my two cigarettes and smoked them. I was indignant; his response was "You are not a smoker, you don't need cigarettes. I was dying for a smoke." He felt no guilt; in his view he was entitled to take my cigarettes because he was in need of a smoke. "I did not take a piece of bread from you," he argued self-righteously.

The rest of our group did not share his view, and the price he paid was not worth the pleasure he got from smoking. He became an outcast. I doubt that he survived; hedonism was not adaptive during the Holocaust. This was the only theft that I remember by a Jew from a Jew during the war.

Imagination is more important than knowledge...
-Albert Einstein (1879 - 1955)

Chapter 16
Budapest Once Again

On July 20, 1944, the Szeged group, as we were known, was ordered to report to the gate office. We were placed in a little room and told to stand at attention. The camp commandant appeared and told us that we would be taken to a special facility in Budapest. It was apparent from his questions that he and his staff were puzzled by the order from Gestapo headquarters in Budapest. He demanded to know what kind of criminals we were to be of interest to high Nazi officials in Budapest. None of us could satisfy his curiosity. We were also in the dark about this unusual development. I wondered if it had something to do with my giving Milan my mother's address. The commandant expressed his frustration by taking off his belt and flaying it around wildly. The blows of the massive buckle were quite painful.

A covered truck pulled up outside. Usually we were transported in open trucks. Another innovation was that we were chained to each other. They did not have handcuffs, merely short pieces of chain and padlocks. Hans and I were the first ones to be chained together. The Untersturmbandfuehrer (lieutenant) who was in charge, had difficulty getting the chain tight enough around our wrists. Hans made the "helpful" suggestion to cross the chain between our wrists. The commandant who was looking on asked us to twist our wrists and the chain fell to the ground. As usual, Hans was planning for an escape. Hans and I got an additional beating. Once we were loaded on the truck, our ankles were also chained together. We were forced to lie on our backs and forbidden to talk. We had no idea why we were getting this special treatment. We did not know our destination. Execution was a definite possibility.

Four SS men guarded us during the trip. One was the driver; next to him was an SS-Untersturmfuehrer (second lieutenant) who was in charge. Two young SS men sat on a bench in the truck with us. They were mean, often poking and hitting us with their submachine guns if we moved or talked.

The truck stopped as soon as we crossed the border from Yugoslavia into Hungary, next to a roadside inn. Our guards, all but one went in for a beer. In

Hungary, the Germans felt welcome. In occupied Yugoslavia, they were hated and feared attacks by partisans. Suddenly, the three SS-men called the one guarding us. They seemed excited. We were left alone. Hans and I dared to sit up and look outside.

The four SS men stood in a huddle and were talking in an animated manner. We could not hear them. Soon after, the guards returned and we dutifully assumed our prone positions. The two young men were quiet and appeared sad. I assumed that a family member or a close friend had died. We moved and they did not shout, we whispered to each other and were not beaten. We even sat up and there were no objections. Finally, one of them said that Hitler had been assassinated. The sadness of these young men at the loss of their beloved Fuehrer was profound. I think of this moment whenever I am told that Nazism and Hitler were imposed upon the German people.

Our elation gave way to disappointment when our guards found out at the next stop that Hitler was alive, and that he had given a speech. Yet they continued to treat us in a relatively decent manner. Something had changed; it was as if Hitler had lost his superhuman powers.

Years later, I found out that an officer named Count von Stauffenberg had left a bomb in a briefcase in a conference room at Hitler's field headquarters at Rastenburg, East Prussia. It was Hitler's good luck that another officer inadvertently shoved the briefcase out of his way, to the far side of the massive oak conference table, which shielded Hitler from the full force of the explosion.

A stenographer and three officers died, but Hitler escaped with only minor injuries. Hitler's survival undermined the plot of the military officers to take over the government and negotiate for peace. The explosion took place at 12:42 PM on July 20th.

I found out later that also on July 20th, the Red Army had crossed the River Bug into Poland. On July 29th, Soviet tanks were 12 miles east of Warsaw.

When we arrived in the city of Budapest, the truck came to a stop and the SS men asked for directions to Columbus Street. We had no idea what was on Columbus Street. At the next stop we were ordered to disembark, the chains were removed and the truck pulled away. To our amazement we were greeted by Mimis and surrounded by smiling, relaxed Jews. We were free.

The Columbus Street camp was located on the grounds of what used to be a fashionable school in the middle of the town. An SS man stood guard at the entrance. This facility, called a camp, was established as the result of negotiations between the Gestapo and Rudolf Kasztner, the head of the Jewish Aid and Rescue Committee, known in Hebrew as "Vaada." The residents of the Columbus camp were to be transferred to Switzerland in exchange for trucks and money. This camp was located in a residential area in Budapest and had a decorative fence around it; one could simply walk out from it. Mimis put his arms around me, "You are the one who did it," he kept repeating.

He explained that our freedom was the work of Milan. The Germans were bribed with dollars and with a letter from my mother written in Russian saying that the Gestapo chief in Szeged was helpful to Jews. The Szeged Gestapo chief was getting ready for the advancing Red Army and wanted a statement that he hoped would save his life. In July of 1944, the shoe was on the other foot. My trust in Milan had not been a mistake after all. He got in touch with Mother and established contact with Mimis through her.

We were taken to a fancy apartment on the second floor and led into a stately dining room. A long table had chairs around it, and as the guest of honor, I was placed at the head. To this day I can vividly see a large tureen filled with soup in the middle of the table. After a good meal, Mimis told me to take a shower so that I would look presentable. Unlike the rest of the group, I was within walking distance of my mother's apartment.

After I took a shower, I was about to hop over the low ornamental fence to walk to mother's apartment, when I heard over the loudspeaker an announcement in German requesting that people who were brought from Topolya should report to the office. I did not like the sound of it and sought out Mimis to ask what I should do. He seemed puzzled and was hesitant in giving me an answer. After some hesitation, he told me to report to the office. A few minutes later, a few SS men walked in and ordered us to follow them. We were placed into a truck. To the best of my memory, there were only four of us at this point. The two brothers once again were not loyal and had deserted the camp. We wondered about our destination, but it did not take Hans and I long to discover that we were being taken to the dreaded Gestapo Foe Street Prison. To our knowledge no Jew who entered this place ever came out alive.

Amikam and I were placed in a large overcrowded cell. There were close to thirty men in it, but only eight bunks; the rest slept on the floor. All were middle aged or older, most of them leading figures in the Hungarian Jewish community. The prison was relatively modern, with flush toilets. One man used a piece of cloth to turn the knob to the toilet door; he was afraid of catching an infection, which seemed amusing under the circumstances. Many Hungarian Jews still did not sense the real danger that was facing them.

The only other fellow close to us in age was Peretz Goldstein who, for some reason, was called "Franz." Amikam was intrigued by the fluency of Franz's Hebrew.

"It is strange. Franz uses words in Hebrew which are known only to people who live in Eretz Israel but he denies ever visiting Palestine," Amikam told me. One day I looked at the boots belonging to Franz; inside was a tag that said, "Made in England." There was also some inscription identifying them as British army boots. In those days this was a dead giveaway as to his identity. We confronted Goldstein with our evidence and he told us an incredible story.

A group of Jewish parachutists from Eretz Israel were trained by the British Armed Forces and dropped into Yugoslavia to organize Jewish resistance in Hungary. He was one of them. Peretz Goldstein and I spent many hours in serious discussions and became friends. He was my first introduction to the expectation that the Jews of Europe should have offered armed resistance to the Germans; an assumption I made clear to him, that was not possible. Goldstein told me about Hannah Szenes, who had also been apprehended. She was being held on the floor below us. I was in awe of the courage of these young people but dismayed by their lack of understanding about the conditions in Europe. Little did I know how famous Szenes and Goldstein would become.

Boredom and anxiety soon dominated our mental life. In the Hungarian prison in Szeged and in Topolya, we had been physically active. In the Foe Street Prison we were never let out of our cell, even during bombing raids, which usually occurred at night. The SS guards went to the bomb shelter during these raids, but the prisoners remained in the cells. I had fantasies that a bomb would hit our prison without killing us and give us an opportunity to escape. I felt strangely invulnerable to the usual dangers of life. My primary concern was to avoid being killed as a Jew.

One day, Amikam and Goldstein were taken out of the cell to be interrogated. They were both amazed that the Gestapo officer who questioned them spoke some Hebrew. His name was Adolf Eichmann; he was familiar to me from Szeged. There was much excitement about his visit to the Gestapo headquarters in Szeged. I was assigned to wash his black Mercedes, which had an elegant black trailer for luggage.

Another day, the iron door to our cell opened with a bang and a young SS man entered. Everyone stood at attention. He stretched out his hand, pointed his thumb down and everybody fell to the ground. He pointed his thumb up and everybody jumped up. This went on for a while. Some of the older men could not keep up. He kicked them until they resumed the activity. I found out that this SS man was nicknamed "Ivan the Terrible." Another time, a different and older SS man appeared in the door and made the same gesture. I quickly fell to the ground, as did the other new arrivals. The old-timers were amused and we were perplexed. With this SS man, all we had to do was stomp our feet. He was merely pretending to torment the prisoners to keep up his reputation. He was called "Istvan," which was not his name.

Ivan the Terrible was likely to visit us if he heard animated voices inside the cell. When he was on duty, we kept quiet. When Istvan was the guard on our block we did not even hide our chessboards. Those of us who played chess donated a portion of our bread rations to make chess figures. The black bread was like clay. The chessboard was a piece of paper. Like my father, I was a good chess player.

We were completely isolated from the outside world. New prisoners were the only source of information. Our main interest was the progress of the Red Army. One new arrival was a simple Hungarian Jew, a window washer. He presented a striking contrast to the bankers, doctors and other prominent Jews in our cell. The Gestapo had arrested him because he was a cousin of Fiorello LaGuardia, the Mayor of New York City.

From time to time, prisoners were taken from their cells. Rumor had it that they were sent to the concentration camp, Mauthausen. My optimism amused my cellmates, all of whom were older men. They watched me shine my shoes and comb my hair every Thursday in preparation for being released or having an opportunity to escape on Friday. "Friday is my lucky day," I would insist. One day, a Wednesday, Amikam and I were told to get ready to be taken out of the cell. We were taken to a holding area where the rest of our small Szeged group was waiting. We were loaded on a truck and taken to Szeged. We anticipated going back to Topolya or worse.

Upon arrival in Szeged at the Gestapo headquarters, we were taken to the familiar makeshift prison where we had been housed on our prior "visit." We had no idea what would happen to us. Before long, Milan made his appearance. "You will be out of here in a day or two," he told me.

The next night, the SS men guarding us disappeared. Milan arrived and told us to follow him. We entered the main building, which was the only way to the outside from the courtyard. Suddenly, we heard loud voices and a group of Gestapo men coming down the steps. These were men who had not cooperated with Milan. He became visibly shaken. We could not go forward nor could we go back to the backdoor because we would be spotted. Milan quickly opened a door leading to a closet and shoved us inside. We could hear him conversing casually with the Gestapo men, who spoke in loud boisterous voices. "They've been drinking," Hans whispered to me.

A little while later, Milan retrieved us from the hiding place and we were on the way to the railroad station. This had been a close call. I found out during the trip that the Gestapo Chief was bribed by the then astronomical sum of $10,000 to facilitate our "escapes," in addition to the letter written by my mother. The money came from Hashomer Hazair.

We arrived in Budapest in the early hours of the morning. Milan gave each member of our group some money and told them to find their way to friends. He delivered me to my mother, a reunion that I have no memory of, as overwhelming emotions, good or bad, are often repressed.

I do remember vividly my next day in town. I was in dire need of a haircut but did not want to go to a nearby barber. The length of my hair could arouse suspicion. I found a barbershop on Rakoczy Street, which was the main boulevard in Budapest. The shop was upstairs, a small one-man operation. I was sitting in the barber chair with a white cloth around my neck when two SS men walked in and sat down to wait their turn. One of them kept looking at me. I recognized him quickly as the SS-man we called "Ivan the Terrible" from the Foe Street Gestapo Jail. I was convinced that he recognized me and lunged up from the chair and ran to the stairs, getting rid of my white cloth along the way. The SS men were after me with the zeal of men pursuing a fugitive from justice. I ran with the fervor of a boy fighting for his life. I lost them in the crowded streets of the city. I was free from incarceration, but I was not free from danger. The law of the land was still that I had no right to live.

While in the Foe Street Prison and even in the concentration camp, Topolya, I used say in jest, "This is like a vacation from fear." In the camp I did not have the apprehension that comes with being on the run. On false papers I was constantly anxious. In spite of the dread of being unmasked now, it was wonderful to be free.

I thought a great deal about Peretz Goldstein and Hannah Szenes and I asked Rafi about them. Rafi was quite annoyed by this undertaking. They caused nothing but trouble for us, he told me. He explained that Peretz, by his inept wandering around Budapest, had endangered our lives. In the past, our concern was primarily the police, but because of this mission, we became an object of interest for the Hungarian espionage agency. This was the reason for our group being handed over to the anti-espionage agency when we were apprehended in June on the border to Romania. They considered us spies for the British Armed Forces. I attributed this then to the overactive imagination of Hungarian border police. Rafi was particularly critical of Hannah, who had been apprehended even earlier than Goldstein. Years later Asher Cohen, Professor of Contemporary History, involved with the Institute for Holocaust Studies at the University of Haifa, would write:

> In June, during the height of the deportations, three Jewish paratroopers from Palestine, including Hannah Szenes, arrived in Hungary. Though they were prevented from contributing to the practical work of rescue, their arrival had a sizable psychological impact on those involved in Halutz Resistance, for whom it symbolized the unity of the Jewish people.[45]

The very opposite was the case. Only a handful of people knew about the futile mission and Hannah Szenes was arrested after she had barely crossed the border to Hungary. Only the Germans and Hungarians knew about her. These "arrivals" increased the risk that we faced in Budapest, but my admiration and affection for Peretz Goldstein was strong and I felt the need to do something for him.

The Hungarian Jewish prisoners in Foe Street Prison received food from relatives. Peretz and I had no official relatives and received no packages. I decided to deliver a food package for him. My sister and I went to the Foe Street Prison to drop off a small suitcase with food for Peretz. I planned to leave it at the gate but the guard insisted that we go inside. He instructed us to empty the suitcase of the food. Prisoners were not allowed to have suitcases. It was scary to be inside the dreaded walls as a visitor delivering a package. However, it was satisfying to leave as one.

My standing in the Zionist underground increased after the Romanian adventure. Rafi, Mimis and Pil treated me with deference. I was praised for my resourcefulness in making the contact with Milan. In the past, I never knew the residence of any leader of our group. I had only "floating" contact with them; we met in parks or on street corners.

Now I knew where each one of the leaders lived. I was pleased to visit the apartment of Rafi, who was in charge of the group. I met his wife and was introduced to his mother. Rafi spoke to her in German about me. It must have been favorable because she gave me a hug. I became part of the inner circle and was treated as if I was much older than 16.

The leaders entrusted me with important assignments. I became the contact person to a group of Dutch officers who had escaped from a German prisoner of war camp. These men instructed us in military tactics and the use of weapons. The meetings took place in our apartment and other safe locations. Our entire arsenal consisted of three revolvers that I carried in a briefcase to each session. I also took part in planning sessions of the coup.

I had access to the "Glass House." This was the name of a building with the address of 29 Vadasz Street, which housed the Department for Foreign Representation of the Swiss Legation. Actually, the members of the Zionist rescue organization staffed the whole place. Rafi Friedel was one of the officials in charge. The Swiss vice-consul in Budapest, Charles Lutz, provided this superb cover for us. To have the headquarters of an illegal organization in a structure with diplomatic immunity was too good to be true.

This comfortable arrangement was destroyed, not by police work, but by an inquisitive reporter. One day, I read with horror a headline in the daily Hungarian paper exposing the "Glass House" as a front for Jewish organizations. To our surprise the police took no action. But our Hungarian Jewish elders demanded that we change our conduct. Arthur Weisz, the owner of the building and the contact man with the Swiss officials, insisted that most of our activities be moved from the Glass House. Document forging could no longer be done in this setting. The Hashomer Hazair members were mostly young Slovaks and a few Hungarian Jews. We often disagreed with the older Hungarian Jewish leadership. I had no direct contact with them, but heard about the tension that existed between the Relief and Rescue Committee (the Vaada), and our leaders Rafi, Pil and Mimis, about the methods. While I had been away in the camp, the 164,000 Jews of Budapest were relocated into specially designated Yellow-Star houses. Naturally, none of our people lived there; all of our members were living on Aryan papers.

Elegant Hungarian men wore long leather coats tailored in the typical "Magyar" way. I casually mentioned once to Mimis that such a coat made one look like a true Hungarian, and he immediately insisted that I order one for myself. These coats were very expensive. It had never occurred to me that I would be given money for such a luxury item. "You deserve it," Mimis told me, in obvious reference to my establishing the contact with Milan. The coat was made to order; and would be ready on October 15, 1944. I know the date because of what happened just before I picked up the coat. On October 15, 1944 the Germans placed Ferenc Szálasi in power as prime minister. Szálasi and his Arrow Cross (Nyilas) party were murderously anti-Semitic.

I met Mimis that day in the park and he gave me the money for the coat. Suddenly, there was commotion in the streets with lots of military activity. "Go home at once," Mimis advised. I hesitated briefly but decided to pick up my leather coat because I wanted its protective value. It made me look Hungarian.

The war news was encouraging but the takeover of the Hungarian Government by the Nyilas party was a disaster for the remaining Jews. The Hungarian Nazis were bent on finding "foreign Jews." Every Polish refugee was suspected of being a Jew trying to pass as a Christian. It again became routine for the police to resolve doubts about a man's identity by an inspection of his penis. Phimosis, a congenital condition making retraction of the foreskin impossible, required circumcision and was, in the beginning, used by some Jews in Budapest, just as in Poland, as an explanation. This story did not work anymore, even for a genuine Christian.

Circumcision, according to God's pronouncement "… shall be the sign of the covenant between me and you" (Genesis 17: 9-11). Benedict Spinoza said that this ancient ritual would ensure that Jews would survive as a separate people. It surely did not enhance survival on Aryan papers. The Jewish nose, the mainstay of anti-Semitic propaganda, was bad enough as an identifying feature, but it left room for some ambiguity. The circumcision was absolute proof. The Hungarian police and the Germans used more and more genital inspection whenever they had a suspicion that a man might be a Jew.

Hungarian Jews were assimilated and could easily pass for Hungarians except for this anatomical difference. Circumcision was resistant to assimilation. A story was told about a Jewish mother from a Polish shtetl who complained about her son's secular clothes.

"Mother that's the way people dress in Warsaw," her assimilated son explained.

"But why aren't you wearing a beard like good Jew?"

"But Mama all men shave in Warsaw."

"And the food? You at least keep a kosher kitchen?"

"Well Mamma it is almost impossible to observe dietary laws in a big city."

Mother then asked anxiously: "Son! Are you still circumcised?"

Contrary to the sentiments of this Jewish mother, the leadership of our group decided to deal with this feature of Jewish identity. We hired a Hungarian surgeon to devise a surgical procedure that would make a "Jewish" penis look like that of a Christian. The operation was simple; the foreskin was cut and sutured, reversing the circumcision. The problem was that the men would get erections during sleep that ripped apart the sutures. For the first 48 hours we watched them and kept them awake. There was a long waiting list for this "lifesaving" operation. Only two or three could be done per week. All of us carried a vial of surgical glue. In certain situations it was possible to glue the foreskin to the head of the penis before the inspection.

Eventually, my turn for the surgery arrived. The anatomical mark of my Jewish identity would be removed by a surgeon's skill. At this point, the Hungarian police and the Nyilas thugs were vigorously searching for Jews, but the sound of Soviet heavy artillery could also be heard. I did not know that the siege of Budapest would last two months. It was prudent to have the surgery but I had an aversion to it. Since Russian artillery was not far from Budapest, I decided to seek an alternative means of protecting myself. My leaders left this up to me.

My documents identified me as Jan Wojcik, a Polish refugee. It was dangerous to be a Polish expatriate unless one was not circumcised. I desperately needed new identity papers. One day a man rung the doorbell and I opened it with apprehension, he looked official. It turned out that he was a magazine salesman. At the door, as required by law, he showed me a document issued by the Hungarian Ministry of Interior to magazine vendors. This hard cover booklet looked like a passport. It had his photo and the Royal Hungarian insignia. I now had an idea of how to shed my no longer useful identity as a Polish refugee.

162

A few days later, I became an official magazine vendor and the proud owner of a document that identified me as Janos Wojcik instead of Jan Wojcik. I no longer carried the Polish refugee card, which gave rise to the suspicion that I might be a Jew. The magazine vendor's license was my new passport to life. The Ministry of Interior document and the leather coat became the backbone of my new Hungarian image. My Hungarian was good enough for a boy born in Kassa (Kocice), which had been a Slovak town until few years ago.

When I showed Mimis my Hungarian "passport" he gave me a hug and grew tearful as a sign of approval for my resourcefulness. Whenever there was a roundup of Polish refugees in the streets of Budapest, I showed my Ministry of Interior document and was presumed to be a Hungarian.

One day, I was in downtown Budapest when a dragnet for Polish refugees took place. A policeman looked at my document and let me get on a streetcar going away from the city center. A few stops later, I noticed a streetcar with a group of Polish Jews going into the city. I did not know them but had no trouble recognizing them as Jews. I jumped off my streetcar, hopped on the one going to the city center, and told them to get off.

Mother was still Aniela Rojek, a Polish refugee. It occurred to me that if mother married a Hungarian she would have a Hungarian last name and Hungarian papers. "Mother, you will marry a Hungarian man," I announced one day to my puzzled mother. When I explained my plan, she agreed, if it was clear that it was a sham. Mimis liked this idea and offered to give me the necessary money for a man willing to go along with this scheme. It was my task to find a bridegroom for my mother. Someone suggested the racetrack was a good place to find a down-and-out a man in need of quick cash.

I had never been to the Budapest Hippodrome. The place was full of animated and prosperous looking men. On my second visit, I spotted a man I thought would be a candidate. He looked like an alcoholic and did not seem affluent. He watched the races intensely but made no bets. I asked him questions about the horse race and betting. Finally I asked if he knew someone willing to help a Polish family. I told him that we were afraid that we might be deported to occupied Poland where conditions were bad. The only way to make sure we could stay in Hungary would be for my mother to marry, but she was a widow of a Polish officer killed during the war and unwilling to consider a real marriage. I mentioned a sizeable sum of money as a reward. He was willing, but he lived with his mother and had to discuss it with her. We agreed to meet the next day in the same place.

When he arrived the following day I observed him from a distance, wondering if he would come with policemen. He seemed alone and I approached him. He had good news. He would go along with the plan, but he had to meet my mother first. We agreed upon a price. He asked for more than I originally offered. It was to be paid after the ceremony. I was reluctant to show him where we lived, but he insisted on meeting Mother before the marriage formality which was to take place in the city registry.

On the streetcar ride I found out that he had been a successful accountant before he developed a method of winning money on the horse races. The coming together of two people who did not know each other, but who would be married in a few days seemed odd. My future "stepfather" got some money out of me before he left my mother's apartment. He claimed that he had to buy a black suit for the ceremony. This was an error on my part. He did not show up at the matrimonial office as agreed upon, and I gave up the idea of getting Mother married to a Hungarian.

The new regime unleashed a reign of terror against the Jews. The Nyilas party members had unlimited power over us. Our landlady's son-in-law, I believe his first name was Gabor, became a Minister in the new government. One day, Mrs. Csorba invited Mother to the opera. Mother sat in a box together with Szálasi. I went to the performance on my own just to be able to see Mother in the company of a Nazi dictator in the presidential box. Mother told us later that he was pleasant and polite. He kissed her hand, which was the proper thing to do when greeting a lady in Hungary. We had a good laugh about this scene.

A few days later, in the middle of the night, there was banging on our window. It was Milan dressed only in his underwear. He had escaped an execution site. The Gestapo had discovered his double agent role. He stayed with us for a few days; Mimis arranged false papers for him and transportation to occupied Yugoslavia. The roles were reversed, and now his survival required our help.

In the fall of 1944, it was obvious that Nazi Germany had lost the war, and we hoped that any day they would surrender. But we underestimated their determination. There was no doubt that the Szálasi regime's days were numbered. And yet the Hungarians were sparing no efforts to kill the remaining Jews. The pursuit of Jews who lived on false papers was relentless. Detectives, uniformed policemen, ordinary citizens and, naturally, members of the Arrow Cross Party, made an effort to ferret out the Jews who were not in the ghetto or the so-called Jew Houses. At the end of November and the beginning of December 1944, about 60,000 Jews living in the Yellow Star houses were herded into a ghetto in the center of town.

One day, while I was walking in the vicinity of the ghetto, a good-looking girl my age asked me for directions. She did not have the yellow Star of David, but because of her furtive manner I suspected that she was Jewish. At first she denied it, but when I told her that I was a Jew on false papers, she admitted that she had escaped from the ghetto. She had no documents and no place to go. Her family had been deported some time ago. I offered to let her stay with us, and she gladly accepted. Her name was Evika. I told Mrs. Csorba that she was a visitor from Kalocsa. Mother did not object to this "guest" and Olenka was delighted with a teenage companion.

Our quarters consisted of a large room that served as living and sleeping space and a small kitchen. Evika slept in the kitchen. During air raids people were confined to shelters. The Csorba villa had no basement and, therefore, the family had to seek protection in the shelter of a nearby apartment building. The public shelters gave anti-Semitic zealots a golden opportunity to look for Jews on false papers. Early in November, the Red Army was just outside of Budapest. Our landlady and her sickly daughter planned to move from the villa to a nearby building that had an air raid shelter. We were invited to join them, but decided to remain in our apartment. Russian artillery was less dangerous than the Jew hunters.

Shortly before the move, Mrs. Csorba had two SS-men as lunch guests. They were ethnic Germans born and raised in Hungary and longtime friends of the Csorba family. My mother, sister and I were also invited. During the meal the young men told us that each of them was in charge of a machine gun nest; they were non-commissioned officers. The frontline was just outside of Budapest. There was a mixture of contempt and admiration in their description of the Red Army assaults.

"We kill them like flies but they keep coming, they have no regard for human life," one of them said. These words made a real impact upon me, as did the next remark. "We have no doubt that we will be killed and the city will fall to the Soviets soon." I found an opportunity to be alone with them. I have an unforgettable image of these two SS-men sitting across from me in Mrs. Csorba's elegant salon.

"Why should you die for a lost cause? You speak Hungarian like natives. You can easily disappear in the city," I told them.

"What about these?" one of them said, pointing to the SS uniforms they were wearing. I offered an easy solution. "At the end of the dinner, drive your car a few blocks and abandon them. Hide in our garage, I will open the side door and in the middle of the night I will bring you civilian clothing. You can stay with us. Mrs. Csorba is moving into the air raid shelter tomorrow morning."

They agreed with expressions of gratitude. Mrs. Csorba's son-in-law had a closet full of suits. After the Csorba family went to sleep, I sneaked upstairs and took two suits and shirts, which I delivered to the garage as promised. My conscious explanation for this undertaking was that I was helping the war effort. Now there were two less Germans to kill the Russians. It is more likely that I responded to the need of two young men for help. My hostility to Nazi Germany did not include these two members of Waffen SS, in fact, we became friends of sorts.

A day later, the Russian artillery shells were falling in our neighborhood. The Csorba family moved into the nearby building with an underground shelter. The two SS deserters moved in with us from the garage. They slept on the floor. The three of us scrounged some wood to protect our ground level windows. They were proficient in building such reinforcements. We did this between the barrages of the "Katyushas," the Soviet counterpart to the familiar German rocket launchers called "Nebelwerfer" (mist thrower) that I saw often on the German newsreels.

One day, a man wearing an official looking hat and an armband identifying him as an air raid warden visited us. Naturally, we were alarmed. Evika and I engaged the man in conversation and offered him a cup of tea. Our fear gave way to concern for we were certain he was a Jew on false papers. It was troubling to us that he was so recognizable because of his facial features. I asked him to follow me into the kitchen and told him that we thought he was a Jew. He naturally denied it at first. I invited him to stay with us and assured him that we were concerned with his safety.

"You are too easy to recognize as a Jew," I told him and he gave up pretending. We now had one more "guest." I did not tell him that I was a Jew. He believed that we were Polish Christian refugees and that he was the only Jew. In reality, out of the seven people in the Csorba villa, five were Jews and two were German.

A few days later, a German detachment of the Wehrmacht established a machine gun nest in front of our villa. They were older men who were surprised to see us in a building without a shelter. The two SS deserters pretended not to understand German, so it fell upon me to talk with them. My ability to speak German was minimal. I asked with pretended concern how we could avoid the Soviets. I was told to sit tight, the whole city was surrounded but reinforcements were on the way. Fortunately, they did not sound very persuasive. How ironic that the two SS men pretended not to speak German and I, a Jew, pretended to be afraid of my liberators.

Two days later, a Red Army unit got into the neighboring villa and opened fire. The Germans climbed into the dugout they had prepared earlier. All of us were huddled under the windows to avoid the occasional bullet or shrapnel that burst through our wooden reinforcement. When there was a break in shooting, the fellows and I would sit at the table and play cards, to my mother's dismay. The picture of two SS men and two Jews enjoying a simple game of cards now seems surreal.

Liberty is always unfinished business.
-Franz Kafka

Chapter 17
The Unexpected Liberators

We awaited the Russian attack of our house eagerly; we were unmindful of the danger of house-to-house combat. The Russians from the villa next door encouraged the Germans to give up. Someone who was more fluent in Yiddish than German was broadcasting through a loudspeaker to the Germans, suggesting that they surrender. A Jew was promising Germans a less harsh captivity if they cooperated. What a difference a few months can make!

The Germans, after an exchange of fire, retreated to the house across the street; our side of the boulevard was no longer German; we were no-man's-land.

I watched the open space between the houses intently. Mother taught me a few words in Russian to use as a greeting to our liberators. When I saw a group of about five soldiers run toward our house, I opened the door. A burst of machine gun fire came from the German side. The soldier who had just reached the door took a bullet to the top of his skull. The others jumped in. They spoke a language I could not understand. They were not the expected Russians. One of them put a gun to my head and shouted angrily. I realized that these were Romanian troops. "Polonaise! Polonaise!" I yelled, pointing at myself. I guessed they would understand my French. They did. The wounded soldier lay at my feet, his brain exposed. He was convulsing. His comrades paid no attention to him; they were busy shooting at Germans. I started dragging the dying man to the back of the house but was stopped by one of the soldiers. He rolled up the sleeve of the wounded man, exposing 4 or 5 watches that he removed and distributed to his friends. I then moved the dying man into the kitchen. This was in the back of the house, away from the combat area, where Evika and I tried to control his violent body movements. His bloody hands left red marks on the wall. The Romanian soldiers moved him out on a stretcher.

A few hours later, the Romanian troops had moved on in house-to-house combat. The sound of gunfire became distant. The Germans were retreating. The next morning I went out into the street and walked to the corner. A blanket of freshly fallen snow covered the deserted streets. It was a sunny January day. The image of this short walk is as fresh in my mind as if it happened yesterday.

Between a few houses I noticed a group of boys playing. I stopped to observe them. It seemed so strangely normal. They were playing soldiers. The bigger boys insisted that they were Russians, relegating the smaller boys to the status of Germans. This scene was a dramatization of our liberation from German captivity.

Our lives were no longer forbidden. It was an end to a dreadful past and a prologue to an uncertain future. We were free of our oppressors. Naturally, I had a sense of triumph, as my will to live had prevailed over the forces of destruction. I was a few months shy of 17 years old and had behind me accomplishments that would be unmatched by the decades of successful life that would follow. When I returned to the house, I noticed that the two SS men had disappeared. I no longer had to deal with the moral dilemma of protecting them. We had become "comrades in arms" during the siege of Budapest, and I would not have denounced them. They believe, no doubt, to this day that we were Poles. My plan had been to announce after liberation "Wir sind Juden" (We are Jews). But things were too hectic with the unexpected arrival of the Romanians to make this triumphant proclamation that I had enjoyed in my imagination.

Liberation did not bring a joyful feeling. How many other Jews were still alive? Were any members of our family, including Father, among them? We were not even free from hunger. My first task was to "organize" food from unoccupied houses.

A Red Army detachment, under the command of a lieutenant, entered our house a few hours after the Romanians had departed. Mother greeted the lieutenant in Russian. It turned out he was Jewish and spoke Yiddish. Mother cried as she hugged him. I noticed tears rolling down his cheeks as he listened to her story. I became emotional watching them in this animated exchange. It was good to see mother again in the role of an independent adult.

The assignment of this group of Russian soldiers was to confiscate privately owned automobiles and ship them back to the Soviet Union. They needed an interpreter to deal with the Hungarians, whose cars they were confiscating. I did not speak Russian but was able to converse with them, based upon the similarity of Polish and Russian. The lieutenant pronounced me the official interpreter and part of the group.

I was given a green military-like jacket and a green Russian hat without an insignia. A pair of woolen riding breaches and officer's high boots completed my impressive outfit. To my amazement, I was also given an automatic rifle and a two-minute instruction on how to operate it. The Jewish lieutenant called me a partisan. The implication of this pronouncement did not become clear to me until much later. It did not occur to me then that being a survivor was less than honorable. I was soon to discover that mere survival was dishonorable in the eyes of our liberators. Only partisans were welcomed.

At Mother's insistence, the first mission of the group was to find a doctor who could attend to a few abscesses on my neck. The SS man's boots on my neck in Topolya had caused a chronic infection. The lieutenant, his group of four or five soldiers and I got into their small truck to look for medical assistance. Ultimately, we ended up at the university hospital where physicians were busy helping the sick and wounded. The lieutenant pointed his rifle at the chief physician and shouted in Russian, "You take good care of his neck or I will kill you." I was supposed to translate this threat but I modified it into a polite request. The surgeon incised the abscess on my neck, which relieved some of the pain. My Russian benefactors gave me a few shots of vodka as an anesthetic.

We returned to our home just in time to save Evika from being raped by one of the Russians who had remained behind. I was the first one to enter the kitchen and found the young Russian struggling in bed with Evika. I grabbed him and we got into a fight. This would have ended badly for me had it not been for Mother's screaming, which attracted the attention of the lieutenant who had made himself at home upstairs. He ordered the whole group to stay away from our apartment.

Evika was a pretty girl who fascinated me. I was bashful with her and did not dare to make any sexual advances towards her, assuming that she was friendly only because I had saved her life. To my amazement, Evika asked me to go to bed with her when I returned from one of our missions. She told me that she loved me and wanted me to be the first man with whom she had sex. I did not believe it. I assumed she was merely trying to express her gratitude for helping her. Be it as it may, I was unable to have an erection. This fiasco ended our relationship. I felt humiliated and she felt rejected.

A few days later, she left our apartment and I had no contact with her until 1949, when I ran into her on the streets of Tel Aviv. She took me to her home and introduced me to her husband as a man who had saved her life. They had one child.

The friendly Jewish Red Army lieutenant and his group left a few days later and we were on our own. A few days after our section of town was liberated, the rest of our side of the Danube River was cleared of German units, though the fighting continued on the Buda side of the Danube. I made my way downtown and checked on the "orphanage" run by Dr. Oscar Osterweil, who I had helped before with the care of the children. Dr. Osterweil, a Polish Jew, had been a well-known physician in Krakow, but in Budapest he became the caretaker of a small group of Jewish children from Poland whose parents had been deported or killed. He was living with them in a small hotel. I was greeted with open arms and persuaded to become Dr. Osterweil's assistant. The first job was to secure food for the children. There was widespread looting going on in the city. I took a group of older boys and went looking for a grocery store to loot.

Dr. Osterweil invoked the biblical principle of Pikuach nefesh, which meant in Hebrew "concern with life." It allowed Jews to break the law to protect life. But we returned from our expedition without food; the food and clothing stores had been picked clean by the looters who preceded us. We did get some cosmetics thrown to us by friendly plunderers. A day or two later the boys and I stood in a long line at a food distribution center operated by the International Red Cross. My mother and Olenka were worried about my daily trips to the center of the city. There was no transportation and I had to walk all the way downtown.

Russian soldiers and some Hungarians attacked and robbed civilians. One day as I was walking home, two Russian military policemen stopped me and asked me for "Dokumenty." I showed them my documents that identified me as a Polish refugee. I proudly explained that I was a Polish Jew who had survived by pretending to be a Christian. I was under the mistaken impression that I had nothing to fear from my liberators. But the two Russian policemen, unlike the frontline soldiers, took a dim view of my being alive, and they accused me of collaborating with the Germans. They made some comments that traitors like me should be sent to Siberia. They debated with each other if I should be arrested. I was permitted to leave after my leather coat was "confiscated." Once again, being a Polish Jew was dangerous.

I was devastated by this encounter. It was bad enough to be robbed of a valuable possession by Soviet military policemen, but being accused of collaboration with the Germans was even more painful. This confrontation was a warning signal. I realized that my liberators could become my persecutors. This called for alteration in plans for the future. Our troubles were not over. Once again, we were in danger, this time from our "friends."

A few days after my confrontation with the Soviet Military Police, I was walking down Rakoczy Street and saw a storefront recruiting station for the Hungarian Communist Party. I walked in. A Hungarian Jew, a well-known Communist whose name I no longer remember, was in charge. I engaged him in conversation, told him who I was, and expressed my bitterness at being considered a collaborator because I was alive. He offered to issue me a document identifying me as a member of the Communist Party of Hungary, which would protect me. I removed a passport-like photo from one of my documents, which he affixed to a Communist Party identity card. The first page of this document had a red star. The inside text was in Russian and Hungarian. I no longer remember my new name. I retained the first name "Janos." This document was of great value to me in the next few months, particularly when I traveled to Poland. The term "identity crisis" was not as yet part of my vocabulary but it was part of my experience. I had to hide who I was even after the liberation. Would there ever come a time when I could safely be myself?

I found out later that a number of survivors were arrested by the Soviets and sent to the Soviet Union as collaborators with the Germans. Animosity to people who had survived enemy captivity was not new. In 1939, Stalin killed virtually all Red Army soldiers who returned to the Soviet Union from Spain after Franco's victory. This included Vladimir Antonow-Oveseenko, the Soviet Consul in Barcelona, one of the heroes of the 1917 revolution, who was executed. All of the generals were murdered. General Smushkevich, the head of the Soviet Air Force, was among them. At the end of World War II, Soviet prisoners of war who survived German captivity were not welcomed; most of them were sent to Siberia and many of them were killed. I did not know then that the Soviets were not alone in their antagonism to survivors.

Home is the place where, when you have to go there, they have to take you in.
— Robert Frost

Chapter 18
Return to Poland

After liberation in Budapest, we wanted to return to Poland as soon as possible. What happened to father, family and friends was uppermost in our minds. Mother was hoping to find her husband and we children expected to see our father in Poland.

It was too dangerous for Mother and my sister to travel under wartime conditions. I decided to go back to Poland by myself. Mother tried to dissuade me from going so soon. "I will have no trouble getting back," I told mother with the bravado of a nearly 17-year-old boy.

So one day in February 1945, I left the apartment alone in an effort to return to Poland. There was no civilian transportation. I set out on foot with a small backpack in which I carried food for the uncertain pilgrimage. I also had a few silk stockings and cigarettes that served as currency. European paper money was worthless at that time.

I sat by the roadside in the bitter cold, hoping to get a lift from one of the occasional Russian trucks. I tried to bite a piece of frozen bread and broke my front tooth. I took this as a bad omen for my trip. Soviet military vehicles did not stop for civilians, so getting on the roof of a freight train was the only alternative to walking.

I walked to the railroad station in Budapest in the hope of getting on a military train going north. To find out where a particular train was going was not easy. Once I found out the destination, getting on the train was another challenge. The trains were guarded by Soviet military police. I managed to get on the roof of a freight car and lay flat for hours before the train began to move. I was hoping that my information was correct and that the train was going to Bratislava, which was east of Budapest, but at least in Czechoslovakia. Once the train left the station, I sat up, holding on to a protrusion, fearful that I would fall asleep.

My train indeed stopped at Bratislava and I climbed down from the freight car. On the streets of Bratislava I met a Jew I knew from Budapest. He told me about a house in the middle of the city where liberated Jews gathered. I stayed there overnight, sleeping on the floor. There was no working toilet and no running water. The only place to urinate or defecate was on the floor in the attic. Many of the men and women liberated from concentration camps suffered from dysentery and had to make many trips to the attic.

It was a long ordeal before I reached the Polish border. I climbed aboard the roof of another freight train car going east. Many hours later the train stopped in the middle of nowhere. But we were in Poland and I was glad to be back on Polish soil. A nearby village was visible on the horizon. It was risky to leave the train not knowing when it would resume the journey but I wanted to visit my first Polish community and I was hungry. As I walked towards the village I passed an elderly woman who smiled strangely and kept looking back after I passed her. It was obvious she wanted to tell me something. I turned back and caught up with her.

"Pan jest Zydek?" (You are a Jew?) She asked. When I told her that I was, she suggested that I should not go to the village but was unwilling to give the reason for her advice. I realized that I would be in danger and returned to the freight train. It had not occurred to me that I would be harmed in a Polish village after the war.

I returned to the roof of the freight car, finding a spot next to a man who was quite a bit older than my usual rooftop companions were. He started talking in a friendly manner. In the middle of the conversation, he inserted a phrase I had never heard before, but I somehow understood that he was telling me that he was a Jew and wanted to know if I was one also. When he got his confirmation, he began to whisper to me that Poles killed returning Jews and I should be careful. I listened but could not believe what I was told.

After nearly a week on the road, I arrived in Krakow. I knew that father had been in the Plaszow concentration camp and somewhere I had heard the rumor that the Jews from Plaszow had been sent to the Mauthausen concentration camp. Whenever I ran into a "Katzetnik", a former concentration camp inmate, I would ask if he had been in Mauthausen and if he had seen my father there. No one had. In Krakow, there was a Jewish committee organized by the few Jewish survivors. They had a board that contained notices from survivors seeking relatives. I posted a message for my father. I looked for a message from him.

A few days later I made my way to Miechow, my hometown. I felt like a stranger in the familiar setting. I did not know the people and they did not know me. The same street corners where we had played as children were empty and dingy. People gave me suspicious and mean looks. I was struck by the absence of any traces of the Jews; thousands of them had lived in this town for hundreds of years.

My purpose in coming to Miechow was to find my father and friends who might have survived. The first Jew I met was Mr. Polsky, who had been a storekeeper before the war and a patient of my parents. He had no information for me about my father.

I also visited Polish friends with whom my parents had left some of our possessions. As I walked from one to house to another, I was met with varying degrees of hostility.

I remember one lawyer who was awakened by his wife when I came in the morning. I was ushered into the bedroom and noticed that the man was wearing my father's silk pajamas and had slept in our custom made bedding. He told me firmly that he knew nothing about my father and that my parents left nothing with him. Another family with whom my parents had left various valuables for safekeeping gave me the same treatment. No one gave a word of welcome or offered me a glass of water. Walking with a sense of gloom in the streets of my hometown, I met the mother of Dzidzia, my childhood sweetheart.

Mrs. Wroblewska was cordial but concerned with my safety. She recommended that I not stay overnight in Miechow. I was not persuaded that I was in danger in my hometown but she insisted: "They will kill you because you are a Jew." She was serious and troubled by what she was telling me. She recounted incidents of survivors being killed by Poles, and she told me about recent killings of Jews in nearby Dzialoszyce. "I thought you could become my son-in-law," she added laughingly, trying to change the subject.

Some Poles lived in our house and Mrs. Wroblewska told me that it was risky for me to visit the place. In spite of her advice, I did go to Pilsudski Street 23. I walked into the hallway without identifying myself. In my mind, the house on Pilsudski Street was still "our home." The initials "E.T." were still on the blue door that separated the upstairs apartment where we lived from the downstairs.

We had taken it for granted that if we survived, we would return to our home in Miechow. The Germans could chase us out of our house but they could not take our home from us. We believed that whatever the Germans did, even though real, was illegitimate and would be undone at the end of the war. After the war, life would become normal again. In spite of the admonition by Mrs. Wroblewska, I entered our building and walked up to the second floor.

I did not knock on the door to our apartment. Instead, I went back outside, tears running down my face. As I walked the familiar but unfriendly streets, I looked over my shoulders. I was in danger but I felt more anger than fear. I accepted being hounded by the Germans, for they were my sworn enemies. I expected to be safe in liberated Poland and welcomed in my native land. The pre-war anti-Semitism was a way of life that all of us accepted as the fate of the Jews in the Diaspora. The wartime anti-Semitism was shameful but these were dreadful times. Now the war was over and most Jews were dead. I hoped that there would be less, not more, hatred of the Jews.

"They will kill you because you are a Jew." These words spoken by the mother of my childhood sweetheart proved that the old hatred of the Jews grew stronger in the Jews' absence.

I soon discovered that it was unsafe to be identified as a Jew on a train. "Morderstwa pociagowe" (Train murders) became part of the new vocabulary of the returning Jews. Groups of Poles killed Jews they encountered on the trains. These murders created no news and remain little known to this day. I have never seen a reference to these killings in literature. The accounts that have come from small towns of assaults and murders of returning Jews could hardly be more horrific. I remember hearing on a train a man declare that Hitler deserved a monument (the Polish word "pomnik" is more evocative) for getting rid of the Jews.

After I witnessed a pogrom in Krakow, I went back to being Jan Wojcik instead of Emanuel Tenenwurzel. I was not about to let the Poles kill me after I had deprived the Germans of the pleasure. The fact that I had to use the German issued Kennkarte in the name of Jan Wojcik is a disgrace for Poland. To hide my identity from the Germans to save my life was a badge of honor. To conceal my Jewish identity to avoid the hatred of Poles during and after the war was reprehensible.

The Jewish community in spring of 1945 consisted of a small number of survivors of death camps and those who had managed to stay alive on Aryan papers. The Polish Jews who survived in the Soviet Union after being deported to Siberia had not as yet returned to Poland.

Years later, I read that Primo Levi had arrived in his hometown in Italy about the same time as I did in Miechow. As he entered the house he was welcomed by a celebratory chant of the concierge, "Ill Dottore!" His mother and family welcomed him. That night, he slept in the room in which he had been born. His friends came to greet him. He suffered 20 months of terrible experiences in the concentration camp, but he, unlike a Polish Jew, did not fear for his life after the war. He had a hometown, his house remained his house and he was welcomed in his country.

Between January 10, 1945 (liberation) and April 12 (President Roosevelt's death), I traveled from Hungary to Poland five times in the hope of finding Father. These trips were also a way to make money by smuggling goods from the relatively prosperous Hungary to the war devastated Poland. Each trip was an adventure. I traveled usually on the roofs of trains. A few times, I had the luxury of being inside a Russian troop train. I had good experiences with ordinary Soviet soldiers who, unlike the officials, were helpful when I traveled between Hungary and Poland. Two episodes stand out. It was forbidden for civilians to enter the trains reserved for the military, but I would tell the soldiers that I was returning to Poland or Hungary, depending which way I was going, and they would accept me as a refuge returning to his homeland.

Military police would go through the railroad cars and look for unauthorized passengers. I always wore a green military-like shirt, which I got from Russian soldiers. One time when the military police were approaching, a Russian soldier took off his hat with the military insignia and put it on my head. On another occasion they protected me by spreading a coat between themselves and playing cards on the coat as if it were a table; I was under the coat.

On my return to Budapest from a trip to Poland, in the Bratislava railroad station, I met a Pole wearing striped concentration camp garb. He was on his way to Poland. He had been liberated in Mauthausen and had met a camp dentist who was blond and blue-eyed. "He looked like a Polish officer," the Katzetnik told me. "Why?" I asked. "He wore black officer's boots," the man said.

That settled it for me. There was no doubt that it was Father, for he had such boots. I was overjoyed. "What a miracle! Our whole family is alive." I said.

My informant shared my feeling of happiness. I can still see his smiling face. I was grateful to him, gave him cigarettes and shared my food with him. I was ignorant then about the conditions in the concentration camp Mauthausen. Jews in that camp worked in stone quarries and died like flies. A Jew in an officer's high boots was unthinkable.

In my enthusiasm, I was ready to turn around and go back to Poland, but I had been gone for two weeks already. Mother would be worried in Budapest. I decided to return, tell Mother and Olenka that Father was alive, and then go back to Poland to find him. After a few days in Budapest once again, I went on the road, certain I would find father in Miechow or Krakow. In Miechow, I spoke again to Mr. Polsky, one of the few Jews who dared to live there. No, he had not seen my father.

I went back to Krakow, to look for the daily postings of lists of survivors prepared by the Jewish committee. Again, I returned to Miechow, determined not to leave Poland until I found Father. "Surely he would come to Miechow," I thought. This time, Mr. Polsky asked me to come back in an hour. He wanted me to meet two Jews who knew something about my father.

When I returned, Mr. Polsky offered me a cup of tea. Two men were sitting at the table next to Mr. Polsky. I recognized them as Miechow Jews but I didn't recall their names. They looked uncomfortable. "You remember Leon Storch," Mr. Polsky asked, "your father's dental technician?"

"Oh yes, I certainly remember him," I told him.

"It is a sad story," they said. "The three of us decided you must be told." Mr. Polsky was having difficulty talking, and he looked at the two other men as if hoping that one of them would continue, but they remained silent and did not look at me. Mr. Polsky had no choice but to continue.

"Leon developed typhus. The German 'cure' for a Jew with typhus was a bullet to the head. Your father hid Leon in his dental office. Amon Goeth from Plaszow was officially in charge of the Jews at the Lotnisko camp (Luftwaffe base). On an inspection, he found out that Leon was in the office, suffering from a high fever. He took out his gun, shot Leon, and then pointed the gun at your father, ready to shoot him also. The Luftwaffe Major who was in charge of the airport camp stopped him. They argued; they even pointed guns at each other." Mr. Polsky stopped briefly and I sensed that the worst was yet to come. "When the Major went on vacation to Germany, Goeth came back and took your father to Plaszow. Your father told him that he had gold buried in Miechow. Goeth sent your father and a few Jews under SS guard to dig in the garden of your house behind the post office. They found nothing. Your father hoped that the Major would come back and save him." Mr. Polsky stopped again and said: "Goeth shot your father in the presence of the whole camp. We did not have the heart to tell you at first," he said quietly.

I stood up, looked straight ahead, shook hands with Mr. Polsky and the two others and walked out without saying a word. I recall clearly that I did not cry.

I have no memory of telling my mother and sister about father's fate. My father was murdered before his 39th birthday.

Forty-two years later, in November of 1987, I returned one more time to Poland. I was invited to lecture at the Polish Institute of Neurology and Psychiatry in Warsaw, and was the guest of Polish Ministry of Health. A few days after my arrival, I once again visited Miechow.

I asked the driver to park in the Town Square and I walked slowly towards our former house. It was a drizzly November morning. I could see the lights in the upstairs windows where the bedrooms and my parents' office had been. The large distinctive balcony was still there, but the flower boxes were gone. When I came closer, I noticed a large sign on the house that read "School of Agriculture."

I entered the hallway, and a pleasant woman in her thirties inquired if she could help me. She was the director of the school. I said that I had lived in this house many years ago and merely wanted to look around. She responded in a huffy a manner. "I know nothing about that. All I know is we purchased this building from the previous owners and made it into a school." At this point, I saw that the door with the initials "E.T." had been removed and I realized, at long last, that this house was no longer my home. I wished the lady a good day and walked away. Strangely enough, I was neither bitter nor angry. I had accepted the reality that though I was born in Poland, I was a Jew and America was my homeland.

There is no sorrow above the loss of native land.
-Euripides

Chapter 19
A Man Without a Country

"Immigration is a desperate move, it should be avoided if at all possible," I told Professor Danuta Fjellestad, a Polish-born Swedish professor of literature visiting Detroit in the 1990s.

"But you chose to immigrate to America," she protested.

"I am different, I was a man without a country," was my reply. Professor Danuta Fjellestad looked at me and said: "I understand." She realized that I was a Polish Jew, not a Pole as she originally assumed.

We met in Detroit when I visited the home of my Polish friend and Professor of English Literature at Oakland University, Kasia Kietlinska. Kasia, whose father was a Holocaust survivor, grew up in Poland not knowing that her father, a Polish official, was a Jew. Professor Fjellestad had immigrated to Sweden after World War II. She met and married a Swede. Poland was still her country; Sweden was the land where she chose to live and work. That was not my situation.

The words of concern spoken by Mrs. Wroblewska in 1945, "They will kill you because you are a Jew," changed my bond to my native land. I lost the illusion that Poland was my fatherland and a void was created in my sense of identity.

A number of Holocaust survivors held on to the fantasy that Poland was their fatherland and remained in Poland. Most changed their names and kept their identity a secret, sometimes even from their own children.

The predicament of these Jews came into focus for me when I read Agata Tuszynska's *Lost Landscapes*, subtitled "In Search of Isaac Bashevis Singer and the Jews of Poland".[46]

"I was late for his death," is the first sentence of the autobiographical reflections of this Polish historian and bestselling author. Ms. Tuszynska was not only "too late for the death" of Singer, she was too late to witness Polish-Jewish culture and did not acquire a Jewish sense of identity. She tells her readers that she did not know "of Singer's existence until that moment in 1978 when he received a Nobel Prize in literature. I didn't know any Jews, or at least I thought I didn't." Her mother was a Jew. Agata was raised a Catholic and did not know about her maternal Jewish roots until she was nineteen years of age. She thought she did not know any Jews because as late as 1978, most of the Jews who remained in Poland concealed their identity. She writes that Singer lived longer in New York than in Poland, yet believes that "He never really made the move to America. He wore the past like an overcoat, whatever the season. His permanent address remained in Poland."

Ms. Tuszynska knows a great deal about Singer, but she is mistaken about Singer's real address. The person Yitshek Bashyevis Zinger (his name in Poland), and Singer the American writer, never had a home in Poland, merely a residence. Singer became an American writer in Yiddish, writing about Jewish culture in Poland. Singer moved from Warsaw to New York, body and soul. It is Tuszynska who has one foot in Warsaw and one foot in New York.

Ms. Tuszynska was searching for her own identity. Singer never lost his. Tuszynska discovered through Singer that she was a stranger to her own background. Thanks to Singer, she knows that on Zabia Street one could find the Jewish hatters, and that on Franciszkanska Street were dealers in leather goods, textiles, rare books and pens. She learned a great deal from Singer about Jewish prayers, the Holocaust, and Polish anti-Semitism.

Exploring Singer's roots, Tuszynska discovered that she was a stranger in Poland. Leopold Wardak, a Pole she met on a train, introduced her to the "Big Lie" of Polish anti-Semitism. Polish anti-Semitism was merely a reaction to Jewish communism she was told. Mr. Wardak offered additional insight:

Before the war there was no anti-Semitism, only some minor harassment. In my opinion, it's a matter of different personalities. A Jew liked to cheat, to trade; he didn't go out with Poles to drink vodka; he followed his own path. They didn't mingle with Poles. They were separate. Our young men harassed them. For example, combating Jews was part of National Unity Camp's program. "Don't buy from a Jew." They set up picket lines in front of their stores. On the other hand, the Occupation was a planned tragedy. Dozens of Jews were shot in front of our eyes.[47]

Tuszynska found another informant in the hometown of Singer - Mr. Stefan Modzelewski, who told her that Jews and Poles got along just fine;

...they leased orchards in the country. Trade was in their hands for the most part. They were very frugal. Sure, they cheated, but that wasn't why they controlled trade. The Jews had their own wholesaler from whom Jewish shopkeepers got a discount, more than the Pole got. That's why the Poles couldn't compete with them. A Jew always sold for less because he paid less at the wholesaler. That's why the slogan "Don't buy from a Jew" was designed to help Poles.[48]

Thus anti-Semitic actions, in Modzelewski's view, were indispensable self-defenses; the Poles were victimized by the Jewish lack of fairness. Others told Tuszynska of the looting of Jewish stores by Poles when the Germans occupied Poland. She found out that Jewish cemeteries were desecrated and that the word "Jew" was an insult. These were not regrets but cherished memories. She was informed,

> ...they (the Jews) started communism everywhere, only not in their own country, not in Israel. ...No doubt if Hitler had taken a different position toward them, they would have served Hitler too.[49]

Tuszynska needed Singer in order to discover what it was like to be a Jew living in Poland. Singer and I experienced it. Living in Poland as a Jew before the war was a life of daily degradation and humiliation. During the war, with rare heroic exceptions, Poles assisted the Germans in its genocidal project.

Even reading Singer's books was offensive to some Poles. Tuszynska experienced the hostility first-hand:

> During my trip back to Warsaw from Lublin, a young man on the train chews me out for reading a book by that disgusting Jew Singer. 'Don't we have enough real Polish writers?' he asked.[50]

We are not told if Ms. Tuszynska informed her train companion that the "disgusting Jew Singer" was the recipient in 1978 of the Nobel Prize for Literature.

Tuszynska believes that Singer left Poland on April 19, 1935, influenced by the "dark specter of Nazism" that was hanging over Europe. In 1935, Polish Jews were concerned with anti-Semitism in Poland. Germany, so close geographically, was far removed from the daily life of Polish Jews.

The discovery of past and present hatred of the Jews in Poland created an identity crisis for Agata Tuszynska, a Polish writer with Jewish ancestors. Had she been in Stockholm on December 8, 1978 she would have heard Singer say, upon the receiving the Nobel Prize: "Children don't read to find their identity. They don't read to free themselves of guilt, to quench thirst for rebellion, or to get rid of alienation."

Singer left his native Poland because his identity there was the cause of constant hostility. I faced the same dilemma when I returned to my homeland. My cultural identity and my ethnic integrity were in irreconcilable conflict. Singer received a traditional Jewish education at the Warsaw Rabbinical Seminary. Yiddish was his language. He was at home in the separate Jewish culture. Unlike him, I was at home in Polish culture and wanted to resume life in Poland after the war. When I returned, it became obvious that I could remain in Poland only if I denied my identity. I was now a man without a country.

Forgiveness does not change the past, but it does enlarge the future.
-Author Unknown

Chapter 20
Germany: The Promised Land

During my trips to Poland in 1945, I met concentration camp survivors who had been liberated in Bergen-Belsen and other camps located in Germany. These Jews came to Poland looking for family members. They told me that in Germany there was food, freedom and safety. Word of mouth was the only source of information. I was told that in West Germany, in contrast to Poland, a Jew did not run the risk of being killed. I decided that we would go to Germany. It was hard to persuade Mother that we had to plan another escape. This time we were running away from our Soviet liberators.

Mother wanted to resume her career in Poland. I, a teenager, had become the breadwinner and family decision-maker, but now that the war was over she expected to resume the role of a parent. In Poland she would again become "Pani Doktor Kowarska-Tenenwurzel."

The reality was that the war against Jews in Poland was still in progress. Mother found it hard to believe that in Poland it was dangerous to live as a Jew. Nothing like this was happening in Budapest. The Soviet Union controlled both countries, she argued. She did, however, accept my judgment that we should not return.

We could not go to Germany directly because we were Polish Jews and were expected by our Soviet liberators to return to socialist Poland. The Soviet military police controlled the borders. My plan was to get to Prague from Budapest and find a way to the West from there. I had heard that Mimis and other members of the Hashomer Hazair organization had returned from Budapest to their native Czechoslovakia. They were active in smuggling survivors to Palestine, via the U.S. zone of occupation.

One day, in the early hours, we gathered a few items of clothing and packed them into a small suitcase with a double bottom, into which I stuffed US Army occupation marks that I exchanged on the black market for dollars. I had earned them by smuggling goods from Budapest to Poland. I felt like a rich man; my treasure was worth about $5,000, a huge sum in those days in Europe. We sneaked out of our apartment without saying goodbye to our landlady. We did not want anyone to know where we were going.

Once again, we had to leave behind most of our acquisitions. I regretted leaving my books and a collection of magazines dealing with the war. Before the war ended I was thinking that if I survived, I would write a book. I had great interest in the influence of anti-Semitic propaganda. In 1944 in Budapest, I started collecting the anti-Semitic weekly newspaper *Der Sturmer,* which had been published in Germany since 1923. My rudimentary knowledge of German grew by reading about the "evil Jews." The editor was Julius Streicher, an elementary school teacher, one of the earliest Nazis in Germany, and a close friend of Hitler. He initiated the campaign of hatred that led to the passage of the Nuremberg laws in 1935. In the 1920s, his paper was so popular that Germans paid scalpers additional money to get a copy.

We took the streetcar to the outskirts of Budapest, hoping that a Russian military truck would give us a lift in the direction of Bratislava and Prague.

No Russian truck stopped, but to our surprise a small truck with a British flag came to a halt at the sight of Mother and Olenka standing by the roadside. I kept myself in the background. We climbed into the truck; we didn't speak English, but we were able to find out that they were going to Bratislava. Sitting in the back of this British vehicle, I underwent one more alteration of identity. I tore my Hungarian Communist card to pieces and threw it onto the road. From now on I would be Emanuel Tenenwurzel again. However, Mother and Olenka continued to call me Janek.

We hitchhiked from Bratislava to Prague and ended up in a camp established for liberated concentration camp inmates who were returning to their native countries. It was located outside of Prague in a section of town called, I believe, German colony. The camp consisted of makeshift barracks, which had been used by the Germans to house prisoners. The Polish Jews in the camp were supposedly all going back to Poland.

In reality, they were seeking ways of going west. In the camp I met Halina Bem, a blond girl with long braids. She reminded me of Gina. Her beauty, charm and competence attracted me. She was two years older and at first paid little attention to me.

Halina was the leader of a "kibbutz," a group of teenagers from Poland who had managed to get to Prague in an effort to go to Palestine. She had survived by pretending to be a Christian, encountering few difficulties in that role because of her fair complexion, light blond hair and blue eyes. We became instant friends and collaborators. I recognized in Halina someone whom I could trust and rely upon. She felt the same way about me.

The various clandestine Zionist groups in Prague looked after their own members, just as they had during the war in Budapest. Halina belonged to the middle-of-the-road Zionist party, but she was not getting much help from them. I got in touch with my old Budapest friends, Mimis, Pil and Rafi, who were in charge of Hashomer Hazair in Prague and active in smuggling Jews from Eastern Europe to Germany. They forged Red Cross documents identifying Polish Jews as returning concentration camp inmates from Germany or Greece, which justified their travel west. The war was over, but the need for clandestine operations continued.

Halina and I took the streetcar to the center of Prague as often as we could. The ancient city was remarkable for its beauty and absence of destruction. A few weeks before, I had visited the twice-devastated Warsaw. The city was mostly rubble. The contrast between the two cities was striking.

My friends in Prague were able to get about twenty false documents for us, which stopped Halina's playful complaining that I was too young for her. We still had the problem that she had possibly as many as 40 in her group. We found out that the document inspections at the border started at the front of the train and proceeded to the end. We decided to split the group in two. I would gather the documents quickly and find a way of delivering them to those sitting down the line. The documents issued by the Red Cross did not have photographs. This time my last name was Pollack and I was a German Jew. I was changing identities like some people change garments.

We were fortunate to get hold of false documents. Other Polish Jews had to rely on more dangerous ways to escape from Soviet-dominated Europe. Many tried to get across the border at night with local smugglers. Some were caught by the Soviet border patrols and sent to Siberia. The movement of Jews from Eastern Europe to Western Germany was known by the Hebrew name "Briha" (flight).

One day, Halina's kibbutz and our family boarded a train taking German and Greek Jews to the West. Nearly all of them were Polish Jews claiming they were German or Greek. During the train trip from Prague to Germany, Mother, Olenka, Halina and I, and Cesia, the youngest member of the group, a girl not older than fourteen, were sitting together. Cesia had survived in a convent and she and I talked about the similarity of our experiences. Cesia asked to speak to me alone and we stepped out of the train compartment into the corridor. Tearfully, she told me of her doubts about leaving Poland. She was a Jew, she said, but she was also a believing Catholic. She missed going to church and saying daily prayers openly. "Look at this," she said, pulling out a medallion of the Virgin Mary hidden under her blouse. I advised her to say goodbye to Halina, get off the train at the next station, and go back to Poland. I told her that among the Jews she would have to hide her deeply held Catholic beliefs. Among the Poles she would have to hide her Jewish ancestors. Since she was completely assimilated and had no family, it would be easier to do the latter than the former. She followed my suggestion in part; she got off the train to return to Poland but could not face her leader, Halina.

Years later, I thought of Cesia when I read Orwell's book *1984*. His character O'Brien said: "When you finally surrender to us, it must be of your own free will...We do not merely destroy our enemies, we change them." How fortunate for me that I was neither neither destroyed nor changed.

When we reached the border between Czechoslovak and Germany, a team of Soviet and American military police inspected our documents. Our plan worked. No one from our group was taken off the train. Next, the Czechoslovak border police searched us for contraband. I became apprehensive when I realized that these policemen were older, and professionals. I was worried about my suitcase with its double bottom full of U.S. occupation marks. Dollars were easily concealed but I had used them to purchase US occupation marks, which were bulky but much more profitable. The Czechoslovak police quickly discovered my trick and confiscated the money. In a few minutes I had lost a fortune. Luckily, I had a small amount of dollars rolled up in a condom hidden in my rectum, a trick I had learned during the war. The Czechoslovak police also took a few ivory figurines that we had gotten in Budapest. Mother began to cry and the border policeman handed her back one of the figurines, which I have to this day. This is the only item I have from before the liberation. It became a relic to me of our past and is still a cherished possession.

After the inspections, the train got under way. When the train entered Germany, members of Halina's kibbutz began to sing Hebrew songs. We had escaped our Soviet liberators and were happy to be away from our murderous Polish neighbors. How strange! Germany, the land of our oppressors, had become our Promised Land.

The beautiful Bavarian countryside changed when the train got into the city of Munich. Ruins were everywhere. At the Munich railroad station, no one expected us. Halina and I went outside the station looking for contacts. This meant finding Jews in the street and asking questions. This was a time-tested method of getting advice and help. We were told that we had to get to the German Museum of Technology and Industry, known as Deutsches Museum, which had been converted into a transient camp for "Displaced Persons." The only means of transportation was the overcrowded streetcars. They looked like beehives, with people hanging onto every external protrusion. I managed to get Mother and Olenka inside one of these cars; I hung on, standing on the running board.

The exhibit halls of the Deutsches Museum had been transformed into dormitories full of former concentration camp inmates, mostly Jews. The United Nations Relief and Refugee Administration (UNRRA) operated the place. It was a mess of disorganized, crowded, confused, and homeless humanity.

Across the street from the Deutsches Museum was an island in the middle of the Isar River. The whole island was a park; Halina and I took walks there, away from the turmoil of the DP camp. We held hands in public, but in the privacy of the park, we hugged and kissed. Every few days, American trucks transported groups of DP's to permanent camps or repatriated them to Eastern Europe. Some people were willing to return to Poland, others were foolish enough to admit that they had been liberated by the Red Army and therefore had no right to be in the U.S. Zone. Halina and her group were sent to the Deggendorf DP camp. Based upon my haggard appearance, one of the officials decided that I must suffer from tuberculosis. I was sent to St. Otillien, a convent and hospital outside of Munich. Mother and Olenka came along.

To be eligible for this hospital, one had to be a "Katzetnik" (someone who had survived in a concentration camp). Survival on false papers did not exist as a category and did not entitle one to any services. Those of us who had escaped the ghettos or concentration camps had to lie and say that we were liberated by

American troops. The need for deception continued. I claimed that I was liberated in the Mauthausen concentration camp. In St. Otillien, I slept in a regular bed, a luxury I had not enjoyed for quite some time. I could take a bath and eat regularly. I took walks in the garden and attempted to converse with the German nuns. Mother and Olenka were in the female section of the hospital and I could see them during visiting hours. After about two weeks, it was determined that I did not suffer from tuberculosis and we were transferred to the Landsberg DP camp. Before being loaded on the trucks, our belongings were searched to make sure that we did not steal anything from the hospital. They found a towel in Mother's bag. She was embarrassed and claimed that it was inadvertent. We had no towels, for that matter, we did not have anything. To lie to our oppressors had not been guilt provoking but to do so after liberation was a humiliating experience. Whenever mother recalled this episode, her eyes became tearful.

The Landsberg DP Camp was located in an old German military barrack. We were placed in a large hall, and each given an army cot and blanket. There were wall-to-wall people; the setting reminded me of the Topolya concentration camp. Some people hung blankets between the cots for privacy. To get to the toilet, one had to stand in line. People were milling around between barracks to avoid the overcrowding. There was nothing to do. The little town of Landsberg was off limits to the DPs by order of the American Armed Forces.

In June 1945, President Harry Truman requested Earl Harrison, a law school dean, to report on the conditions in the DP camps. Dean Harrison wrote to the President:

> They (the Jews) have been 'liberated' more in a military sense than actually." He observed that "many Jewish displaced persons and other possibly non-repatriables are living behind barbed fences in camps of several descriptions (built by the Germans for slave laborers and Jews), including some of the most notorious of the concentration camps amid crowded, frequently unsanitary and generally grim conditions, in complete idleness, with no opportunity, except surreptitiously to communicate with the outside world, waiting, hoping, for some word of encouragement and action on their behalf.[51]

Our second liberation was not a bed of roses. Living in a DP camp was an ordeal. It was time to make another choice.

According to rumors circulating in the camp, in nearby Munich one could get a room by going to the German Housing Authority (Wohnungsamt). Word of mouth was still the only source of information. It was against regulations to leave the camp, which was guarded by American soldiers. Once again, we escaped our benefactors and decided to place ourselves in the hands of the Germans. We could not board the train in Landsberg; American military police patrolled the station. We walked to a nearby community to catch the train. In the city of Munich, German refugees seeking housing besieged the Wohnungsamt. My German vocabulary was limited, and I had to rely on Mother's Yiddish to understand the German words. We stood in line for many hours. It was uncertain where we would sleep the next night. Shortly before the closing hours, we were assigned to the apartment of Miss Louise Bogenrieder, who lived on Clemens Street 63, in the district of Schwabing. We went back to the overcrowded streetcars to get to our new residence.

We had a piece of paper in our hands compelling Miss Bogenrieder to surrender two of her three rooms to us. We would share the kitchen. The apartment was on the second floor above a tavern. Miss Bogenrieder was in her late 50s; her appearance seemed unreal. Never before or since have I met a woman so qualified by looks to play the role of a witch. Miss Bogenrieder was a spinster who had always lived alone. She did not hide her surprise that she would have to share her quarters with "foreigners," yet she was appropriately polite and cooperative.

In Poland, it was not safe for us to stay overnight in our hometown. In Germany, a piece of paper issued by a German clerk entitled us to living quarters. We had a roof over our heads but no beds. We had access to the kitchen but we had no food. We were sharing the hardships with the Germans, who had lost the war. Yet these burdens were preferable to living in a DP camp operated by the Americans. There was plenty of food in those camps but the living conditions were degrading. There were thousands of German refugees from Soviet-occupied Germany in the city, in addition to the Displaced Persons. Food was hard to come by.

Within the next few days, we combined the best of all possible worlds. We returned to the nearby DP camp, Foerenwald, and became residents on paper, but continued to live in Munich. I traveled to the camp by train to pick up the weekly food package. This was not a legal arrangement; people who lived outside the camp were not entitled to these packages. Military police at the railroad station in Foerenwald searched the DPs and confiscated the packages, but I had little trouble eluding them. Deceptiveness continued to be essential to our well being. The care packages contained canned foods, but most important were the cigarettes. American cigarettes were the currency of the land. We paid for furniture, various goods and services with cigarettes.

Before long, our two rooms felt like home. Mother got a job in Foerenwald as camp dentist, but did not live there. At long last, she was "Pani Doktor" (Madame Doctor) and I became a normal 17-year-old boy.

I often read about the devastation, anarchy and starvation in occupied Germany after World War II. When I arrived in Munich sometime in the summer of 1945, there was no anarchy. Streetcars were running, restaurants were open, trains were operating. True enough, the Germans had to live within the limited food rations. When you went to a restaurant, they clipped the meat coupon if you ordered a dish containing meat. Many people no doubt were hungry, but there was no starvation.

When our lives in Munich became relatively normal, I became depressed and utterly exhausted. For about two weeks I lay on the army cot that was my bed. It was as if the years of being pursued and of carrying the responsibility of my mother and sister, had caught up with me. An anguished awareness of the enormity of the events that had taken place in the last few years dawned upon me. I now had the luxury of entering a period of mourning. My father's tragic death became more of a reality. The horror of what had happened to the European Jews hit me. Mother and Olenka took care of me as if I were physically ill. Yet rest and loving care were of little help.

Mother suggested that I visit Halina at the Deggendorf DP camp and I took her advice. It was the first pleasure trip I had taken since 1939. This time, I was not on the run or seeking survivors. I was a traveler sitting in the compartment of a passenger train, looking at the scenery with the eyes of a tourist. The beauty of the Bavarian countryside was uplifting.

Halina and the members of her kibbutz received me with open arms. The decrepit old German army barracks looked wonderful to me. There was a joyous atmosphere in the group. They worked in nearby fields expecting any day to go to Palestine. One of the boys had "organized" a motorcycle. (To "organize something" in the parlance of the survivors, meant to get it under nearly impossible circumstances.) I was given a five-minute lesson on the operation of the machine and felt confident enough to invite Halina for a spin. We had an exhilarating ride through the nearby country roads. On the way back, making a turn at a very slow speed, I lost control and we ended up in a ditch. Neither one of us was injured but Halina cried. I hugged her and she calmed down. We sat by the roadside for a long time and talked. This incident became a turning point in our relationship. It united us as if it were a bonding ceremony. We acknowledged that we were in love with each other. Halina made plans to leave the kibbutz and come to live in Munich.

Falling in love was like a rebirth and my depression lifted. But I had a sense of admiration for Halina that made her unapproachable sexually. The lack of privacy at Deggendorf provided a convenient rationalization for not making sexual advances. I was aware of my inhibition and troubled by it. Being in love with Halina did not stop me from thinking about Gina. Contrary to reason, I believed that she was alive.

Upon my return to Munich, I ran into a girl I had met on my first trip to Krakow. She too had survived by living on false papers. We had wandered around in Krakow and I had had someone take a picture of us in front of the Wawel Castle. I have the photo to this day, but I do not remember her real name, only her Polish first name, which was Zosia. When I met her in Munich, I told her about the photo and we walked over to our apartment to see it. She was amazed that I had a mother and a sister. No other member of Zosia's family survived. She was a pretty girl without the saintly look of Halina and she was not blond. Years later, I became aware that in my unconscious mind, blondes were Christians who would denounce me as a Jew if they saw my circumcised penis.

Zosia had a two-bedroom apartment by herself, which in those days was an exceptional luxury. I stayed overnight with her. With Zosia I was not timid or sexually inhibited, she was a Jew and therefore not dangerous. This was my first lovemaking experience without the fear that my penis would reveal my fatal identity. Once again, a sexual experience was a turning point. A few days later I swapped a pack of Camel cigarettes for an old pair of German Army skis and went to Garmish-Paterkirchen to ski. The cable cars were reserved for the use of

186

American troops, with the exception of an hour or two in the early hours. In order to get onto the cable car when it opened, one had to be there at 5:00 a.m. at the latest. It was worth getting up before dawn and standing two hours in line to enjoy the magnificent skiing from the top of Zugspitze back into town.

One sunny day in the late afternoon, I was skiing down from Zugspitze to the town of Garmish-Paterkirchen, when I heard joyous band music. It did not sound like a German orchestra. When I got closer, I came upon an American military band. The soldiers moving along behind the band were not goose-stepping or strutting, they were just marching American style, which to me seemed like strolling. There was nothing militaristic about the music or the marching. Later, I found out that they were playing "Stars and Stripes Forever." This was clearly a citizen army.

American army uniforms had little in common with the threatening outfits worn by most militaries of Europe. American uniforms were functional, concerned with the comfort of the soldiers. This was the beginning of my love for America. I detested militarism and its devotion to intimidation. I accepted the need for going to war, but I rejected the degradation inherent in the militaristic tradition. Total obedience, perfection in military drills and techniques of presenting the weapons is claimed to be necessary to ensure effectiveness in combat. But more often than not, it provides an opportunity to humiliate friend and foe and to gratify the sadistic needs of totalitarian minds.

When we arrived in Munich in 1945, my sister Olenka was 13 years old. She was tall, beautiful and highly articulate. She looked 18. Boys my age and older treated my sister, who was merely a child in my eyes, as a young woman. I expected my little sister to play hopscotch and tag, but she was interested in Jewish boys and the American songs played on the Armed Forces Radio.

"No lipstick," I demanded with the authority of an older brother in a fatherless home. I was determined to protect the chastity of a young girl. I objected to her listening to American songs. American music was considered to be too erotic for a young girl. "I am learning English by learning the songs," Olenka argued. She had a point. Listening to American radio, with her talent for languages, had made her nearly fluent in English. Near our apartment, the Jewish Committee was opening a Jewish school. I welcomed this and saw to it that Olenka was one of the early registrants. After all, she was 13 and had never spent a day in a classroom.

The school was located on Moehl Street, the center of black market activity. The street was teeming with young Jewish men and an occasional Jewish woman. Among survivors, women were a rarity, particularly attractive ones. This was before the influx of Polish Jews who came from the Soviet Union. Among the Germans, the situation was different. There were lots of young women. Most young German men had been killed or were in prisoner of war camps. It was considered disgraceful for Jewish men to become romantically involved with German women but many did. It was unheard of for a Jewish woman to socialize with a German man.

My efforts to turn my sister into a schoolgirl failed. She dropped out after a few months. Thanks to her proficiency in English, she got a job as a telephone operator working for an American agency. She lied about her age, claiming to be 16, which was believable. Working for the Americans gave her access to the American Army store (PX) and she dressed in fashionable American clothing. My little sister became an American working girl. She skipped the transitional period of development between childhood and young womanhood. Before long, she was the chief operator.

In addition to her attractiveness, Olenka also had a brilliant mind. Throughout her life she made the impression of someone with a college education, though her education consisted of a few months in a makeshift elementary school taught by amateur teachers. I have always believed that Olenka's intelligence and resourcefulness were superior to mine. But the abrupt switch from wartime adversities to American affluence was harmful to her. My transition was more gradual. I lived among the Germans and struggled with the hardships of post-war conditions. In Munich, our lives diverged.

My sister often realized her short-term goals but never attained the good life. Many of my wishes have not been fulfilled, but I have had a long and satisfying life. Olenka suffered all of her adult life from depression and conflict with the people she loved. She died in her forties a painful death of breast cancer, undiagnosed until it was too late.

*

"How could you, a Holocaust survivor, study in Germany?" This question is often posed to the nearly 700 Jews who, after liberation, gained academic degrees at German universities. The accusatory tone usually reveals that this is not a question but an indictment. The question presumes that we had a choice.

The reason we stayed in Germany for so many years after the war was not our affection for the Germans, but the indifference of the world to survivors. Germany became our place of refuge because no one else was willing to accept us. In Nazi Germany, Munich was called "The Capitol of the Nazi Movement." It is a strange twist of history that it became the center of Jewish life in post-war Europe. It is a sad irony that the Germans, for whatever reasons, became significant players in the healing process of the wounds they had inflicted upon us. It is a paradox that I did not feel secure in my hometown in Poland, but was completely safe everywhere in postwar Germany.

The American War Department wanted to know what to expect in occupied Germany after victory in Second World War. The American Historical Association prepared a forecast. Here is a short excerpt:

> The military defeat of an army does not necessarily mean that the cause for which it fought will be abandoned by every follower. No one supposes that just because Hitlerism has been utterly crushed in battle, every last Nazi will suddenly have a change of heart. On the contrary, there are Germans, especially among the young men imbued with fanatic Nazism, to whom the teachings of Hitler and Goebbels and Rosenberg are a sort of religion. To them the dead

leaders will live as martyrs; defeat will only strengthen their resolve to achieve the aims of Nazism another day. Like the defeated German generals of the First World War, they will wait and work for the day of revenge and victory."[52]

Dr. Condoleezza Rice no doubt relied on such historical sources when she spoke about American casualties in occupied Iraq. Dr. Rice told the Veterans of Foreign Wars in San Antonio, Texas, on August 25, 2003:

There is an understandable tendency to look back on America's experience in postwar Germany and see only the successes. But as some of you here today surely remember, the road we traveled was very difficult. 1945 through 1947 was an especially challenging period. Germany was not immediately stable or prosperous. SS officers—called 'werewolves'—engaged in sabotage and attacked both coalition forces and those locals cooperating with them—much like today's Baathist and Fedayeen remnants."[53]

I lived in Germany from 1945 until the end of 1951 and never witnessed or heard of Americans having problems with the German population. In *The History of Germany Since 1789,* the distinguished German historian Golo Mann writes, "The [Germans'] readiness to work with the victors, to carry out their orders, to accept their advice and their help was genuine; of the resistance which the Allies had expected in the way of 'werewolf' units and nocturnal guerrilla activities, there was no sign..."[54]

Many American Jews say that they are unable to visit Germany. They find it incomprehensible that thousands of Holocaust survivors flocked to Germany from Eastern Europe and lived among the Germans in harmony until they could emigrate to America or Israel.

If those of us who lived in post-war Germany believed that Adenauer's Germany did not differ from Hitler's Germany, we would have been unable to live a full life in that country. While living and studying in Germany, I remembered Hitler, but I lived with the reality of Adenauer. Hitler was painful history; Adenauer was welcome actuality. Historical reality and existential reality are worlds apart.

The United Nations Relief and Rehabilitation Administration (UNRRA) established a university in Munich for displaced persons. One day in 1945, Halina asked me to accompany her to an admission interview. Unlike me, Halina had a "matura," a certificate of having completed a secondary education in Poland. Professor Studinsky, the Dean of Admissions who also was the Dean of the Faculty for Political Science, interviewed Halina. She was applying to the School of Pharmacy. Professor Studinsky, a Ukrainian who spoke Polish, engaged me in a conversation that developed into a heated discussion on political issues. "What faculty are you matriculating into?" he asked me.

"None at this time but political science has been my area of interest," I answered cautiously.

"I can tell you have talent for this field. I would be pleased to have you as a student. Where did you get your matura?" he asked. It did not occur to him that a young man could converse intelligently and not have a matura, the equivalent of a junior college diploma, in his pocket. My education had stopped at the level of 5th grade in Miechow's elementary school.

"The Polish Secondary School of Hungary in Balaton Boglar," I lied. I also told him that I did not have the certificate from my school.

"That is very common among the refugees," he told us. All that he required was a sworn affidavit by two witnesses that I had received a matura.

Halinka (I no longer called her Halina) and I made a quick trip to a Notary Public. She declared under oath that I was a graduate of Balaton Boglar. My second witness was a total stranger. In those days, it was common to ask a fellow survivor to provide such assistance. We did not consider it lying or perjury, we broke many unjust laws to survive. It seemed that this skill was still necessary.

I became a university student in political science by the use of a fake document. In Germany, political science and political economy were combined. I found the subject fascinating and studied it with enthusiasm. It gratified my need to understand what makes society and individuals function. Professor Studinsky became my mentor and I was his star student. The close relationship between a Ukrainian and a Jew was puzzling to some, as Ukrainians were known for their intense anti-Semitism.

Within a few months, I was the only teaching assistant in the whole university. Dean Studinsky announced that my grades were excellent and that I was exempt from taking examinations. The absence of formal education prior to entering the university did not seem to be an impediment to my success. I was experienced in covering my ignorance. I read incessantly and rapidly attained a good command of German, which was the lingua franca among the various nationalities of the UNRRA University.

A few months into the academic year, there was a celebration of the establishment of the University. The High Commissioner for the U.S. Zone of Occupation and the Commander of the U.S. Forces in Europe, General Lucius Clay, attended. A student from each nationality was to speak briefly at the ceremony. I was chosen to represent all of the Jewish Students. My "speech" consisted of a few English sentences that I had memorized, since I did not speak English. An American female officer attached to the Armed Forces Radio became my instructor. She drove an American car (not a Jeep), smoked cigarettes, and was very pretty. She was the first American woman I had ever met.

The ceremony took place in the largest auditorium of the Deutsches Museum. The public consisted of a mixture of Americans, UNRRA University students and dignitaries from various ethnic organizations in Germany. The proceedings were broadcast on Armed Forces Radio. My "speech" began with: "I am Emanuel Tenenwurzel..." I repeated the "I am" two or three times.

Shortly after the ceremony in the Deutsches Museum, a student called Jozef Silverman organized the Jewish Students Organization. I was one of the founding members and initially the youngest member. I was in charge of social activities and every few weeks I organized an outing to the lakes, mountains and castles surrounding Munich. These short trips provided much needed recreation and an opportunity to make friendships. We took long walks, climbed mountains in the summer and went skiing in the winter. My biggest coup was securing a number of rooms for us at the Four Seasons Hotel in Berchtesgaden, which in the Third German Empire had been reserved for "Partei Bonzen," the party big shots. It was now under American control. From the terrace of the hotel, which was our favored spot, we could see the imposing peak of Watzman, Germany's highest mountain. I persuaded a few students to join me in climbing to the top. A dentistry student named Kastner resisted. "Why should I climb to the peak to be able to see the valley if I can see the peak from the valley," he argued.

The primary purpose of the organization that we called "Zwiazek" (Polish for "Association") was self-help. The leadership negotiated food packages from the American Joint Committee and our office became a distribution center for food and clothing. We organized a soup kitchen for our members, which became a daily gathering place.

The Jewish students in Munich were a diverse group. Most came from Poland, though a number were Hungarian and German Jews. In 1945, the group consisted mostly of men and women who had been liberated from German captivity. In early 1946, our ranks increased by the arrival of Polish Jews who had survived in the Soviet Union and had never been directly exposed to Nazi persecution. The American and German authorities presumed that all of us were former inmates of concentration camps. The concept of "survivor" was not in our vocabulary. The word survivor does not exist in Polish or German.

Getting our people admitted to the German University in Munich was a major function of the Zwiazek. The German University had a policy of admitting only the oldest applicants. This was designed to help those Germans whose education had been delayed by service in the German Army. We negotiated an exemption for our members from this regulation. Our organization functioned like a social service agency. In 1947, at the age of 19, I was elected Secretary General of the association. We employed two full-time German secretaries who were kept very busy.

In the fall of 1946, the representative of the Jewish Agency asked to address the entire membership, and a special meeting was called. The Jewish Agency was, for us, the Jewish government of Palestine; it was admired and respected. We were told that the American official in charge of the American Joint Distribution Committee would also speak to us. This committee was formed by American Jewish organizations to assist Jews worldwide. To us, they were the source of the food packages that we relied upon for our existence. They wore impressive American military uniforms. Dr. Otto Auerbach, a German Jew who was the head of the Bavarian Reparations Agency for the victims of Nazi persecution was also coming.

There was an air of mystery about the meeting because we were not told the purpose of it. To our amazement, the representative of the Jewish Agency began by telling us that it was a disgrace for Jews to study in Germany. Socializing with Germans and being taught by German professors was shameful, he said. We should, instead, try to go to Palestine illegally. "We don't need intelligentsia, we need chalutzim" (Zionist pioneers) was the passionate ending of his speech.

The Director of the "Joint," as we called it, expressed similar views and told us that in the future, students would not be receiving food packages. Dr. Auerbach made some threats that his office would no longer assist us.

"Our education is a form of compensation the Germans are paying to the Jews" was my comment. Our protestations only increased the condemnatory fervor of our "friends" from America and Palestine. "There will be no more packages of food for the students," was the parting message of the American Joint director. There was an air of disappointment and anger among the students when these men departed. It was painful to be chastised by people we expected to be our helpers. We were still in a state of convalescence, yet these men were demanding sacrifices from us. Attempts to get to Palestine in those days were usually hopeless. The Jews who tried the illegal route often ended up in a British camp on Cyprus.

Packages of food were the lifeblood of our organization and the basis of subsistence for our members. It was hard to accept that Jewish bureaucrats would deprive us of the necessities of life. We waited in vain for the delivery of the packages on the appointed day. The Executive Board, known to all by its Polish name "Zarzod," met for an emergency meeting. We decided to occupy the villa that was the headquarters of the Joint. This luxurious house was located in a park-like setting. A contingent of the boys surrounded the building. An American military police vehicle in front of the building made us reluctant to storm the place. I climbed a nearby tree and watched the villa, which was surrounded by high shrubs. Once the police vehicle departed, we entered the offices and forced our way into the Director's office. He was told that we were not leaving until he canceled his order depriving students of the packages.

"I am calling the MPs, you better leave at once," he yelled in Yiddish and reached for the phone on his desk.

"No, you are not," I answered and ripped the phone cord off the wall. A few other fellows approached him in a threatening manner, letting him know that he should not get out of his chair. He realized we were serious and changed his tactic. He expressed willingness to talk to Silverman, our president, if the "hooligans" left his office. We did, and shortly afterwards, delivery of our food packages was promised.

We decided to educate people about the merit of our efforts to gain an education. We distributed leaflets showing that "Sherit Hapleita" (Hebrew for Living Remnant) was in dire need of an intelligentsia since the Germans had killed most Jewish professionals. One such flyer had a graph showing the Jewish population of Europe before and after the war and the proportion of professionals. The caption read in Yiddish: "Help create a Jewish intelligentsia."

We also decided to seek new students. We had 200 members when the effort was made to eliminate us, but before long, our membership exceeded 400 active students. This was a distinctive contribution of the Munich group; it makes us proud to this day. There were handfuls of Jewish students in other German universities, namely Heidelberg, Frankfurt, Erlangen and Mahrburg. We

192

published a newsletter called "Wiedergeburt" (Rebirth); Roman A. Ohrenstein was the editor.

The Jewish Students Organization in Munich prevailed upon the Bavarian Ministry of Education to establish a special commission that would examine and certify a Jewish applicant for admission as being qualified to enter a university. Some did have the necessary education but had no documents to prove it. Others had not had a chance to attend a secondary school in a camp or on false papers. The new administrative entity was called "Verifications Commission"; it was empowered to issue certificates after successful completion of an examination in a wide range of subjects.

I was recognized as an outstanding student in political science, but my education was highly deficient. I began an intensive preparation program for the examinations that were to take place in three months. My greatest challenge was the exact sciences; mathematics, physics and chemistry. I found a German professor of astronomy who became my tutor in mathematics and physics. He lived in a bombed out house without heat. I paid him for instruction with cigarettes. Once, I invited him for lunch to our house and discovered that he must have been starving. He showed more than a keen appetite for my mother's mediocre cooking. From that time on I paid him with food and cigarettes. I was interested in physics but disliked mathematics. I once asked him how many times I should repeat a mathematical drill. "Do it until you begin to like it," was his answer. I do not recall his name or the math he taught me, but I have never forgotten this advice.

A chemistry professor from the famous Munich Engineering School was also my tutor. I passed the examinations by the Commission without any difficulty and received a certificate. This reduced my feeling of shame for not having attended a gymnasium. It took many years in the United States to realize that Americans are not shocked by this black hole in my education. My European upbringing made me feel like an intellectual fraud because I never attended a secondary school.

Reading had been my entertainment since childhood. Collecting books, lead soldiers and stamps were my hobbies before the war. In Munich, buying books became possible once more. I was no longer fighting for my life and leading the nomadic existence of a fugitive. Soon, I had a small library. I fell in love with Heinrich Heine. His poetry and prose were my introduction to German literature. My *Goethe's Werke* (Works of Goethe) in 24 volumes is no longer complete. I have the works of many German classics, the Brockhaus encyclopedia and naturally, a copy of Hitler's *Mein Kampf*. I can still recite the satirical poems written by Erick Kaestner. In Germany, theater was a vibrant cultural institution. My rapid learning of German was in large measure the result of weekly visits to the theater. As a student, I could get excellent seats for very little money.

In Munich, I became a proud owner of a bicycle. At the end of Clemens Street was the English Garden, which was an enormous park, and a biker's paradise. The bike also became my main transportation in the city. It was an old bicycle and I was forever patching the inner tubes, but I preferred the beat-up bike to the crowded streetcars.

In Munich, we lived an almost normal bourgeois existence. Work, education, and love affairs were on our minds. Being in danger, political developments and military operations were no longer our concern. To live a normal life was our goal. We avoided the reality that we suffered from emotional scars that affected our interactions with people and undermined our self-esteem. Marriages and choices of occupations took place in the shadow of the mind-altering past. The Jewish students as a group defined themselves more by similarities of goals than by differences of experience. Some of us had survived death camps, some survived by living on false papers, and others came from the Soviet Union and had no contact with the Germans before arrival in occupied Germany. We all focused on rebuilding our lives.

One day, Mother brought a man named Nathan Rottenberg to the house. She had met him in the Foerenwald DP Camp. He was a good-looking fellow, and younger than Mother. It was obvious that they were romantically involved. Mother introduced him to me with some apprehension. She expected disapproval from me because Nathan was a simple, uneducated village Jew from Poland. I took a liking to him instantly. He was an illiterate but dignified and purposeful man. I did not expect Mother to be a widow forever. Nathan treated Mother with respect and affection. That is all I expected from her future husband.

Mother and Nathan were married within a year. Nathan had survived some of the worst concentration camps, but remained one of the most benevolent people I have ever met. He was generous, helpful, hard working and fiercely loyal. He was the sole survivor of a large family from Klimontow, a shtetl in Poland. A laborer before the war, he became a truck driver in Germany, an occupation he held for the rest of his life.

Nathan was as different from my father as a duck from a swan. Father was a sophisticated, handsome and urbane man, fluent in four languages, well read in Polish literature and quite knowledgeable in Jewish studies. Nathan was a skinny, inarticulate man who spoke Polish like a peasant and was never exposed to Jewish learning. He was unassuming, sincere and goodhearted. He showed complete deference to Mother. I never knew him to disagree with anything Mother said. Over the years, he and I formed a bond of true affection. And yet for Mother, it was a marriage of desperation. She never complained. Nathan symbolized her acceptance that her former status could never be regained.

Nathan, unlike most of the Jews in Munich, was not involved in the black market, which was quite lucrative. All survivors, including the students, participated indirectly in the underground economy. We sold our cigarettes and coffee from the food packages to these black marketers for cash and they, in turn, sold them to the Germans. This was illegal and the American Military Police arrested a few students for it.

My life in Munich revolved around my studies and the activities of the Student Organization. This group was like an extended family, bound by a similar past and by the determination to get an education. Concern with the future made me doubt that political science was a good career choice. I believed that this esoteric subject that I loved would be useless in America, Australia or Israel. I tried to persuade my best friends, Natek Birman and Israel Borenstein, who studied political science, to abandon the field. Medicine seemed more practical, but we had little interest in it. We, in the social sciences, viewed medical students with disdain. They were parochial, preoccupied with passing examinations in anatomy, histology and other boring subjects. I decided to transfer to the German University where I would study medicine and political science at the same time. Birman and Borenstein agreed that the shift to the German University was a good move, but they did not intend to study medicine in addition to political science.

The transfer to the German University required a recommendation from the Jewish Student Organization, which was based upon examination. An older student named Piekarczyk, with an engineering degree from Poland, was in charge of the examination. My friend Borenstein failed the examination and was refused the necessary certificate. The next day, the disappointed Borenstein took a train from Munich to Landsberg. On the train, a group of Jews were being rude to some German women. Borenstein threatened to beat them up if they did not behave properly. At the end of the trip, an elderly gentleman handed Borenstein a business card and said, "You are a nice young man. Call me if I can help you." Borenstein stuck the card in his pocket without reading it. He looked at it later and found that the man was the Rector of Ludwig Maximillian University. The Rector of a university in Germany is the equivalent of a Cardinal or a Four Star General in America. Borenstein called his train acquaintance and became a student of political science without the certificate from Piekarczyk. He received his Ph.D. magna cum laude and had a distinguished career as an official of the United Nations in New York and Geneva. He, like I, had never entered a secondary school.

I am an autodidact, which relieves the educational systems of Poland and Germany of responsibility for my shortcomings. I had no access to schools and had to educate myself on the run at my own initiative. Even when I did have access to teachers, I continued with the do-it-yourself approach. The system of examinations at German universities suited my post-Holocaust symptoms. I was unable to concentrate, I was anxious and restless. To sit through a lecture was an ordeal for me and I rarely attended any of them. The professors demanded knowledge of subjects but did not care how you got it. Albert Einstein writes in his memoir that freedom is essential to learning. We certainly had that freedom; there was no compulsion to attend lectures.

In the study of medicine there were essentially three formal examinations. They dealt with basic science after the first few semesters, and then a halfway exam called Physicum, and the final exam for the licensure.

My examination by a famous physics professor at the Institute for Physics was scheduled for 8 o'clock one Saturday morning. I was somewhat late, hopped on my bike and rushed to the Institute. I knocked on the locked door and was greeted by a little man who had a pronounced hunchback. I told him that I was here to be examined by Professor So-and-So. I don't remember the name but I believe he received the Nobel Prize. "Come in, come in," the man said in an agitated manner. "I can see that you have not attended any of my lectures. I am Professor So-and-So."

I told him that I had attended only one of his lectures two years ago. I had concluded it was way above my head and decided instead to rely upon self-study. "We will see how well you have done it," the famous man responded. To his credit, he did not penalize me and I received a very good grade in physics. The professor was impressed with my discussion of the controversy about the wave versus the corpuscular theory of light. This was not the product of my preparation for the examination, but a result of casual reading.

In Munich, I led a social life with fellow survivors, engaged in graduate studies, and followed my passion for reading and sports. Freedom from life-threatening danger and the absence of persecution had a beneficial influence on my mind and body. I no longer looked sickly as I did on arrival in Germany.

During my seven years of living in Germany, I stayed in youth hostels when climbing the Alps in summer or skiing in winter. I stood in lines with Germans waiting for ski lifts and sat in crowded lecture halls with them at the university. I was taught and examined by German professors, and German doctors treated me when I became ill. A well-known German surgeon operated on me. The procedure was performed at the Jewish Hospital in Munich.

As the Secretary General of the Jewish Student Organization, I negotiated with German officials, and traveled extensively and frequently throughout Germany. I roamed about the country without any concern for my safety. Curiosity was all it took to explore Western Germany. I was never met with any hostility. The Holocaust survivors in Germany were understandably provocative at times, and yet I never heard of a Jew attacked or even verbally abused by a German.

I remember German inhumanity during the Holocaust, but I have not forgotten German politeness and considerate behavior in relation to the survivors after the war. They were barbarians in "Eastern Territories" during the war and good neighbors after the war. My attitude toward Germany is puzzling to some of my American friends. A fellow Holocaust survivor has called me "an apologist of Germany" when I called attention to the fact that in Germany, Holocaust survivors were safe after the War.

Living in Munich after World War II, I witnessed the transformation of Western Germany into the Federal Republic of Germany, an enlightened democratic state, but the murderous Third Reich was Germany also. The two are separate entities for me. I remember the murderous Nazi Germany and I admire modern Germany. In the book *Hitler's Willing Executioners*, Goldhagen writes:

> The Germans were Dr. Jekylls as occupiers and Mr. Hydes when occupied. The German war behavior was horrendous but they showed repentance in words and deeds after the war. Germany has undergone a dramatic transformation in political structure and national spirit. They have repudiated their past and reached out to the victims of Nazi Germany.[55]

After World War II, Germany was no longer seeking vengeance against the winners and held no animosity to the victims of Germany. Germany collectively and most Germans individually, accepted responsibility for the Holocaust. A sense of shame became the prevailing mood. We, the victims of the Third Reich and the vanquished perpetrators, lived in harmony among the ruins of the "Hauptstadt der Bewegung" (Capitol of the Movement).

In Munich, I established close friendships, but my love life was a problem. I was bashful and insecure with women. My relationship with Halina was characteristic. She was beautiful, bright, and kind—but blonde. There was no doubt that we were in love. One day, we were at the Island Park near the Deutsches Museum. It was late fall, we were lying on the ground covered with yellow leaves. I wanted to make love and she was very willing. But my desire was not matched by my performance. This was the end of a promising relationship, and I began to avoid her. On one of our excursions into the Alps, I watched Halina being courted by Edek Langer, a student of dentistry, and immediately assumed that Halina was in love with him. He was handsome and self-assured; a real man, not just a boy, like me.

Sabina Schwartz, whom I visited often, had an upstairs neighbor, Marion Landau. She too was a medical student and they did their homework together. I met Marion frequently on my daily visits to Sabina. She was a German Jew, pretty without being beautiful like Halina or Gina, and she was not blond.

We were drawn to each other. However, she had a boyfriend and was seven years older than I. Her boyfriend, whom I shall call "Alfred," was a husky 30-year-old, a handsome man with thick, wavy hair. He was a German-educated Lithuanian Jew who was the founder and manager of the Sherit Hapleita orchestra. I did not feel that I could compete with such a rival. And yet, I found Marion's serenity and thoughtfulness irresistible. Unlike the rest of us, she had both parents, and her education had not been interrupted by the war. Her mother was German and her father was an assimilated Jew; which had made Marion a Jew in the eyes of Nazi Germany. If her mother had continued to be married to her Jewish husband she would be guilty of a crime. So the whole family moved to Klaipeda (Memel in German), Lithuania's second largest city after Kowno. In 1941, the Germans occupied that city and began anti-Jewish measures. Marion and her mother returned to Berlin, rented a small apartment and smuggled Mr. Landau into it, where he remained hidden for the duration of the war. During the frequent air raids on Berlin, he could not go into the air shelter because of his striking Semitic looks. When he traveled from Klaipeda to Berlin, his face was bandaged as if he was injured.

I admired Marion for her resourcefulness, courage and loyalty. I still divided people into those I would want to be with on false papers and those who were unsuitable for clandestine life. This was an intuitive judgment that served me well during the war and never failed me throughout my life.

Marion made it obvious that she preferred my company to that of Alfred. Before long, we were in love and spending a great deal of time together. Since she was not blond, I did not have any sexual problems with her. But she was reluctant to break up with Alfred; her parents liked him and expected her to marry him. Marion's mother was not delighted with me. I was barely an adult and, to make matters worse, I was an "Ostjude" (Eastern Jew). Marion's parents lived in the town of Landsberg. As German Jews, they were never required to live in a DP camp.

For the time being, our love affair was a secret. Only Sabina knew. Alfred still visited Marion daily. A towel hanging from her windowsill was a sign that he was upstairs and I had to stay away.

Marion was two years ahead of me in medical school and had the benefit of a formal education in German schools. In her gentle way, she helped me in my studies. I never felt put-down because of her superior knowledge of literature or medicine. She had the ability to be instructive without being didactic. Unlike me, she was systematic and orderly. We got along very well in spite of our differences in background and personality. We took frequent excursions to the lakes and mountains in the vicinity of Munich. Marion broke up with Alfred and we decided to get married.

I was in love with Marion, yet my devotion to Gina did not vanish. But I considered Gina unattainable. I first heard that Gina was alive some time late in 1946. One day, I was told that an officer from the Jewish Brigade of the British Armed Forces was looking for Betty Tenenwurzel, my mother, on Moehl street, which was a spot where many survivors were roaming. It was a challenge to find him. But I did, and he had messages from our relatives in Palestine. He helped me to find Gina, who lived in Tel-Aviv, and gave me her address. We wrote letters to each other every week. Marion was aware of my attachment to Gina and my ongoing correspondence with her.

In October 2000, Gina came to our home in Eastport, Michigan for a visit and brought with her about 100 letters that I had written to her. The first letter is dated December 18, 1946. The envelope has a postmark from Tel Aviv, which means that I had given it to someone; I believe that I gave it to the officer of the British Jewish Brigade, who had brought the news that Gina was alive. These letters are written in Polish. Here is my translation of the first letter:

Dear Ginus (a diminutive of Gina)! I don't know how to begin to describe my joy and express the entirety of my feelings evoked by your letter. I will not even try out of fear that I would not adequately reflect them. I have always tried to find out where you are. After I was liberated, I wrote to Bucharest and received conflicting responses. Once I was told that you were on a ship that sank. I never believed it; I was convinced you were alive. Later I found out that you are in Palestine. I always believed in the depths of my soul, that one day we would meet.

You write about the times we have spent together...Your memories of all the details moved me deeply. I too remember various details of our life. I remember clearly when I first saw you digging antiaircraft shelters. I remember how we played cards, fearful that my father might come. I never will forget the wonderful and naïve ways of trying to express my love for you. Do you remember the little note that I handed you with one question? (I am making reference to asking who the boy she likes the best is.)

… Ginus! Imagine my feelings when after liberation I got through from Budapest to Miechow. Our house on Pilsudski Street looks like in the past and yet it is so different after all these years; it is empty and silent and yet so many memories are attached to this structure. I was overcome with sadness when I saw our old playground, my monogram E.T. on the doors is a bit faded out, but not as much as the memory of all of us. Dzidzia and her mother could not recognize me. Everything looks so different; in the garden of Weissfisch grow potatoes. Only one Kozlowski is alive and they no longer have a goat. The house on Glowacki Street #4 shows a variety of changes; it is quiet and peaceful in "our" gatehouse. [I am referring to an entrance hall in the building in the ghetto where we used to play]

… In my album of various photographs, your photos are in the first place. I have two of your pictures, one taken in the garden of (illegible) and the second one taken shortly after arrival in Budapest. These photos and the little pig and calendar as well as a half of a pinecone endured with me all my prisons and similar troubles [these were items given to me by Gina]. It was strange that these items were not taken from me after I was arrested. They removed even my shoelaces. In the concentration camp in Yugoslavia, everyone knew that Rojek (my name at the time) had a Talisman and this was the theme of a number of jokes. But, if anyone wanted to know a date I was the only owner of a calendar. Shortly after I was arrested they found one of your photographs, the big one that was taken shortly before our departure from Budapest. You look like the ideal Nordic type.

The Nazi who interrogated me asked how I came into a possession of a picture of an Aryan girl. When I told him that this was my girlfriend who is Jewish, I was given a beating. A few other Gestapo men confirmed unanimously that this was a form of "Rassenschande." Your photo found its way to the wallet of the Obersturmfuehrer. At the end I received one more kick.

I remember how one day they brought to our camp Mr. Blatt and Mr. Abramczyk and I found out that you succeeded to escape. My joy had no limits…I decided to study at the university, knowing my "education" - ha! ha! You can image how hard it was, but the first ice has been broken. I passed an equivalent of a matura and I am a university student. I have the honor to have the title of the youngest student of "Verband der Juedischen Studenten in der US Zone" (Organization of Jewish Students in the US Zone). Ginus, study is nothing but a means and not a goal. I can distinguish the two with mathematical accuracy and therefore it is a given that Emanuel Tenenwurzel one day will land in Eretz Israel.

I hope that you will be in the port waving your handkerchief in a similar manner as I did when we departed for Uszod and you remained on the railroad station in Budapest. ... I would like to write more but it is after 1 a.m. and in the morning I have to rush to lectures. In a few days we will have our winter vacations during which our student organization will go into the Alps to ski. I will then have time and will overwhelm you with letters whether you want to me or not. ... Ginus! Be healthy and remember your old friend ... Shalom Janek, Munich, December 18, 1946

My love for Gina had an unreal quality; she was emotionally unattainable and physically unreachable. Marion was real and I was certain of her love for me. In August of 1948, Marion and I were married in a civil ceremony conducted by the German equivalent of a Justice of the Peace. Our families did not attend and we did not ask any friends to be present. My mother was not thrilled that I was marrying a German woman seven years my senior. Marion's parents were not happy about the marriage of their only daughter to a penniless Polish Jew. There was no festivity to mark the occasion and no honeymoon.

When we returned from the office of the Justice of Peace, my mother had a meal for us. We had to hurry and help Mother and Nathan with last minute packing chores. They were leaving Germany for Sydney, Australia, and would soon be embarking on the long sea journey. It was a bittersweet occasion. The plan was that we would join her in Australia in the future. My father's two sisters who lived in Australia had sent us landing permits that made us the envy of our friends. I decided to delay going to Australia because I wanted to finish my medical studies in Munich.

Shortly after my mother and Nathan left, Marion's parents moved into our apartment. The two rooms were adjacent; one had to pass through the first one to get to the next. They occupied the second room, which meant that we had no privacy in the first room.

The second room had furniture that I was very proud of. It was new, manufactured by a German furniture factory that normally sold only to Americans. It had taken considerable effort on my part to get it. It was light in color, reminiscent of my parents' bedroom furniture. I got a job for my father-in-law, Mr. Landau, in Munich as a manager of the Bogenhausen Hospital, which had been taken over by the Jewish Committee. Dr. Osterweil, who I had helped in Budapest, was the hospital director.

The Landaus were to stay with us for a short time but they showed no inclination to leave. Marion's mother was a typical Berliner; vocal, opinionated and aggressive. I admired her for her loyalty and courage during the war but I resented her domineering attitude.

One evening, we were walking down Clemens Street and, as usual, we were arguing about her mother. At one point, I said, "Your mother is a real witch." Marion slapped my face. I said nothing but continued to walk. I walked across the English Garden to Bogenhausen where Olenka and her husband Oscar lived in a small apartment. I stayed with them for a few days. Marion let me know that she had her parents move out and wanted me to come back. But I was determined to get a divorce. Living with Olenka and Oscar was not easy; their lifestyle was different from mine. Fortunately, a fellow student, Giza Zieman, and her husband Yitzchak, offered me a room in their large apartment. They insisted that I should pay no rent, which was important for me. I supported myself by being a security guard at an American storage facility outside of Munich. Giza was the daughter of Mr. Bawnik, the undisputed king of the black market. Rumor had it that he manufactured counterfeit American cigarettes in Berlin. He had a diplomatic passport from a South American country and traveled throughout Europe. The Bawnik family had an apartment in Tel-Aviv.

The Zieman apartment on Stengel Street in Munich was spacious and quiet. This was important for study and helpful when I suffered my frequent migraine headaches. Whenever I had one of these episodes, I was nauseated, vomited and could not tolerate light or noise.

My first attempt to establish a family had failed. Marion and I met many years later, first in Chicago and then in Tel-Aviv. She blamed herself for the breakup of our marriage, but I am quite certain that my emotional problems were the cause. My admiration and affection for Marion have endured to this day.

After the divorce, which took place around my 21st birthday in 1949, I was determined to reunite with Gina, visit my relatives and see the miracle called Israel.

If the facts don't fit the theory, change the facts.
-Albert Einstein

Chapter 21
Israel: The Promised Land

On May 14, 1948, the State of Israel was established and we, the stateless Jews living in Germany, could travel there without a passport. We could not believe there was a country where we would be let in just because we were Jews.

Shortly after my separation from Marion, the Jewish Student Organization received notice that in July 1949, an International Jewish Student Convention would take place in the newly-formed State of Israel. The organizing committee would pay all the expenses for ten delegates from Munich. Others could go if they paid their way, which was not within the means of most of us. Nearly everyone of the 400 of us wanted to be a delegate. We decided to distribute the ten places by lottery. I hoped that I would be one of the winners. This would be my opportunity to see the Jewish State, which was a dream come true. On a more personal level, I wanted to see Gina and my aunts and other relatives with whom I kept up correspondence. Unfortunately, I was not among the ten lucky members, and tried in vain to come up with the money.

One day, I was approached by Felek Korn, another member of the leadership of the Student Organization, who told me that an 11th free ticket had been made available to us and that the group had decided that I would be the recipient of it as a reward for my work on behalf of the organization.

I notified Gina and my relatives that I would soon be visiting the state of Israel. Even though I was the youngest in the group, I was elected to be in charge of the trip and had access to the travel documents. I saw in the papers that among the 30 students traveling, the organizing committee subsidized not 11 but 10 delegates. My passage was paid in cash, which was a large amount in dollars. I was puzzled and curious as to who my anonymous benefactor was. It turned out that Giza Zieman had secretly paid my fare.

We traveled by train from Munich to Marseilles, where we were to board an Israeli ship and go to Haifa. The ship we were looking for was named "Cadima" meaning "forward" in Hebrew. It was exciting to know that we would travel on an Israeli ship. I became weepy when I saw the blue and white flag of the State of Israel, with the Star of David flying from the stern of the ship. This was the first time that the existence of a Jewish state became a reality for me.

The Cadima was a small ship, and the students traveled in steerage. We slept most of the time on deck but in spite of it, we had a great time. When the ship pulled into the port of Haifa, I was on the bow; the first person I saw on the pier was Gina. The scene was exactly as I had described in my letter to her. I noticed that she no longer had her blond braids, but she looked even more beautiful than I remembered.

I was the first one to get off the ship, and hugged Gina. Next to her were my Uncle Alexander and his wife Bracha. Alexander was my father's older brother, in Palestine he adopted the name Tenen. My reunion with Gina was cut short because a truck from the kibbutz of S'Day Nachum, where Alexander and Bracha lived, was waiting. I had little choice but to go with my uncle and aunt to the kibbutz. I told Gina that I would visit her soon in Tel-Aviv.

Alexander and Bracha had come to Palestine as pioneers in the early 1930s. I had a vague recollection of Alexander from my early childhood. Bracha was a Russian Jew whom Alexander had met in Palestine. She did not speak Polish, and I conversed with her in a mixture of Russian and Yiddish. I was trying to pass my German as Yiddish and my Polish as Russian. Alexander and Bracha had four little boys with whom I communicated by sign language. They were a wonderful family and I loved being with them.

Alexander worked hard in the fields, while Bracha was in charge of the poultry farm. I was used to chickens wandering around Polish farmyards; here they were kept in indoor chambers, which I thought was cruel. I worked in the fields. Every morning I was picked up by a truck driver, who turned out to be a general in the Israeli army and a well-known archeologist. My stay on the kibbutz was fascinating but I was eager to see Gina in Tel Aviv and visit my mother's four sisters—Klara, Kacia, Rywa, Sonia—and their families.

Before I left the kibbutz, Uncle Alexander insisted that I wear my American army surplus shirt and pants from the DP camp, instead of the elegant German shirt and fashionable slacks that I had bought for the trip. He also gave me a typical Israeli hat. "Now you look like a Sabra" (a native-born Israeli), he said with satisfaction. At this point I did not realize that my uncle was concealing the fact that I was a survivor. Israel was flooded with survivors who were viewed with contempt by fellow Jews of Israel.

In those days in Israel, the Army operated most of the vehicles. Hitchhikers gathered on the outskirts of town and hoped to get a free ride. It was on a first-come-first-serve basis. I joined such a group outside the town of Afula, expecting to take my turn to get a ride. But a military jeep pulled up, the driver pointed to me to hop in and I was on my way.

The young soldier spoke only Hebrew and I could not find out why he had singled me out. He was not going all the way to Tel Aviv and dropped me off at another hitchhiker gathering spot. There the same thing happened. A military truck full of soldiers stopped and I was the only one who was picked up.

The mystery was solved a few days later in Tel Aviv. The city bus drivers regularly refused to accept payment from me. One time, I insisted on paying and the driver said, "Ata Hajal." This time I understood that the words meant, "You are a soldier," and told him "Lo" ("no" in Hebrew) and paid my fare. In the early days of its existence, the Israeli Army wore surplus American uniforms just like what they had given us in the DP camps. My uncle's design became clear to me. I changed into "civilian" clothing. In Israel, I was not about to pretend that I was someone I was not.

It was wonderful to see my aunts, their husbands and children. Uncle Yehoshua and Aunt Klara came from Jerusalem to meet me. The next day a party was held in my honor, attended by 70 relatives. The Kowarski family had many dedicated Zionists who had come to Palestine as pioneers. Sonia and Rywa, identical twin sisters, were no longer indistinguishable. Sonia, who survived the death camp Stuthof, looked younger than Rywa, who had lived in Palestine since the late 1920s and worked as a nurse with her gynecologist husband, Ravitz. Before the war, not even close friends could tell them apart.

Uncle Yehoshua Kowarski was a well-known painter and a man about town. I remembered him well from his visits to Miechow. We developed a close friendship during my three-month stay in Israel. My admiration for Klara was intensified during this visit. Just like in Warsaw, she was surrounded by interesting people.

In Tel-Aviv, I lived with Sonia and her husband, Kalman Avineri. Kalman was a chemist from Wilno who received his education at the Sorbonne. Both treated me with great affection. They lived a few houses away from Ben-Gurion, whom I saw a few times in the street. Aunt Kacia was married to Jacob Wapnik, also from Wilno. He was an electrical engineer and he, too, had been educated in France. I spent time with my cousins with whom I could not talk without an interpreter.

On the second day after my arrival in Tel-Aviv, I went to see Gina. She lived in a one-bedroom apartment not far from the beach. In the middle of the living room was a round table with a carved wooden box on it. "Guess what is in the box?" Gina asked with a mysterious smile. After a few failed attempts on my part, she opened the box. Inside were all the letters I had written to her. This and other signs of her love for me did not penetrate my defensive belief that my love for her was unrequited. In my view, she was solicitous only because I had saved her life. We met many times but our connection remained platonic; I did not dare to approach her.

Giza Zieman had a younger sister who lived with her mother in a fancy apartment in Tel-Aviv. She still used her Christian name, "Krysia," a diminutive of Kristine. She had survived on false papers, thanks to her Aryan looks. She had blond hair, blue eyes and a fair complexion. The rest of her family had to be hidden, because they looked Jewish. Krysia, whose real name was Nechama, was two years younger than I. Little did I know that Gina was determined to bring about a romantic relationship between us. It worked. Krysia and I became infatuated with one another. I was not aware that I was seeking an escape from my inability to accept Gina's love. There was talk of marriage, and we decided that Krysia would go back with me to Munich. We were informally engaged. I did not know that Krysia's romantic relationship with an older man, a physician named Leon Tec, perturbed the Bawnik family. They considered me preferable.

The Israeli army arranged a tour of the country for the student delegates. We traveled in a convoy of five military trucks from the Lebanon border in the North to the Negev desert in the South. It was amazing to see flourishing agriculture in what used to be desert. Historical places became a reality. Our excursion ended in Jerusalem, coinciding with the burial of the founder of political Zionism, Theodor Herzl, whose remains had been brought to Jerusalem from Vienna. He had died in 1904, the year my father was born. It was a moving ceremony, which I attended with Aunt Klara and her husband. The final resting-place of this visionary was a hill west of Jerusalem, which is now known as Mount Herzl. In my childhood, his Zionist ideas had been Utopian, but a mere dozen years later, I stood at his graveside in the State of Israel. I read Herzl's novel "Altneuland" (Old New Land) before leaving Germany. In this work of fiction he fantasized the creation of a Jewish state. The book ended with the sentence: "If you will it, it is no legend."

As I stood by Herzl's gravesite, I thought about my father.

I know how and by whom my father was killed. I don't know when he was murdered or what happened to his body. There is no monument marking his gravesite and there was no burial ceremony to commemorate his life.

Burial practices have deep psychological significance. How the burial ritual is conducted reflects the feelings of the living for the dead. Psychologically, at least viewed from the perspective of the living, individual burial of a loved one represents a way of relating to the deceased. Burial ritual is an expression of feelings of the bereaved that is public and therefore shame provoking if not appropriate.

The vast, empty ground of the concentration camp Plaszow is no longer a cemetery, but the site of an atrocity. My father is one of the many unknown victims murdered at that location. The Germans killed him and the memory of him. Not even his name remains, as I changed my name from Tenenwurzel to Tanay.

People of all cultures erect some marker on the burial site of a loved one. In Buddhism there is a tradition of erecting a burial mound called a "stupa." The ancient Egyptians built a structure called a "masteba" in which to keep the mummies, to say nothing of the magnificent structures created for the pharaohs. According to Greek legend and a play by Sophocles, Antigone was condemned to die because she performed the burial rites for her brother Polynices. Creon forbade the burial of Polynices as punishment for an act of rebellion. Out of the seven known tragedies of Sophocles, two deal with the subject of respectable burial.

In December of 1991, I visited my mother's grave in Sydney, Australia. Nathan, my mother's second husband, pointed his cane to a space next to my mother's gravesite and said, "I bought this plot a few years ago so I will be buried next to Betty." He made all the necessary arrangements for his burial. Nearby, a burial ceremony was being conducted. Nathan pointed to a man and said, "That is the president of the Burial Society. I want you to meet him." Nathan, who was then an 80-year-old concentration camp survivor, was facing his death with equanimity. He considered it an event requiring preparation and planning.

In 1997, Nathan Rottenberg, unlike all of his family, died a natural death. He was taken to a hospital by ambulance with a coronary occlusion. Within hours he believed that he was in a concentration camp and insisted on leaving against medical advice. I could not persuade him otherwise. He is buried next to my Mother, his beloved Betty.

To live in the State of Israel and to have the love of Gina was the fulfillment of my adolescent dreams. But at the end of the three-month visit, I no longer wanted to settle in Israel and I believed that Gina had no interest in marrying me. It was my feeling that neither wanted me. There was some reality to the feeling of rejection by Israel; survivors were treated with pity and ambivalence.

The survivors were the disdained newcomers in Israel and outcasts in Poland. One cannot shed one's identity or acquire one on request. The pioneers transformed the desert into gardens; they expected to do the same with people.

Israel wanted me on its own terms. Uncle Alexander's compliment, "Now you look like a Sabra," acquired a new meaning. I was expected to become a pseudo-Sabra and reject my Holocaust survivor identity. I was astounded by Gina's avoidance of the past; she wanted to be like a Sabra.

I realized that my need to live a life of authenticity could not be fulfilled in Israel. I felt like a stranger among my own people. Surviving the Holocaust was to me an identity-transforming experience, which I would not disown.

The attitudes of the Israelis to the Holocaust survivors have changed greatly in the last 50 years. It is popular to claim that survivors have been significantly assisted by emissaries of the Yeshuv and the Jewish Brigade to leave Eastern Europe. The 1945 and 1946 escape of Polish Jews from Poland to West Germany was not the result of an organized effort that came from the outside. It was an individual action and not a collective undertaking.

I heard Yehuda Bauer, a respected Israeli historian, assert in a speech to nearly 1,000 people attending the Conference on Jewish Displaced Persons on January 14, 2000 that a "Briha commander" was in charge of the exodus of Jews from Eastern Europe to West Germany.

In 1945, I went five times to Poland from Hungary and then to Germany. No one assisted me. I have not seen nor heard about a single Israeli who was active in those years in Eastern Europe. I came to Munich in the early summer of 1945. I never heard of the term "Briha" and never saw a Jew from Palestine until about six months after I was in Munich. Throughout the time that I was in Western Germany, I laid eyes on two or three members of the Jewish Brigade.

Tom Segev, a respected Israeli journalist, wrote years later that the reports by the members of Jewish Agency described "the refuges as a formless, faceless mass, human debris, a huge community of beggars, degenerate, backward, diminished not only physically and psychologically but also morally."[56]

The negative attitudes to the survivors are now forgotten; we are no longer objects of pity and contempt. I was always aware of my identity as a survivor. I

206

did not choose this identity and cannot choose to give it up. I am the eternal outsider.

The return voyage from Haifa to Marseilles was pleasant; this time we felt like tourists on a cruise. My headaches vanished. Krysia and I enjoyed each other's company. Paris, where we spent a few days, was glorious.

In Munich, I filed for divorce from Marion. Mr. Bawnik, Krysia's father, came to visit us, and to look over his prospective son-in-law. We got along very well. He suggested that I finish my studies in Switzerland and offered to pay for them. When I declined, he said, "I am a businessman, you will pay me back with interest." I did not take him up on the offer.

Yet, the relationship with Krysia did not work out. After all, she was blonde, which limited the scope of my erotic activities. Krysia left Munich after a few weeks. Both of us knew that it was over without admitting it. As a parting gift, Krysia gave me a complete set of medical textbooks, something I could not afford, and each contained a mushy inscription. We liked each other, but our true loves were in Israel. I loved Gina Olmer and Krysia loved Leon Tec.

After Krysia left Munich she resumed her relationship with Leon Tec, and has been happily married to him for nearly 50 years. Nechama Tec (Krysia) is a well-known Holocaust researcher and a professor of sociology in Connecticut. We remain good friends to this day.

Love is all very well in its way, but friendship is much higher. Indeed, I know of nothing in the world that is even nobler or rarer than a devoted friendship.
                              -Oscar Wilde

Chapter 22
Love and Friendship

The books that Krysia gave me made the study of medicine easier. Memorizing endless details was boring; attending medical lectures was an ordeal for me. The joy of learning I had experienced in studying political science was gone. It was customary for two or more medical students to get together and prepare for the examinations. I began to study with Tosia Hechtkopf, an attractive girl my age with pitch-black hair. Our examination schedules coincided. She had the good fortune to have an intact family; a father, mother and younger sister. They lived in a spacious apartment on Troger Street 52 in the Bogenhausen district of Munich. By our standards, they were rich. Her father established a small shirt factory in Munich. Tosia and I had different backgrounds and personalities. She did not have my Holocaust experiences but both of us were Polish Jews.

Tosia and I would start early in the morning, be served lunch by her mother, followed by a midday break which, as time went on, developed into a sexual interlude. Afterward, we would resume the boring memorization for the examination. I liked Tosia but was still in love with Gina. I continued to correspond with her. It became obvious that my feeling of rejection by Gina was a figment of my imagination based upon my selective sexual inhibition in relation to her.

Gina wrote that she would come to Europe, but could not visit Germany. Israel and Germany did not have diplomatic relations at that time. Israeli passports were stamped "Not valid for travel to Germany." In order to meet me, she got a job in Vienna, but I could not travel to Austria. I was still stateless and did not have a passport. The Austrian consulate was sympathetic to my predicament, but that was the extent of their help.

I knew that there was smuggling going on between Germany and Austria. Cigarettes were the primary contraband. I asked Gina to meet me on a specific date at the railroad station in Salzburg, which was over the mountain from Bad Reichenhal, on the German side. My plan was to hire a smuggler in that city. But when I arrived in Bad Reichenhal, I discovered that the smugglers were asking too much money for the guidance into Austria. I had to get across on my own. It was spring of 1951 and there was still snow at the higher elevations. I could not take the easy way out for fear of apprehension by Austrian border patrols, which would result in a criminal conviction and preclude my emigration to America. I would also miss seeing Gina.

I took a route that required mountain climbing. It was arduous, but I arrived safely at the railroad station in time to meet Gina's train from Vienna. Just like in Haifa a few months before, we fell into each other's arms and talked for a long time, sitting on a bench at the railroad station. The bond between us was much more than romantic love; we were attached to each other like two frontline soldiers who have faced death side by side. Finally, I went to a counter with a sign saying "Tourist Accommodations" and asked for a hotel room.

"Two rooms or one," the elderly clerk asked, looking at the two of us. I hesitated and was about to ask for two rooms, assuming that Gina would not want to share a room with me. Before I could answer, Gina quickly interjected: "One room please." I was astonished, pleased and intimidated.

More than 50 years later, I have a vivid picture of the sunny room with a large bed in the middle. I also have a clear memory of my inability to make love to Gina. I felt devastated. My sexual inhibition in relation to Gina was undeniable. I expected rejection from her but she was as loving and serene as ever. However, I was convinced that she felt contempt for me. Youth is wasted on the young, said George Bernard Shaw. An obstacle that a few minutes of patience could have solved destroyed my dream of marrying Gina.

We nevertheless managed to have a pleasant time sightseeing for the next two days. Gina even took the bus with me to the German border when the time came to go back. This time I was more daring. I simply walked up to the border crossing and sneaked to the German side when the guard was not looking. After a few minutes, I returned to the barricade separating Austria from Germany and said farewell to Gina, who had waited for me at the barrier. We delayed the parting as long as possible. We both knew that it was a turning point in our relationship. I had given up Marion and now I was losing Gina.

To this day, Gina and I regularly cross the Atlantic for the sake of spending a few days with each other. We talk on the phone often. I have had a few girlfriends and three wives, and all of them have encouraged my relationship with Gina. My wife Sandy and Gina are the best of friends. Whoever loves me, loves Gina. She remains an enduring presence in my life. Did the lifelong love and friendship endure in spite of or because we never became lovers? I will never know. However, one thing is certain; Gina is the center of wonderful memories and a never-ending source of warm feelings. Both of us have been sustained by a friendship that endures and nurtures.

After the Salzburg expedition, I returned to Munich feeling defeated. The long held dream of marrying Gina ended. Before I left for Salzburg, Tosia was eager for us to get married, and we had long discussions on the subject. I did not plan to marry her because I was in love with Gina, and Tosia had personality traits I found thorny. She was highly emotional and often difficult to deal with.

But after Salzburg, I changed my mind. I could not marry Gina because of my sexual problem with her, and I persuaded myself that Tosia's personality would change. Her parents were opposed to our marriage. To them I was not a Jew. I was not religious and worse than that, I was not "learned" in the Talmud. Mr. Hechtkopf, Tosia's father, came to see me with a famous rabbi. They argued that it was not appropriate for a person of my background to marry a girl from a religious family. I acknowledged my ignorance of Talmud but rose to the defense of my family.

"My great-grandfather was the famous Radoszycer Cadyk," I told them. Suddenly, I became respectable and desirable as a son-in-law. My ancestry was the basis for some people to hate me and for others to respect me. The rabbi and my future father-in-law would have been shocked if I had told them that I saw a similarity in their views and those of the Nazis.

The wedding day was scheduled for September 25, 1951. In the summer of 1951, I received a notice that I must report to "Funk Kaserne" (Funk Barracks), a transit camp for DPs programmed for departure to the United States. If one did not report for departure on the day scheduled, one lost the chance to go to America. Leaving Germany was the highest priority, and I reported as required for the preliminary procedures.

Going to America would require changing our marriage date and would prevent my graduation from medical school, which was to take place, at the earliest, in December 1951. Many of my friends, who had left for the United States before graduating, had to work menial jobs in New York to get enough money to return and finish their education. Waiting my turn to be processed in the Funk Kaserne DP Camp, I walked into the office of an American female official. I explained my situation, and she understood enough German to get an idea of the problem. She took a piece of paper and wrote on it: "Abraham Benjamin Shmulewsky," and told me to see him. This was the American vice consul in charge of the immigration of Displaced Persons.

It took some effort to see such an important official. Mr. Shmulewsky was a handsome, dark-haired man with a mustache. He listened to my story through a German interpreter, and reached for the phone. "Emanuel Tenenwurzel's file please," he said.

A secretary brought my file and Mr. Shmulewsky opened the bottom drawer of his desk, put the file into it and said, "Your file has just gotten lost. It will be found after you let me know that you have gotten married and passed your examinations."

I thanked him, and he smiled like a man who had found a simple solution to a complicated problem. He warned me: "If your story is not true, you will never go to America." A German official would have asked for documentary verification. As proof of my veracity, I invited him to our wedding. To my astonishment, he accepted.

Our wedding was a festive occasion attended by many students and the American and Israeli consuls. At the time, I was a night watchman at the Israeli consulate. Shmulewsky and I became friends in spite of the language barrier. Thanks to him, we were able to get on one of the last ships taking displaced persons to America. The DP Immigration Act was expiring on December 30, 1951. My dissertation for the doctoral degree would not be completed until after Christmas.

In Germany, one becomes a medical doctor upon completion of the licensing examination as a physician. Then one can present a doctoral thesis that may result in the granting of the academic title of a Doctor, the equivalent of the American Ph.D. degree. Many German physicians practice without getting this honorary title.

The day after I had my last doctoral examination, Tosia and I were on the train to the Bremen DP transit camp, from there we went aboard the US Navy Ship *General Blatchford*, a liberty type cargo vessel.

These mass-produced ships were known for their poor performance at sea. Most troops on board would get seasick and would be unfit for combat on arrival. I was designated to be in charge of the DPs during the voyage. I had the imposing title of "Commandant" and the responsibility for organizing everything from food distribution to the assignment of sleeping bunks. I assumed that the captain had chosen me to be in charge on the recommendation of Shmulewsky, or because I was the only male physician on board.

The Navy personnel were concerned with the nautical phase of crossing the Atlantic. All other functions had to be performed by us. The captain made daily inspections of the human cargo; otherwise we had no contact with the Americans. The ship was terribly overcrowded, and stormy weather made it impossible to get on deck. If everyone got out of their bunk, there wasn't enough room to stand. Most passengers were Ukrainians or from the Baltic countries. Americans considered them Displaced Persons; they had to flee the Soviets as Nazi collaborators. Many had served in Baltic SS units; some were involved in special units dealing with extermination of the Jews. One Hungarian Jew came to me to report that one of the passengers was a Hungarian ethnic German, known for persecution of the Jews. It so happened that this man was the only English-speaking person among us. He had some special connection with the Americans. He was the interpreter whenever I communicated with the captain. I could do nothing against him as he was under American protection, assisting in ferreting out communists.

We hold these truths to be self-evident, that all men are created equal, that they are endowed by their Creator with certain inalienable rights that among these are life, liberty and the pursuit of happiness.
–Thomas Jefferson

Chapter 23
Home at Last

It was a bitter, cold day in early January 1952 when the USN ship *General Blatchford* pulled into New York harbor. It was almost seven years to the day since liberation.

An immigration agent interrogated me as soon as we got off the ship. The documents clearly stated that I was liberated in the Mauthausen concentration camp by American troops but he asked: "How long did you serve in the Red Army during the war?" The German interpreter was the Hungarian ethnic German who had been identified to me as a Nazi on the ship. He turned out to be an American agent. I was enraged by this trick question and answered in an irritated manner. "Children did not serve in the Red Army during the war."

The country was in the grip of anti-Communist hysteria. But the unwelcome reception by a suspicious communist hunter did not diminish my joy of stepping onto American soil. I was about to enter the country I hoped would become my home.

The sight of the Statue of Liberty evoked a "home at last" feeling. Almost 50 years later, these three words sum up my feelings about living in this country. America fulfilled its promise. It has become my home. In the United States, I do not feel like an exile, which I am certain would be my experience had I immigrated to any another country.

"Emek! Emek!" someone yelled as we were walking from the ship to the bus, which was to take us to the refugee shelter. It was incredible to hear my real name, which I had not heard since I left home in Miechow.

I recognized my uncle, Yehoshua Kowarski, and his wife Corrine Chochem standing behind a barrier. Corrine was holding a bouquet of flowers. They looked half frozen. After some hugging, we were in a taxicab instead of an immigrant bus. I never expected that there would be someone to welcome us in America.

My uncle Yehoshua, a well-known modern painter, to my knowledge lived permanently in Israel. Before leaving Bremen, I had sent postcards to various relatives telling them that we were leaving for America. The only address I had for Yehoshua was at the Hotel Alamac in New York. I was certain that he was no longer in the hotel but I had sent it anyway; as it turned out, he had indeed received it.

The taxi pulled up to a grand building on Park Avenue. A doorman rushed to open the door and a few minutes later we were in a large apartment that belonged to Pauline Koner, a ballerina, and her husband, a symphony conductor named Mahler (a nephew of Gustav Mahler). They were on tour in the Soviet Union and Yehoshua and Corrine had the key to their plush apartment. We spent a week in New York before going on to Chicago, which was our destination. We fell in love with New York. It was like the European cities we knew, except it was bigger and very American.

I remember taking a walk in Central Park early one morning. Skyscrapers dominated the horizon but I was enjoying an oasis of nature. The park was empty. The occasional car would come to a standstill at the stop sign even though there was no other car visible and there were no policemen to enforce the law. America was a land of law-abiding people. Freedom and adherence to rules gave me a sense of security.

Corinne and Yehoshua introduced us to many interesting people, mostly artists and writers. One evening, a writer tried to persuade me to stay in New York and work with him on a book about my experiences. Yehoshua encouraged me to do so. I was determined to write a book about "The War." The term Holocaust was not yet used to describe what had happened to the European Jews. I told him that I wanted to write it myself in English, which I hoped to learn soon.

After our week in New York, Yehoshua and Corrine placed us on a railroad car headed for the "Windy City." Our stay in New York did not prepare us for the city of Chicago and the reception we would receive there.

The HIAS (Hebrew Immigration Aid Society) placed us in the home of Mrs. Saloway, on Chicago's west side. This old woman had left a Polish village at the turn of the century, and assumed that Poland had remained the same as she left it. She tried to explain to us what a radio was. It did not occur to her that two greenhorns, both of whom were physicians, would be familiar with such advanced technology as a radio. The apartment was run-down and the neighborhood a slum.

One day, in the empty streets I searched for a public toilet. I ran into Dr. Victor Platt, a fellow student from Munich, and he told me that there was no such thing as public toilets in America. The absence of public toilets was striking to me. In all European cities, one was always within walking distance of a public facility.

In the towns we had known, people interacted with each other on the street and in apartment buildings. In Chicago, families were isolated in their single-family homes and their cars. In my view, a place where streets were full of cars and virtually no people did not deserve to be called a city. Chicago's downtown, the Loop, was not an urban center but a cluster of stores and offices. In those days, there were no large apartment buildings in downtown.

After living in Chicago for a few months, I noted that my socks did not have holes in them, since I walked so little. Public toilets and holes in socks were to me part of living in a city. So were theaters, opera and concert halls. The theaters and the Lyric Opera of Chicago were not impressive in the 1950s. Chicago was not what the Germans called a Gross Stadt (big city). After Munich and a brief stay in New York City, being in Chicago was a disappointment. It was my first encounter with urban sprawl and its twin, the slum.

Our first concern was for both of us to be admitted to an internship in an accredited hospital. In those days Michael Reese was the best hospital in Chicago and we were eager to be accepted there. But Michael Reese Hospital, according to the grapevine, did not accept foreign graduates. On March 5th, my 24th birthday, I received a letter from Uncle Yehoshua addressed to: Emanuel Tanay c/o Emanuel Tenenwurzel. We were just about to leave for Michael Reese Hospital to be interviewed by the clinical director. I stuck the envelope in my suit pocket. Uncle Yehoshua had persisted in his effort to have me modify my name to one that Americans would be able to pronounce.

The Yiddish-speaking medical director of Michael Reese Hospital, Dr. Morris Weiss, talked to us for a long time. The hospital had no female interns and the interns' quarters housed males only. Dr. Weiss seemed to think that Tosia would not seek the internship. However, when he was told both of us were applying, he accepted us for the internship on the condition that before July 1st, I would master enough English to take a medical history from a patient. Tosia, unlike me, knew some English. We had to agree to become assistant interns immediately without any assurance that in July we would become regular interns. There was also the problem of a name.

"Tenenwurzel is a name that no one will be able to pronounce and it will not fit on the paging board," Dr. Weiss told me.

I pulled out the envelope with the name Emanuel Tanay from my pocket. "How about this?" I asked. "Perfect," was his reply. Once again, my new life required a new name.

Three months later, I was called to the director's office. Dr. Weiss instructed me. "Here is the name of a patient. Go and take a medical history from her. I have her chart and we will compare your history with that of her English-speaking intern," I was back in an hour with a few pages of medical history. "You have a more detailed account of her illness than the American intern," he said approvingly. I began to laugh. He was puzzled by my reaction; I told him that the elderly women spoke only German. He too began to laugh. I was accepted to the most desirable internship in Chicago.

Being an intern, next to surviving in wartime, was the most difficult time of my life. The demands were incredible. We worked 36 hours and had 12 hours off. We were paid $15 a month. When dealing with indigent patients we were, as a practical matter, in charge of the entire care of the patient. I felt inadequate for the task and often too tired to think clearly. Most memorable and troublesome were the two months I spent in the Emergency Room.

The Emergency Room at Michael Reese Hospital was a world unto itself. It resembled a war zone. The intern on call was the only physician. In theory we could call residents or even attending physicians, but in practice this was rarely done. Residents were busy and attending physicians were inaccessible. Even if called, they would come too late; most of them lived in far away suburbs. Gunshot wounds and victims of stabbings had to be taken care of. A never-ending supply of DOAs (dead on arrival) had to be pronounced dead. The DOAs were not brought into the hospital. I had to walk out to the patrol car and confirm the policeman's diagnosis. Police were the only resource for poor people. Emergency Medical Services were nonexistent.

My signature then entitled the policeman to take the body to a funeral home of his choice, where he would receive a $10 "reward." "Doc, take a look at mine, I was first," the competing cops pleaded. I would climb into the squad car, shine my flashlight into the unresponsive pupils and declare the person legally dead. Most troubling to me were the bleeding victims who could not be taken care of in our emergency room and who could not be admitted to the hospital because they were too poor, and had to be taken instead to the Cook County Hospital, which also required an intern's approval. I would go out to the patrol wagon, stop the bleeding by applying a hemostat or two, and send the policeman on his way to Cook County Hospital. A nurse would make the policeman sign that he was responsible for returning the valuable instruments.

The first time I ever delivered a baby by myself was in the back of a police cruiser outside of our emergency room. The indigent patient was then taken to the Cook County Hospital downtown. A mere few feet away, paying patients received excellent care from competent staff. Even in the war torn Germany, the disparity of care between the haves and have-nots was not that pronounced.

Dealing with dying patients and their families was a challenging and maturing experience. I learned that it is futile to use heroic measures to postpone death by days or hours. At first I participated in these medical exhibitions of grandiosity. An elderly doctor whom I admired greatly took me aside and told me that people have the right to die without being used for our grandstanding. German medical education and American clinical experience was a good combination. The former stressed exactness, the latter taught acceptance of the fallibility of human nature and human institutions. The emergency room was my introduction to what could be called American pragmatic idealism.

Reflections

Why shouldn't truth be stranger than fiction? Fiction, after all, has to make sense.
-Mark Twain

Chapter 24
I Do Not Believe What I Remember

It is Friday evening, November 8, 1996. I am in the apartment of my cousin Louis Bernstein, a Sydney cardiologist. The whole family is sitting down to a traditional Friday night meal. For a Holocaust survivor, I have a large family. Sandy and I arrived in Australia at 6:40 a.m. on Air New Zealand from Los Angeles. My cousin Harold Kerr met us at the airport and my niece, Danita Needleman, joined us shortly after.

Aunt Pola Bernstein, my father's sister and Louis' mother, sits next to me. She is 94 years old and is served first by one of the granddaughters. She pushes the plate towards me: "He is the guest of honor."

Leah, the lady of the house, with the help of her three daughters, prepared a great meal. We are enjoying the food and above all, each other's company. I recall such festive meals at the home of my grandparents in Kielce. The beautiful gathering in Sydney is a reminder that the Jewish culture of Europe is dead. There are no Jews in Kielce, where the large Tenenwurzel family lived for generations.

The conversation around the table turned to the headline of the day. Australian officials had refused an entry visa to an English historian named David Irving, who denies that the Holocaust took place. My Australian relatives are pleased and proud of their government. They are surprised that I, the only Holocaust survivor at the table, don't share their views. I tell them that I find it amazing that so many people, fifty years after World War II, believe that the Holocaust did take place. I do not believe what I remember. The Holocaust is unbelievable. The Jews in Poland, before and during World War II, did not believe that there was a Holocaust in the making. "People who deny the Holocaust are useful. They stimulate discussion, bring history alive, and provide an opportunity to explore doubts," I said.

"What doubts?" Danita asks with some indignation; everyone at the table agrees with her.

"I am a forensic psychiatrist and I like to be cross-examined. It gives me the opportunity to address the inevitable doubts about my prior testimony that any jury is likely to have." I respond. As a final point, I told my relatives that I believe it is a waste of time to debate if the Holocaust happened with people who deny the reality of it.

The literature on the Holocaust does little to make the Holocaust credible. Elie Wiesel wrote a book called *Night*, but did not claim that he was writing about reality, even though he was. Steven Spielberg made a powerful movie about Plaszow, a small concentration camp located on the grounds of an old Jewish cemetery in Krakow. A death camp on the grounds of a cemetery shows dramatic flair, but this is not believable even though it is factually true.

It is hard to believe that Oscar Schindler, a German businessman, card-carrying Nazi and a notorious womanizer, would risk his life to save Jews. It is also hard to believe that a cultured German officer named Amon Goeth would, while eating breakfast, step out onto his balcony and shoot people at random, then return to his table to continue the meal. Who can believe that a German officer Amon Goeth shot my father in front of the assembled inmates of the camp Plaszow? Even less believable is the fact that Goeth gathered the entire camp population to watch his dogs kill Mr. Olmer, Gina's father.

That is just as unbelievable as the account that I, a teenage boy, saved my mother, my sister, Gina and myself from being killed by the Germans.

It is not believable that the Germans "exterminated" the Jews of Europe by using Cyclon B, a poison manufactured by I.G. Farben, Germany's largest chemical company. Vermin are exterminated, but people are killed. People, after they die, are buried. The murdered Jews of Europe were incinerated in "Kremas" built by Topfer & Sons, a German industrial establishment. This sounds more like gruesome science fiction than historical reality.

The indignation about the Holocaust denials is inconsistent with the widespread view that the Holocaust is unbelievable, unimaginable and indescribable. A state sponsored program to exterminate a whole nation should be greeted with disbelief. I am more concerned about indifference of the many than denial by the few.

A misguided historian is less troubling to me than the schoolteacher from Tennessee who sat next to me on a flight from Chicago to Tampa in January 2000. She asked me enough questions to find out that I am a Holocaust survivor.

"I know all about it, my best friend went through the same thing," she said.

It turned out that her friend was an ethnic German who had to leave Eastern Europe when Nazi Germany lost the war. Time and again, I have met Americans who fail to see the difference between the hardships suffered by the citizens of Nazi Germany, their collaborators, and the genocide of the Jews. The ignorance of the well-meaning majority is more distressing than the willful distortions of the mean-spirited minority. The plausible myth is a much greater danger to historical accuracy than the grotesque falsehood.

Jews are obsessed with revisionism of the Holocaust, as if this was a prevailing view. More Americans accept that extraterrestrial beings in flying saucers visited the earth than hold the view that the Holocaust is a hoax invented by German-hating Jews. Some questions raised about the Holocaust are appropriate, since it is inevitable that some of our information is inaccurate. All historical events require never-ending revision by research.

The word "revisionism" is derived from the Latin and it simply means to look at something from a different point of view. Taking a different approach to old theories is the method pursued by all sciences. New discoveries require revision of old theories. My professor of Political Science in Munich used to say, "A good theory is like a suitcase as long as it accommodates all of the facts. If you require more facts, you get a new suitcase." The trouble with the Holocaust Revisionism is that it has no new facts, only new fantasies.

At this time, the Holocaust is very well remembered and acknowledged in the Western World. In May of 2001 in Sarasota, Florida, I lectured about the Holocaust on three separate occasions, to a total of 3,300 middle school and high school students. The questions asked by these youngsters demonstrated their great interest in and knowledge of the Holocaust.

The kids asked, "How did you eat? How did you wash your clothes? How did you find where to live? Did you have money? Were you scared? Were you able to sleep?" Such real life issues were the least of my problems. Suddenly, I felt skeptical about my past. How did I manage to overcome all the dangers that faced me in those five long years? Did I really survive all those challenges? Are my memories merely a figment of my imagination? My past is unbelievable even to me.

In Munich, shortly after liberation, most of us were thinking about writing an account of our survival. One of us, a man named Jacob Littner, did it. In 1947, he left his manuscript with a German publisher in Munich who assigned a German writer named Wolfgang Koeppen, the task of editing it. The book was published in 1948 as a work of fiction, giving Koeppen as the author. Littner died in New York in 1950 and Koeppen died in 1996. Literary research "unmasked" the work of fiction as an autobiography. It is likely that Koeppen recognized that in the 1940s, Littner's account of Holocaust survival would not be believable unless presented as a work of fiction.

It is understandable that many young Germans find it hard to believe that their forefathers perpetrated horrendous atrocities and accepted the bizarre ideology of Nazi Germany. Race and blood had a supernatural significance in Nazi mythology. Nazi dogma maintained that the combination of the "bad blood" of the sub-human Jews with the blood of the noble Aryans would result in the death of the superior race. This notion became the canon of a new belief system that was embraced with passionate intensity by millions of Germans. Nazism elevated keeping Aryan blood pure to the Most Holy Obligation ("heiligste Verpflichtung") of the German nation.

The concept of race claims biological divergence among people. Georges-Louis Leclerc De Buffon, a brilliant French naturalist, first applied the term "race" to humans in the eighteenth century. There is a consensus among physical anthropologists and evolutionary biologists that race is not a biologically valid way to separate human beings. It is generally accepted that all humans share the same origin (Monogenesis). Polygenesis is a theory that some of the races have separate beginnings. The Bible tells us that all human beings were descended from Adam and Eve; therefore, Christians should have rejected the divergent theories of origin.

By no stretch of imagination could the Jews be considered a race. The fact that educated, intelligent people accepted this deserves to be subject of psychological research. The metaphorical blood of poets became the biological reality of Nazi Germany.

Dr. Von Fritz Lenz (1887-1970), a German physician-geneticist was a pioneer in race purification pseudo-science. The "racial hygiene" policies of Nazi Germany have deep roots in Germany. The Kaiser Wilhelm Society (KWG) was Germany's most prestigious scientific institution and focused a great deal of its attention on eugenics. The KWG operated between 1911 and 1945.[57] Dr. Von Fritz Lenz argued that race was "the ultimate principle of value." He was a leading ideologue in the Nazi race purification programs. One year after the end of World War II, Von Fritz Lenz regained his position as Professor of Genetics in Germany.

It would be foolish to assume that the intellectual content of Hitler's *Mein Kampf* generated the enthusiasm that was essential for the creation of the racist Nazism. A long history of militarism, the horrors of the First World War, and the notion that Germany was robbed of victory in that war by a conspiracy of liberals and Jews, made the Germans receptive to Nazi propaganda and ready to follow Hitler, a charismatic fanatic.

What Robert Lifton called the "medicalized killing" of sick German children and mentally ill Germans, was a pseudo-medical activity that laid the moral, methodological and quasi-legal foundation for the Holocaust. I say pseudo-medical, even though doctors were active participants in this crime. There were doctors who objected to it.

It is, indeed, difficult to imagine that physicians could become executioners. And yet a French physician, Joseph-Ignace Guillotine, devised the first modern technology of killing "bad people." His motives were "humanitarian." Both Dr. Guillotine and Dr. Brande, the organizer of the T-4 program of exterminating disabled Germans, claimed to be motivated by humanitarian concerns. The proponents of the death penalty in the United States prefer injection to the electric chair because it is more "humane."

Robert Lifton, in his classic study of these Nazi doctors, writes that after 10,000 sick Germans were killed, the doctors and the "medical personnel" of the German medical facility known as Hadamar, celebrated the occasion with a party. It is unbelievable but true that German doctors murdered German children by starvation, slow poisoning and later by gassing.[58]

Millions of Germans believed that survival of mankind required the elimination of Jews; this was a collective delusion that achieved the status of social consensus. The Holocaust, like slavery, is not believable. And yet slavery existed among humans for thousands of years. We find it in ancient India, Europe and all of Asia. Slaves played a significant role in Egypt. Slavery was widespread in Africa. The status of the Jews in German captivity had some similarities to slavery. The slaves and the Jews were subhuman in the eyes of their oppressors. However, the Holocaust in many respects differed from slavery.

The goal of slaveholders was exploitation of the slaves. The measure of success for the slaveholder was the quantity of work performed by the slave. Some sadistic slaveholders worked their slaves to death, but most protected their investment. A slave was mobile property; a Jew in Nazi Germany was "life unworthy of living."

A slave was bought to fulfill a pragmatic need of the slaveholder. The Jews had no property value to the Germans; they could not be bought or sold. A slave could be freed. The Hebrew Bible made it mandatory that slaves be liberated after six years (Exodus 21:2, Deuteronomy 15:12).

The death of a slave was an economic loss to his owner. The death of an able-bodied Jew was realistically a similar loss to the Third Reich. However, ideological dedication superceded economic interests in Nazi Germany. The primary objective of the Germans, even outside of the death camps, was "extermination" of the Jews. Work was a method of extermination. The cardinal measure of success of a facility was the number of Jews killed in a given day.

The situation of the Jews in German confinement was unparalleled because it was almost entirely based on ideology and hate.

We hate some persons because we do not know them; and we will not know them because we hate them.
-Charles Caleb Colton (1780 - 1832)

Chapter 25
Why Do People Hate?

The French singer Charles Trent captured one of life's blessings with his song, "I wish you Love." To wish someone to feel hate would be a curse. It is worse to hate than to be hated. I am grateful to have survived being hated without suffering the burden of hating. Hate transforms ordinary people into ruthless killers.

I spent my professional life as a forensic psychiatrist trying to understand why people kill other people. Killing people may be perceived as necessary, noble or evil, heroic or sadistic, but there is no controversy that intra-species killing is a unique human characteristic. Mark Twain observed: "The joy of killing! The joys of seeing killing done -- these are the traits of the human race at large."[59]

CONSCIENCE

Conscience is the need to behave consistently with recognized ethical principles. Behavior contrary to conscience leads to feelings of guilt. Conscience, ethical values, a capacity for empathy, the ability to love, to name but a few human attributes, have to be developed and nurtured in a child. The capacity to love and empathize comes with development and maturation. Narcissism and rage are primal emotions. Parents, peers and society create individual and collective conscience.

Adam Smith, long before Sigmund Freud, formulated a concept similar to Freud's Super Ego. In The Theory of Moral Sentiments, Adam Smith postulated the existence within each of us of an "inner man" who acts like an "impartial spectator" and passes judgment upon our behavior and that of others. Freud introduced the term superego to describe the same phenomenon. Killing the Jews did not violate the conscience of people who felt justified by religion or ideology to hate them.

An institution, unlike an individual, does not have a conscience; it has a policy or a program. Societies that promote hate suffer the consequences of raising children who hate. "Hitler Jugend" in Nazi Germany and the "Komsomol" in the Soviet Union taught children to hate. In 1995, I was asked to discuss a documentary the showed Palestinian school children being taught arithmetic with the help of a textbook that illustrated computations by showing dead bodies of the Israelis. The Palestinian children who attacked Israeli military forces are viewed as little heroes by the Palestinian society. They are called little soldiers.

More people in the United States oppose making abortion a crime than those who demand that it should be illegal. The anti-abortion organizations don't need police protection; they can promote hatred in tranquility. It is significant that the movement that calls itself "Pro Life" has inspired a great deal of hate and some murders. The people called "killers" by the Pro Life movements do not advocate hate and have no need to murder their antagonists. The opponents of peace in Israel and the opponents of abortion in the United States have absolute conviction that they are right, zero tolerance for people who oppose their point of view, an inability to compromise and the need to punish and take vengeance. They also have a clear conscience.

EMPATHY

As Fyodor Dostoyevsky famously said, it is easier to denounce the evil doer than to understand him. It requires little effort to have empathy for victims; empathy for perpetrators of atrocities is an act of will that is essential to the comprehension of genocides. Dr. Mengle was a contemporary of mine, a fellow physician who was educated like I, in a German university, but is more a stranger to me than an Australian aborigine. Nevertheless, I have tried to understand what motivated him.

The term empathy is relatively new in the English language; it differs from sympathy. The German equivalent "Einfühlung," was an everyday expression, which a German physician and the founder of scientific psychology Wilhelm Wundt (1832-1920) used as a technical term. E.G. Tichener, a student of Wundt, coined the English translation "empathy" in 1910.

One has to have an ability to feel separate from the subject in order to identify with his or her feelings. When the subject is a target of projection of feeling empathy becomes impossible. Empathy may serve benevolent or malevolent impulses. Selective absence of empathy is a characteristic of a dogmatist.

Empathy is not a matter of individual psychology alone. It involves cultural factors. Shared community values are a significant element in the ability of an individual to experience empathy. The cheering crowds in Islamic countries in response to the September atrocities had no empathy for the victims; they empathized with the Islamic suicide-martyrs.

Seduction and propaganda require empathy, as do psychotherapy and education. Diplomatic negotiations are successful if both parties have empathy.

The 1938 Munich conference was a disaster because Hitler had empathy and the British Prime Minister Neville Chamberlain did not. Chamberlain projected his qualities of fairness unto Hitler. The fair-minded British conservative assumed that Hitler was his German counterpart. Had Chamberlain been capable of empathy, he would have recognized that Hitler was an ideologue whose appetite was insatiable. Why did the English diplomats fail to recognize Hitler's personality? He revealed himself in *Mein Kampf* and his speeches. He showed by his actions that he meant what he said.

My father, a dentist in a small Polish town, had no difficulty to see Hitler for who he was. He ridiculed the Munich agreement from the moment that it was concluded.

MILITARY TRAINING AND HATE

One of the attributes of a good soldier, it is claimed, is hatred of the enemy. It was considered necessary to subject young men to abuse to make them into good soldiers. Abuse generates sadistic feelings. Military leaders understand that cruelty transforms placid young men into angry young men. Resentful soldiers become ferocious fighters. It is overlooked that hostile people are dangerous, not only to enemies, but also to friends and relatives. Inclusion of women into the military has reduced abusive training and will with passage of time eliminate it.

My brother-in-law, William McGrath, is a retired Marine Corps Colonel. I have heard him tell stories of training (euphemism for torment) of the US Marines. Bill remembered that when he was a young Lieutenant, if someone whispered after the lights were out; a non-commissioned officer would punish the whole dormitory. He would flip on the lights and yell "out of the rack", which meant that everyone had to jump out of the three layers of bunks and stand at attention. "In the rack," would be the next command. This continued for about twenty minutes until everyone was completely exhausted.

In the mess hall, Bill recalled, everyone stood by the table, next to their chairs. The non-commissioned officer would then command, "One, two, three - sit." Quite often the auditory result would displease the drill sergeant, who would instruct the few hundred hungry young men, "When I say sit, I want to hear one ass slap." The routine of getting up and sitting down would continue for about twenty minutes until the quality of the sound generated satisfied the tormentor disguised as a trainer.

I have heard similar accounts of "making men out of boys" in the few decades of being a consultant to the Veterans Administration. I have heard of "training" practices that had lethal consequences. Sadism disguised as training is still sadism.

William Styron, a distinguished American novelist, enlisted in the Marine Corps in World War II and was recalled to active duty during the Korean War. He characterized the boot camp as "one of the closest things in the free world to a concentration camp." Philip Caputo, the famed author of *A Rumor of War*, was a

Marine Lieutenant in Vietnam. He recalls a Drill Sergeant who made the troops chant at the top of their lungs, "Ambush is murder and murder is fun".

The Vietnam War has demonstrated that Americans are not immune to being perpetrators of atrocities. Shortly after the Tet offensive, I spent 10 long days in Danang at a Marine Corps base.

In spite of my opposition to the Vietnam War, I agreed to accept the so-called Presidential Invitational Order to go to Vietnam. I testified at a court martial of a young man named Alvarez, who was charged with six counts of first-degree murder. Before the trial, Alvarez was flown to the United States in order to be examined by me. This young man had had an episode of malaria, received a "Dear John" letter from his girlfriend and became depressed. A few of his buddies were killed in an ambush and there was a firefight at his outpost. The combination of these factors brought about a dissociative state during which he perpetrated the atrocity of killing six Vietnamese civilians.

On the military flight to Okinawa, I heard young Americans returning to Vietnam talk casually about "gook hunting". I assumed that this was a reference to looking for Vietcong. I later discovered to my horror that this was a term describing shooting from a truck or jeep at unsuspecting Vietnamese civilians working in the fields.

In Okinawa I was given an escort officer. He was a highly decorated Marine who got battlefield commission in Vietnam. He told me stories that gave me nightmares. Captain Fricker referred to the Vietnamese always as "gooks."

In Danang, I examined a number of marines who perpetrated atrocities against Vietnamese civilians and fellow Americans. I discovered the meaning of the term "free fire zone" which as a practical matter meant that any American could kill any Vietnamese. It was evident that the Vietnamese in the eyes of many soldiers were not quite human and the usual rules of conduct did not apply. Torture of Vietnamese civilians was common.

Americans who I told about the atrocities upon my return from Vietnam did not believe me. In 1969, I submitted a paper to a psychiatric journal describing the observations I made in Vietnam. The paper was not accepted for publication. A different paper I wrote on the *Dear John Syndrome*, dealing with the plight of American soldiers whose girlfriends wrote them letters dissolving the relationship, was published and received a great deal of attention.

My stories on the atrocities perpetrated by our soldiers became more credible 32 years later, after disclosures about the atrocity committed by the unit of Senator Robert Kerrey. On April 25, 2001, *The New York Times* published a lengthy article on the Thanh Phong massacre, perpetrated by the elite Seal commando of Lt. Kerrey. The piece was thoroughly researched and written by Gregory L. Vistica, who observed, "For 32 years, former Senator Bob Kerrey of Nebraska has been haunted by a memory he kept to himself: He and his squad killed more than a dozen unarmed women and children in Vietnam. Kerrey told the reporter: "Standard operating procedure was to *dispose* of the people we made contact with," and "Kill the people we made contact with, or we have to abort the mission...It does not work to merely bind and gag people, because they're going to get away" he explained. They used knives to avoid betraying their presence with gunshots. This is the story as told by the former Senator, which is bad enough. It gets far worse if one believes another Marine, who testified that the Vietnamese were herded together and killed on the order of Kerrey.

In April 22, 1971, John Kerry, a decorated 27-year-old Navy veteran of two tours in Vietnam, gave the Senate Foreign Relations Committee testimony about the conduct of some Americans in Vietnam. Senator John Kerry is, as of this writing, a candidate for President. He told the senate that these Americans "had personally raped, cut off ears, cut off heads, taped wires from portable telephones to human genitals and turned up the power, cut off limbs, blew up bodies, randomly shot at civilians, razed villages in a fashion reminiscent of Genghis Khan, shot cattle and dogs for fun, poisoned food stocks and generally ravaged the countryside of South Vietnam."[60]

HOLOCAUST AND 9/11

The body count of the Holocaust and the death toll of 9/11 differ due to the present technological limitations of radical Islam. "Only" 3,000 Americans were killed, but the target of the September atrocity was the entire Genus Americanus. The September atrocity was, like the Holocaust, *genocidal*. The victims of the 9/11 atrocity and the victims of the Holocaust were killed not for what they did, but whom they represented to the killers. All genocides are motivated by hate. September 11th may turn out to be the equivalent of Kristallnacht ("the Night of Broken Glass"), as the 1938 pogrom organized by Nazi Germany against the Jews is called, a harbinger of things to come. The Holocaust taught us that appeasement of a culture of hate is futile. Failure to face the reality of the clash between the Islamic and western cultures may turn out to be a disaster for western civilization. In the 20th century, culture of hate was ideological and confined to Europe. In the 21st century, the culture of hate is religious and global in scope.

In our rationalistic age, everything has to have a rational reason. After 9/11 there was widespread soul-searching about American behaviour in relation to the Islamic World. "What did we do to make them hate us?"—Americans have asked themselves.

In the fall of 1999, 300 people were killed in Moscow and other Russian cities by the terrorists. One hundred and twenty eight hostages died as a result of the hostage taking by Muslim terrorists in the House of Culture in Moscow. Christian Cayrl, Moscow Bureau Chief for Newsweek Magazine who reported these atrocities writes:

> Again and again, during the crisis, I heard Russians wondering aloud what sort of atrocities their troops must have committed to drive the young women among the hostage-takers, to take such a desperate action.[61]

Self-blame for being hated is a Judeo-Christian characteristic. What did the young Australians do to be killed by Islamists in 2002 in a nightclub in Bali? What did the Germans do who were killed while visiting a synagogue in North Africa? These are but few of the atrocities perpetrated by the Islamists against the infidels.

The Islamic holy warriors demonstrate the murderous power of hate. The Muslim clerics inspired countless volunteers to sacrifice their lives and become human delivery systems of explosives. It is doubtful that the promoters of martyrdom would be as successful if their message invoked love. Hatred is not a reaction to the behavior of the target of hate; it is an expression of the repressed rage of those who hate.

LOVE AND HATE

Love is celebrated in word and song; hate is not acknowledged as a motivator of human behavior. "Do you love me?" is a common inquiry. "Do you hate me?" is a question rarely asked. We want to know that we are loved and prefer to be unaware about being hated. And yet it is easier to inspire action by hate than love. The ability to love, to be decent, kind, fair and just are not inborn traits, they have to be acquired. Rage and hate are primitive responses. We see them in all children. "You have to be Carefully Taught to Hate" is a song from the musical "South Pacific." In reality, you have to be carefully taught not to hate. The notion of innate goodness of a child goes back to Jean-Jacques Rousseau (1762), who idealized the primitive state uncorrupted by influence of civilization.

To teach children to hate is easy; all one has to do is reinforce their tendency to project rage. You don't have to teach children to be selfish and ungrateful. You don't have to teach children to blame others or to lie. A child who runs into a table blames the table; a bit later he blames the mother. When he grows up he may become an anti-Semite and blame the Jews for his troubles and those of the world. Whoever was a child has the potential to be an anti-Semite or some other bigot, i.e. a person who blames others for his or her own shortcomings and misfortunes.

The emotion hate precedes the reasons given for it. Some people said they hated Jews because Jews were communists. Other anti-Semites hated Jews because they were capitalists. Some explained their hatred by claiming that Jews controlled commerce, the professions, and were very rich. Others hated Jews because they were poor and spread diseases like typhus and tuberculosis.

Hate is not intensification of anger; it is qualitatively different. Anger seeks redress, hate calls for destruction. When the cause of anger disappears, anger vanishes. Hate is relentless. Hatred of a Jew did not cease with slaughter of the Jews, the corpses of the Jews had to be desecrated. Jewish cemeteries were defiled.

Ungratified hate, like ungratified love, is a burden. A union with the object of love and the destruction of the object of hate is gratifying. Hate murderers are not concerned with the future; like all avengers, they need to gratify their current passion. Hatred is dangerous to others and to self. Suicides and homicides are the harvest of hate. Hate of others and hate of self are two sides of the same coin.

People don't hate for rational reasons; therefore, rational arguments are not likely to overcome this emotion. Hate is resistant to persuasion. Hatred invokes reactive hostility, which proves to the hater that his or her hatred was a defensive response. It is futile to argue that it was a response to their behavior.

Jewish history is tale of adaptation to hate. Jews did not have the ability to resist hate by force. Assimilation, conversion and adherence to Jewish religious traditions were the approaches taken by Jews in the last 2,000 years. None of them proved to be an effective method of preventing hatred. Jewish history proves that it is futile to appease those who are consumed by hate. The Jews were hated because they were suitable scapegoats.

Developmentally, rage, anger and hate appear in this order. Rage is a mindless explosion of aggression. The prototype of rage is the state of an infant in distress. An infant lives in a two-dimensional world: complete bliss or a tantrum. There is nothing intermediate between these two states. A mature adult lives emotionally in a world with many transitional states. Every infant falls into a state of rage when frustrated. Fortunately children have little power to cause much damage.

Anger is a measured response of a mature person to a real situation. Hate has the destructiveness of rage and the facade of anger. Those who hate demand redress of their grievances. However, even if the demands are fulfilled, it is unlikely that their hate will disappear. They are unable to accept amends that fall short of destruction of the target of hate.

"I lost my temper," an adult will admit sheepishly. Display of rage is cause for embarrassment for a mature person. Hate on the other hand is embraced with pride. "Die Juden Sind Und Unserer Unglick" (The Jews are our misfortune) was a sign proudly displayed all over Nazi Germany. To hate Jews was a badge of honor. The Germans believed that they were reacting to the evil nature of the Jews. They were in essence saying, "If the Jews were not evil, we would not hate them."

Anger and friendliness are responses to behavior. Hate requires no interaction with the object of hate. The Poles and Germans who helped me survive had a relationship with me. The Germans and Poles who wanted me dead did not know me.

Hate dehumanizes the object of hate. The hater has no sense of empathy for the person he or she hates. The human quality of empathy is selectively suspended by hate. Hate is an intense emotion that has as its goal the desire to injure or destroy the object of hate. Interactions with a person or a group may lead to indifference, pleasure, distaste, anger or hostility, but not to hate. Hate is independent of the conduct of the object of hate. All that matters is his or her identity. People hate human beings they have never met. The most menacing images of the Jews emerged from the imagination of people who never met a Jew. Shakespeare was not likely to have met a role model of the despicable Shylock. There were virtually no Jews in England in his time. Hitler saw his first Jews as an adult in Vienna.

Hatred and anger are dramatically different. Anger is the consequence of being harmed and is directed at the real cause of the harm. Anger is proportional and perpetrator directed. Hate is the result of being oppressed and abused; it is directed not at the perpetrators of the abuse and oppression, but at scapegoats. Hate is more intense than anger, but unlike anger it is irrational, maladaptive, relentless and not likely to be resolved.

Religion successfully creates the cultural myth of a scapegoat by hiding the hate, which is an integral part of the myth, under the mantle of the sacred. The function of a scapegoat is to channel society's destructive impulses. The sacrificial system of a religion is structured around rituals that symbolically gratify violent impulses. Participation in these rituals satisfies and contains violence.

Powerless African Americans suffered discrimination and abuse by the powerful white society and predictably were in need of scapegoats. Anti-Semitism in America, according to a survey commissioned by the Anti-Defamation League, stood at an all-time low in the 1990s. However, the survey found blacks three to four times more likely than non-blacks to be anti-Semitic. Reverend Jesse Jackson, who once called Jews "Hymies" and New York City "Hymie-town", actively campaigned with Al Sharpton on behalf of the anti-Semitic Congresswoman Cynthia McKinney. In 1991, Reverend Sharpton turned a traffic accident in Brooklyn involving a Hasidic Jew and a black child into a pogrom. Sharpton led 400 protesters through the Jewish section of Crown Heights. There were four nights of rock and bottle throwing, and a young Talmudic scholar was encircled by a mob shouting, "Kill the Jew," and was stabbed to death.

Minister Louis Farrakhan has a three-decade long record of hate-filled Islamic evangelism against the Jews. The Black religious movement called Nation of Islam and its ministers regularly churn out anti-Semitic, anti-white, homophobic and anti-Catholic propaganda in their sermons. A number of other Black leaders continue to spew hate speeches about Jews. Black Congresswoman Cynthia McKinney, a Georgia democrat, lost her primary election in August 2002 to another African American woman, a former judge. McKinney's father, State Representative Billy McKinney, was asked to explain the defeat. His answer: "Jews, J e w s."[62] This comment should have been expected. In 1996, Rep. Billy McKinney made anti-Semitic remarks during his daughter's re-election campaign for Congress.

"Why does Black pride mean bashing Jews?" Abraham H. Foxman, national director of the Anti-Defamation League and a Holocaust survivor asked. The answer is that oppressed people are prone to scapegoat the most vulnerable members of a society. Anti-Semitism has been a time-tested vehicle for recruitment of supporters. Christianity, Communism and Fascism relied upon hatemongering to gain the support of suffering masses. Islamic societies are also boiling with rage and seeking scapegoats.

Before September 11th, it was inconceivable that Islamic holy warriors would be able to kill thousands of Americans. Killing motivated by ideology or religion is consistent with individual and collective conscience.

Nearly all people have powerful inhibitions against killing human beings. However, history abounds with people whose inhibitions against killing have been suspended by political or "cultural" dispensation.

In the Third Reich, genocidal killing was a category of killing that was socially approved and legal. Societies that approve of genocide, governments that organize them, and ordinary citizens who participate in them, are a phenomenon that is not created by a decree of a dictator. Hatred of that magnitude has to be cultivated for many generations. Societal and individual values must be congruent if the genocidal project is to succeed.

Every society has an ethos, an ideal. Societies based on hate create people who hate. Political leaders often cultivate hate as the motivating force of a nation. Hate and dehumanization of a group create the genocidal state of mind.

HATE MOVEMENTS

The first phase in the evolution of a movement is creating an ideology that justifies hate under an idealistic cover. The next step is dehumanization of the target group. A group demonized into The Enemy of the People becomes an acceptable object of hate. Violence then becomes necessary as self-defense against the conspiracy of "them" against "us."

Bin Laden proclaimed on videotape: "We will see again Saladin carrying his sword with the blood of unbelievers dripping from it." Other fanatical believers, religious and secular, are convinced that the unbelievers must be killed for the glory of God or in the name of a good cause. Noble causes often give opportunity for gratification of sadistic and masochistic needs. Religious and secular belief systems gave rise to many atrocities in history. Sadistic behavior justified by a noble cause is still a manifestation of sadism. Masochism and sadism are an element of most religions and social movements.

Noble cause and hate of the unbeliever create group cohesion. Sharing a common enemy produces a bond between the members; it eliminates distinctions based upon class, gender and age. Scapegoating an external enemy diverts attention from "us" to "them." Projection of evil makes us good; we are good because they are bad. All movements exploit hate to gain political power. They create false reality through propaganda.

Hitler's phenomenal rise to power was accomplished through hate propaganda. His attempt to seize power through force failed. He realized that the word is mightier than the sword. Within a short time, he was a democratically elected leader of Germany, which he transformed into a brutal dictatorship. Propaganda is an essential element of all movements. "One of the great

232

conditions of hatred," the wryly-cynical Thackeray observed, "is that you must tell and believe lies against the hated object in order to be consistent."

Hitler has become a symbol of the misuse of state power. He should also be a symbol of the misuse of the power of persuasion. Americans do not sufficiently appreciate the power of propaganda and confuse it with public relations. Propaganda motivates hate of the other; a public relations effort inflates the image of a person or institution.

In the spring of 1944, I, a Jew on false papers, attended in Budapest the showing of a German anti-Semitic film called "Jud Suess" (The Jew Suess). It was based upon the life of Joseph Suess Oppenheimer, who at the end of the seventeenth century became a banker and a protégé of Karl Alexander, the prince of Wurtemberg. The prince replied upon Oppenheimer to manage his finances and ultimately bestowed upon him the title of Secret Counselor. Karl Alexander converted to Catholicism. When the prince died suddenly, Oppenheimer was charged with the damage to the Protestant religion and other "crimes." He was convicted and hanged at the gates of the City of Stuttgart. In the movie he was portrayed as a lecherous old Jew who seduced Christian girls. Lascivious sex and fraudulent moneymaking are time proven themes of anti-Semitism. The Hungarians who emerged from this entertainment beat up Jews they encountered in the streets. I placed myself in danger of being unmasked as a Jew on false papers by not joining all the other teenagers who were screaming anti-Semitic slogans.

When it comes to hate, there is no rational "because." Hate is irrational. Suppose irrefutable proof was found that Jews did not kill Christ. Would Christians who claimed that they hated Jews because Jews crucified Jesus, no longer hate Jews? "Hier gibt's kein warum" (Here there is no why) was a slogan of the concentration camp guards.

Hatred accounts for the success of many mass movements, including religion. The source of hate is often overlooked. Ideas alone do not create hate. Hate attaches itself to ideas.

God wishes that one should put aside all humanity
when it is a question of striving for His glory.
-Calvin

Chapter 26
Religion, Ideology and Genocide

The 20th century could be called the century of genocide:

- 1915, 1.5 million Armenians killed and starved in Turkey

- 1928-37, 7 million Kulaks starved or executed in Soviet Union

- 1933-45, 6 million Jews exterminated by Nazi Germany. There are no precise figures on the numbers of Gypsies that were murdered by the Third Reich. The range of estimates is between 250,000 and 500,000.

- 1975-79, 750,000-1.5 million Cambodians killed by Khmer Rouge.

- 1994, 500-800,000 Tutsis hacked to death by Hutus in Rwanda.

Genocide is inspired by three sources: Religion, Nationalism and Ideology. Quite often all three promote murderous action against real or imagined enemies. Genocide is a systematic mass murder of a group of people based upon their collective identity. Some people speak of "attempted genocide of the Jews and Armenians" as if the term genocide means complete annihilation of a national or religious entity.

The Turks perpetrated genocide by killing a significant number of Armenians because of their identity. The Nanking atrocity was genocidal even though the Japanese were in no position to plan a complete annihilation of all the Chinese.

Most perpetrators of interpersonal violence explain that they were in a state "outside of myself." This is a common phrase in German and French to depict impulsive aggression. In psychiatry, we call it a "dissociative state." Religious and ideological violence is not of this variety. Fanatical believers are themselves when they kill or torture the heretics or the infidels; they have a "noble reason" and social approval.

Rational people as a rule give rational explanations for irrational conduct. These justifications are the first layer of the onion that hides the underlying motives that come from the deeper layers of personality structure. Freud used the onion analogy to illustrate the complexity of behavior.

"I am a bad guy and I will kill you," my then barely 3-year old grandson Aaron said to his mother as he pointed a stick at her as if it were a rifle. Not a single person from the hundreds of killers I examined called him or herself a "bad guy."

Adults who kill other people usually have a "noble reason" for doing so. They view themselves as "good guys" and the victims they kill as "bad guys." The Germans who were trying to kill me did not think that they were "bad guys"; they were merely trying to eliminate the cause of evil, the Jews.

The Holy Inquisition tortured and killed heretics by the thousands to serve God. Auschwitz was built in the name of a "good cause." The Islamic suicide bombers invoke the name of Allah before they kill people who have done them no wrong.

Father Joseph, the Catholic priest who participated in an effort to have me delivered to the Gestapo, acted consistently with his beliefs that Jews are evil and should be eliminated. It was God's will that Jews should suffer - was the Catholic teaching before the 1965 Vatican II declaration.

Stefan Jagodzinski, a devout Catholic who risked his life to shelter me, had to keep it a secret from other Christians that he was helping a Jew. He could not tell his family, his girlfriend or his priest that he was protecting a Jewish youngster from being murdered.

I asked Stefan forty years after the Holocaust why he risked his life to help me. "Because I am a Christian," he answered without hesitation. Father Joseph and Stefan Jagodzinski invoked the same belief system to justify diametrically different behaviour.

Religion or ideology has been a major factor in all genocides. Religion has been part of every known society on the globe. A phenomenon which is so pervasive cannot be the product of cultural forces alone; it must have biological (instinctual) roots. People have a need for a religion, particularly in childhood. If you ask a little child: What is the sun made of? You are likely to get an answer. Children answer nearly every question that begins with "Why?" Rarely does a child say, "I don't know." Religious people have retained this attitude. "God is the answer" they tell us. Billboards and bumper stickers all over America proclaim it.

Religion is a system of beliefs held by a large group of people about ultimate issues. The source of religious authority is a supernatural being called God. The all-encompassing influence of religion creates a distinct religious culture. Religion influences the formation of personality and the development of social structures within a society. The personality makeup and a belief must be in harmony to create a believer.

Religions go through three phases in relation to a society. The first is the *theocratic phase*, where king and religious leader are one. The second phase is the *political phase*; religion controls or has strong influence on the secular authority. The third phase is religion in a secular state based upon the *separation of church and state*.

Religion is dangerous to non-believers in the first two phases. The major difference between the Western and Islamic civilizations is that most Islamic countries are in the first or second phase of the evolution of the relationship between state and religion.

Western culture accepted separation of religion from significant aspects of life. Religion no longer controls limits of knowledge in the West. God on Sunday, and reliance on science and technology the rest of the week, is the way of the West. In the Islamic World, God dominates life every day.

Christianity's hate of the Jews played a significant role in making the Holocaust a reality. Islam's Jihad against Western culture motivated the perpetrators and organizers of the September 11th atrocity. Islam is rarely mentioned as the adversary of the West. We are at war with terrorists, deplore actions of the anti-Semites and communists. We blame the Pope Pius XII for his silence. Hitler is responsible for the Holocaust and Stalin is the perpetrator of many atrocities. Bin Laden and Saddam Hussein are the current poster boys of evil. But we miss the point when we substitute individuals for institutions. Christianity's problem was not the Jews, but modernity. The pope was not silent alone, the Church was. Hitler was not the cause of the Holocaust, Germany was. Stalin was a tyrant, but it takes a state to bring about the killing of millions.

In *Clash of Civilizations*, Samuel Huntington wrote that, "a major war involving the West and the core states of other civilizations [read Islam] is not inevitable, but it could happen."[63] A mere five years later, the September 11th atrocity prompted President Bush to declare that we are at war with terrorism. [Read Islam]. When a society approves an activity, it is more than terrorism. The failure to recognize what motivates one's enemies diminishes effectiveness.

Adolf Eichman once said, "I will leap into my grave laughing, because the feeling that I have 5 million Jews on my conscience, gives me extraordinary satisfaction." This was a boast, 60 millions Germans have legitimate right to share the credit for this deplorable "achievement."

Not all Germans shared Eichman's beliefs, and not all Christians approved of the Inquisition and the Holocaust. Not all Muslims supported Bin Laden. Yet, there was no significant opposition in the Christian world against the Inquisition or the Holocaust, in Nazi Germany Adolf Eichman was admired, and Bin Laden is a hero in Islamic countries.

A belief held by an individual that is based upon imagination and is not validated by experience or science will be ignored or declared a symptom of mental illness. If the same belief resonates with the emotional needs of a large group, it becomes a myth, a religion or an ideology.

Religion and ideology are similar to falling in love. Most human beings are familiar with the gratifying and energizing experience of being in love. Fanatical believers derive the same rewards from religion or ideology. Religion gives the believer an ecstatic feeling.

236

Religion and ideology offer the opportunity to gratify altruistic and sadistic impulses. It is a virtue to love members of the in-group and despise the enemies of God or the enemies of The People. The images of God and the devil gratify the need to love and hate. Religion has been the foremost belief system through the ages and a powerful force in the history of humanity. In modern times, secular religions called ideologies became, at times, equally important. A belief is a blend of ideas, emotions and rituals. Beliefs in witchcraft and the power of the devil were just as intense and powerful as the beliefs in God, Communism and National Socialism.

Religion is an awesome psychosocial force. Will Durant's observation identifies one reason for the power of religion. He writes:

> Most men are harassed and buffeted by life, and crave supernatural assistance when natural forces fail them; they gratefully accept faiths that give dignity and hope to their existence, and order and meaning to the world; they could hardly condone so patiently the careless brutalities of nature, the bloodshed and chicaneries of history, or their own tribulations and bereavements, if they could not trust that these are parts of an inscrutable but divine design. A cosmos without known cause or fate is an intellectual prison; we long to believe that the great drama has a just author and a noble end.[64]

Religion was the dominant belief system in the Western world prior to the twentieth century; it promoted hate of evil, sin, and the infidels. The combination of religious passion and secular power has caused immense suffering in Europe and continues to do so to this day in some parts of the world. Each monotheistic religion, at certain times in its history, imposed severe frustrations upon the believers. These sacrifices created anger. These feelings could not be directed at the source without arousing feelings of guilt. The repressed rage needed scapegoats, which, in many instances, have been the Jews or other infidels.

Religious institutions of Christianity have in the past promoted hatred of the Jews. At the present time, Islamic institutions advance hatred of the Westerners, and most likely will continue to do so for decades to come. One of the leading newspapers of Saudi Arabia dared to question the hate mongering of the Muslim clerics in May of 2003. In response, a senior Muslim cleric ruled it a sin to buy this paper. (*New York Times*, 05-28-03, p. A14). Mr. Kashoggi, the editor of the paper, was dismissed.

Religions and ideologies are harmless at low intensity. Ardent beliefs, like all ecstatic pursuits often escalate to a level of fanaticism. Religious triumphalism and bellicose evangelism are the next step. No criminal is as dangerous as a fanatical idealist with absolute power. More people are killed by idealists in the name of God and in the name of a good cause than by criminals. At one time or another, each one of the monotheistic religions has been at war with the infidels, the unbelievers and the heretics. Judaism has caused the least harm in the last 2,000 years, for the simple reason that it had no worldly power. This is changing with the establishment of Israel, where the religious radical minority exerts increasing influence. In the summer of 1995, Yitzhak Rabin, the war hero who led the Israeli Army to victory in the Six-Day War and Prime Minister of Israel, was killed by a religious Jew who believed that Mr. Rabin deserved to die because he violated a religious precept by negotiating with the enemies of Israel. Orthodox rabbis in America took the lead in demonizing Mr. Rabin. Yitzchak Rabin was called a Nazi at public rallies; radical Orthodox rabbis cursed him. There are hundreds of thousands of Israelis who believe in negotiation, but none of them have ever killed a fanatically religious Jew. Seven years later, another Prime Minister of Israel is in danger from the same religious radicals. Ariel Sharon, a radical in his own right, is not radical enough for the religious minority of Israel who call for his murder.

The threat of the radical right has become a matter of terrible urgency in the Israeli government. Avi Dichter, the chief of the Israeli internal security service, has been for months running around - to borrow a phrase from George Tenet - with his hair on fire over the threat. He has warned of the potential for attacks against the Dome of the Rock and the Al Aksa Mosque, on the Temple Mount; such a strike, he said, would set off a global war between Muslim and Jew - a goal the radical yeshivas of the West Bank share with Al Qaeda.[65]

Christianity no longer has the power to conduct crusades against infidels or set up inquisitions against heretics. Islam, however, has remained outside modernity. It continues to have the fanaticism that the two older predecessors have lost. Theocracies based upon religion have caused as much suffering as dictatorships based upon ideology.

Though religious people love God and fellow believers, religions have supported such social evils as absolute monarchy, slavery, intolerance and the oppression of women. Torture and killing of heretics, wars against infidels and the suppression of schismatic movements have also been inspired by religions. Religions prefer the authoritarianism of monarchy and dictatorship. Ethics and theology are often at odds.

Fear is my dominant response to fundamentalist religion. Whenever I see people pray fervently, I wonder, whom do they hate? Everyone on this globe is somebody's infidel. Since I am a non-believer, I am an infidel to all religious people and have good reasons to be fearful of them.

Elie Wiesel begins his book *The Gates of the Forest* with an epigram; "God made men, because he loves stories." I think the reverse is true. Men made God, because men love stories. The German philosopher Ludwig Feuerbach writes in *Das Wesen Des Christentums* (*The Essence of Christianity*) published in 1841, that "man is not a shadow of God; it is God who is the shadow of man, an illusory phantasm that man nourishes out of his own substance".

In Munich I became fascinated with the writings of Friedrich Nietzsche, whose views reinforced my attitudes on religion. He writes:

> I hear the church bells.... How is it possible?! All this for a Jew who died on a cross two thousand years ago and who maintained he was the Son of God.... What a religion! A God who begets a child from a human wife.... A so-called just God who accepts an innocent person as sacrifice instead of the sinner. A

teacher who is supposed to give his blood to his followers to drink. Prayers to have miracles done Sins committed against one God, expiated by another God.... The symbol of the cross in a time when the penalty and shame of crucifixion are no longer known—how abhorrent is all this! Like ghosts of an ancient past visiting us from the grave". [66]

BELIEF SYSTEMS AND PERSONALITY

Personality determines the belief system one chooses. Even more importantly, personality dictates *the means* a person selects to implement his or her belief system.

I use the term belief system to describe all non-empirical convictions based on faith, be they secular or religious. Religion, political science and philosophy have been the source of most belief systems that have attracted millions of followers. The belief system of a person is like an iceberg; there is more to it than what is visible on the surface.

At the core of every belief system are feelings. People have a need for rituals, fellowship and adherence to a belief system. A variety of organizations gratify these needs. It is not surprising that Hitler and Stalin created successful movements; they used elaborate ceremonies and rituals that they borrowed from their prior religious training.

Religion and ideology have a profound impact upon personality formation. A culture of fundamentalism fosters authoritarian mentality. There is a parallelism between personality and a belief system. A person who relies upon revelation as a frame of reference will not be persuaded by reasoning. The acceptance of revelation indicates an emotional need for dogmatic pronouncements. One can coerce fundamentalist believers, but one cannot persuade them to be tolerant. A tolerant fundamentalist is a contradiction in terms.

Organized religions and ideological movements are totalitarian; they attempt to govern all of human behavior. Religious belief systems tell people who they are, what they should do, what they should eat, and how they should relate to other people. They control such activities as sex and mating and promise eternal salvation and explain complexities of existence.

Total commitment to an idea is a virtue that fanatical believers value above everything else. Fanatical believers are by nature radical, since they know "The Truth." Radical Christianity, radical Islam, radical Judaism and radical ideology are radical first – everything else is a distant second. Therefore, religious and ideological fundamentalism and Western culture are natural antagonists. Western culture evolved from Christianity. Modern western culture is post-Christian, just like Israel is post-Judaic. Heritage should not be confused with contemporary reality.

239

The ultra-Orthodox Jews of Israel, called Haredim, are an ever-increasing aggressive minority, which tries to impose its beliefs upon the passive majority. Intensely religious Jews, like all religious fanatics, feel entitled to resort to violence in the name of God. I remember years ago visiting a middle class neighborhood where my aunt and uncle lived, called Kiryat Shalom, meaning "neighborhood of peace." This neighborhood has been transformed by the invasion of the Orthodox Jews.[67] This peaceful, secular neighborhood accepted a religious summer camp and allowed them to use the public pool. Within a few years, the neighborhood was transformed. The pool was closed to women, the roads are blocked on the Sabbath, and the secular residences are cursed and harassed.

Personality of individuals is not created but exploited by demagogues and the founders of movements. An idea can become an emotional fetish. A "fetish" is an object that has magical or spiritual powers. Religions and ideologies rely upon the power of fetishism. Fetishistic practices are part of mass movements. The swastika certainly gained the status of a fetish in Nazi Germany.

Religious and ideological beliefs are pseudo-rational. They are rational in form but irrational in content. An observant Jew will explain dietary laws as based upon "the Bible." Animals – and the products of animals – that do not chew the cud and do not have cloven hoofs (e.g., pigs, horses); fish without fins and scales, shellfish (e.g., clams, oysters, shrimp, crabs) and all other living creatures that creep; and those fowl enumerated in the Bible (e.g., vultures, hawks, owls, herons) are prohibited.

Keeping a kosher kitchen requires separation of dishes that are used for milk and foods that were exposed to milk from dishes used for meat. The underlying "rationale" for this injunction is a passage that says that one should not cook a calf in his mother's milk. These explanations raise more questions to which there are no rational answers.

The New York Times reported on May 14, 2004, a manifestation of Jewish fundamentalism that reached across the ocean. A few excerpts from this article follow.

The modesty regulations have given rise to a thriving Brooklyn trade in wigs, along streets like 13th Avenue in Borough Park. Wigs of human hair are particularly prized, and can cost several thousand dollars. They not only look better, some women say, but they also last longer.

For thousands of Orthodox women, one of the most fundamental practices of daily life — adhering to the code of modesty that prohibits a public display of their hair after marriage — was thrown into turmoil this week by a ruling from a distant authority. More than 5,700 miles away in Israel, several rabbis issued a ban on wigs made in India from human hair, which is used to make many of the wigs sold in Brooklyn. The rabbis said the hair may have been used in Hindu religious ceremonies, which like other pantheistic practices are considered idolatrous in Orthodox teaching.

240

As a result, many of the women felt obliged to put aside their costly wigs, flocking instead to stores that sold acceptable replacements. "You have to hope whatever you have is good, otherwise you put a thousand dollars in the garbage," said a woman named Mindy, who declined to give her last name for fear of what her father-in-law would think. "The way Orthodox people live their lives is very complex to begin with," said Chaya Lewis, an administrative assistant at a school in Crown Heights. "We do everything everybody else does, yet we have guidelines. If this is a problem, we're going to find a way.

Narratives also contribute to the formation of personality and are a significant element in the creation of the prevailing attitudes of a society.

The nomadic tribes called "Israelites" created a narrative that endured for a few thousand years and captured the imagination of millions of people all over the globe. Jesus, who in his lifetime left virtually no historical record, has, by the power of a narrative, become the center of a belief system shared by a third of humanity. Mohamed, an illiterate merchant from Mecca, shared his revelations by word of mouth and became accepted as the final prophet by another billion people.

The followers of a movement are not a creation of the leader; the leader is more spokesman than creator. There is a symbiotic relationship between the leader and the followers. The identity formation of a large group of people does not take place in adult life. Hitler, Stalin and Osama bin Laden did not brainwash millions of people. They provided leadership that assisted believers to express themselves in action.

I had the opportunity to study the relationship between a leader and his followers in the case of the religious leader Prophet Jim Jones, who established a movement called the Peoples Temple. Jim Jones founded the Peoples Temple in the 1950s as an independent congregation in Indianapolis, Indiana. In 1960, the Peoples Temple became affiliated with the Christian Church, and four years later Jones was ordained. In 1965, the Peoples Temple moved to Ukiah, California, where members became active in Protestant Churches and were involved in state politics. Branch congregations opened in San Francisco and Los Angeles, and an agricultural settlement was established in Jonestown, Guyana in 1974.

Many relatives of Jones' followers complained to the authorities about the movement, and on November 14, 1978, U.S. Congressman Leo Ryan of California, arrived in Guyana to conduct an investigation. He was accompanied by a group of newsmen. When Representative Ryan departed, he took with him 14 defectors of the cult. Prophet Jones commanded his lieutenant Layton to lead a party that assaulted the Congressman's group and the airstrip near Jonestown. Congressman Ryan and seven other people were killed.

After the news reached Jones that the Congressman was killed, Jones ordered his followers to commit collective suicide; 913 people died. There were 276 children among them. The leader of the assassination group named Layton survived and was tried in the Federal Court in San Francisco. I was the defense expert in that case. As part of my preparation for trial, I reviewed the literature dealing with the movement, which, at that point, was called a cult. I also listened to many hours of tape recorded sermons of Jones. I was struck by the similarity of the intonation and delivery to the speeches of Hitler. The response of the crowd was equally enthusiastic.

The critical issue is not if a belief system is rational, but if it resonates with a given population at a specific time in history. There was social harmony in Germany after the First World War on the issue of the Versailles Treaty; it was considered unjust. After 1933, there was social harmony in Germany on the mythology of the Nazi Party about the Jews.

A belief system that acquires secular power is fundamentally different in its impact upon the lives of believers and non-believers. The relationship to power is an important criterion for the evaluation of a belief system. Karl Marx was a profound thinker whose contributions have made a lasting impact on the social sciences. Adolf Hitler was a shallow ideologue who made no contributions to political science. Marx and Hitler have in common a coercion to implement their ideology. True philosophical belief systems never seek to acquire coercive powers. A book reinforced by a sword or a gun becomes part of a weapon system. Love of wisdom and coercive power are two incompatible concepts. A lion and a lamb can live in peace provided that it pleases the lion. Neville Chamberlain's "peace in our time" lasted as long as it pleased Adolf Hitler.

The level of dedication to a belief system has geopolitical implications. The willingness to die and kill for the glory of God or victory of an ideology represents a global danger in our age of advanced technology of death. Extremism no longer dominates Western societies. This accomplishment may also turn out to be our undoing. Fanaticism combined with modern technology has the tactical advantage of being able to take the initiative.

Given an even playing field, there can be little doubt that Islam would once again gain the upper hand in relation to the Western World. The fervent faith of a billion people, combined with weapons of mass destruction, would assure victory of Islam. Technological superiority of the West is the only remaining obstacle to worldwide hegemony of Islam. If Islam fails to win technological parity, it may gain victory by the not-so-secret weapon of demographics. It is estimated that by the year 2040, France and Italy will have Islamic majorities.

RESISTANCE TO CHANGE

A strict adherence to a doctrine is self-destructive and dangerous to others. It is self-destructive because it is unable to adapt to the ever-changing world. It is dangerous to others because it often justifies contempt, coercion and cruelty against the deviants and the heretics. Religious fundamentalism is most dangerous because it is based upon irrational premises and therefore it is immune to refutation.

Faith, unlike reason, is not kindly disposed to divergence of opinions and change; faith proclaims eternal principles and enduring symbols. For 1,900 years, Christianity dominated European thinking. Modern Christianity has limited coercive powers; it has to rely upon persuasion. Islam, on the other hand, continues to dominate the lives of Muslims through coercive powers of the Islamic clerics. In the Islamic world to this day, the Koran is the controlling source for proper behavior and belief.

Human history can be viewed as a struggle between the forces of constancy and change. One can see this in the life of an individual and in the history of a culture. Successful individuals and cultures create a balance between these conflicting trends. Religion, once formed, claims to have the final word of God and is naturally resistant to change. In politics, the conservatives resist change, and the progressives want to reform the society. The revolutionists want to destroy the old societal structure and replace it with a new one. Religion aligns itself with the conservative political forces. However, every religion was at one time an innovation.

Religious people have an aversion to change. "BIDA"-innovation, is a cardinal sin in Islam. Yet change is the only constant feature of human existence. There is a never-ending and universal human conflict between the need for stability and adaptation to change. A changeless universe beguiled even the early scientists. Newton's absolute time and absolute space gave way to Einstein's relativity. Religion's answer to the question "When were human beings created?" has been the same for hundreds of years. The shelf life of scientific knowledge is short. In the year 2,000 it was believed that biological anthropology answered definitely the question as to when the oldest hominid emerged. A mere two years later, this was proven to be wrong.

The social sciences are particularly offensive to religion, since they focus on the "here and now" of human existence. Adam Smith and Karl Marx share a materialistic view of the world of work and production. The science of economics teaches that people work not for the greater glory of God or to advance an ideology; they are motivated not by eternal salvation but by far less noble reasons, like gaining a livelihood or making a fortune. Social sciences try to empower the individual and society to influence the present and future conditions of life. The rewards will be reaped on this earth and not in the hereafter. It is not surprising that Christianity opposed science and modernity, and the separation of church and state.

THE TRIUMPHANT RELIGION

The history of the Islamic civilization is an example of the destructive power of a victorious religion. In 1453, with the conquest of Constantinople, Christianity ceased to be a rival to Islam. Islam as a religion and civilization was triumphant. A few hundred years later, the Islamic culture was stagnant and in decline. It was defeated, not by external enemies, but by the religious opposition to change and the rejection of modernity. Orthodoxy and abhorrence of modernity endangered the Christian world in the Middle Ages, but the Reformation and Industrial Revolution transformed Christendom into an ever-evolving civilization.

Islamic Turkey carried out the first genocide of the 20th century. The government claimed that the Christian Armenian population of about 1,750,000 was "dangerous" because they conspired with the pro-Christian tsarist enemy during World War I. First the Armenians in the Turkish army were disarmed, placed into labor battalions and killed. As the next phase, the Turks rounded up and killed the Armenian leaders.

The rest of the Armenian population was assembled and told they would be relocated, and then marched into the desert between Jerablus and Deir ez-Zor, where they starved to death in the burning sun.

In the Black Sea region, the Turks placed the Armenians on barges and sank them far out at sea. The death toll of Armenians in Turkey has been estimated to be between 600,000 and 1,500,000 in the years from 1915 to 1923 (Encyclopedia Britannica).

To this day, Turkey denies the genocide of the Armenians, though in January 2001, France passed a law branding as genocide the mass murder of Armenians at the hands of the Turks. Armed resistance was used by the Turks to justify the genocide of the Armenians. The reason of all genocides is not the behavior of the victims, but the mentality of the perpetrators. James R. Russell, Professor of Armenian Studies at Harvard University writes:

> Armenians were mostly unarmed: they could not defend themselves against Turkish depredations. Like the European Jews, Armenians were prominent in the big cities, but powerless. Many Armenians fled to the US in the 1890s but most remained. Armenian reformists supported the Young Turk revolution and served in their new government. Soon after the latter came to power there was a pogrom in Adana: by 1912 American consular officials were warning Armenians to send children abroad. I know some who survived this way.
>
> In April 1915, the leaders of the Armenian community at Constantinople were arrested and murdered, leaving the nation headless. Telegrams to provincial governors then coordinated the extermination of the Armenians: young men were drafted into slave labor battalions and worked to death or killed. The rest were assembled at collection points for deportation. In vain there was some warning: Armenians resisted till the Russians came. Everywhere else, from Izmit to Erzurum, the genocide was total. In towns far from any border, death marches ("deportations") were the means of murder; on the Black Sea coast, it was drowning. Nearer Russia and escape, people were burned in barns. In 1918 Turkey invaded Russian Armenia and Iran to finish the holocaust. In the

east, Azeris began to massacre Armenians in Artsakh (Karabagh). But the campaign stalled.

Turkey lost the war. But war crimes trials at Constantinople stopped when Mustafa Kemal ejected the Allies. He declared the Ottoman leaders heroes: there had been no Armenian genocide; there had never been any Armenians. Their towns were given Turkish names. Monuments were destroyed, and continue to be: in 1994 I visited the monastery of Narek, near Van, and found a Cross-stone of the tenth century, which I photographed – when I returned in 1997 the Kurdish villagers told me the police had come soon after my visit and destroyed it. Turkey uses the struggle for self-determination in Karabagh as a pretext for blockading the Armenian Republic. Tens of thousands have died as a result, and hundreds of thousands more are emigrating. This is a continuation of the genocide.[68]

The Armenian genocide is the prototype of the persistent hostility of the Islamic world toward the Christians. Mustafa Kemal, who adapted the name Atatürk "Father of the Turks," did not repudiate the Armenian genocide. Christianity and the West are to this day the "Crusaders" to the religious Islamists. The secular Islamists find other explanations for their hatred.

In 1974, the overthrow of Portuguese dictator Marcelo Caetano led to self-government for East Timor, a Portuguese colony. In 1975, the Indonesian army invaded East Timor and took over control of the country. About 100,000 of the original population of 600,000 died during the first year of occupation. The victims were Catholic, the perpetrators were Muslim.

Intellectuals are viewed by Islamists as promoters of Western Culture and enemies of Islam. Algerian novelist and poet, Tahar Djaout, was killed on May 26, 2001, outside of his apartment by Islamic fundamentalists. Many Algerian intellectuals have also been murdered.

Christian fundamentalism is no longer a major force in Western Civilization, though in the Islamic world, fundamentalist religion remains a dominant power. It is beside the point that the Americans and the rest of the Western World have no hostile intentions in relation to Islam; our very existence makes us "the enemies of Allah."

Modernity came late to the Islamic world. It began with the Young Turk Revolution and still has not been achieved in the 21st century. Politically and technologically, Islamic countries are where Christianity was in the Middle Ages. Radical Islam declared war on the leader of Western culture, the United States of America and, on the outpost of Western culture, Israel. The United States, in response, declared war on terrorism. What is needed is, in addition to the military response, an educational ideological campaign against the theology of hate that is promulgated by Islam. One can debate if advocating violence against infidels is true Islam or not, but the reality is that killing infidels and heretics is acceptable to many people who follow Islam.

In some of the countries of Islam, the ruling minority would like to maintain friendly relationships with the West. However, they are under pressure from what has been euphemistically called "the street." In countries like Pakistan, Indonesia, Iraq, Saudi Arabia and Egypt, truly democratic elections at this time would have a devastating impact on the relationship between the West and Islam. Democracy is a state of mind, not merely a method of electing leadership. Most democratic societies evolved through three stages: secularization, modernization and industrialization. The Islamic world acquired modern technology without even undergoing the industrial revolution. Medieval mentality with 21st century military technology is a recipe for disaster.

Imagine what would have happened to the Western world had the Ottoman Empire succeeded in conquering Europe as it nearly did. Germany's greatest philosopher, Dr. Gadamer, in an interview published on September 25, 2001, was asked by the magazine *Die Welt* for his reaction to the 9/11 atrocity. He said: "I feel quite perturbed that that this kind of a power [Islam] not so long ago was on the outskirts of Vienna."[69]

He was referring to the 1683 siege of Vienna that threatened the existence of Western culture. The Turkish army was repelled by the intervention of the Polish King, Jan Sobieski. He defeated the Turks at the Kahlenberg on Sept. 12, 1683 in one of the crucial battles of European history. It should be remembered that more than a hundred years before, Islam had nearly conquered Europe. After the siege of Granada in January 1492, Christians believed that they might triumph over Islam. After the fall of the Twin Towers in New York City, Islamists feel encouraged that they can still triumph over the infidels.

JEWS AND CHRISTIANITY

Christianity as we know it is based upon Jesus, but it was founded by Paul, a Hellenistic Jew who had no contact with Jesus. Paul of Tarsus taught that there were two versions of Christianity, one he called the "gospel to the circumcised" and also entrusted to him by God was "the gospel to the uncircumcised."

Paul's Christianity was not a form of Judaism but universal (Catholic) salvation to be accepted by all humanity. Paul was a revolutionary determined to replace the old with the new belief system. Thus, being non-Jews became part of the identity of Christians. Christianity as an offshoot of Judaism, had an identity crisis. The early Christians, like rebellious adolescents, resolved it by negative identity formation.

The name Jesus (Hebrew) Christ (Greek) reflects the duality of the origins of Christianity. It represents the Greco-Roman and the Hebrew roots of Christianity.

Paul's position was not acceptable to the fledgling Christian Church of Jerusalem. He was compelled to travel to Jerusalem and face James, and the other leaders. He was nearly killed, but was rescued by the Romans from the anger of his fellow Jerusalem Christians. He declared himself independent of the Jerusalem Church. Ultimately, the mother church of Jerusalem repudiated Paul.

The old conflict of Rome and Jerusalem emerged once again. Rome became the capitol of Pauline Christianity.

The early Christians rejected Judaism and the Roman Christians rejected the Jerusalem version of Christianity. The alleged rejection of Jesus by the Jews has been a preoccupation of Christian theology. At the time of the crucifixion of Jesus there was nothing as yet to reject.

Karen Armstrong, in her *History Of God*, writes that scholars agree that Mark's Gospel, "which is the earliest, is usually regarded as the most reliable, presents Jesus as a normal man, with a family that included brothers and sisters. No angels announced his birth or sang over his crib. He had not been marked out during his infancy or adolescence as remarkable in any way. When he began to teach, his townsmen in Nazareth were astonished that the son of the local carpenter should have turned out to be such a prodigy. Mark begins his narrative with Jesus' career."[70]

Christianity in Roman times was a challenge to the existing order. Jesus was a revolutionary who defied the status quo. The Gospel of John, Chapter 5, describes how Jesus made an infirm man who was unable to walk, "whole" on the Sabbath. "And therefore did the Jews persecute Jesus, and sought to slay him, because he has done these things on the Sabbath."

This is an early example of the displacement of blame from the powerful Roman Empire upon powerless fellow Jews. Ultimately, the crucifixion of Jesus becomes a Jewish responsibility. The Vatican-sponsored website on Christian-Jewish dialog has a paper by Lloyd Gaston entitled, "Transformations in Telling the Passion Story." He writes:

> The historicity of the titulus on the cross, the charge against the accused, is virtually certain: The King of the Jews. Jesus' crime was seen then to be political... Jesus died as part of a group: two others crucified with him are called guerrilla fighters ("robbers") and one who may have been (Barabbas) is described as "a rebel who had committed murder in the insurrection" (Mk 15:7). Jesus was arrested, probably by Roman soldiers (Jn 18:12) as a robber, i.e., a Zealot (Mk 14:48). Although Jesus certainly did not have a trial before Pilate, he may have had a brief hearing. In any case it is quite certain that Pilate passed sentence and ordered the execution.[71]

The fact that Jesus was called King of the Jews was an extreme political offense. Pilate had to take the title "king" as a threat to the Roman State. Gospel according to John tells us:

> Pilate therefore said to him, "Are you a king then?" Jesus answered, "You say that I am a king. For this reason I have been born, and for this reason I have come into the world, that I should testify to the truth. Everyone who is of the truth listens to my voice."

However, the gospels, especially Matthew and John, present Jesus as damned by the Jewish mobs against Pilate's better judgment. Pilate pleaded with the "perfidious" Jews to spare Jesus. In the end, he gave in to demands of the Jews and ordered the death sentence. The New Testament left no doubt that blame for killing Jesus is extended to all future generations of Jews throughout all time. The reluctant Pilate is assured by the Jews, "We take his blood upon ourselves and our children!" In the documentary "Shoah," by Claude Lanzmann, a group of Poles who have just emerged from Church tell him that these words justified the Holocaust.

The cross, next to Jesus, is the most common faith-related symbol of Christianity. The cross was an instrument of torture and execution in the Roman Empire. Why did Christianity focus on the cross and the suffering of Jesus? Why did the Jews become responsible for an execution carried out by the Romans? The fact is that Romans tortured and killed Jesus and thousands of other Jews.

The narrative about torture of the beloved and venerated Son of God reenacted repeatedly is likely to generate hate of his supposed tormentors and killers. That answers the first question. It was safe to stigmatize the helpless Jews and dangerous to hate the powerful Romans, is the answer to the second question. The fledgling Christian movement in Rome found it useful to forgive Pilate's action and blame the Jews for the execution of Jesus.

In I Thessalonians 2:14-16, Paul writes:

...Even as they have of the Jews, who both killed the Lord Jesus, and their own prophets, and have persecuted us; and they please not God, and are contrary to all men, forbidding us to speak to the Gentiles that they might be saved, to fill up their sins always; for the wrath is come upon them to the uttermost!

Christianity professes to be a religion based on redemption and forgiveness. When asked how often a sinner could be forgiven, Christ's answer was seventy times seven. And yet Catholicism cultivated for nearly 2,000 years vengeance against the Jews for their alleged guilt in the crucifixion of Jesus, that which was ordained by God.

Whenever people overlook inconsistency, powerful emotions are at work. God, in his infinite goodness and omnipotence, decided to sacrifice his only son to redeem the sins of humanity. How could the Jews and Romans reject to carry out the will of God? This question was often on my mind whenever I was lectured about "His blood being upon Jewish hands." Did even God use the Jews as scapegoats? He first created a problem for Abraham by making him willing to slaughter his son Isaac. Then God had his own son killed and allowed it to be blamed on the Jews.

The Koran, just like the New Testament, lends itself to various interpretations. For example, there is a passage in the Koran that states:

And when the sacred months are passed, kill those who join other gods with God wherever ye shall find him; and seize them, besiege them, and lay wait for them with every kind of ambush. ...Believers!

248

Wage war against such of the infidels as are your neighbors and let them find you rigorous.

The interpretation a person gives to the scriptures is like a Rorschach test; it reveals his or her personality traits. Father Joseph denounced me because he was a Christian, but Stefan Jagodzinski told me that he risked his life to protect me for the same reason.

SCIENCE AND RELIGION

Science begins with "I don't know" and ends with "All knowledge is tentative." The three-dimensional world of Euclid gave way to the fourth dimension of Einstein. Newton's axioms became Einstein's relativity. Many people are uncomfortable with the ambiguity of science and cherish the certainty of religion. Theology was the queen of sciences because it offered certainty. Religion and law offer certainty because they are based upon fictions.

Comprehension of reality threatens the mythical world of religion. In the 19th century, religion found itself at a disadvantage in competition with science. The value of science could not be dismissed because even the uneducated masses could see the benefits of secular knowledge. The writers of the Bible recognized the danger of the comprehension of reality to religion. Adam and Eve were cautioned, on penalty of death, not to eat of the fruit of the "tree of knowledge."

Milton begins Paradise Lost with:
Of Mans First Disobedience, and the Fruit
Of that Forbidden Tree, whose mortal taste
Brought Death into the World, and all our woe.

Paradise was lost by the pursuit of knowledge. Supernatural Revelation, defined as disclosure by God of himself, is the fountain of truth for the monotheistic religions. The monotheistic narratives, unlike those of ancient Greece are anti-scientific; they oppose a spirit of inquiry.

Cicero said, Socrates "brought down philosophy from heaven to earth." Moses, Jesus and Mohamed reversed this achievement.

Religious dogma has been a major obstacle to scientific knowledge. For centuries, science was subordinated to theology. The publication of Origin of the Species in 1859 liberated science from religion. The basic tenets of Christian theology, that the world and its creatures were created as a finished product, were no longer tenable. The same happened to the dogma that the world was created a few thousand years ago and that living creatures were distinct and constant. Evolution and the myth of perfect creation could not coexist. In religion there is no room for new knowledge, all important questions have been answered. In 399 Socrates was indicted for "impiety." His crime was "neglect of the gods whom the city worships and the practice of religious novelties."

In the Western World such views have been called heresy, revisionism, dissent, heterodoxy, sectarianism and apostasy. Religion and ideology do not tolerate opinions that oppose established doctrines.

Religion and science address similar questions. Religion provides definite answers; science gives hypotheses and theories that are forever changing. If Newtonian physics were a religious dogma, the Theory of Relativity would result in Einstein's excommunication or worse. Einstein undermined what has been considered the immutable role of gravity. The scientific community was not outraged; Einstein's innovation was celebrated.

In the religious view, a supernatural power, God, rules the universe and his representatives on earth control human society. The humanistic-scientific approach tells us that natural forces rule the universe and people govern human society. C.P. Snow made the celebrated observation of the two cultures—humanities and arts on one side, and science on the other. This is a valid distinction. However, humanities and science are not negating each other. The humanities do not deny the truth of science and vice versa. Albert Einstein and Sigmund Freud were humanists and scientists. Religion and science on the other hand, cannot coexist in the same mind with consistency. It takes intellectual and ethical craftiness to combine the two.

Science offers the opportunity to seek the truth, but religion gives the certainty of knowing the truth. Some people are able to tolerate inconsistent ideas. Others require constancy, in which case they must choose between religion and science. If you accept the Bible as the source of all knowledge about creation, you cannot, at the same time, accept geological evidence that the earth is millions of years old. The Bible stories, if taken as metaphors, promote philosophical thinking. However, those who take them literally may suffer an atrophy of critical thinking. Pragmatic principles are maintained, provided that they work. Dogmatic principles do not require empirical validation, they are true eternally. Pragmatic principles emerge from their environment and disappear in it again; dogmatic principles have an unnatural stability.

Science and technology have drastically accelerated the rate of change in the West. The Islamic theocratic societies, dominated by dogmatism, were unable to keep up. They remained economically stagnant and poor. Most of the Islamic countries have not yet entered the scientific industrial-capitalist stage of development. From a socioeconomic perspective, the Islamic World suffers from arrested development. This is the fate of all orthodoxy; it is inevitably overtaken by history.

"The Truth" in religion and truth seeking in science have little in common. In religion, "The Truth" is revealed and everlasting. In science, the truth is the ever-changing pursuit of discovery of the mysteries of the universe. The truth of a scientific conclusion depends upon two conditions: it must logically follow from the premises, and the premises must be true. The truth or falsity of the premises is determined by scientific methodology appropriate to a given field. The basic principle of religion, the existence of God, must be accepted on faith. There is finality, perfection and certainty in "The Truth" of religion. Religion, like art offers perfection that can be embraced or rejected. In religion and ideology, one is required to accept the entire belief structure. The wrong belief or an incorrect opinion does not endanger the reputation of a scientist. In a theocracy or dictatorship, whoever has doubts about a doctrine is a heretic or a dissenter.

The unbelievers and the dissenters are fit subjects for excommunication, expulsion, imprisonment or extermination. The Jews were the eternal out-group and ideal scapegoats for the resistance to change.

Western Modernism accepts change and imperfection; rejects absolutism, tolerates uncertainty and rebuffs orthodoxy.

Western culture evolved from religious and secular sources. Judaism, Catholicism, the Reformation, scientific revolution, industrialization and secularism are developmental stages of Western culture. Whatever flaws Western secular societies have, they are the only hope of humanity. Imperfections are the key to survival of a species; this is the message of Darwin's theory of evolution. That is also the reason for the success of the American experiment, it tolerates diversity.

THE PROBLEM OF EVIL

In July 2000, I flew to Washington to attend the funeral of my friend and hero Jan Karski, I was a houseguest at the home of my friends Patricia and Robert Simon. Bob and I discussed the subject of evil. People who hate, he felt, should be called evil. I do not like the term evil because it is elastic, I told him. Bob, an eminent forensic psychiatrist, said to me, "You have come face to face with the ultimate evil. You are a Holocaust survivor and a forensic psychiatrist; you must tell us more about the nature of evil." Bob has given a great deal of thought to the subject of evil. His book *Bad Men Do What Good Men Dream* explores clinical aspects of evil. I am skeptical about the notion of evil. The word has a tone of righteousness about it. Evil is a synonym for social disapproval. It would be hard to argue with the validity of Nietzsche's statement *"there are no moral phenomena, only moral interpretations."*

"You will agree that Hitler and Stalin were evil." Bob insisted. "It was not evil to kill Jews in the Third Reich, but a civic duty of German citizens." I answered.

Saint John Chrysostom preached that it is a duty of a Catholic to hate Jews. Was he evil? From the perspective of the Catholic Church in those days he was virtuous and the Jews were evil. The Crusaders massacred Jews and Muslims and in the eyes of the Church of those days they were not evil, but pious Christians.

Evil is a synonym for moral disapproval. When hating Jews was "Christian duty" anti-Semitism was a sign of devotion and not immoral or evil. After Vatican II anti-Semitism became a sin. The concept of evil inspires hatred against people declared evil. Evil is the secular equivalent of sin. Evil, just like sin, is parochial and regional, but it claims universality. What is needed is a globalization of values. To take care of children is a universal value from Afghanistan to Zambia.

Patricia, Bob's wife, did not take part in our intense discussion about evil. The next day, she drove me from their home in Potomac to the National Airport in Washington D.C. We were engaged in small talk when suddenly Pat said, "Would you mind if I ask you a personal question?" "Please go ahead," was my reply.

"Do you believe that faith in the goodness of some people helped you to survive the Holocaust?" she asked. I responded with a resounding "Yes." Pat, in her benevolent way, focused the debate about evil on the reality of human conduct. Her words reminded me of Jan Karski, who told Jewish audiences "You should remember that the Jews were abandoned by human institutions but not by individual people."

Many Catholics helped Jews at the risk of their own lives; they did so as individuals, guided by their own interpretation of the teachings of the Church. Do isolated acts of individuals redeem an institution? I do not think so.

In the Judeo-Christian tradition, religious doctrines are divine. By attributing a divine origin to morality, the priests became the interpreters and guardians of morality, and thereby secured for themselves the power to control behavior. This link between morality and religion has been so firmly forged that it is still sometimes asserted that there can be no morality without religion. In reality, conscience formation is a psychosocial process independent of religion.

Evil presumes an absolute frame of reference. Good or bad for what? Something can be good in one context and bad in another. Heavy snow is bad for the traveler, and good for the skier. The opposite of evil is not useful, but pious or noble. Good and bad, unlike evil and noble, are instrumental and contingent.

From the perspective of the PLO, suicide bombers are noble. Koran, the sacred scriptures of Islam, condemns suicide, but blowing oneself up in order to kill infidels is not considered suicide but martyrdom; a martyr is assured of entrance into heaven. He is admired on earth for his piety. "The virgins are calling you," Mohamed Atta wrote reassuringly to his fellow hijackers just before 9/11. It has long been a staple of Islam that Muslim martyrs will go to paradise and marry 72 black-eyed virgins. (*New York Times*, August 4, 2004)

The term "suicide bomber" does not reflect Islamic and Western perceptions of self-sacrificing terrorism. Martyr-murderer is a more accurate term. Suicide in Western culture is a symptom of an illness. Killing civilians in the name of a cause is considered murder in the Western world. Thus, the term "martyr-murderer" represents a cross-cultural designation of the same behavior.

"Mutual Assured Destruction" was an insurance policy against nuclear war with the Soviet Union. Mutual assured destruction has no protective value when dealing with Islamic nuclear powers. In a culture of martyrdom, death is not a deterrent, but an incentive. Nuclear non-proliferation is not a negotiable issue. It is a life and death matter for the Western culture.

Psychiatric News, June 15, 2001, reported that at the annual scientific meeting of the American Psychiatric Association, a paper was presented that will help courts define "Evil Behavior." The author of this contribution was Michael Welner, M.D., the "inventor" of the Depravity Scale. This "instrument" was designed to give scientific validity to such concepts as "atrocious, outrageous, and vile." I firmly believe that these concepts have no place in psychiatric nomenclature. In decades of practicing forensic psychiatry, I have never been called upon to define evil and hopefully never will.

Deliberate infliction of suffering and death is sadistic and yet it is often not seen as evil if done under the cover of religion, nationalism or another belief system. Clinical, ideological and religious sadism differ in the interpretation of identical behaviour. Being tortured in the name of God, ideology or individual psychopathology makes little difference to the victim. Preoccupation with death and killing gratifies sado-masochistic needs. Calvin, in his *Meditating on the Future Life* said: "If heaven be our country, what can earth be but a place of exile? Let us long for death and constantly meditate upon it."

The Germans devised sadistic ways to humiliate and torment the Jews in the name of "racial justice." Cleaning sidewalks with toothbrushes, cutting off the beards of pious Jews and beatings were common. The concentration camps were institutions dedicated to sadistic torture. Eugene Kogon, the German politician, was imprisoned in Buchenwald before the Holocaust. He reported that the latrines were open pits, 25 feet long; the prisoners would defecate by squatting at the edge and holding on to the railings. "One of the favorite games of the SS was to push the defecating prisoner into the pit, in Buchenwald ten prisoners suffocated in excrement in this fashion in October of 1937 alone."

Overt sadism attracts some people and is repugnant to most. A belief system offers an excuse to gratify sadistic strivings without guilt or shame. Good men can do bad things in the name of a "good cause" and remain righteous. People professing belief in Jesus as Christ the Savior, humiliated, tormented and killed the Jews for hundreds of years. Father Joseph's smile when he unmasked me as a Jew showed pleasure based on the knowledge that I would be tortured and most likely killed. His sadistic needs were hidden in the fabric of a belief system. He had nothing personally against me; I was evil by definition. His hatred was not interactive; it was based upon an abstraction called "The Jews."

The Holocaust was the result of combining the ideology of "Death to Evil" with technology of mass murder. This is an issue that goes beyond the fate of the Jews of Europe. Many atrocities were perpetrated under the banner of a fight against evil. The handwriting is on the wall. The next step could be total annihilation of humanity.

Most genocide is the product of theocratic or dictatorial societies based upon religious or secular totalitarianism.

These two forms of government are the creations of an absolutist belief system. Religion and ideology are the most common foundation for an absolutist belief system. The term '"absolute" acquired the meaning of something being perfect and pure. Thus, absolutism is a belief system characterized by the conviction that one has the perfect answer to human problems.

Groups, societies, and the whole of humanity are engaged in a race between capacity to destroy and capacity to control aggression. When remote tribes practiced cannibalism, the civilized world was aghast but not in danger. When the so-called "rogue" States acquire atomic weapons the whole globe is at risk. A "Star Wars" defense system, even if it is feasible, is like the proverbial finger in the dyke. In the psychosocial evolution of Homo Sapiens, cannibalism and incest became taboo and are nearly extinct. Bloodshed to promote ideology or religion has to join these sacred prohibitions. We are too powerful to pursue armed conflicts that can lead to humanicide. Globalization of values of democracy, pluralism and tolerance is a necessity if humanity is to survive. This is the message of the Holocaust and the September 11th atrocity.

From a historical perspective, the recent modifications of Catholic doctrine in relation to the Jews are impressive, but not sufficient. Religious beliefs can be viewed as God given and exempt from scrutiny. Or they can be studied the way we approach such natural or historical phenomena as hurricanes, climate change and wars. Secular beliefs are analyzed and the followers are held accountable for the consequences they produce.

Religion may be entitled to tax exemption, but it should not claim an exemption from moral responsibility for the destructive actions, which it inspired. Religion sees the world in Manichean terms – as a confrontation between good and evil. The beneficial consequences of religious teachings are praised, but a veil of secrecy covers the harm religion has inflicted upon individuals and societies.

If it's a burnt offering to God, then I don't want to know the God at the other end.
-Michael Berenbaum, leading Holocaust scholar

Chapter 27
Distortions of Holocaust History

History is a bridge from the present to the past; it is constructed of facts, imagination, wishful thinking, it is at times determined by religion or ideology.

As a Holocaust survivor and a student of Holocaust history, I am aware of the twin dangers of remembrance: the failure to remember what happened and remembering what did not happen. Both distort history. History as found in historical texts is not reality; often it is a distorted reflection of the past, designed to gratify the needs of the present. The memory of those who witnessed history in the making is not free from distortion, but is often more reliable than history written by those who were not there.

Some historians say that the Holocaust began on November 10, 1938. Others insist that it began in June 1941. Yet others say that it started with the Wannsee Conference on January 20, 1942. For me the answer is simple, genocide is about actual killing and that begun on a mass scale in June 1941.

Truth and accuracy are always an issue when dealing with history. Historians rely on sources. It is essential to examine the basis that these sources have relied upon.

In this book, I have described living in a United Nations Relief Organization Camp, located in the Deutsches Museum in Munich. I arrived there in the summer of 1945. A few months later, I attended the UNRRA University, which was located in the same building. Fifty years later, I read in a publication of the Jewish Historical Institute that the German Museum had supposedly been destroyed during the time that I lived and was a student in that building.

I wrote a letter to the Institute stating this fact. I received a response from a professor of history, who cited a variety of *sources*. I thought I could easily refute him and contacted a member of the staff of the University of Munich, with whom I had correspondence on other matters. To my surprise, she also wrote that bombing destroyed the Deutsches Museum. When I questioned her, she replied with some indignation, "I took the information from a good source, the museum's web site. The museum would have no purpose to lie."

Clearly, everyone was telling the truth. At issue was not honesty of belief, but accuracy. When I shared this story with my fellow alumni of the UNRRA

University, some found it amusing, and others just shrugged their shoulders. A few years from now, there will be no one to contradict the "fact" that the Deutsches Museum in Munich was destroyed by bombing.

On October 9th, 2003, I attended a lecture at the Jewish Community Center (JCC) in Ann Arbor. The presentation was given by a Polish historian, Ania Cichopek. During the discussion, a number of participants made reference to the fact that during a visit to Poland in August of 2003, organized by the Ann Arbor JCC, they saw a monument honoring Dr. Janusz Korczak, a Polish hero who protected Jewish children and went to death with them.

They were surprised when I informed them that Dr. Korczak was not a Polish Catholic, but a Polish Jew. They insisted that their tour guide, Professor Zwi Gitelman, the head of The Institute of Judaic Studies at the University of Michigan, informed them about Dr. Korczak. I called my friend Nancy Margolis, who was on the trip and who was the head of the Ann Arbor Jewish Community Center. She confirmed that they were informed that Dr. Korczak was a Pole.

When I read books dealing with the Holocaust in Poland or Hungary I am often astonished by the misinformation that is communicated or implied based upon "historical sources". History, like all data, is often distorted in transmission. Harald Welzer, Professor of Social Psychology at the University of Hannover, conducted a research project entitled "Traditions of Historical Consciousness."[72] The research began in October of 1997. The Institute of Psychology at the University of Hannover interviewed three successive generations from 40 German families. A few thousand interviews were collected. The transformation of stories was remarkable. Memories were changed with time and each generation. "Along the way, from generation to generation, anti-Semites become resistance fighters, Gestapo agents are transformed into rescuers of Jews."

Even when all the members of the family heard descriptions of German atrocities, children and grandchildren remembered only the good things that parents and grandparents had done. Professor Welzer calls this "cumulative heroization" (Kumulative Heroisierung). This process occurred in two-thirds of the cases. Children and grandchildren grossly exaggerated the danger of opposition to the Nazi regime. For example: the 17 year-old grandson in the Groothe family said, "I believe that most people, in spite of everything, thought the Jews were human beings. But an individual could do nothing against it. An individual could simply do nothing. One could say, in my view, this is bad. But then one would be arrested and, most likely, shot."

Professor Welzer describes the evolution of an episode described by Joseph Renz. Mr. Renz served in the East and told his family about shootings of civilians carried out by his unit. Then he commented, "Had I been ordered to do it, which was quite possible, I have wondered what I would have done?" No one in the family asked Mr. Renz about the circumstances. When individual members of the family were interviewed later, their stories had changed significantly. The daughter, Vera Young, described the incident as involving self-defense. The grandson, Ulrich Young, had a different version. "Grandfather never shot anybody and would have never done it." Then he added, "That my grandfather could have taken part in these things is beyond my imagination."

Members of the family had to reconcile family loyalty and the reality that "the Nazis" and "the Germans" committed terrible war crimes. The conflict between present day values and past behavior is resolved by remembering for the present.

In the 1970s, I petitioned Yad Vashem to honor Stefan Jagodzinski, one of my heroic helpers. I enumerated his many acts of heroism on behalf of myself and my family. As a result, he received an award from Israel's Holocaust Remembrance Authority and a tree was planted in his honor. In 2002, I discovered that my account had been grossly exaggerated by the authors of Yad Vashem's *Encyclopedia of the Righteous Christians.* Someone had shaped my narrative to fit the present-day image of a passive Jewish youngster being taken care of by a heroic Polish rescuer. The Encyclopedia states:

> Toward the end of 1942, when the ghetto was about to be liquidated, Dr. Tenenwurzel, with the aid of a Polish acquaintance, succeeded in placing his fourteen-year-old son, Emmanuel,(sic) in a monastery in *Mogila.* In order to conceal the boy's Jewish identity, it was decided to teach him the tenets of the Christian faith and to train him as a priest.

In reality, I was not placed, but escaped the ghetto and was forced by bullets to return and try again. I escaped by climbing a roof of a house and going down the rainspout onto the Aryan side. No one taught me the tenets of the Christian faith; I learned on my own. When I became aware that I was about to be arrested in the monastery, I hid in the Church organ when the Gestapo came. However, the Yad Vashem's account says "the Polish acquaintance that assisted him (Emanuel) in the past came to his aid once again, and gave him into the care of his friend Stefan Jagodzinski."

After I escaped from Stary Korczyn, where I lived with Stefan, I was entirely on my own, but according to Yad Vashem, "Stefan decided to continue to protect his Jewish friend and even to share his fate." The following entry is a complete fabrication:

> Rumors that Emanuel was Jewish filtered through to the new place of residence, however, and the day before the Gestapo came to arrest them, they escaped to Krakow. From there, through his contacts with the underground, Stefan succeeded in smuggling Emanuel across to Hungary where he was liberated in the spring of 1945 by the Soviet Army."

Another entry does not even remotely resemble anything that I have provided to Yad Vashem. The entry states:

> Stefan also assisted Emanuel's mother and sister, who had escaped from the Miechow Ghetto, and supplied them with "Aryan" documents that saved their lives. His efforts to transmit forged documents to Emanuel's father, *Bronislaw Tenenwurzel,* failed however, and the latter was shot in the Plaszow camp."

My mother and sister escaped from the Ghetto long before they or I met Stefan. My father had false documents when he visited me in the monastery, which was also before we met Stefan, though it is true that Stefan tried to get some papers to father later. The concluding line of the entry reads: "Emanuel, who later became Professor Emanuel Tanay, immigrated with his mother and sister to the United States after the War and hosted his friend Stefan in his house in 1989."

My mother and sister emigrated from Germany to Australia in 1948. I remained in Munich and came to the United States in 1952. It is, however, true that my wife and I hosted Stefan in our house in 1989.

For most people, Holocaust and the history of the Holocaust are one and the same concept. It is history that Wallenberg saved 100,000 Hungarian Jews from being killed. It is history that Jews were passive and went to death like sheep. It is history that Jews mounted armed resistance against being killed by the Germans in the Warsaw Ghetto. However, this is not what happened in reality. Wallenberg did not save 100,000 Hungarian Jews from being killed. The Jews in German captivity were not passive; nearly all- those who survived and those who did not- struggled to survive. The Warsaw Ghetto Uprising was a collective suicide; the few hundred men and women of the "Jewish Fighting Organization" decided to die in Warsaw instead of Treblinka.

The social behavior of the Jews in German captivity was determined by the enormous disparity of power between the Jews and the Germans. The reconstruction of the personality of lions, based upon observations in the zoo, would have little resemblance to reality.

PASSIVITY AND RESISTANCE

For decades it was a cultural past time among American Jews and Israelis to preach about the evils of Jewish submissiveness during the Holocaust. Compliance with the oppressors was not a character flaw but an expression of the *courage to endure*. The genocide of the Jews by the Germans was not an assault upon a national entity living on its own land. The Jews were an oppressed minority before they became captives of Nazi Germany. German bureaucratic ingenuity slowly destroyed the social structure, such as it was, and debilitated the individuals. The next step of delivering them to the factories of death was easy.

It has never occurred to us to blame our brethren for meekness and conducting "business as usual" while we were tortured and murdered. A great deal more could have been done for the Hungarian Jews prior to March 1944, since they were clearly at risk and the statesmen in the United States, Great Britain and Palestine had easy access to them and could have warned them and arranged for their immigration. Neither the Allies nor the Jews of Palestine did so. After March 1944, the situation of Hungarian Jews became desperate.

The contemptuous passivity claims were a wall behind which the American Jews and Israelis were hiding from the painful past. It was strange to hear and read the bystanders accuse the victims of passivity. I have never heard a survivor mention passivity as a feature of the Holocaust experience.

The notion that survivors were passive is erroneous. Passivity and survival are incompatible. Passivity was deadly. Relentless activism and a capacity for adaptation were essential to survival. Decisions had to be made based on imagination; experience had little value. Misguided expectations, distortions of history and feelings of guilt, created the image of the Holocaust survivors.

The absence of armed resistance by the Jews in German captivity should surprise no one. Millions of Red Army soldiers died in German camps without armed resistance. The conditions in the ghettos were at least of equal barbarity. In the Warsaw Ghetto, there was an average of 13 people per room. Starvation and disease (especially typhoid) killed thousands each month. When helpless prisoners attacked their armed keepers, the outcome was not in doubt. The great disparity of power made resistance self-defeating.

The pursuit of unlikely survival was at least as honorable as seeking certain death in a suicidal clash. I am still amazed by the expectation that Jews could mount armed resistance to the German efforts to kill them. In 2002, in Sarasota, Florida, I gave a talk on the Holocaust to a junior high school audience. Somewhere during my presentation I made mention of the fact that I was a member of an underground group in Budapest. At the end a young boy asked, "How many Germans did you kill as a resistance fighter?" "Underground group" in his mind meant an effort to kill the Germans. I answered, "Our objective was not killing the enemy but frustrating his goal of killing us."

The question "Why did you not fight the Germans?" has a simple answer: "We did not want to commit suicide." The Jews in the imprisonment facilities called ghettos or camps could stage suicidal riots, but they could not engage in military operations.

The theme of passivity was reinforced by Dr. Bruno Bettelheim's writings. He claimed to be a Holocaust survivor, but he arrived in the United States in 1939. In the spring of 1957, Adolph Haas, Richard Hicks and I played host to Dr. Bettelheim. As young psychiatrists, we were delighted to meet the famous psychologist. He was the visiting speaker at the Ypsilanti State Hospital where the three of us worked. During a dinner, Dr. Bettelheim discovered that Haas and I were Holocaust survivors. He informed us that the Germans were able to murder millions of Jews because there was no armed resistance. "If a few Germans were shot when they came to get the Jews, the Germans would have given up the project" he said.

Dr. Bettelheim talked as if having guns was as common in Poland as it is in America. I doubt that any Jew in my hometown had a gun. Even if we had had guns to offer, armed resistance would have been self-defeating. The Germans were eager to find "reasons" to murder the Jews, they looked for real or imagined provocation to respond swiftly, and ruthlessly – we told him. Dr. Bettelheim hardly listened to our arguments.

I was amazed that a psychological scholar judged human behavior without empathy or knowledge of the existential reality of Polish Jews. We tried to convince him that heroic armed resistance was an exercise in futility and an expression of suicidal desperation.

I even invoked in his native German, a quote from *Faust* by Goethe: "Dasein ist die erste Pflicht" (To exit is the first duty). He was not persuaded.

Dr. Bettelheim's speeches and writing reflected the widespread view that the Jews of Europe "went to death like lemmings." Dr. Bettelheim wrote that failure to resist was the result of "yielding to the death instinct." Bettelheim mistook survival strategy for passivity and a death wish. Passivity, a code word for cowardice, was the catchword of Holocaust discussions in those days. Bettelheim did not understand that the actions of individual Jews, no matter how heroic, could not change the collective fate of European Jews. Yet, his ideas were popular because they resonated with the need of American and Israeli Jews to find heroes. His opinions received lavish publicity, not because his arguments were compelling, but because they appealed to the intellectual vice of seeing the past in terms of the present.

Jewish armed resistance could have only symbolic meaning. The Germans lost only 15 soldiers as the result of the heroic efforts of the Warsaw Ghetto fighters.

Marek Edelman, one of the surviving leaders of the Uprising, writes: "I wasn't nervous - perhaps because actually nothing could happen. Nothing greater than death. It was always *death that was at stake, not life.*" He also writes,

...There were 220 of us in the ZOB (Jewish Fighting Organization). Can one call that an uprising? What mattered is not let them slaughter us when they came to get us. The choice of the manner of death was the issue...everything that followed April 19, 1943 - was a longing for a beautiful death.[73]

According to Edelman, on April 19th, 21-year old Mordechai Anielewicz announced, "we will perish together... we are going to die, there is no going back, we will die for honor and for history."

On May 9th, Anielewicz shot his girlfriend Mira and then killed himself. Lutek Rotblat, another of the leaders, shot his mother and sister. Eighty fighters committed suicide on Mila Street. When Edelman and his group got there, they found only a few still alive. Jews killed more Jews than Germans during the Warsaw Ghetto Uprising.

Kazik, my friend and the husband of Gina, was part of the Uprising, and his resourcefulness and courage led to the rescue of a group of the fighters. Kazik told me that the Warsaw Ghetto fighters had some revolvers and homemade Molotov cocktails. This was the result of many months of intense efforts to acquire weapons. After the war, the Polish underground claimed that they gave the ZOB a few hundred revolvers, but Kazik says that they received only fifty and bought some on the black market. It is a tribute to the determination of the young fighters that with such meager resources they were able to fight the Germans for many days.

If these young men and women had had hundreds of revolvers, more Germans would have died, but the uprising would have remained a symbolic act devoid of military significance.

In August 1944, like their Jewish counterparts in the ghetto, the Polish Underground organized the Warsaw Uprising. The Red Army was on the outskirts of town and the Polish Underground Army wanted the honor of liberating the city. The uprising lasted two months, and when it was over, about 200,000 Poles were dead, and the entire city was in ruins. During the hostilities, most of the city's buildings were destroyed. Important monuments of the national culture were lost forever. After the final surrender, the Germans expelled the 500,000 remaining inhabitants and turned the city into a heap of rubble.

The Polish Warsaw Uprising in 1944, like the Warsaw Ghetto Uprising, is an epic event in the respective communities. They have in common being examples of quintessential futility. Both events resulted in foreseeable carnage and military and political irrelevance. Polish General Wladyslaw Anders, the commander of Polish troops outside of Poland, said, "I was completely shocked by the outbreak of the Rising. I regard it as the greatest misfortune in our present situation. It didn't have the slightest chance of success...no words can express our pride and wonder at the heroism of our Home Army and of the capital's population."[74]

In November of 1997, forty-four years after the Warsaw Ghetto Uprising, while driving, I was listening to the University of Michigan radio station. A young author (I did not catch his name) was interviewed. He had written a novel about the Holocaust to counteract the image that Jews went to slaughter like lemmings.

"I was bothered that my ancestors went to death like cowards," he complained. So, he researched the literature and discovered that the Jews did fight the Germans. "Jews did not go to death like cowards," he said proudly. His book is about Bernard, a Jew and a member of the French Resistance. The book, written by this young American Jew, has more to do with him than the situation of his ancestors in German captivity. He rejoiced in the exploits of Bernard against the Germans, but he did not know about the heroism of survival. My children, grandchildren and their children are a more significant victory than killing a few Germans.

As I drove and listened to the time tested lamentations about the absence of armed resistance, I recalled my visit to the "Holocaust Martyrs' and Heroes' Memorial" created by the State of Israel (Yad Vashem). The year was 1964; my mother, her husband Nathan and I approached the entrance in a solemn mood. Life size photographs of young men and women in heroic postures and holding automatic weapons greeted us. The large inscription in Yiddish read: "MIT NAGANEN IN DI HANDS" (With Rifles in our hands). These well-fed, triumphant and smiling faces were not typical of the Jews in German captivity. They did not look like victims of German oppression or survivors of the Holocaust.

My mother, Nathan and I had little in common with the images of these heroic warriors. We were survivors; they were guerilla fighters.

The name "Holocaust Martyrs' and Heroes Authority" gratifies the bystander's need for heroic images. The name contradicts the historical reality and the survivors' memories; armed resistance was, after all, suicidal.

The Jews were slaves in Egypt, but in Nazi Germany they were martyrs and heroes? The dreadful reality of genocide is transformed into a glorious myth. A martyr, by definition, is someone who voluntarily suffers death rather than denies his religion. Very few Jews among the millions killed during the Holocaust qualify for the martyr's status.

To declare the nearly six million Jewish victims as martyrs is a religious takeover of history. The Jews did not go to the gas chambers in the spirit of martyrdom (*mesirut nefesh*) described in the Talmud or as the *kedoshim* (the holy ones). The Jews who were murdered in the Holocaust and those who survived did not live up to the secular standards of military heroism or the religious criteria for martyrdom. The resistance seekers created a myth of heroic Jewish armed combat and neglected the brave struggles of the survivors.

Neither monuments nor words celebrate the heroism of survivors who did not "rebel" in the ghettoes or who did not "fight in the forests."

THE SEARCH FOR HEROES

If my father had been a Catholic, his death would have made him a candidate for beatification. My mother was offered my release from the concentration camp if she became an informant; she refused. Rafi, Mimis, and Pil, the Budapest underground leaders, saved hundreds of lives and would have had monuments erected in their honor if they were Christians. If I were not a Jew, the fact that I saved seven lives would entitle me at least to a tree in Jerusalem's Avenue of Righteous Christians.

The extent of Christians helping Jews to survive is often magnified and the heroic help given by fellow Jews is neglected.

Raoul Wallenberg, a resourceful and courageous Swedish emissary, was transformed into a superhuman rescuer. Wallenberg needs no embellishment to deserve our admiration. Wallenberg, like the Swiss diplomat Dr. Lutz, was active on behalf of the Hungarian Jews. My first hand knowledge of Wallenberg's efforts and the present day image of his activities are in stark conflict.

The Jewish rescue efforts in Budapest and the role of the Zionist underground are described in the memoir of the underground leader and hero, Rafi Friedel. Rafi described in his memoir a variety of efforts designed to save the Jews of Budapest, but makes no mention of Raul Wallenberg. Dr. Lutz, the Swiss consul is mentioned several times. Reading Rafi's manuscript, prepared shortly after the liberation, was a conformation of my own memories that the role of Wallenberg has been exaggerated and the rescue efforts of the Jews neglected.

The Raoul Wallenberg legend helps to avoid facing the failure of the civilized world to come to the assistance of the Hungarian Jews. It is a disgrace that by July of 1944, the rescue efforts of the Allies and of the American Jews consisted of sending to Budapest one brave Swedish businessman who pretended to be a diplomat.

The Raul Wallenberg story creates the appearance that Hungarian Jews were rescued by a humanitarian intervention. In reality, those who survived did so for reasons that have little to do with the efforts of this young man or any other endeavor from outside. The fate of Hungarian Jews and the efforts to assist them should be considered in historical context. On March 2, 1944, Soviet troops were 100 miles from the Hungarian border. [75]

A book put together by a committee of University of Michigan professors begins by stating that on January 17, 1945, Raoul Wallenberg vanished from the streets of Budapest and "left behind 100,000 Hungarian Jews, alive because of Wallenberg's fearless and ingenious efforts over the preceding six months to save them from Nazi mass murderer Adolf Eichman."[76]

The reality is that Wallenberg arrived in Budapest on July 9th. Regent Horthy ordered the deportations halted on July 6, 1944; at this point most of the Jews were already in Auschwitz.

The historian Jim Powell tells us how Wallenberg's Schutzpass saved 100,000 Jews:

Soon after the courageous Swede Raoul Wallenberg arrived in Nazi-controlled Budapest, July 1944, he conceived a bold scheme to save Jews. He knew the Nazis had a bureaucratic mind, so he designed impressive looking documents which basically said that the bearer wants to get out of Budapest, but because it's a war zone departure is impossible. Until departure becomes possible, the bearer is under the protection of the Royal Swedish Legation. Wallenberg rented several dozen Budapest buildings where he provided sanctuary for Jews. He brought them in at night, so the Nazis wouldn't know how many there were. Of course, the Nazis could have seized the Jews at any time, but Wallenberg's strategy was delay. The Allies had landed in Normandy, and the Russians were advancing from the East. The more Jews he could protect in his buildings, the more Jews were likely to be alive when the Nazis surrendered. This beloved man was credited with saving almost 100,000 lives.[77]

The idea of protective passes was linked to the so-called *Jew Houses.* Isolating the Jews of Budapest was a problem in logistics for the Germans and Hungarians. The large number of Jews living in Budapest and the fact that Hungary was still a quasi-independent country precluded the formation of a ghetto in Budapest. It was not feasible to clear a large section of town and designate it as a Jewish Quarter, as it was done in occupied Poland. The Hungarians established "Zido Haza" (Jew houses) instead. Most people lived in

Budapest in large apartment buildings. These mini-ghettoes were marked with a yellow star at the entrance.

The Jews who anticipated traveling to a foreign county lived in separate houses marked with the yellow star and the insignia of the country to which they expected to journey. To qualify to live in such a house, one had to have a certificate from a consulate of a foreign country stating that one was considered for a visit. These were creatively called Schutz-Pass.

The concept of a Schutz-Pass was a fiction that impressed some Hungarian functionaries, and did not have an impact upon others. If the Hungarians or the Germans had the inclination, they dragged the Jews out of the protective houses if the Swiss or Swedish sign was on the door or not.

The number of Hungarian Jews that Raul Wallenberg "saved" has increased with the passage of time. The total number of Jews who were in all so-called Protected Houses was less than 20,000. We also know that these houses were established before Wallenberg arrived in Budapest, when the city was still full of Jews.

A few Hungarian Jews have told me that they survived thanks to Wallenberg. When I asked them a few questions, it became obvious that they only assume that they are alive due to Wallenberg's arrival in Budapest.

The exaggeration of Wallenberg's contributions is not unique. Holocaust literature has many examples of this tendency.

"Nicholas Winton: The Power of Good" is the title of a documentary produced by a Czech filmmaker. The movie credits Mr. Winton, a British stockbroker, with rescuing 669 Jewish children.

In 1938, Mr. Winton visited Czechoslovakia and saw the persecution of the Jews. He arranged for the children to go to British Isles. His efforts were altruistic. The result was that the children escaped being in occupied Europe during the Holocaust. The few hundred Jews in Ann Arbor, Michigan in whose company I viewed this film, celebrated Mr. Winton as a Holocaust rescuer.

In 1938, neither Mr. Winton nor the parents of these children could or did anticipate the genocide ahead. Not even Hitler knew then what would happen to the Jews of Europe. It is not accurate to call Mr. Winton, as many did, the English Schindler. The Schindler Jews were at risk of being killed when Schindler intervened and he risked his life to protect them.

Mr. Winton was an altruistic man who does not need to be endowed with clairvoyance to be admired for his compassion for the persecuted Jews. The exaggeration of virtue and heroism does more harm than good. The inflated claims breed cynicism and undermine the credibility of history.

The Zegota story is one more illustration of the search for heroes. On September 1st, 1999, I arrived in Prague to speak at the World Meeting of Child Holocaust Survivors. As I entered the hotel lobby, a man approached me. He was Rene Lichtman, a child survivor from Detroit. We had never met before but he recognized me, having attended some lecture I gave. Rene told me that he and a filmmaker named Siegel were involved in a project of making a film about child survivors of the Holocaust. He wanted to schedule a filming session with me. Lichtman and Siegel had just returned from Poland where they attended a conference on Zegota, the Polish organization that "has saved thousands of Jews," he said.

Lichtman and Siegel were not happy with my comment that Zegota was a small group of Poles who did little to help the Jews. "There is research to show that saved many Jews," Lichtman insisted. There was no more talk about scheduling a filming session with me. I did not fit the theme that these two filmmakers had adopted. Zegota has become part of the rescue mythology.

The purpose of Zegota was not assistance for the Jews, but expression of the moral rejection of killing the Jews. I have so far encountered one Jew who was helped by Zegota.

The *Encyclopedia of the Holocaust* tells us that Zegota was an underground organization in occupied Poland and operated from December 1942 until the liberation in January 1945. It was founded on the initiative of Zofia Kossak - Szczucka, who also became its chairperson.[78] In September 1942, she circulated a leaflet. Whoever read this document has to conclude that it had more to do with anti-Semitism than rescue efforts. The leaflet states, in part:

> We are speaking up, we Catholic-Poles. Our feelings in relation to the Jews did not undergo a change. We did not cease to consider them political, economic and ideological enemies of Poland. Moreover, we are aware that they hate us more than the Germans; they make us responsible for their misfortune. Why, on what basis – this remains a mystery of the Jewish soul, a fact constantly confirmed. Consciousness of these feelings does not free us from the duty to condemn crimes. We do not wish to be Pilates. We do not have the capacity to actively counteract the German murders, we are unable to help, to rescue anybody, but we do protest from the bottom of our hearts filled with pity, indignation, and horror. God, who forbids killing, demands this protest from us. Christian conscience demands it.
> We protest also as Poles. We do not believe that Poland should benefit from German cruelty. On the contrary. The stubborn silence of the international Jewry and the efforts of German propaganda tried to place the blame of the slaughter of the Jews upon Lithuanian and Poles. We see in this planned hostile action against us.

Nechama Tec wrote,

> The stated aim of this document was to protest the Nazi crimes committed against the Jews. In reality, this leaflet is a strange mixture of outrage against German atrocities, indignation against the indifference of the Free World, and reiteration of anti-Jewish sentiments.[79]

The respected American statesman Zbigniew Brzezinski writes: "Zegota is the story of extraordinary heroism...tantamount to 'Schindler's List' multiplied a hundred-fold".[80]

Zbigniew Brzezinski was born in Warsaw in the same year and month as I was. Did he forget the virulent anti-Semitism of his native land? Does he have access to some historical evidence inaccessible to the rest of us? With the passage of time, the heroism of the few who assisted Jews during the Holocaust was exaggerated to epic proportions.

Wer Jude ist bestimme Ich (I determine who is a Jew).
-Herman Goering

Chapter 28
Who is a Jew? Who is a Survivor?

Defining who was a Jew was an industry in Nazi Germany. German Jews, like Hungarian Jews, were so assimilated that one had to do genealogical research to determine who was a Jew, or in Nazi terms, who had "Jewish Blood." In Budapest, I could rarely recognize a person as a Jew either by name or by appearance. That changed in April of 1944. It seemed that half of the city was wearing the mandatory yellow star. Not even the converts to Catholicism, some of whom were priests and nuns, were exempt.

The Primate of Hungary, Cardinal Seredi, fought hard to get an exemption for the Catholic Jews. Prime Minister Stojay ruled against this request. The Cardinal argued that the Star of David "was a symbol of religion and not of the Jewish *race* and, consequently, wearing it by Christians would be a contradiction."[81]

Prime Minister Stojay argued that the yellow badge was not to be construed as a symbol of Jewish religion but "a convenient means to the necessary identification from the administrative point of view of those of the Jewish race."[82]

He assured the Cardinal that he would not object to the converts wearing a cross. The Cardinal did not dispute that the Jews were a race and yet he argued that being baptized changed a Jew into a non-Jew. In the Nazi mythology, being a Jew was a biological reality that could not be modified.

However, Herman Goering, in his capacity as the commander of the German Air Force, was less rigid in defining who was a Jew. He was told that Luftwaffe Marshall Erhard Milch had a Jewish mother and therefore was a Jew by Nazi standards. "Wer Jude ist bestimme Ich" (I determine who is a Jew), declared Goering, and Milch remained a non-Jew. He continued to occupy one of the top positions in the Luftwaffe. He was not the only German soldier who had "Jewish blood."[83]

Orthodox Jews define a Jew as someone born to a Jewish mother. Under the Israeli Law of Return, it is *not* the religious faith that defines Jewishness but

Jewish parenthood. The Nuremberg laws defined as a Jew a person who had one Jewish grandparent. Thus, being Jewish for the Orthodox Jews and the Nazis is an *accident of birth*, not necessarily a religious commitment. If being committed to religion were the definition of Jewishness, then a majority of the Hebrew speaking population of Israel would not be Jewish.

Dr. Editha Stein considered herself a Jew, even though she converted to Catholicism. In 1922, she entered a convent and became Sister Theresa Benedicta. The church accepted this distinguished scholar with open arms. The Nazis, in 1936, decreed that Sister Theresa Benedicta, a Carmelite nun, was a Jew. In 1943, she was sent to Auschwitz where she was killed. The Catholic Church pronounced her to be a martyr of Catholic faith and a saint. However, the Pope declared that she died "as a daughter of Israel." The Jews objected that a woman killed as a Jew was declared a Catholic Saint. However, had she lived and came to Israel like Friar Daniel; she would not have been considered a Jew by the State of Israel.

Friar Daniel, born as Oswald Rufeisen, a Polish Jew, survived the Holocaust by claiming to be a German (ethnic German). He worked for the German police in the occupied Soviet Union and saved a number of Jews and Christians from being killed.

After the war, he converted to Catholicism, became a priest and joined a Catholic Order in Israel. Brother Daniel, as he was known in his Order, applied for Israeli citizenship under the Law of Return that grants automatic citizenship to any Jew who comes to Israel. He was not a Jew because he was a Catholic, declared the Supreme Court of Israel.

One day, during a conversation with my then 16 year-old son David, I told him, "You answer a question with a question, like a Jew", I said.

"I am a Jew," David replied. I asked him why he considered himself a Jew.

"Because my father is a Jew," was the instant response.

I did not tell him that in the eyes of the Orthodox rabbis, he was not a Jew because his mother is a Christian. David received no Jewish or Christian religious educational indoctrination, and yet, he feels that he is a Jew.

In my view, Sister Theresa Benedicta, even though a devout Catholic had rational and cultural reasons to say that she was a Jew. Brother Daniel, a hero of the Holocaust, had every reason in the world, except religion, to insist that he is a Jew. The same holds true for my son David.

My involvement with Judaism has been a cultural one. Even though I am not religious, I doubt that anyone would maintain that I am not a Jew. I am an agnostic Jew from Poland, and an American. These identities are not in conflict. I share the feelings of Alan M. Dershowitz, who wrote:

> Though I am a doubting Jew, who identifies primarily with the secular aspects of Judaism, I love attending traditional Jewish religious services - and not only because I enjoy the music or because it brings back positive memories of my youth. Participating in the Jewish minyan - a communal prayer service - moves me in ways that I cannot fully explain. It connects me to the Jewish people of the time and also throughout the world today.[84]

It is gratifying to embrace cultural heritage as the basis of ethnic identity, but it is painful to recognize that persecution was also a factor in shaping our characteristics. The psychosocial sense of identity is the result of interactions with other human beings. Jewish history and individuality was shaped by encounters with persecutions. Oppression, expulsions and ghetto existence are central to the understanding of the development of Jewish identity.

*

Who is a survivor? Survival is a noun describing confrontation with death. A person who could have been involved in a life-threatening event has a different emotional experience than someone who was actually exposed to it.

There are survivors of a multitude of disagreeable experiences that have little to do with exposure to the immediate risk of being killed. Who is a survivor depends upon the definition of the term. We could say that a survivor of the Holocaust is any Jew who, if he or she were under Nazi Germany's control, would have been killed. This definition makes every Jew a Holocaust survivor. We could limit the definition to all Jews who were in Germany in 1933 or in Poland after September 1939 until liberation.

A survivor of the Holocaust, in my view, is a Jew who was in German captivity and faced concrete danger of being killed. A survivor is someone who was exposed to the genocidal process and succeeded in staying alive.

"I am also a survivor," a woman with a slight Hungarian accent told me at a party. "Were you also liberated in Budapest?" I asked, assuming we had that in common. The strange look on her face signaled that this was a wrong question to ask. Her family came to the United States in 1941. The Germans did not occupy Hungary until March 1944.

Encounters with death, like exposure to fire, traumatizes by proximity. When survivors gather at parties or meetings, I can easily distinguish what I call the "front line survivors" from others who had the good fortune not to be in German captivity during the Holocaust.

The experiences of the Jews in German captivity were determined by geography, history and chronology. On March 18, 1944, the 15-year-old Elie Wiesel was one day away from living in a German occupied land. On the same day, I, a 15-year-old Polish Jew, was in my fifth year of living in German captivity. In June of 1944, Elie Wiesel was in a death camp in occupied Poland, while I was in a relatively benign concentration camp in former Yugoslavia. In August of 1944, after an escape from the camp, I lived as a free man in the city of Budapest, while Elie Wiesel was near death from starvation in Buchenwald. Efforts to comprehend the Holocaust must begin with the question "Where?" and "When?"

Prior to 1941, Nazi Germany subjected the German Jews to discrimination, persecution, imprisonment and torture. Hannah Arendt was deprived of academic advancement because she was a Jew, and had to leave her native Germany. She immigrated to the United States, where she made great contributions to social science. In Germany she did not experience the imminent danger of being killed because she was a Jew.

Otto Bettelheim was persecuted and imprisoned in the Buchenwald concentration camp, but he came to the United States in 1939, before the final solution became operational. Dr. Bettelheim became an acclaimed child psychologist in this country, and a prolific writer. I do not consider Drs. Arendt and Bettelheim Holocaust survivors. The term "Holocaust survivor" should reflect experiences endured by a given individual. Did he or she suffer danger of being killed as a result of the "Final Solution" is the criterion, I believe, for being a Holocaust survivor. The Jews who escaped Nazi Germany before the genocidal project was initiated are not Holocaust survivors; they are victims of Nazi persecution.

Making distinctions in the degree of suffering is unavoidable for a psychiatrist who treated and evaluated hundreds of fellow survivors. The Jews who survived the death marches and death camps, are in my clinical experience, the most severely traumatized. Next are those who endured concentration camps. Those of us who lived on false papers suffered, by comparison, less severe traumatization; we were less helpless and experienced less horror.

It does not require the skill of a psychiatrist to identify survivors who lived on false papers as being different from those who survived in a concentration camp. The "refugee" survivors are also affected by the experiences they suffered. However, they did not have direct confrontation with death. It is all a question of degree of trauma.

Most German Jews who left Germany because of Nazi persecutions are refugees who have never been subjected to incarceration but suffered persecution. Some victims of Nazi persecution have no experiential knowledge of the events called the Holocaust. I have evaluated a number of Jews who escaped being exposed to the Holocaust by finding refuge in Shanghai. Their resourcefulness, courage and resilience were remarkable. They endured many hardships. However, they did not have direct confrontation with the sadism and destruction that was the Holocaust.

To this day, we do not have a term to describe the Jews saved by the Soviet deportation to Siberia. They do not fit the definition of "refugee" because they were *deported* to the Soviet Union.

During the short-lived German-Polish War, many Jews from Western Poland escaped the advancing German Army to eastern Poland. On September 17th, 1939 as the result of a secret agreement between Germany and the Soviet Union, the Red Army occupied eastern Poland. The Jews from Western Poland who avoided German captivity found themselves under the control of the Soviets. The Soviets did not send these refugees to the German occupied Poland, but instead deported them to Siberia. This banishment turned out to be the biggest unintended "rescue" operation of Polish Jews during World War II.

After a relatively brief stay in Siberia, the Polish Jews were transferred to the Far East and lived in relatively good circumstances. They enjoyed relative freedom and comfort till the end of war. Their children attended schools and the adults worked. Many attended secondary schools, some gained academic degrees, and others served in the Polish Army organized in the Soviet Union. Nearly all of the Jews who survived in the Soviet Union returned to Poland after 1945. They found their communities destroyed and their relatives and friends "exterminated." Some of them maintain that they are Holocaust survivors because had they not been in the Soviet Union, but remained in occupied Poland, they would have been killed. These people are victims of Nazi Germany, but they are not Holocaust Survivors in my view.

Some Holocaust survivors intensely oppose making distinctions based upon different degrees of suffering. Time and time again, I have heard the phrase "pain is pain" or "suffering is suffering." They object to any distinctions, as that could create dissension within the ranks of survivors.

I was invited to present the history of the Jewish Students in Munich at the international gathering of survivors called "Life Reborn." The conference was organized by the Holocaust Memorial Museum in Washington, D.C. To the group, I defined a survivor of the Holocaust as someone who was exposed to the actual danger of being killed during the German genocide of the Jews. Many in the audience disagreed with me. They protested that my definition excludes those who were deported from eastern Poland to Siberia and, later, relocated by Soviet authorities to middle Asia. It excludes German Jews who "emigrated from Germany before 1939." I was accused of divisiveness and worse. The designation victim of Nazi Germany did not satisfy people who would be excluded from the definition of a Holocaust survivor.

Some stressed the lack of any useful purpose in my definition. One woman, who I believe was a child of survivors, expressed a surprise that I, a psychiatrist, was such a rigid person and did not have the flexibility to be inclusive. Pamela Trieb, a social worker whose work with survivors I admire, argued with great intensity that people who left Poland to escape the advancing German army and experienced great hardships in the Soviet Union are Holocaust survivors because "had it not been for Nazi Germany, they would not have suffered this ordeal." She invoked a specific client who lost a child in Soviet Union. "Why would you deny this man the distinction of being a Holocaust survivor?" She asked in an accusatorial voice.

A few people invoked The Shoah Foundation definition of survivor which, they claimed, included all Jews who were under Nazi control from 1933 to 1945. Michael Nutkiewich, Ph.D., the senior historian of the Shoah Foundation, wrote to me in response to an inquiry:

> The Shoah Foundation interviews anyone who was under Nazi Germany's direct authority between 1933-1945, or under any of the official allies of Germany between 1933-1945. In addition, we have interviewed Sinti and Roma (gypsies), participants in war crime trials, liberators, rescue and aid workers, and homosexuals under Nazi authority.[85]

There may be no moral distinction between various forms of suffering imposed upon people, but there is an experiential difference for the victims. Happiness, pain, joy, and despair very in intensity. After the War, I was in the fortunate position to have a mother and a sister. In 1945, many of my friends had no living relatives. My friend Sophie Schor had both parents. My stepfather Nathan Rottenberg survived some of the worst camps and a death march. He experienced macabre scenes and was tortured. My mother survived on false papers and never saw a camp.

Who is a Holocaust survivor is linked to the question, when did the Holocaust begin? Did it start with the persecution of the German Jews in 1933? The Encyclopedia Britannica has the following entry under "Holocaust":

Holocaust Hebrew SHO`AH, or HURBAN, the 12 years (1933-45) of Nazi persecution of Jews and other minorities, which was marked by increasing barbarization of methods in the expanding territories under German rule; it climaxed in the Final Solution (die Endlösung), the attempted extermination of European Jewry.

On November 7, 1938 the German diplomat Ernst vom Rath stationed in Paris was shot by Herschel Grynszpan, a young Polish Jew, whose parents were abused in Nazi Germany. Hitler ordered "spontaneous" protest during which 91 Jews were killed and hundreds were seriously injured. About 7,500 Jewish businesses were destroyed and 177 synagogues were burned. The mass of broken glass gave rise to the name Krystallnacht (Night of Crystal). Was Krystallnacht the beginning of the Holocaust, as some people claim? I do not think so, which is not to minimize the barbarity of that day.

The respected British historian Sir Martin Gilbert gives a different date:

The German invasion of the Soviet Union in June 1941 was the start of the Holocaust as we know it. Messages reaching Churchill through his intelligence services told of the murder, in groups, of thousands of Jews. He made powerful reference to these killings when he broadcast on November 14, 1941:

'None has suffered more cruelly than the Jew the unspeakable evils wrought upon the bodies and spirits of men by Hitler and his vile regime. The Jew bore the brunt of the Nazi's first onslaught upon the citadels of freedom and human dignity. He has borne and continued to bear a burden that might have seen beyond endurance. He has not allowed it to break his spirit; he has never lost the will to resist. Assuredly in the day of victory the Jew's suffering and his part in the struggle will not be forgotten."[86]

*

In January 1952, I disembarked the ship General Blatchford and set foot on American soil for the first time. I was called by social workers of the Hebrew Immigration Society "a refugee." When I had stepped aboard the same ship in Hamburg, Germany, I was called a "Displaced Person." The United States Immigration Service gave me a card designating me as a "Resident Alien." The American Jews called me "a greenhorn." I called myself a Holocaust survivor.

One should, for example, be able to see that
Things are hopeless and yet be determined to make them otherwise.

-F. Scott Fitzgerald

Chapter 29
Trauma and Triumph

Isaac Bashevis Singer begins *Enemies, A Love Story*, with: "I did not have the privilege of going through the Hitler Holocaust." Was it a privilege? The depiction of survivors in his writing is more consistent with a curse than a privilege. Singer's disdain for survivors was relatively gentle when compared to that of General George S. Patton, commander of the Third Army and liberator of Nazi concentration camps. This representative of the United States wrote in his diary: "Others believe that the Displaced Person is a human being, which he is not, and this applies particularly to the Jews who are lower than animals . . . a subhuman species without any of the cultural or social refinements of our time."(emphasis mine) He described in his diary one DP camp,

> where, although room existed, the Jews were crowded together to an appalling extent, and in practically every room there was a pile of garbage in one corner which was also used as a latrine. The Jews were only forced to desist from their nastiness and clean up the mess by the threat of the butt ends of rifles. Of course, I know the expression 'lost tribes of Israel' applied to the tribes which disappeared -- not to the tribe of Judah from which the current sons of bitches are descended. However, it is my personal opinion that this too is a lost tribe -- lost to all decency.[87]

In reality, Holocaust survivors are people whose love of life triumphed over the forces of hate. They are a bridge between life and death, love and hate, despair and hope.

Claude Lanzmann, the creator of the classic documentary "Shoah," is quoted in the German newspaper *Die Tagszeitung* (May 2001); Lanzmann told the interviewer: "Spielberg collects personal stories, which do not convey the deeper meaning. His Shoah Foundation made a terrible film: 'The Last Days.'"

Lanzmann found Spielberg's celebration of survivors distasteful; he proudly declared that his documentary "Shoah" was "about death and not about survival." He claimed that in his film there is not a single survivor. "There are returnees, who have already been in the hereafter swinging over the crematoriums and came back. These people never say 'I', they do not tell their own story. They say 'we,' because they speak for the dead. These are modest, simple people. What they say does not become an adventure novel."[88]

In truth, we are neither simple nor modest. We have a sense of accomplishment that fills us with pride. If Lanzmann considers people who lived through the Holocaust to be the walking dead, he is dead wrong. Holocaust survivors did not let their past kill their future. The optimism that sustained us in times of horror inspired us in times of the post-war hardship in Germany. We remained alive in body and spirit, in spite of the ordeal. It is hard to believe this could be possible.

The DP camps of 1945 were places of misery transformed by survivors into thriving communities. The camps of Landsberg, Bergen-Belsen, and Foerenwald became vibrant centers of education and cultural life within a few months after liberation.

The survivors, through their own efforts, became productive citizens of various countries. General Patton would no doubt change his mind if he saw us in Israel, the United States and countless other lands. The attributes that were essential to survival made us successful in business, professions and other pursuits.

David Chase, born David Ciesla, is an international entrepreneur of immense wealth and a respected philanthropist. He is the younger brother of my dear friend Helen Covensky, who herself is an accomplished artist. At age 14, David was one of the youngest inmates of Auschwitz. He survived the death camps and the death marches, and arrived in New York at the age of 17, with 25 cents in his pocket.

My former fiancée and lifelong friend Nechama Tec, is a professor of sociology at the University of Connecticut and an author of many books. She survived on false papers in Poland. She, like I, did not have the benefit of formal elementary education but has become a respected scholar. My friend and colleague, Henry Krystal, survived Auschwitz, and later became a professor of psychiatry and an authority on psychic trauma. Elie Wiesel won the Nobel Prize.

These are but a few of the hundreds of survivors I know who have attained success after liberation. This is the untold story of the Holocaust.

In April of 1993, I attended the dedication of the National Holocaust Memorial Museum. The President of the United States, William Clinton, and the President of Israel, Herzog, as well as other dignitaries, attended. Elie Wiesel gave a memorable speech. The horror of the Holocaust was discussed by all of the speakers. What was missing was any mention of survivors.

I was pleased when the Museum organized a gathering in November of 2003, entitled "Tribute to Survivors." It was a major undertaking, which was beautifully organized. It concluded with a moving ceremony at the same location as the dedication of the museum 1993. Once again, Elie Wiesel gave a moving speech, and, once again, the horror of the Holocaust was powerfully conveyed. The significance of remembering the catastrophe was stressed. Yet, what was missing in the "Tribute to Survivors" was a tribute to survivors. The suffering of survivors was mentioned, but the heroism of survivors received no attention.

All survivors represent triumph of life over death and most are alive as the result of heroic efforts. They are the forgotten heroes of the Holocaust. They are heroes because they succeeded to stay alive in a culture of death. They have a story to tell worth listening to. Courage to endure and the skills to adapt to terrible situations are admirable qualities. I have known for a long time that it took uncommon courage to survive but only recently did I recognize the extent of it.

I, like most survivors, believed in those days that I had nothing to do with being alive. It was an accident or luck that I survived. I have examined and treated many Holocaust survivors, countless American Veterans of World War II, the Korean War and the Vietnam War. Virtually all survivors of natural and manmade disasters insist that they are alive due to luck. They deny their own contribution to the favorable outcome. The same people will take credit for less significant developments in their lives.

If I said that I became associate director of a university psychiatric hospital and professor of psychiatry because I am lucky, people would laugh. No one laughed when I used to say that I survived as the result of luck. Survival during the Holocaust was the result of luck that happened to people who were resourceful, had courage and the will to live.

In October 1978, Elie Wiesel and I were part of a lecture series at Mercy College of Detroit. At dinner we sat next to each other and talked about our survival. He said to me: "I never did anything to stay alive." There was a time when I felt the same.

In September 2000, I attended a gathering of child survivors in Seattle. I conducted a workshop for members of the group. My group consisted of about 30 survivors seated in a circle. I invited each one to describe how they survived the Holocaust and to tell the group about their lives after the war. Most were liberated in the camps, many were in death camps. I and two or three others were in a camp only briefly. The matter of fact manner in which the stories were told showed an incredible capacity to endure horrifying circumstances. Every member of the group became a successful professional or entrepreneur after the war. Everyone in the group married, had children and grandchildren.

After listening, I expressed my admiration for their courage and resourcefulness. The first person that spoke objected to my saying that survivors were resourceful and courageous. She pointed out that those who did not survive were also resourceful and courageous. She then described her own life after liberation, which was a story of remarkable success. She became an academic educator, a mother of two children and a number of grandchildren.

A man from Holland spoke up next. He too took issue with my opinion that survivors contributed to their survival. However, his story confirmed my view. Dutch peasants hid him and his mother in the last few months of the war. Germans were searching for Jews in the village and it became apparent that the peasant would denounce them. The mother secretly fashioned a nurse's uniform for herself, escaped with the 10-year-old boy in the middle of the night, walking through the snow to a highway. She stopped a German car, told the officer that she was a nurse taking the little orphan boy to Amsterdam to reunite him with some relatives. They were given a ride to the city, where the Dutch underground helped them.

A good-looking, articulate woman said, "I am neither resourceful nor lucky, it was my destiny to survive." She described a life that was a vivid testament to her resourcefulness and luck. Destiny was a common explanation for survival and I was tempted to call them "Children of Destiny."

Survival was not a random event, unconnected to the survivor's actions. No Jew survived without his or her active participation in the process. The outcome was multi-determined. S.J.Gould writes in *Wonderful Life*:

> I am not speaking of randomness, but of the central principal of all history—contingency. A historical explanation does not rest on direct deductions from laws of nature, but an unpredictable sequence of antecedent states, where any major change in any step of the sequence would have altered the final result. This final result is therefore dependent, or contingent, upon everything that came before—the inerasable and determining signature of history.[89]

The liberated Jews of Europe were confronted with two disasters; the calamity that became known as the Holocaust, and the reality of being homeless. Most asked themselves: "Why did I survive and others did not?" The poem "Could Have," by the Polish poet Wislawa Szymborska comes to mind.

> You were saved because you were the first.
> You were saved because you were the last.
> Alone. With others.
> On the right. The left.
> Because it was raining.
> Because of the shade.
> Because the day was sunny. [90]

All survivors are burdened by "survivor guilt," superimposed upon the harm they suffered as the result of traumatic experiences. I have never seen a veteran who did not feel guilty when one of his buddies was killed. I have never seen a Holocaust survivor who did not have survivor guilt. Survivor guilt was shown by the countless survivors of car, plane and other accidents that I have examined in the last 50 years.

Survivor guilt is one of the reasons why most Holocaust survivors insist that they played no role in staying alive. Any Jew in German captivity could, by his or her conduct, bring about instant death. No strategy insured survival. I cannot say that I survived because I went on false papers. This decision could have easily resulted in my death. Did Elie Wiesel survive because he went to Auschwitz? Every choice was potentially deadly and in every setting some Jews survived. Courage to endure, resourcefulness and will to live were necessary but not sufficient.

All of us paid a price for the miracle of survival; it is now called "Post Traumatic Stress Disorder," a term introduced to psychiatry in 1980. The essence of this syndrome is reliving, not merely remembering, the past. We have suffered from this condition for decades before it became a recognized diagnosis. I have examined hundreds of survivors and have not seen one who did not show symptoms of this illness. I have treated dozens and have not seen one who has been cured. That includes me.

Survivors have the notion that surviving the war made us stronger. The opposite is true. To survive extreme stress, one has to be resilient and have the illusion of invulnerability. Denial of vulnerability is adaptive in a life and death struggle. However, common sense tells us that severe trauma leads consistently to injury of the mind and body. A person run over by a truck expects to suffer harm, not enhancement of his or her coping skills. Training improves performance; injury impairs the victim but is not necessarily disabling.

When I became aware that my Holocaust experiences had caused me harm, I sought treatment. My first therapist was Dr. Editha Sterba, a well-known Viennese psychoanalyst practicing in Grosse Pointe, Michigan. During the three-year long analysis (1956-1959), the Holocaust was never discussed. I did not want to talk about it and Dr. Sterba did not want to hear about it. The center of attention was my childhood. I terminated the treatment against Dr. Sterba's insistence. I believed that it was of no value to me. I knew on some level that talking about the Holocaust was unavoidable.

In 1960, I began analysis with Dr. Harry August. I saw him five times a week for the next ten years. This time, my Holocaust experiences were dealt with in detail. It was a mutual education. Dr. August was a classic analyst whose misconceptions about the Holocaust surfaced occasionally. He viewed my lack of hatred of the Germans as denial. As time went on he recognized that the absence of hate was a personality trait that made my survival possible.

Dr. August showed me that I survived, not by luck, but in part due to my own resourcefulness and courage. I also realized that I felt guilty for not having saved my father and took little credit for my contributions to the survival of my mother, my sister and my childhood sweetheart Gina, and others. None of that reduced the feeling of guilt for my father's death.

A Holocaust survivor has one foot in the here and now and another entangled in the past, a precarious position. To us, history is past and present. Einstein said that the distinction between the past and future is an illusion. For the survivors, the separation of the past and the present is more a wish than reality. We do not view the Holocaust as a symbol, but an experience that is relived in some way every day.

In June 1991, I wrote a description of my life in the Miechow ghetto. I intended to read it during a talk I was to give at the Grosse Pointe Unitarian Church. I read the text aloud to Sandy. After two pages, I broke down crying. I regained control of myself after a few hugs and a drink of water and resumed reading to the sympathetic audience of my loving wife. Once again, a crying fit put an end to my reading. "Why should the memories of that period be so painful?" I asked. Sandy was less perplexed. "You were a little boy whose world was shattered," she said, as she put her arms around me.

We survivors can't help but guard against the ever-present danger of being overwhelmed by the memories that are always with us. I agree with Joyce Carroll Oates, who wrote in the novel *Foxfire*, "For writing a memoir is like pulling your own guts inch by slow inch. I didn't know this when I started this book but I know it now."[91]

Acknowledgements:

Many people have helped me in the writing of this book. I can mention but a few. The heroic helpers described in the book deserve credit for my being alive. My wife Sandra and my children Elaine, Anita and David have been supportive and encouraged me to continue this project and more importantly, to finish it.

My cousin Deborah Tannen provided advice and help in efforts to get it published. Robert Jay Lifton was one of the first people who told me that it was my obligation to write this book. Elie Wiesel has been an inspiration and encouraged me to write when he and I first met in 1972. Carol Rittner, Nechama Tec, Theodore Souris, James Graves, Frank Kelley, Robert Simon, Stewart Hubbell, Ralph Slovenko, Kasia Kietlinska, Lisa Van Sustern and many others gave me helpful feedback after reading the manuscript. My daughter Elaine read the manuscript in its early form and made useful suggestions.

My analyst, Harry August M.D., helped me to cope with the traumatic past. Last but not least, my parents made this book possible by giving me the optimism that was essential to my survival.

Over the last 30 years, my secretaries, Rose Russ, Judy Van Gheluwe, Amber Johnson, Yvonne Tonn, Hannelore Foster, and Tracey Payne typed various segments of the manuscript. I am grateful to Ms. Sally Arteseros, whose editorial help was invaluable to me. Ms. Katie Wilson proofread and made valuable editorial suggestions; she was also my publishing assistant. I greatly appreciate her work.

Holocaust Bibliography:

Anger, Per. *With Raoul Wallenberg in Budapest* (Washington, D.C.: United States Holocaust Memorial Library, 1996).

Arendt, Hannah. *Between Past and Future: Six Exercises in Political Thought.* New York: Viking, 1961.

Armstrong, Karen. *A History of God: The 4,000- Year Quest of Judaism, Christianity, and Islam.* New York: Ballantine, 1994.

Baron, Salo Wittmayer. *A Social and Religious History of the Jews*, Columbia University Press, 16:9-10, New York, 1976.

Bartoszewski, Wladyslaw T. *The Convent at Auschwitz.* New York: George Braziller, 1991.

Berenbaum, Michael, *Witness to the Holocaust*, HarperCollins Publishers, Inc., New York, 1997.

Cargas, Harry James, ed. *The Unnecessary Problem of Edith Stein.* Lanham, Md.: University Press of America, 1994.

Cargas, Harry James. *Shadows of Auschwitz: A Christian Response to the Holocaust.* New York: Crossroad, 1990.

Carlen, Claudia, I. H. M., ed. *The Papal Encyclicals, 1939-1958.* Raleigh, N.C.: McGrath Publishing, 1981.

Carroll, James. *Constantine's Sword: The Church and the Jews.* Houghton Mifflin Co., New York, 2001.

Chrysostom, John, *Eight Orations*, 6.

Churchill, Winston. *The Gathering Storm*, Bantam Books, New York, 1961, p. 376 .

Cohen, Eli. *Human Behavior in the Concentration Camp,* Horton; New York, 1953.

Cornwell, John. *Hitler's Pope: The Secret History of Pius XII*. New York: Viking, 1999.

Crossan, John Dominic. *The Birth of Christianity: Discovering What Happened in the Years Immediately after the Execution of Jesus*. San Francisco: Harper San Francisco, 1998.

Dawidowicz, Lucy S. *The War Against the Jews, 1935-1945*. New York: Bantam, 1975.

Deak, Istvan. "The Pope, the Nazis, and the Jews." *New York Review of Books 47*, No. 5 (March 23, 2000), 44-49.

Dershowitz, Alan M. *The Vanishing American Jew: In Search of Jewish Identity for the Next Century*. New York: Little, Brown, 1997.

DesPres, Terrance. *The Survivor*, Oxford University Press, New York, 1975, p. 5.

Dimsdale, Joel E. *Survivors, Victims, and Perpetrators: Essays on the Nazi Holocaust*. New York: Hemisphere Publishing, 1980.

Engel, David. *Facing a Holocaust: The Polish Government-in-Exile and the Jews, 1943-1945*. Chapel Hill: University of North Carolina Press, 1993.

Encyclopedia Britannica. 2002.

Fitzpatrick, Sheila and Robert Gellately, Eds., *Accusatory Practices*, University of Chicago.

Freud, Sigmund. *Moses and Monotheism*. Translated by Katherine Jones. New York: Vintage, 1967.

Gilbert, Martin. *The Atlas of Jewish History*. New York: William Morrow, 1993.

Gilbert, Martin. *History of the Twentieth Century,* Avon Books, 1998

Gilbert, Martin. The *Holocaust*, Holt, Rinehart and Winston, 1985.

Goldhagen, Daniel Jonah. *Hitler's Willing Executioners: Ordinary Germans and the Holocaust*. New York: Knopf, 1996.

Gribetz, Judah. *The Timetables of Jewish History*. Simon & Schuster, 1993, p. 468.

Hilberg, Raul. *The Destruction of European Jews*. 3 vols. New York: Holmes and Meier, 1985.

Hochhuth, Rolf. *The Deputy*. Translated by Richard Winston and Clara Winston. New York: Grove Press, 1964.

Hoffman, Eva. *Shtetl: The Life and Death of a Small Town and the World of Polish Jews*. Boston: Houghton Mifflin, 1997.

Katz, Steven T., *The Holocaust in Historical Context*, Vol. 1, "The Holocaust and Mass Death before the Modern Age", Oxford University Press, Inc., New York, 1994, p. 259.

Keegan, John. *World War II*, p. 91.

Kogon, Eugene. *The Theory and Practice of Hell*, Farrar, Straus New York: 1953, p. 56.

Lemkin, Raphael. *Axis Rule in Occupied Europe*. Washington, D.C.: Carnegie Endowment for International Peace, 1944.

Littell, Franklin H., and Hubert G. Locke, eds. *The German Church Struggle and the Holocaust*. Detroit: Wayne State University Press, 1974.

Marrus, Michael R. *The Holocaust in History*. New York: New American Library, 1987.

Marrus, Michael R. *The Holocaust in History*, Hanover and London: University Press of New England, pp. 30-50.

Marton, Kati. *Wallenberg: Missing Hero* (New York: Arcade Publishing, 1995).

Meier, John P. *A Marginal Jew: Rethinking the Historical Jesus*. New York: Doubleday, 1991.

"Memory and Reconciliation: The Church and the Faults of the Past http://relations.com.stmnts/vatican12-99.htm."

Mitterrand, Francois; Elie Wiesel, *Memoir in Two Voices*, Arcade Publishing, 1996, p. 5.

O.R. Mendes-Flohr, Jehuda Reinharz, eds, *The Jew in the Modern World: A Documentary History*, New York, 1980, p. 482.

Pawlikowski, John T. *Christ in the Light of the Christian-Jewish Dialogue*. New York: Paulist Press, 1982.

Powell, Jim. "Colossal Courage" in *The Triumph of Liberty* (New York: Free Press, 2000).

Rittner, Carol and John K. Roth. Editors. *"Good News" after Auschwitz?* Mercer University Press, June 2001.

Roth, John K. and Michael Berenbaum, eds., *Holocaust*, p. 122.

Rubenstein, Richard L. *The Cunning of History: The Holocaust and the American Future.* New York: Harper and Row, 1975.

Ruether, Rosemary, Radford. *Faith and Fratricide: The Theological Roots of Anti-Semitism.* New York: Seabury, 1974.

Sartre, Jean Paul. *Anti-Semite and Jew.* Translated by George J. Becker. New York: Grove Press

Shatyn, Bruno, *A Private War*, Wayne State University Press, 1985.

Swearingen, Ben E., *The Mystery of Hermann Goering's Suicide*, 1984, p. 87.

Thayer, H. Standish, editor. *Pragmatism.* New American Library, May 1970, p. 63.

The New Testament in Modern English, translated by J.B. Phillips, Macmillan Paperbacks, 1962, pp. 63-64. University of Nebraska Press, 1987.

Tuchman, Barbara W. The Guns of August, Macmillan Company, New York, 1962, p. 173.

Waite, Robert G.L. *The Psychopathic God Adolf Hitler*, New American Library, 1977, pp 300 and 450.

Weber, M: *Economy and Society*, G. Roth and C. Wittich (EDS) New York: Bedminster Press.

Wiesel, Elie. *All Rivers Run to the Sea: Memoirs*, Alfred A. Knopf, Inc., New York, 1995, p. 79.

Wiesenthal, Simon. *The Sunflower: On the Possibilities and Limits of Forgiveness.* New York: Schocken, 1997.

Wills, Garry. *Papal Sin: Structures of Deceit.* New York: Doubleday, 2000.

Zaleski, Carol. *Otherworld Journeys*, Oxford University Press, 1987

Zuccotti, Susan. *The Italians and the Holocaust: Persecution, Rescue, and Survival*. Lincoln:

Notes

[1] Arnold Toynbee, Armenian Atrocities, The Murder of a Nation, (London, New York : Hodder & Stoughton, 1915).

[2] Anna Cichopek, "Pogrom Zydow w Krakowie," *Zydowski Instvtut Historiczny*, 2000.

[3] Elie Wiesel and Francois Mitterrand, *Memoir in Two Voices*, (Arcade Publishing, 1996).

[4] Isaac Bashevis Singer, *Shadows on the Hudson Farrar*, (Straus and Giroux, 1997).

[5] Czeslaw Milosz, *Native Realm*, (New York: Doubleday and Company, 1968).

[6] Milosz, *Native Realm*.

[7] Milosz, *Native Realm*.

[8] Martin Gilbert, *History of the Twentieth Century*, (Avon Books, 1998).

[9] "Polish Society Through Jewish Eyes", *The Jews in Poland*, Uniwersytet Jagiellonski, Krakow, 1992.

[10] Antony Alcock, *A History of the Protection of Regional- Cultural Minorities in Europe*, (New York: St. Martin's Press, 2000) 83.

[11] Milosz, *Native Realm*.

[12] Henry Grynberg, *Res Publica*, (Poland, 2003).

[13] Milosz, *Native Realm*.

[14] Gilbert, *History of the Twentieth Century*.

[15] Gilbert, *History of the Twentieth Century*.

[16] Milosz, *Native Realm*.

[17] My friend Miriam Winter entitled her Holocaust memoir "Trains."

[18] Adolf Hitler,"Reichstag Speech" 1935. The Avalon Project:
<http://www.yale.edu/lawweb/avalon

[19] *The New York Times*, March 29, 2003.

[20] William Shirer, *Berlin Diary: The Journal of a Foreign Correspondent*, (Alfred Knopf, 1941).

[21] Milosz, *Native Realm*.

[22] Adolf Hitler, *Mein Kampf*, (Houghton Mifflin Co., 1943) 140.

[23] Doris Kearns Goodwin, *No Ordinary Times,* (New York: Simon & Schuster, 1995).

[24] Winston Churchill, *The Gathering Storm*, (Bantam Books, 1961).

[25] AJP Taylor, *The War Lords*, (Penguin Books, 1977) 74.

[26] Goodwin, *No Ordinary Times*.

[27] In 1973 bank robbers took hostage a number of people in Stockholm. During the siege the hostages developed affection for the captors. One of the hostages eventually became engaged to one of the captors. The Stockholm syndrome is very rare.

[28] Raul Hilberg, Stanislaw Staron and Josef Kermisz, editors, *Warsaw Diary of Adam Czerniakov: Prelude to Doom*, (New York: Stein & Day, 1979).

[29] Raul Hilberg, *The Destruction of European Jews*, 3 vols. (New York: Holmes and Meier, 1985).

[30] "Egosyntonic homicide" is a term I introduced into psychiatric literature based upon my studies of homicide perpetrators. ("Psychiatric Study of Homicide" by E. Tanay in American Journal of Psychiatry, 1969).

[31] "Righteous Gentiles", *Frontline*:
<http://www.pbs.org/wgbh/pages/frontline/shetl/righteous/>

[32] This was a prelude. / Where they burn books / in the end they also burn people.

[33] Years later, I found out that the German who was stabbed was Dr. Friedrich Schmidt, who was the deputy county executive (Kreishauptman).

[34] Steven T Katz- "The Holocaust and Mass Death before the Modern Age", *The Holocaust in Historical Context*, Volume I, (New York: Oxford University Press, 1994) 259.

[35] Katz, *The Holocaust in Historical Context*.

[36] James Carroll, *Constantine's Sword: The Church and the Jews*, (New York: Houghton Mifflin Co., 2001) 213.

[37] *The Summa Theologica of St. Thomas Aquinas*, Second and Revised edition, 1920. Literally translated by Fathers of the English Dominican Province Online Edition Copyright © 2000 by Kevin Knight.

[38] Red Army commanders made a tactical error when a large part of their force diverted north of Warsaw in order to cut Polish supply lines from the Baltic Sea. Pilsudski had set a trap and sprung it, taking full advantage of the Russian error. The result was that the diverted Red Army force itself became cut off from its supply line, and the remaining Red Army force was decimated. This was regarded by many as a miracle, and became known as the "Miracle on the Wistula."

[39] *The New York Times*, March 17, 2001.

[40] Zyd was officially neutral, but most Poles considered it an insult. Many Poles used the diminutive Zydek, which was patronizing; Zydowisko and Zydlak were most offensive and hateful.

[41] Randolph L. Braham, *Politics of Genocide: The Holocaust in Hungary*, (New York: Columbia University Press, 1981) 125.

[42] Randolph L. Braham and Scott Miller, eds., *The Nazis' Last Victims*, (Detroit: Wayne State University Press 1998) 179.

[43] Hilberg, *The Destruction of the European Jews*.

[44] Daniel Jonah Goldhagen, *Hitler's Willing Executioners: Ordinary Germans and the Holocaust*, (New York: Knopf, 1996).

[45] Braham and Miller, eds., *The Nazis' Last Victims*.

[46] Agata Tuszynska, *Lost Landscapes: In Search of Isaac Bashevis Singer and the Jews of Poland,* (New York: William Morrow, 1998).

[47] Tuszynska, *Lost Landscapes.*

[48] Tuszynska, *Lost Landscapes.*

[49] Tuszynska, *Lost Landscapes.*

[50] Tuszynska, *Lost Landscapes.*

[51] "The Harrison Report" 1945, The United States Holocaust Memorial Museum:
<http://www.ushmm.org/museum/exhibit/online/dp/resourc1.htm

[52] "Will Post-War Germany Want to be Re-educated?" American Historical Association:
http://www.historians.org/projects/GIRoundtable/GermanReEd/GermanRe Ed_3.htm>

[53] Daniel Benjamin, "Condi's Phony History", August, 2003.
<http://www.slate.msn.com/id/2087768/>

[54] Golo Mann, *The History of Germany Since 1789,* (New York: Praeger, 1972).

[55] Goldhagen, *Hitler's Willing Executioners.*
[56] Tom Segev, *The Seventh Million: The Israelis and the Holocaust*, (New York: Henry Holt and Co., 2000).

[57] Monika Renneburg and Mark Walker, *Technology and National Socialism*, (New York: Cambridge University Press, 1993).

[58] Robert Jay Lifton, *The Nazi Doctors: Medical Killing and the Psychology of Genocide*, (Perseus Books Group, 1986).

[59] Mark Twain, *Following the Equator*, 1897.

[60] Testimony of John Kerry to Senate Committee on Foreign Relations:
<http://www.nationalreview.com/document/Kerry200404231047.asp

[61] *The New York Review of Books*, December 19, 2002, page 50.

[62] *The Wall Street Journal*, August 22, 2002.

[63] Samuel Huntington, *Clash of Civilizations*, (New York: Simon & Schuster,1996)

[64] Will Durant, "The Power of Religion": <http://www.willdurant.com/religion.htm

[65] *The New York Times*, August 5, 2004.

[66] NIETZSCHES WERKE, *Menschliches Alzumenschliches,* Bergland-Buch,Salzburg.

[67] Noah Efron, *Real Jews: Secular versus Ultra-Orthodox and the Struggle for Jewish Identity in Israel,* (New York: Basic Books, 2003).

[68] James R. Russell, "Massacres of the Armenians" *The New York Review of Books,* August 9, 2001.

[69] On file with author.

[70] Karen Armstrong, *A History of God: The 4,000-Year Quest of Judaism, Christianity and Islam,* (Ballantine Books, 1994).

[71] Lloyd Gaston, "Transformations in Telling the Passion Story" *Jewish-Christian Relations:* <http://www.jcrelations.net/en/?id=749

[72] *Frankfurter Rundschau,* January 6, 2001.

[73] Hanna Krall, *Shielding the Flame: An Intimate Conversation with Dr. Marek Edelman, the Last Surviving Leader of the Warsaw Ghetto Uprising* (Henry Holt: New York, 1986).

[74] Norman Davies, *Rising 44: The Battle for Warsaw,* (Viking, 2004).

[75] Hilberg, *The Destruction of European Jews.*

[76] Penny Schreiber and Joan Lowenstein, eds., *Remembering Raoul Wallenberg: The University of Michigan Celebrates Twentieth Century Heroes,* (University of Michigan Press, 2001).

[77] Jim Powell, "Colossal Courage," *The Triumph of Liberty,* (New York: Free Press, 2000).

[78] *Encyclopedia of the Holocaust,* (New York: Macmillan, 1990).

[79] *Encyclopedia of the Holocaust.*

[80] Zbigniew Brzezinski quote, <http://www.holocaustforgotten.com/zegota.htm

[81] Cardinal Seredi quote, <http:www.catholicleague.org/pius/piusnyt/moralorder.htm

[82] Hilberg, *Destruction of the European Jews.*

[83] Bryan Mark Rigg, *Hitler's Jewish Soldiers, The Untold Story of Nazi Racial Laws and Men of Jewish Descent in the German Military*, (University Press of Kansas, Modern War Studies, 2002).

[84] Alan M. Dershowitz, *The Vanishing American Jew: In Search of Jewish Identity for the Next Century*, (Little, Brown, 1997).

[85] On file with author.

[86] Sir Martin Gilbert, "Churchill and the Holocaust" BBC History: <http://www.bbc.co.uk/history/war/wwtwo/churchill_holocaust_01.shtml

[87] "General Patton's Warning" : <http://www.natvan.com/national-vanguard/assorted/patton.html

[88] On file with author.

[89] S.J. Gould, *Wonderful Life*, (New York W. W. Norton, 1989).

[90] Wislawa Szymborska, Polish poet., "Any Case," lines 6-11 (1948); translated by Grazyna Drabik and Sharon Olds (1993).

[91] Joyce Carroll Oates, *Foxfire*, (New York: Penguin Books, 1993).